The Ethics
of
Intercultural
Communication

Intersections in Communications and Culture

Global Approaches and Transdisciplinary
Perspectives

Cameron McCarthy and Angharad N. Valdivia
General Editors

Vol. 32

The Intersections in Communications and Culture series is part
of the Peter Lang Media and Communication list.
Every volume is peer reviewed and meets
the highest quality standards for content and production.

PETER LANG
New York • Bern • Frankfurt • Berlin
Brussels • Vienna • Oxford • Warsaw

The Ethics

of

Intercultural

Communication

Edited by Bo Shan & Clifford Christians

PETER LANG
New York • Bern • Frankfurt • Berlin
Brussels • Vienna • Oxford • Warsaw

Library of Congress Cataloging-in-Publication Data

The ethics of intercultural communication /
edited by Bo Shan, Clifford Christians.
pages cm. — (Intersections in communications and culture:
global approaches and transdisciplinary perspectives; vol. 32)
Includes bibliographical references and index.
1. Intercultural communication. 2. Communication—Moral and ethical aspects.
3. Mass media—Moral and ethical aspects. I. Shan, Bo (Professor of journalism)
editor. II. Christians, Clifford G., editor.
HM1211.E94   303.48'2—dc23   2015016453
ISBN 978-1-4331-2962-9 (hardcover)
ISBN 978-1-4331-2961-2 (paperback)
ISBN 978-1-4539-1643-8 (e-book)
ISSN 1528-610X

Bibliographic information published by **Die Deutsche Nationalbibliothek**.
Die Deutsche Nationalbibliothek lists this publication in the "Deutsche
Nationalbibliografie"; detailed bibliographic data are available
on the Internet at http://dnb.d-nb.de/.

The paper in this book meets the guidelines for permanence and durability
of the Committee on Production Guidelines for Book Longevity
of the Council of Library Resources.

© 2015 Peter Lang Publishing, Inc., New York
29 Broadway, 18th floor, New York, NY 10006
www.peterlang.com

Printed in the United States of America

Table of Contents

Foreword

STEPHEN J. A. WARD

Distinguished Lecturer of Ethics
University of British Columbia

The Ethics of Intercultural Communication is a timely and substantial contribution to the study of how cultures do, and should, communicate with each other through news media, art, imagination, dialogue, and other means. In a global world, linked by global media, there is an urgent need for scholars and others to think and act in the domain of intercultural and global communication.

The background for this book is nothing other than the future of humanity on this small blue planet. As cultures come into tension, and as global problems challenge a massively unequal world, how can the peoples of the world communicate and cooperate ethically to promote global peace, understanding, and justice?

This question is not another plaintive cry about the state of the world by well-meaning but naive idealists. It is not a purely theoretical question fit for the philosopher as she dreams about a perfect world in her study. It is a practical question that calls for the mobilization of ethical citizens for reform, guided by deep theory, revealing facts, and humane philosophizing.

To put the matter darkly: We, as an international community, will either figure out how to address our differences or we will live in a world of increasing violence instigated by injustice, ignorance, intolerance, and parochial values. We must summon all of our energy to this task or we will live in a world of environmental and militaristic threats to our species and other sentient creatures.

I view the ethics of intercultural communication as an important part of the construction of a global ethics of communication and journalism, in principle and in practice. The field does concern itself with the ethics of particular problems and contexts. However, intercultural communication also should be part of this wider world-building project for philosophers, ethicists, journalists, and communicating citizens.

Therefore, a crucial issue is to what extent this book is a contribution to its field and to global ethics. Is it clear about the aims of its field? Does the book ask the right questions and study the right themes, given some conception of the field?

I examine the book in light of these broad questions rather than comment on each of the 19 chapters. The book ranges from philosophical discussions about the principles of communication ethics to case studies of news coverage. My conclusion is that the book asks good questions and rigorously explores important themes. It raises, and challenges us to answer definitively, normative questions about the aim and nature of intercultural communication ethics. I organize my discussion around three major questions.

The first major question is: How should ethical issues in intercultural communication be discussed systematically?

In the book, three types of writing fall under the flexible rubric of "ethics":

- Philosophizing about ethical traditions, as carried out eloquently by the book's two editors. They explain the lack of ethical theory in Western journalism, compare ancient Greek philosophers with Confucius, and present alternate, communitarian ethical views as a corrective to a Western stress on rationality and individualism.
- Empirical studies of news coverage, with an implicit (or explicit) normative intent, for example, studying group language prejudice in reports. Such studies presume that misrepresentation, in its many forms, is unethical and therefore a basis for criticism.
- Articles from media ethics on the intercultural competence of journalists and the relevance of virtue theory and casuistry to media ethics.

These three types of writing point us toward the systematic and well-focused discussion of ethics and ethical theory that the field needs. The contributions of the editors are good examples of philosophical ethics. Ethics in the rest of the book tends to be dispersed among many types of writings. In particular, a significant number of chapters in the two sections on case studies are background material; they do not provide extended ethical analysis. Ethics here amounts to value judgments that media coverage was prejudiced or unbalanced. The book needs more discussions such as Chapter 11 that bring together the many interesting points made in the cases so the reader can see the overall implications for intercultural ethics.

The book also is not "an ethics" in the sense of a unified ethical theory that unfolds logically and is applied to cases. As an edited collection, this type of book was probably not possible. Yet this underlines the need for ongoing systematic discussions linking the many moving parts of an ethics of intercultural communication.

Further, only in the first and last sections, and in a few other chapters, does it appear that "the ethics" in the book's title refers to a complex ethical structure. For instance, in the journalism ethics of Sections II–IV, "the ethics" of journalism largely refers not to fundamental principles but to values and prescriptions of varying generality. The content ranges from supremely general principles and mid-theoretic precepts to concrete guidelines on how to address recurring situations. Does this book think of intercultural communication ethics as having, or striving to achieve, such a structure? If so, what would be its main components?

Therefore, I arrive at this question: In the final analysis, what does this book mean by *the ethics* of intercultural communication? What would an ethics of intercultural communication look like? This book opens a pathway for us to follow in answering those questions.

The second main question is: To what extent is the book balanced and diverse in its discussion of issues, use of methods, and inclusion of participants?

One restrictive feature is the predominance of analysis and case studies related to the United States and China. It chooses for depth of comparison to concentrate on this juncture, but in doing so it calls for further research on intercultural issues in other countries such as South Africa, Guatemala, or India. Also, there is an imbalance in criticism. There is plenty of criticism of Western values and media. Such criticism is needed. But where is the balancing criticism of non-Western values and media? In terms of method, the case studies tend to focus on negative examples—cases where news outlets misrepresented an event or did not critique mainstream values. Where are the positive case studies of good intercultural reporting?

There are a few studies of interesting attempts to dialogue across cultural and national borders, but there could be others. What can intercultural ethics learn from truth and reconciliation processes, building ethnic bridges after civil war, and the employment of conflict-reduction journalism? We can learn as much from positive (or significant) attempts at dialogue and dialogic journalism as we can from negative examples of questionable coverage by some Western mainstream media.

The book does not include extended discussions of the ethics of intercultural communication in a digital world. How is social media, and a journalism practiced by citizens, affecting intercultural communication and theories of intercultural communication? Media ethics is wrestling with issues created by digital global media. Is the ethics of intercultural communication undergoing similar developments?

Scholars in this volume use general terms such as *media, journalism, communication,* and *Western culture.* Too often such terms are used in a sweeping, unqualified sense. Sometimes, Western media is identified with professional mainstream journalism, or a subset of the latter—well-known media organizations in the United States, such as CNN or the *New York Times.*

In addition, many case studies use methods—for example, text analysis—that leave little room for the important voice of the journalist or news outlet. As a result, the journalist or the news outlet is an abstraction analyzed from a safe academic distance but rarely spoken to or allowed to address the criticisms or theories. If we take this book as representative, the message is that intercultural communication ethics must build on it to further diversify the range of participants, the types of media, and the types of cases.

My final and third major question is a question the book itself asks: Is true intercultural communication really possible? Is an ethics of intercultural communication possible? There are many obstacles, from hostility to strangers to economic (and other) factors, that support a news media that is parochial and culturally intolerant.

The book has the great virtue of fearlessly asking this question, in several chapters.[1] Shan asks the question directly in the final chapter and Christians outlines an ethics of human dignity for a multicultural world. Roberts wonders about the likelihood of a media ethics code "for all time zones." I believe this question will not go away. Rather, it will continue to raise difficult questions about the study of intercultural communication ethics.

One of the most difficult questions is whether theorizing within academia is a sufficient response to the problems of communication in the outside world. I said at the beginning that global ethics needs thinking *and* acting—the right type of theorizing *and* the right type of reforming actions. But what actions and what theory?

Can experts be content to theorize about intercultural communications, perhaps multiplying the number of case studies and strengthening its ethical theory? Or does the state of the world require these experts to take action? Should they join efforts in their societies, and the global society, to reform communication systems and challenge unethical communicators?

I suspect that many scholars would reject any engagement that constituted a form of activism as incompatible with analyzing communications in an objective manner. I believe that objectivity and certain forms of activism are compatible, but I won't argue the point here. Rather, I simply predict that it will become increasingly difficult to separate theorizing in academia and practical reform in the world. Calls for engagement will grow as the impact and importance of cross-cultural communication grows.

In posing these basic questions, I am addressing the field of intercultural communication ethics as a whole, not limiting myself to the book in particular. As an editor of essays on global media ethics (Ward, 2013), I know the challenges that faced the book's two distinguished editors. No book can cover everything. Hopefully this book will inspire a series of books like it from around the world.

Despite the limitations of one volume addressing a complicated topic, this book is indeed a significant addition to the field of communication and ethics in a global age. Many chapters are insightful and rigorous. They will provide invaluable material for the teaching and discussion of intercultural communication and ethics. There is immense learning distilled into this book, and there is immense learning to take from it.

The fact that the book raises difficult questions without offering definitive answers is, from one perspective, to be expected. From another perspective, it is a strength of the book. It is to be expected because of the evolving state of intercultural communication. Firm answers are illusive in the rapidly changing world of communication. It is a strength in the sense that one of the book's positive contributions is to make us think hard about its topic. By reading this book, we are prompted to keep asking these questions and to pursue research into areas where we need new ideas, better methods, and stronger evidence.

The Ethics of Intercultural Communication points us toward the future, providing a platform to launch further investigations. It invites us to improve our understanding of global communication society and to support those who construct a more open, diverse, and compassionate world.

NOTE

1. I addressed this question at length with respect to the creation of a global media ethics in Ward (2015, ch. 8).

REFERENCES

Ward, S. J. A. (2013). *Global media ethics: Problems and perspectives.* Malden, MA: Wiley-Blackwell.
Ward, S. J. A. (2015). *Radical media ethics.* Malden, MA: Wiley-Blackwell.

Introduction

Moral Reasoning in Intercultural Media

DIALOGUE: PROFESSOR CLIFFORD CHRISTIANS
AND PROFESSOR BO SHAN

In this age of globalization, journalists have increasingly entered the inter-cultural context. How do we transform traditional principles of media ethics? How do we resolve moral conflicts through ethical convergence? How to construct a new media ethics? How can media professionals become moral subjects who carry moral responsibility? In this introduction, the two editors have an academic dialogue on these issues faced by the media. They reflect on classic moral concepts such as values, principles, and rights, as well as how to use them appropriately within an intercultural background.

Shan: As a Chinese scholar, I'd like to discuss with you an important issue: how to do moral reasoning. Specifically, what is moral reasoning—the details and processes of moral reasoning—in the intercultural context?

Christians: The question of how to do moral reasoning in an intercultural era requires our learning from each other. This is an interest of many of us in different parts of the world. We conclude together that the media are creating a global age that is realigning the world not around politics but language and culture; clearly politics and economics are included, but the realignment is deeper than that. So the question of how we help each other do moral reasoning in this context is of great interest to me, and I deeply appreciate that you are focusing on it.

THE POTTER BOX AND CHINESE MORAL REASONING

Shan: My first question is, How does media ethics become an issue from historical and realistic perspectives? According to my understanding, in 1888, Charles A. Dana, the chief editor of the *New York Sun*, created eight codes of ethics for journalists. Is that, then, the time in the ethics of journalism when journalism changed from a trade or craft into a profession?

Christians: This is correct history, with the professional societies assisting by their development of codes in the early 20th century. The reality is that media ethics did not arise from philosophy but came from media practice. Certain leaders of journalism saw ethics and codes in medicine and in law and concluded that if journalism wanted to be a profession with status, it must follow medicine and law. Journalism education was inspired by that idea: We need educated journalists, not just those who learn it on the run. Codes of ethics were seen as the internal standard for journalism as a profession.

Shan: So can we say that introducing media ethics was a turning point in the development of American journalism?

Christians: Yes, you can understand codes of ethics as motivated by status, and therefore an indicator of journalism's turn to professional standards. There are a few references in history to reporters and editors who wanted ethics because of failures in the field, who felt that journalism was not doing its job right. They didn't fret about status, first of all, but complained that journalism had too many weaknesses, and they wanted to correct them. There was some incentive for ethics from journalists who were morally good, but that was a minor stream. The primary motivation was gaining status by the imitation of medicine and law. Journalism was on a new professional pathway that it still follows today.

I have written about this from the perspective of philosophy. From 1888 to 1924, philosophers such as G. E. Moore were doing important work on moral reasoning. But philosophers had no interest in journalism; they were not consulted on journalism education. There are three periods in the United States in which ethics emerges in journalism. And in each of these three major turning points, philosophy is nowhere to be seen. Its resources are not used or made available to journalism ethics. Philosophers became interested in medicine and there was tremendous work on bioethics, for example. Philosophers became interested in law and some in business, but not in journalism. This means that within journalism, we were doing our best in ethics, but we did not use all the educational resources that were available to do it right.

Shan: In reviewing this development of ethical codes, can we say that the core values of journalism morality include five points: press freedom, truth telling, social justice, the principle of nonmaleficence, and the responsibility for the media to make profits for its organization? Is this understanding correct? But when we talk about the last core value, isn't that contradictory to the former four values? As a private entity, society doesn't give newspapers any rights, so the newspaper does not have any responsibility to it. Therefore, media organizations become private profit-earning enterprises, and the practice of journalism is more about following the rule of journalism internal standards. What do you think about the contradiction between the last core one and the former four values?

Christians: Yes, your reference to core values resonates with me. Core values, to be acceptable for a public enterprise such as the press, must be core values that the public would verify. The only way that journalism can receive recognition as a profession is that its core values find agreement with the public at large. And if you say to the public, "this enterprise we call journalism has core values and therefore it should be treated as a profession," the public would definitely say yes to the first four values. But now we have the fifth one, and you are right, it's contradictory. If you use the public test, professional status is granted when its mission is recognized as crucial to society. In that sense, the fifth one, which does seem contradictory, is also acceptable to the public. A contradiction may arise over what media profit means. Should this program be chosen only because it generates the biggest audience? Someone could argue that the media should be administered according to common carrier rules, like the statutory profit regulations for the American trucking industry. So there is some controversy, but I think that in general the public will agree with the profit value. The media are businesses and have the right to survive. What the public accepts is that profits guarantee the other values.

Shan: Your book *Media Ethics* uses the Potter Box to analyze moral reasoning. Here is a Chinese case I'd like to share with you. In the Wenchuan earthquake, a female teacher didn't have time to look for her own daughter because she had to take care of her students. On the second day, when she finally had time to rescue her daughter, she could only find her body under the ruins. The media reported this again and again and finally drove the lady insane. The media covered the lady as a moral model who had sacrificed her daughter to save other students. However, traditional Chinese morality has also said that you should take care of your own child. The lady had to retell the story how she did not look for her daughter first, over and over again, to the public under great psychological pressure, and it led to the sad result of her suicide. How would you analyze this case with the Potter Box?

Christians: We are doing step number 1 now, that is, defining the facts. This means we should know all the details and take every aspect into account. We need to discuss the details more, but at least the basic issues are underway. The Potter Box says that on the left-hand side, that is, steps 1 and 2, you are asking what actually happened. What is the case and situation in step 1? Then in step 2 values need to be examined. You have to identify what values people held in the situation. Clearly for the teacher, she valued teaching as her personal and primary duty in the earthquake. The public values motherhood, and this is what the public values as the first responsibility, regardless of the social situation at stake. A different value in step 2 is obvious for the press. At this time in its history, the press values human interest stories; they consider them to be of public interest and newsworthy. Obviously values of the teacher, the public, and the press are in contradiction here. Certainly the press's assumption, that the teacher-mother's terrible personal distress is newsworthy, is debatable.

The Potter Box wants to teach that ethics is more than value clarification. When we are dealing with the overall topic today, ethics and the intercultural, one of the basic issues is whether we should only compare values in two different cultures. In this case, we see the contradiction between the values of the public, the values of a teacher, and the values of the news profession. But rather than merely clarifying these values further, with the Potter Box we do not stop at step 2. There are additional steps that must be taken before we can decide, especially in a relativistic age in which it is assumed there are no universal principles. Step number 3 on the right side of the Potter Box asks what we ought to do about the left-hand side, after the facts are taken into account and you know what values motivate all the actors. Step 2 must be taken seriously, but we realize that some values are negative or contradictory. So you need step 3, which asks about principles. In step 3, you identify the ethical principles or theories that illuminate the facts of the case and the values that are held. Which one of these values is right or wrong? What should the press have done? So far we only know that the press published the teacher-mother's deep distress and suicide because they considered them newsworthy. The press undoubtedly said, "She committed suicide under clinical depression; her depression is not our responsibility, we were just doing our job." Instead of leaving all the debate over values, we should go to step 3 and ask what the press should have done in this case.

Basically there are five different principles that are possible, five different categories. Of the five theories of quadrant 3, the one that is the most prominent in journalism in the United States and in most democratic societies is utilitarianism. Journalists following this principle would say that their responsibility is to speak to the largest number of people as possible who are affected by this case, and to do it with the least amount of harm. In John Stuart Mill, it was always "maximum good" and "minimum harm." So most journalists would say that their publishing of this case regrettably caused some psychological harm to the mother, but their coverage only embarrassed her a little while making people know that teaching is a difficult profession and has many heroes; in this the public was served. Many ethical theorists have recognized that utilitarianism's appeal to consequences, to results, is too ambiguous; it's a single-strand theory that has only one appeal, that the largest number of people are served the best results. It was a sensation in John Stuart Mill's day because he didn't have to appeal to God or to formal law. It is just a straightforward practical standard of consequences. This is the same idea as majority rule in modern democracy. I consider it the weakest possible theory for media ethics, but some of the smartest ethicists in the world still follow utilitarianism when they sort through conflicting values.

THE VEIL OF IGNORANCE AND INTERCULTURAL ETHICS CONVERGENCE

Christians: For step 3, the principle that I believe the most applicable is the theory based on minorities, which in the Potter Box system is John Rawls. Rawls argues that the utilitarian appeal to the majority has all the weaknesses I've talked about. So he designed a theory in which the final test is the minority. It's the minority and their rights, their thinking, their identity that are crucial. Rawls's *Theory of Justice* has its own specific strategy for getting to the minority; it means going to the original position behind the veil of ignorance.

Rawls is an illustration of several theories at present that reject utilitarianism's appeal to the majority and make the minority the critical question. For journalists, the otherness of the other, the bleeding other, ought to come first in theory and practice. A Levinas example would go like this: "If a person with a bloody face bursts into my office when I'm talking with my students, everything will stop and the bloody person will be my preoccupation." I believe that the ethical theory of the minority is the right theory when there is a power difference between media professionals and a grieving, suffering human being. The powerless person is the teacher who was not only accused of neglecting her child but made responsible for the dead child. It's at the time of our grieving that we are the most vulnerable. In these situations, we need a theory that doesn't emphasize the rights of a generic public or a powerful press but gives priority to the childless mother.

Now back to the Potter Box. Which theory one chooses in step 3 is sometimes debatable. Some people will follow the utilitarian principle to excuse the press and think they are not responsible for the woman's going insane. But whenever there are inequalities in power—when there is the powerless, the vulnerable, the suffering, the beaten down versus the massive press—then you need either John Rawls or a similar theory that says you do the right thing when the suffering person is served. Rawls argues that when you are in a state behind the original position, the first thing everybody agrees on is freedom. Then behind the veil, everybody agrees secondly that the most vulnerable are to have priority. He imagines that when making decisions behind the veil of ignorance, people will act as human beings who could emerge from this veil as not the journalist but the mother. Thinking in that way, you will always be disposed toward the weak in case you are the weak in real life when the veil is opened. The theory has more complications, but basically it's an argument against utilitarianism, one that gives priority to the minority instead.

Shan: However, there are many people who criticize Rawls's veil-of-ignorance theory. One argument is that it's not applicable in the real world. Because everybody is socialized, they cannot go back to their original position. What's your comment on this criticism?

Christians: This is a pertinent criticism. Rawls's theory assumes an abstraction, that is, the original position. And within that abstraction, ethics is done. But not knowing who you are is not the usual way of making decisions in real life. Those who defend Rawls would say that he means we should think sympathetically in the other person's shoes, and when we do, we avoid risk for ourselves and therefore think in terms of weakness, the suffering. You may not have lost a child, you may not even have a child, but you can sympathetically take the position of the mother who has lost hers. It is true that stepping behind the veil of ignorance into your original position is a process of abstraction. But the idea behind it strikes me as defensible and important for intercultural communication. Assume now I'm a journalist; I have a responsibility to the public. Ideally I have freedom of expression, which is so precious that I can't possibly hide what I have come to know in my reporting. I've been trained for my profession to give an account of what is newsworthy. Rawls would say to the journalist, "yes, but imagine you are the woman; your daughter has just died during the process of your covering a big story. Today you are at the Wenchuan earthquake scene, and meanwhile your own family just had a major tragedy. Then you can understand this woman's tragedy and let it guide you rather than follow a professional definition of newsworthiness."

We can't lose Rawls's main point in spite of the criticism about the nature of the original position. That is, whenever we want to write principles of ethics, and there is a major differential between the powerful and the suffering, then the weakest are the optimum test of rightness or wrongness. Clearly Rawls is working against the tradition of utility's majoritarianism. Therefore, some people will prefer Levinas's ethics, for example, which is revolutionary in starting with the Other rather than beginning and ending with the decision maker. When we discuss media ethics, the appeals have always been to either virtue like Confucius and Aristotle; to results such as John Stuart Mill or in contract theory; to duty, for example, Kant or Islamic ethics; or to love, either feminist ethics or some religious forms of ethics. Rawls's *Theory of Justice*, or similar emphases on justice, belong to this list also. With justice a central issue in intercultural communication, his kind of theorizing has special appeal. Regardless of how you understand various theories of justice, justice at its core means that the vulnerable, the weakest are the beginning point.

Shan: With my special interest in intercultural communication, I can actually see how the veil of ignorance is workable in this field. In international reporting of intercultural affairs, the veil of ignorance means that as a journalist, you should walk in another's shoes to report from different perspectives. Journalists following this principle would seek for the real cultural truth to understand more about other cultures and to provide general facts from a more complete perspective.

Christians: I agree totally with that. In my teaching Rawls through the Potter Box, I include him because I want my students to have read a philosopher's theory of justice. But the challenge for us who are interested in intercultural communication is to say how we can articulate an ethics that enables us to actually make the minority, or the weak or the suffering, the optimum standard. It's hard for journalists who haven't lived in another culture to think sympathetically out of their own culture to another. So rather than saying that this principle can't work, I believe it is better to conclude that this is the most powerful of the five ways of thinking about ethics, but it still needs more refinement. To summarize, the Potter Box does not say that it always has to be Rawls of the five theorists for step 3, but it's the proper theory when the weak and the powerful are at odds in box 1. For intercultural communication more generally, I believe it is also the kind of theorizing we need and where we should concentrate.

This could be stated differently. For those who have special competence in intercultural communication, the challenge is how one articulates a theory of justice that is sophisticated enough for the complicated world of intercultural communication. One of Rawls's influential colleagues, Martha C. Nussbaum, argues that Rawls defines what justice means in Western terms, but in the current global, media-saturated world, there are three areas in which Rawls needs to be rethought or advanced. And the second of those three is, in her terms, "disability." That is, Rawls's theory of justice needs more development in the case of the disabled, those who can't participate and who don't have a voice. Thomas Cooper believes that the best strategy now for ethics in universals is to study the indigenous people, the Aborigines in Australia, the Polynesians in the Pacific, the Shuswap in Canada. That is, we should study those who live close to the ground and not in a capitalist society or a socialist one, or in a marketing economy or an industrial order, with all the trappings that go along with different social systems. Instead, study societies that are organized by people who are close to our common humanity. That's at least one way to implement a theory of minority justice or social justice in which the suffering aren't just accounted for but become the core of our ethics.

Shan: I appreciate the priority on the weak and the powerless. However, I wonder whether it's possible in the real world. Is it actually possible to give priority to the weakest people or to minorities? In intercultural communication, is it possible for us to develop a kind of negotiation relationship among different values and different cultures? Take Chinese and Americans, for example; collective Chinese will give priority to communal values, and we always talk about building a harmonious society. However, individualist Americans give priority to personal rights; they emphasize more the right to know and the personal right of communication. We don't need to judge which of these values are right or wrong. A better way might be to make the different values of the two cultures converge. Then it would promote intercultural communication around the world. What's your opinion on this kind of ethical convergence?

Christians: Very good in terms of the dialogic. We negotiate, we try to understand each other better, and we look for common values or agreements between our cultures. Step 4 of the Potter Box does something like this. The question for step 4 is this: Who are you loyal to? In the Wenchuan case, if the principle of minority preference has priority, then journalists have to decide on their loyalties. Who is newsworthy, and if so, why? Ultimately, following the principle of justice, the person you are covering, the vulnerable would have to agree that you have chosen a reasonable alternative as a responsible journalist. The negotiation then is over what is legitimate news. Journalists have their internal standard; they think the story of the teacher is of human interest and it lets people know about teachers and the demands of education.

But feminist theories tell us that for the loyalties question of step 4, we should have motivational displacement. The journalists' motivation cannot be from their organization or profession. When there are the weak in the situation, journalists should displace their motivation with the motivation of the suffering other. The only way one can do that is by learning, by dialogue, by hearing their voice. In intercultural communication research, when we do scholarship we can hear each other and we can come to clarity about what others really value. In the news, when we are facing tremendous deadlines, then it often is a matter of understanding the frame of reference of the victim and asking ourselves, "What if I were in that position?" And then you write the story following the preferences of the suffering felt by your inner self. Yes, in looking for common values and trying to understand better what other cultures are like, hearing the other's voice is an important aspect of intercultural studies and research. I believe that to make the ethics of the minority a reality depends on the kind of research and study and teaching we do in the intercultural field. Clarifying the larger context, in interaction with professionals on the ground, is an important step forward.

Incidentally, I take positive notice of your reference to China and the United States within the global context. For clarity and sharpness, we are centering our discussion on Oriental and Western cultures, while the complex world is on our mind at all times. Your reflection makes China and North America a working laboratory for dealing with the intercultural issues of our increasingly borderless planet. Your thinking and research are teaching us how to concentrate on particular cultures and analyze them from a cross-cultural perspective simultaneously.

Shan: I'm very interested in the Potter Box and would like to make a proposal for making it into a cross-cultural Potter Box. That means from the very beginning of the Potter Box, the definition phase, people may sense or see the facts from different cultural perspectives. So at the next levels of values, of principles and of loyalties, we could change every level of the Potter Box into cross-cultural reasoning. Do you think that is possible?

I'd like to share with you a reflection on Murdoch's *News of the World* scandals. Although the behavior of the journalists is immoral, why does it happen again and again in the press? I think that is because morality or ethics is weak in regulating or guiding people's behavior. But I also believe that this is due to the prevailing preference for utilitarianism in ethics. When you always justify your behaviors by ends—in other words, when the results can justify means—then journalists can always say that they're doing it because of the public interest. Do you think this is a reason for such phenomena happening again and again in the press?

Christians: I basically agree with your analysis, but I'd like to say it in slightly different terms. Ethics does make the distinction between ends and means, and we analyze their connection in different ways in the West and in the East, but basically the importance of that distinction is maintained cross-culturally. As you suggest, it's a good framework for understanding our different approaches. Agreeing with you that the utilitarian way of considering ends is the reason for what the *News of the World* did—its immorality and failures—I focus on means and ends in big institutions. Means become so dominant in technological organizations that means is their preoccupation instead of ends. When you have in Murdoch's empire more than 60,000 employees, and you are dealing with budgets of billions, then your preoccupation with means, with organizational management, becomes so paramount that ends are trivial. The editors, the owners, the people who run the operation become specialists in means, efficiency, and instrumentalism. Huge corporations demand a focus on means, administration, cost effectiveness, finance, making technology run like an efficient machine. In such massive corporations, means always stand in the center and ends somewhere at the margin.

Theorists of technology, such as the French thinker Jacques Ellul, have made a claim that when technology, instruments, efficiency, and machineness dominate, then ends disappear. In the structure of technological regimes, ends play no meaningful role. Max Weber, the German sociologist, had a version of this in his concept of bureaucratization, that is, when you have a massive institution and have to organize it systematically, you divide it into explicit units or snippets where no one is responsible. Therefore the ultimate end, whether you are doing the right thing—justice, ethics, keeping your promises—is somewhere in the environment, but that's not central. What we've seen in the *News of the World* is an example of massive empires that are enormously successful financially because that is where they have put their emphasis; they are specialists in the techniques of costs and revenue. It's the mystique of means, the values driven by means that make ends marginal, and therefore press organizations keep repeating the same mistakes. Ends are not directly relevant for running big machines. The new technologies are international—ICTs, data clouds, communication satellites, the cyber world of search engines—but we live in communities and practice our professions within them. Ethics needs to work effectively on the ground as research and lived experience indicate. We need a media ethics that is actionable and pluralistic.

IGNORANCE OF ETHICS IN MEDIA AND INTERCULTURAL APPROACHES

Shan: Those are very inspired thoughts. Let's continue with a discussion about the character of present ethics, particularly the ignorance of ethics in Western media. I propose three reasons for what I call the "cold ignorance" of ethics. First of all, I believe that the Western media are dominated by the utilitarianism that you mentioned, so that they justify their preoccupation with means. Let's think of the example of the "hidden camera" or the behavior of hiding your real identity when you are reporting. Journalists will argue that they are doing this in the public interest, because of the people's right to know. This claim about good ends can justify the immoral means of deceiving. The second reason why the media are cold to ethics is because, among the five core values that were mentioned earlier, the last one is profit oriented. Even when we talk about objectivity, impartiality in Western journalistic codes, the purpose of those codes of ethics is basically to attract a larger audience to make more profit. The third reason is that nowadays in Western news reports, journalists are still trying to promote Western values. Maybe this is unconscious, but it's true; negotiation with or different perspectives from other cultures is lacking. For example, in the 1996 code of ethics for journalists in America, although it gave priority to and put emphasis on the weakest or the minority, it lacks an emphasis on negotiating with people from other cultures. Based on these three reasons, I think the possible solution to solve these problems is that we should have a cross-cultural turn in research on media ethics. Do you agree?

Christians: I couldn't agree more. You've presented a good analysis of why Western ethics is unfit for international journalism. You said that there were primarily three reasons for "cold ignorance," and I agree with those reasons. I also believe that more and more journalists are recognizing these problems. I think that what you are calling for, among the best of our journalists, would also be welcome rather than their insisting Western journalism and Western ethics are the right answer. I believe that more and more, there is a recognition of the weaknesses in Western journalism and ethics. And, yes, you mentioned correctly in the third reason that there is too much self-promotion and not much willingness to negotiate. That's true in general for the majority. But I hear among journalists, certainly among students in our programs, and more and more from professors, that journalism values have helped us keep free from government control but not from business control. Increasingly with giant international corporations, it becomes obvious that the media ethics that focuses on freedom from government, no censorship, and freedom of expression only speaks to one kind of threat and does not speak well to the business threat; core value 5 is distorted. I affirm your analysis, and I believe that as a new kind of ethics is developed, Western journalists will recognize that responsible reporting needs a different, bigger international and cross-cultural ethics rather than one that is Western oriented.

One additional point is that on the second problem in your analysis—that the commitment to objectivity leads to business priorities—various versions of objectivity are crucial to Western journalism, and that value will be the hardest to overcome. I'm agreeing that your analyses are right and that Western journalism has these three weaknesses; therefore, international journalism finds Western media ethics unacceptable. Objectivity is still the centerpiece and is so important to Western journalism that your idea that objectivity must be called into question, and we need a different way of thinking about it, will be the most difficult for Western journalists to admit and certainly to give up.

Shan: About the difficulties of objectivity that you just mentioned, actually in 1992, I published a paper reconstructing news objectivity. I'm not saying that we ought to give up objectivity but rather that we should go beyond objectivity by developing a kind of dialogic style of objectivity from the perspective of intersubjectivity.

Christians: Your work here is valuable. In parallel, I have been working on the idea of "interpretive sufficiency," that is, telling enough about the story, the history, the meaning, the background, so the reporters' interpretation of the advent is complete. It's a version of moving beyond objectivity, though not saying that precisely. But as we develop an ethics of intercultural communication, your thinking on a dialogic style of objectivity will be crucial. I understand what you are saying, that we don't abandon objectivity as a core value, but we move to something beyond it or we define it in a deeper way.

HOW TO BE A RESPONSIBLE SUBJECT IN THE INTERCULTURAL CONTEXT

Shan: The last issue that I would like to discuss with you regarding the cross-cultural context is this: How can we become responsible subjects who can bear the responsibility of media ethics? On this issue, I especially prefer the opinions of two American scholars, John Martin Fischer and Mark Ravizza. They think that there are two premises before you become a responsible subject: One is that you must have freedom to be yourself and another is that you have to be reasonable and rational; together this means you can't be influenced or controlled by a dominant ideology or some outside force. Well, my question is, What do you think are the key issues for us to become responsible subjects in cross-cultural communication? Especially in the context of the Internet, where there are more than professional journalists but netizens who become reporters.

Christians: I assume that the responsible subject you are talking about here refers to international journalists. To my mind, what it means to be responsible in intercultural journalism or ethics requires the press to understand the general morality rather than be limited to a professional morality. Journalists must learn moral principles from within society as a whole and not narrow their thinking to their own familiar professional values. Responsible journalists must learn the ethics of public life. I call this the ethics of the general morality, so that their thinking and society's understandings of ethics are the same. To be responsible to society, to live by one's duty to the public, particularly in the intercultural and transnational world, requires a social ethics that is not just media ethics. Therefore, the question that frames everything in intercultural communication is what ethical principles belong in common to the human race, or at least those principles that research is identifying in regions or across societies. If journalists say they have a responsibility to society, then they need to understand how society thinks.

One important concept in social ethics is keeping your promises; when a vow is made, when you make a promise to someone, you should keep it. A reporter can say that within the journalist's morality, "I make a promise to my sources to keep their information confidential; that is, if they tell me private information, I promise it will be confidential." Then the journalist says later, following one of journalism's core values, that "this information is so important I have to break my confidentiality promise and I will publish it now." You can see there are two different ethics here: the social morality says to keep your promises; in the journalist's morality, my promise of confidentiality is subject to my own rules if I think the private information is important. I'm illustrating a response to your question by arguing that the duty of the journalist is to understand responsibility in society's sense of the term. To be responsible means to follow the principles that come from the public, not from a media organization. There was a movement in the United States called public journalism that defined responsibility this way. What stories to write and how to write them were determined by living among the public to hear the public's point of view and then representing their analysis of problems, their concerns, and their solutions. The issue here is that the public establishes responsibility and therefore journalists must know the general morality and be accountable to it.

Shan: Building on this, I'd like to share my thinking on the word *responsibility*. There are two dimensions of responsibility. The first one is when someone is questioned or blamed for some bad results, the responsible subject will be accountable for it. The second dimension is that as responsible subjects, they should explain the reasons why they did it. Within the intercultural context, we could add one more dimension to that. We could develop responsibility into a "responsibility of subjectivity," which means that apart from being responsible for results and explaining reasons, the third thing we could do is to let people from different cultures understand what we are doing or why we did this. And we could also listen to the different voices of different cultures to make things better.

Christians: That third aspect is very good. What it says is that rather than journalists making judgments based on their freedom of expression, they are now engaging in interaction, dialogue, listening so that the judgments of those in the culture being covered become crucial. That's a way of implementing the idea of the general morality. Journalists should want the public to instruct them, to help them understand what responsibility is. So it's not just responsibility from their own conscience but responsibility to their peers, to the ethical principles central to society. Your adding the third dimension is a great insight.

—translated by Jiamei Tang

—edited by Xinya Liu

Comparative Research ON Chinese AND Western Communication Ethics

CHAPTER ONE

The *Analects* OF Confucius AND THE Greek Classics

A Comparative Approach[1]

BO SHAN AND JINCAO XIAO

The *Analects* demonstrates the wisdom and characteristics of the spiritual communication of the Chinese people. For communication systems in the contemporary world, the Chinese people can review this wisdom to revive the communicative spirit of intersubjective benevolence in an era of multiculturalism. This forms complementary relationships with the spirit of Western communication based on rationality. The opportunities for comprehension, reflection, and insight in Confucius are complementary with the accurate expression of meaning and rational persuasion in the West. The construction of moral political relationships in Confucius is parallel with the transcendence of moral political relationships in truth-seeking activities in Socrates, Plato, and Aristotle. The stress in Confucius on situations and emotions in interaction is placed alongside the stress in ancient Greece on the guiding role of rationality in interpersonal communication. Establishing these complementary relationships manifests the integrity of human communication as a whole. In the process, the communicative wisdom of the *Analects* is creatively transformed.

Lunyu, also known as the *Analects of Confucius* (hereafter referred to as the *Analects*), is a record of the words, acts, and thoughts of Confucius by his disciples and his followers. The thinking about communication connoted in the *Analects* has been perceived by the academic circle (Cheng, 1987; Shao & Yao, 2014a, 2014b; Wu, 1988; Zhu, 1988) more on the macro level than on the micro level, more for the exploration of moral concepts than for communicative wisdom, and more from a purely Chinese perspective than from a comparative perspective. This perception makes it difficult for the *Analects* to be the wisdom that can be shared about the communication of humankind.

The communicative wisdom of the *Analects* centers around "benevolence" (*Ren*). The basic contents of benevolence include mutual affection, mutual respect, and mutual love, which are communicated among people. There is no equivalent for "communication" in the *Analects*, but words such as *Chuan* (spread), *Yan* (words), *Jiao* (communicate), *Feng* (culture), *Ca* (observance), and *Guan* (look) touch upon the connotations of symbols, speeches, comprehension, interactions, relationships, and influences from different perspectives. Together they display Chinese communicative wisdom. On the basis of understanding the texts and the contexts, and with reference to ancient Greek classic texts, this chapter constructs the dialogic relationships of communicative wisdom between China and the West by explicating the communicative wisdom displayed in the *Analects*.

DIALOGIC WISDOM: CREATING OPPORTUNITIES FOR UNDERSTANDING, REFLECTION, AND INSIGHT

Communication is the process of exchanging ideas or notions with symbols, as well as the process by which human beings understand and are understood by each other. Dialogue is the main form of verbal and semiotic communication. In dialogue, speaking, listening, observation, and feedback are important modes of mutual influence and mutual comprehension. The 500-odd chapters of the *Analects* are the result of dialogues between Confucius and his disciples, 141 of which are actual dialogues. Compared with the dialogues of Socrates and Plato, dialogues in the *Analects* are short and have fewer exchanges. There are more than 70 single-exchange dialogues, and few with three or more exchanges. The theme of the dialogues is benevolence, but they also involve such topics as "rites," "politics," and "gentlemen." The participants include Confucius, his disciples, emperors, officials, friends, and hermits. In the dialogues, on the one hand, Confucius spreads the value of benevolence while letting other people accept its spirit and related ideas; on the other hand, he guides people to practice benevolence.

What are the characteristics of Confucius's dialogues? First, Confucius seldom uses logical deduction and rational persuasion to communicate values; instead, the dialogues guide people to experience life and reflect on life to gain inspiration from it. People need to "seek the cause in themselves" during the dialogue or after it to gain insight. The dialogues serve as an opportunity for comprehension and insight rather than a display of the content of communication with strict reasoning and persuasion to accept. This process is not purely rational thinking; instead, it involves factors such as emotions to pursue the peaceful, reasonable, and amenable spiritual realm. The dialogue that best represents this mode is the one about "the three-year-mourning period" (Yang Huo, *Analects*, Book 17). In it, Zai Wo thought the mourning period of three years will lead to the collapse of rites and music as well as serious social consequences. Confucius doesn't agree with the opinions of Zai Wo. But he doesn't look for the loopholes in Zai Wo's reasoning, nor does he exemplify the importance of the three years of mourning or retort with rational debate. Instead, he asks Zai Wo whether he has emotional peace or not. This process requires people to "examine their conscience" to recall, to release their emotions, and to compare. After asking whether Zai Wo is emotionally peaceful, Confucius points out the proper behavior of emperors during mourning and the fact that it takes a baby three years to leave the parents' arms. He seeks to help the participants in dialogue to realize the value of mourning for the practice of benevolence. If the participant remains indifferent and fails to comprehend mourning, extra words would be meaningless.

Another evidence of his nondeductive style in the *Analects* is that Confucius often uses rhetorical questions to inspire thinking. At first, these questions cause the ones questioned to pause and keep distance from their usual beliefs and thinking, thus creating opportunities for reflection. Next, Confucius usually introduces some kind of foreshadowing as a starting point of thinking. There are more than 50 rhetorical questions in the *Analects*. The following few are representative: "Is it not a pleasure, having learned something, to try it out at due intervals? Is it not a joy to have like-minded friends come from afar? Is it not gentlemanly not to take offence when others fail to appreciate your abilities?" (Book 17), and "What can a man do with the rites who is not benevolent? What can a man do with music who is not benevolent?" (Book 3). This kind of reflective questioning is an important mode to evoke thinking and promote understanding.

The second characteristic of the *Analects* is the qualification of "words." According to the statistics of Yang Bojun's *Annotations to the Analects*, "words" appears 126 times: 59 times as the noun form "speech" (1980, p. 246) and 8 times as "eloquent" (p. 240). However, the *Analects* uses "words" cautiously, requiring a consistency of words with acts and objecting to the abuse of language. The spread of values not only relies on reasoning and inspiration but also requires the communicator's personal involvement for values to be accepted by the audience in practice. "Flowery words" and "inconsistency between words and acts" manifest a lack of virtue, which is not conducive to the spread of values. So Confucius says, "what need is there for a facile tongue? A man quick with a retort will frequently incur the hatred of others. I cannot say whether Yong is benevolent or not, but what need is there for a facile tongue?" (*Analects*, Book 5); "It is rare, indeed for a man with cunning words and an ingratiating countenance to be benevolent" (Book 17); "unbending strength, resoluteness, simplicity and slowness of speech are close to benevolence" (Book 13); "the mark of the benevolent man is that he is loath to speak" (Book 12); and "artful words will ruin one's virtue" (Book 15).

Confucius requires a match between form and content, which is described this way: "only a well-balanced admixture of the two will result in gentleman-liness" (Book 6), and "it is enough that the language one uses should get the point across" (Book 15). In other words, language is not the home of Being in the *Analects*, but the bridge and stage of inspiration. Understanding is gained in life's experiences and reflection, so the status of language is not fundamental, as expressed in "what does Heaven ever say? Yet there are the four seasons going round and there are a hundred things coming into being. What does heaven ever say?" (Book 17).

The third characteristic of the *Analects* is that it reminds us to accept wisdom. Dialogue not only includes speaking but also "listening," "hearing," "looking," and "observing." First, a person should listen more and learn to distinguish wherever there is doubt. For example, "Use your ears widely but leave out what is doubtful; repeat the rest with caution and you will make few mistakes" (Book 2), and "I use my ears widely and follow what is good in what I have heard" (Book 7). In dialogue, one should not be too eager to speak or refute but should think more and excel at extracting the essence and learn to "question," to "look at the means a man employs, observe the path he takes and examine where he feels at home" (Book 2). Therefore, in Confucius's eyes, it is Yan Hui, who is good at listening and thinking, who can best understand his sublime words rather than Zai Wo and Zi Gong, who are good at rhet-oric.[2] Second, apart from verbal communication, dialogues also include the communication of moods and emotions. The speakers should be good at all-round observation, namely, "sensitive to other people's words and observant of the expression on their faces" (Book 12) and "now having listened to a man's words I go on to observe his deeds" (Book 5).

The main characteristic of Socratic dialogues is the use of "midwifery" to define things.[3] Socrates discusses the definition of virtue in the *Meno*, the definition of bravery in the *Laches*, real rhetoric in the *Phaedrus*, piety in the *Euthyphro*, and what is justice and what is good in the *Republic*. As David Bohm (2004) points out, dialogue suggests a "stream of meaning" flowing through, among, and between us; it enables all speakers to participate and share it and makes it possible to create new understanding and consensus in the entire group (p. 6). New consensus and new understanding appear in the form of knowledge. Through dialogue, Socrates seeks to explore the defini-tions of things in the human world, to form knowledge through obtaining definitions and to reach consensus through knowledge.

Different from the dialogue of questions and answers between Confucius and his disciples in the *Analects*, the characteristic of midwifery is that the participants in the dialogues ask and answer questions concerning the same theme[4] to reveal the absurdity[5] and loopholes in people's daily beliefs, that is, in "the derivation of something universal from the particular (Hegel, 1996, p. 58). "The particular is the experience or presentation of whatever is in our consciousness in a naive way" to advance the understanding of phenomena by turning from specifics to the general (Hegel, 1996, p. 58).

In *Memorabilia* and the *Republic*, Socrates typically used this model to discuss justice:

> Socrates asked, "lying, deceiving, enslaving, none of these things will be laid by us next to justice, Euthydemus?"
>
> "Clearly under injustice," Euthydemus said.
>
> "What if someone should enslave an unjust and hostile city? Will we say that he does an injustice? And what if he should use deception when he is at war with them?" Socrates asked.
>
> "Surely not," Euthydemus said.
>
> "Then can we say that while it is just to do such things to enemies, it is unjust to friends?" Socrates asked.
>
> "Certainly," said Euthydemus.
>
> "If some general who sees that his army is dispirited should lie and say that allies are approaching and by this lie put an end to the soldiers' lack of spirit: under which shall we put this deception?" Socrates asked.
>
> "Under justice, in my opinion," said Euthydemus.
>
> "And if someone, whose son needs medicine but will not allow it near him, should deceive him by giving him the medicine as food and by using the lie in this way to make him healthy: where, again, should one put this deception?" Socrates asked.
>
> "In my opinion," Euthydemus said, "this too goes in the same place."
>
> "Are you saying," Socrates asked, "that one should not be straightforward even with one's friends in all circumstances?"
>
> "Surely not," Euthydemus said. "Rather I change where I put the things mentioned, if it's permitted."[6] (Xenophon, 1994, pp. 145–148)

The above example shows that "midwifery" attaches importance to the clarity of expression. It understands discussion and logical reasoning as striving for accurate expressions, the gradual transcendence of complex concrete phenomena, the grasp of common stuff, and the enhancement of understanding among people.

Midwifery is used for the exploration of knowledge while rhetoric for spreading it. The Sophists who are the academic competitors of Socrates and Plato are good at using language skills to take advantage of the audience's emotional and psychological factors for persuasion. The spread of knowledge is not the purpose of rhetoric. Socrates, Plato, and Aristotle object to the so-called rhetoric that disregards truth, confuses right and wrong, and even abandons true knowledge to cater to the public (*Republic*, 267A–269C, 272C–273C). In their opinion, true rhetoric on the one hand studies the characteristics of the audience, knowing how to "classify the kinds of speech and of soul there are, as well as the various ways in which they are affected, and explain what causes each. True rhetoric will then coordinate each kind of soul with the kind of speech appropriate to it. And true rhetoric will give instructions concerning the reasons why one kind of soul is necessarily convinced by one kind of speech while another necessarily remains unconvinced" (271B). On the other hand, true rhetoric needs to know the essence of things, that is, know how to classify things according to their essence and how to put individual things into a general type to be understood by the audience (273E). True rhetoric respects and spreads true knowledge. Aristotle inherits and develops Plato's views on rhetoric. In the *Rhetoric*, he analyzes the various factors of communication and relationships among them, such as the character of the communicator and the audience, the emotional and psychological features of the latter, the communication themes, and the styles and methods of communication.

In summary, in Confucius and in Socrates, Plato, and Aristotle, there are different styles of dialogue.[7] To Confucius, the function of dialogue lies in creating opportunities for comprehension, reflection, and insight. The interlocutor needs introspection to understand meaning, so the communication of meaning is characterized by ambiguity and openness. As a result, meaning is not completely fixed in language. It can be said that in the dialogues of the *Analects*, "meaning is implied" and "words are finite while meaning is infinite." On the other hand, Socrates, Plato, and Aristotle emphasized reasoning and logic, striving to clearly and accurately clarify meaning in language and to fix meaning within language and to analyze the various factors and their relationships in the process of communication. To them, "meaning is in the words."

In fact, both sides object to "letting the words interfere with the meaning." The *Analects* abstains from inconsistency between words and acts, which gives the impression that the communicator cannot practice the values being emphasized. The ancient Greek thinkers abstain from the deviation of words from knowledge and from blind catering to the audience. They demand that the mode of expression match the content. Socrates, Plato, and Aristotle all study the wisdom of speech from the perspective of communicators, while the *Analects* pays attention to the perspective of the audience and the wisdom of listening.

RELATIONSHIP WISDOM: EXTENDING KINSHIP TO INTERPERSONAL RELATIONSHIPS

Communication is the process of linking all unrelated parts of the real world, so it is also the process of building relationships. Though the word *relationship* does not appear in the *Analects*, it is discussed in many passages, involving emperor-subject, father-son, friends, and teacher-student relationships. The vertical father-son relationship is the focus of the *Analects* as well as the basis of some social relationships. In the *Analects*, the political human relationship is the main topic of discussion, while economic and commercial relationships are basically not touched upon.

What, then, is the significance of human political relationships for life? The *Analects* maintains that secular relationships are the origin of the meaning of life, which are inherent in people (An Lezhe & Luo Siwen, 2003). Positively speaking, "benevolence means people" (The Book of Rites, *Doctrine of the Mean*). Etymologically, *benevolence* means "two people," that is, it represents interpersonal relationships. Confucius said, "a benevolent man helps others to take their stand in that he himself wishes to take his stand, and gets others there in that he himself wishes to get there" (*Analects*, Book 6). Here "helps others to take a stand" and "gets others there" occur during the same process as "taking his stand" and "getting there himself." It is in this process that the meaning of life, which is rooted in relationships, increases. Cultivation of one's mind and body not only aims at upgrading one's personal morals and state of being but also aims at taking some actions to push the development of other people. So when Zi Lu asked what constituted a gentleman, Confucius replied that it is he who "cultivates himself and thereby achieves reverence"; "cultivates himself and thereby brings peace and security to his fellow men"; and "cultivates himself and thereby brings peace and security to people" (*Analects*, Book 14).

In terms of building relationships, Confucians take human relationships as the basis and "benevolence," which originates from such relationships, as the norm regulating relationships so that social relationships are gradually extended outward. Because China at that time was a patriarchal kinship society, in which social relationships were structurally similar to patriarchal relationships,[8] and because "filial piety" was the source of "benevolence," the improvement of kinship relationships was important to the development of other interpersonal relationships. Therefore, "it is rare for a man whose character is such that he is good as a son and obedient as a young man to have the inclination to transgress against his superiors; it is unheard of for one who has no such inclination to be inclined to start a rebellion" (*Analects*, Book 17). In addition, because the words and acts of governors were exemplary, their being loving and filial were of special importance to the maintenance of social relationships.[9]

In terms of relationship itself, the *Analects* attaches great importance to emotions. First, the *Analects* demands that a person should have a loving attitude and be affectionate to other people, as illustrated by these sayings: "the benevolent love of other people"[10] and "love the multitude at large but cultivate the friendship of your fellow men" (Book 17). "All within the Four

Seas are his brothers" in the *Analects* (Book 12) becomes "treat all elders as if they were your own parents and treat all youngsters as if they were your own children" in the *Mencius* (1A: 7). This means that the kinship based on blood relationships is extended to various interpersonal relationships. As a result, there is warmth between all people. Later Confucians even develop the broad worldview that "all men are my fellows and all things are my type." Second, the *Analects* stresses the support of moral sentiments for relationships. Good relationships demand that the other party has a corresponding morality, while virtues demand that the people originating the relationship have corresponding moral sentiments. In the dialogue about "three years mourning," Zai Wo is against "three-year mourning," not feeling guilty and lacking the correspondent moral sentiment, so Confucius concludes that Zai Wo is not benevolent. When discussing "filial piety," the *Analects* thinks it not enough to show acts of supporting parents; children should have the moral sentiment of respecting them,[11] so that acts and emotions match each other.[12]

In the *Analects*, the meaning of life is rooted in secular moral political relationships, but ancient Greece had the tradition called the "love of wisdom." The pursuit of the pure application of reasoning and of knowledge for the ancient Greeks opens up new meaning space beyond secular life and makes it possible for life to transcend secular relationships. The typical example is the philosopher king in the *Republic*. After he perceived the supreme good, he was reluctant to return to political life but willing to lead a meditative life. Plato's philosophy makes people transcend secular relationships in the Platonic realm of Ideas, while Aristotle's philosophy makes people transcend secular relationships in meditation. Christianity thereafter guides people to transcend secular relationships in heaven.

Different from the *Analects*, which attaches great importance to emotions, Plato and Aristotle believe that rationality is the force for constructing relationships and the measurement of them.[13] In that sense, relationships themselves are no longer the model and basis for various social relationships.[14] Plato and Aristotle indicate in many places that rationality should be the measurement for constructing relationships. In the *Republic*, Plato maintains that the most rational people should become rulers of city-states, that those with lesser rationality should become soldiers, and that those with the worst rationality should become husbandmen and craftsmen. Rationality is the ruler of the individual spirit; passion is the ally of rationality and desire should be ruled by it. Only when rationality becomes the measurement for deciding the relationship of ruling and being ruled will relationships be harmonious and upright (*Republic*, 427E–445A). In Aristotle's *Politics*, rationality is also the criterion for deciding relationships. For example, in the relationship between men and women, Aristotle maintains that men's rationality is stronger than women's, so women should be ruled (1254b13). In the relationships between master and slaves, Aristotle believes that the master can use rationality, while slaves can only accept the master's rationality, so the slaves should be ruled (254b20).

For Plato and Aristotle, the main morality regulating interpersonal relationships is justice. Justice is represented more as rationality than emotions. Justice demands the rational proportion of distribution and exchange of various resources.[15] Besides, even in emotional friendships,[16] all parties concerned should maintain an equitable proportion of communication. More importantly, Aristotle thinks that real friendship is based on virtues, which means that people can use rationality well and emotional desire should obey the order of rationality. Therefore, whether all parties have sufficient or corresponding rationality is the basis for establishing friendly relationships, while emotional factors do not have a prominent role in friendly relationships.

In summary, the fundamental spirit of the *Analects* is benevolence, which stresses political moral practices in the secular world and holds the worldview of "one world." Confucians place the meaning of life in human political relationships while the ancient Greeks have the tradition of seeking truth and loving wisdom, thus opening up the possibility of transcending human political relationships in truth-seeking activities. So the two parties choose different paths in constructing relationships. The *Analects* stresses the outward extension of kinship sentiments and the support of moral sentiments, while the ancient Greeks take rationality as the basis of relationships.

INTERACTIVE WISDOM: "CULTURALIZATION BY RITES AND MUSIC" AND THE "DOCTRINE OF LOYALTY AND FORGIVENESS"

Generally speaking, interaction is the mode of existence of living organisms; without interaction, there will be no common action. Interaction naturally means communication, which manifests itself as ceremonies of social communication and mutual influence among people.

Interactive ideas in the *Analects* are mainly embodied in the concepts of "culturalization by rites and music" and the "doctrine of loyalty and forgiveness." The former is the mode of influencing other people advocated by the *Analects,* while the latter are the behavioral norms in interpersonal interaction.

"Culturalization by rites and music" can be understood from two aspects. The first is "rites and music," by means of which the participants can cultivate their social emotions and enhance their sense of belonging and responsibility to the community so that values are spread. The second is "culturalization," which advocates that the disseminator of values should teach by personal example and verbal instruction to influence the audience's emotions and psychology. Exemplary modeling is needed so that the values communicated are actively accepted and acknowledged. In the interactive model of "culturaliza-tion by rites and music," the disseminator takes the dominant role and is the guide of interaction. The disseminator should not only stick to the advocated principles but at the same time be flexible with the interactive mode and com-municated content according to specific situations.

The communicative function of "rites and music" is embodied in building emotions. On the one hand, they evoke emotions and, on the other hand, they produce resonance in the participants so that they are mutually con-firmed emotionally. When a disciple asked him the essence of rites, Confucius replied, "A noble question indeed! With rites, it is better to err on the side of frugality than on the side of extravagance; in mourning, it is better to err on the side of grief than on the side of indifference" (*Analects*, Book 3). Confucius means that ritual words, appearance, and music are merely means to manifest and evoke these emotions; the key is the emotions. Therefore, Confucius said, "surely when one says 'the rites, the rites', it is not enough to mean presents of jade and silk. Surely when one says 'music, music', it is not enough merely to mean bells and drum" (*Analects*, Book 17). Music is an important component of rites and has very strong power to shape emotions.[17] Good music can not only convey a sense of beauty but also express people's moral intentions.[18]

The *Analects* records that Confucius sang with other people. When the others sang well, he would surely ask them to sing again, and he himself would do the same.[19] To Confucius, music is the builder of emotions. Only by repeated singing can the emotions be solidified and the correspondent struc-ture be formed. However, this kind of solidification is not the result of simple repetition but of mutual emotional confirmation of the participants, that is, of enhanced resonance. Among the numerous rites, Confucius stressed, "Conduct the funeral of your parents with meticulous care and let not sacrifices to your remote ancestors be forgotten" (*Analects*, Book 17), thus attaching great impor-tance to sacrifices and funerals. Because sacrificial and funeral rites establish the emotional links between individuals and family history, it is not only conducive to cultivating moral sentiments concerning "filial piety" but also weaves individ-uals into the history and genealogy of the community.[20] Cultivating the indi-vidual's responsibility to the community results in the historic fact that people become participative and experiential.[21]

Culturalization is the situational interactive mode advocated by the *Analects*. First, culturalization relies on the demonstrative function of the disseminator, and demonstration requires that all parties be in similar situa-tions. Confucius believes that "by nature the gentleman is like wind and the small man like grass. Let the wind sweep over the grass and it is sure to bend" (*Analects*, Book 12). Another way of stating it: "If a man is correct in his own person, then there will be obedience without orders being given; but if he is not correct in his own person, there will not be obedience even though orders are given" (Book 13). To set an example by one's action is a good way to spread value and beliefs. For it to function, the imitator should have a "pre-comprehension" of the disseminator's behaviors and beliefs to be able to interpret the symbolic meaning of actions. Besides, the audience needs to establish a connection with the disseminator to observe the actions.

Furthermore, culturalization requires interaction that is individualized. The *Analects* seldom preaches. Confucius teaches his disciples according to their abilities. As mentioned in *Annotations to the Analects* by Yang Bojun, Confucius understands his disciples well, so he often uses different modes and content to answer the same question from different disciples. Five disciples including Yan Yuan, Zhong Gong, Sima Niu, Fan Chi, and Zi Zhang ask the meaning of benevolence seven different times, and Confucius does answer them in a general way. For example, "return to the observance of the rites through overcoming the self constitutes benevolence" (*Analects*, Book 12); "do not impose on others what you yourself do not desire" (Book 15); and "love your fellow men" (Book 12). Or he focuses on the way of morality ruled by benevolence, such as, "they are respectfulness, tolerance, trustworthiness in word, quickness and generosity" (Book 17).

But Confucius is specific to situations also: "When abroad behave as though you were receiving an important guest. When employing the services of the common people behave as though you were officiating at an important sacrifice" (*Analects*, Book 12); "While at home hold yourself in a respectful attitude; when serving in an official capacity be reverent; when dealing with others give of your best" (*Analects*, Book 13); "The benevolent man reaps the benefit only after encountering difficulties, and that can be called benevolence" (Book 6). Since disciple Sima Niu is talkative and impetuous, Confucius directly tells him that benevolence is to speak slowly. In the Hsien Tsin (Book 11), Confucius gives the opposite answer to the same question according to the characters of his disciples:

> Zi-lu asks, "Should one immediately put into practice what one has heard?" The Master said, "As your father and elder brothers are still alive, you are hardly in a position immediately to put into practice what you have heard." Ran You asked, "Should one immediately put into practice what one has heard?" The Master says, "Yes. One should." Gong-xi Hua says, "When You asked whether one should immediately put into practice what one had heard, you pointed out that his father and elder brothers were alive. Yet when Qiu asked whether one should immediately put into practice what one had heard, you answered that one should. I am puzzled. May I be enlightened?" The Master says, "Qiu holds himself back. It is for this reason that I tried to urge him on. Ran You has the drive of two men. It is for this reason that I tried to hold him back."

When Zi-lu and Ran You ask whether one should immediately put into practice what one has heard, because Zi-lu is daring, Confucius's answer is to hold back; since Ran You is cowardly, Confucius encourages him to take prompt actions. Besides, the *Analects* already includes the idea of audience classification. Confucius once says, "you can tell those who are above average about the best, but not those who are below average" (*Analects,* Book 6), and "it is only the most intelligent and the most stupid who cannot be budged" (*Analects,* Book 17). The communicative mode of knowledge is related to the qualification of the audience.

The "doctrine of loyalty and forgiveness"—which means that "a benevolent man helps others to take their stand in the way that he himself wishes to take his stand, and gets others there in the way that he himself wishes to get there" (Book 6) and "do not impose on others what you yourself do not desire" (Book 15)—is the basic norm of interaction defined by Confucius and regarded as consistently embodying the spirit of benevolence.

The "doctrine of loyalty and forgiveness" is also situational. It does not appear as a commandment, such as in "no killing other people" and "no lying." When applying it, the practitioner should judge, analyze, and deduce from the situation, so that the doctrine falls into the situation in some specific manner. Moreover, as Confucius seldom mentioned an abstract humanity,[22] "people" in the *Analects* refers to specific others. When we think about "not imposing on others what you yourself do not desire," we need to consider if we are in the same situation as others, and whether we are willing or unwilling to accept certain treatment. When considering "helping others to take their stand" and "getting others there," we also need to live into the others' situation to consider how to help them and how to participate and regulate. Compassionate understanding is the prerequisite to implementing the doctrine of loyalty and forgiveness. Therefore, we can explain why Confucius used different contents and modes when facing different disciples to express his ideas.

The "doctrine of loyalty and forgiveness" is inclusive. First, taken as an interactive principle, it is not easy to avoid giving the impression that one is imposing one's standard on others. On the one hand, its negative principle is this: "do not impose on others what you yourself do not desire." On the other hand, the positive principle—to "help others to take their stand" and "get others there"—refers to specific others who have their own characteristics and backgrounds. We help others to develop according to their own characteristics instead of measuring and transforming others according to our standards. Second, this doctrine also reminds people not to lose themselves. When Zi Gong asks about friends, Confucius says, "Advise them to the best of your ability and guide them properly, but stop when there is no hope of success. Do not ask to be snubbed" (*Analects,* Book 12). When talking about how to treat the Lords, he said, "to be importunate with one's Lord will mean humiliation. To be importunate with one's friends will mean estrangement" (*Analects,* Book 4). Also, "The term 'great minister' refers to those who serve their Lord according to the Way and who, when this is no longer possible, relinquish office" (*Analects,* Book 11). In interacting with others, one needs to respect the other party and respect oneself to strike a balance. This is true "agreement with others without being an echo."[23] Third, Confucius's affirmation of filial piety means his affirmation of the giving and conserving of life. When it is extended to relationships beyond kinship, it means the affirmation of the conservation of all lives. The value stressed is life itself rather than certain features of life, such as rationality, emotions, or will. We should neither be extremists and take a certain quality as the only standard for value judgment nor formulate norms of human interaction according to this only standard.

Different from the *Analects,* which stresses situations and emotions in interaction, Plato and Aristotle emphasize the guiding role of rationality in interpersonal interaction. Aristotle thinks that matters related to practice should be tackled by prudence.[24] In *The Nicomachean Ethics,* Aristotle analyzes virtues that regulate interpersonal communication such as justice, love, restraint, bravery, generosity, magnanimity, and honesty. The nucleus of these moral virtues is to use rationality to guide and regulate emotions and desires in the process of practice, so that emotions and desires are in a moderate state, avoiding excess and inadequacy. Justice is moderation between an excessive preoccupation with the good and inadequate preoccupation with the good and between inadequate loss of evil and excessive loss of evil. Bravery is moderation between fear and confidence when facing danger on the battlefield. Excessive bravery is impertinence, and inadequate bravery is cowardice.[25] Generosity is moderation in giving wealth; its excess is extravagance, and its inadequacy is meanness. Magnanimity is moderation toward honor. An excessively magnanimous person is vain, while an inadequately magnanimous person is self-effacing. All these immoderations result from either the fact that emotions are not regulated by rationality or the fact that subjects fail to make correct judgment. Overall, abiding by rationality is the criterion for interaction.

It should be noted that the stress on rationality is not equivalent to an insensitivity to practices or the inflexibility of interaction. When discussing moral virtues, Aristotle points out that practical moral virtues should take a specific time, occasion, object, reason, and mode into consideration (*Nicomachean Ethics*, 1106b20). This means that there are no fixed methods for improving moral norms, so one can only learn from people with virtues.[26] The difference between the *Analects* and Aristotle is that "the doctrine of loyalty and forgiveness" involves a process of empathy and reciprocity, while Aristotle is more concerned about whether certain acts are appropriate from the subject's perspective.

The stress on rationality makes interaction possess "a sense of scale."[27] This scale requires establishing clear boundaries in communication practice and a demarcation of communication space. In the discussion of justice, Aristotle introduces the concept of "desert."[28] It requires clarity of what is yours and what is mine, asking people to justify and defend their own demands and establish clear communication space. Comparatively speaking, if strong emotions are involved in interpersonal interaction, then what both parties can or cannot do is flexible, and the interpersonal boundary will be vague and loose. This stress of "a sense of scale" and the boundary of communication naturally makes laws. Whatever is mandatory, clear, and operative becomes a major norm for regulating interpersonal interaction.

In summary, the emphasis on the influence of emotions, introduction of historical factors, and mutual magnanimity are the interactive features of the *Analects*. By contrast, Socrates, Plato, and Aristotle highlight the decisive role of rationality in interaction,[29] thus creating the trend of stressing the boundaries of communication and using laws to regulate interaction. All parties pay attention to situations, but with different degrees of intersubjectivity.

TRANSFORMATION OF WISDOM

By comparative analysis, we have found that Confucius is cautious about the use of language. He creates opportunities for understanding through dialogue, not completely fixing the meaning within language and hinting that we must pay attention to the wisdom of receiving. Confucius emphasizes relationships, placing the meaning of life in moral political relationships, expanding various relationships based on family relationships, and paying attention to maintaining and consolidating relationships by cultivating moral sentiments. "Culturalization by rites and music" operates in the interactive mode with Chinese characteristics, and the "doctrine of loyalty and forgiveness" is the fundamental norm guiding interaction. Both combine emotions with history, situations, and rationality to form a three-dimensional interactive model.

The communicative wisdom of the *Analects* demonstrates the wisdom of the spiritual communication of the Chinese people and their communicative characteristics. In communication systems of the contemporary world, Chinese people can construct communicative subjectivity by reviewing this wisdom to revive the communicative spirit of intersubjective "benevolence" in an era of multiculturalism. This forms complementary relationships with the Western communicative spirit based on rationality, namely, opportunities for comprehension, reflection, and insight versus the accurate expression of meaning and rational persuasion; the construction of moral political relationships versus the transcendence of moral political relationships in truth-seeking activities; and the stress on situations and emotions in interaction versus the stress on the guiding role of rationality in interpersonal communication. Benevolence actually manifests the integrity of the human communication spirit, in the process of which the communicative wisdom of the *Analects* is creatively transformed. In contemporary terms, the wisdom of the *Analects* is one that transcends communication restrictions. It includes the following two aspects.

On the one hand, it is wisdom to face others. In contemporary society, various grand narratives have collapsed, the world is becoming more diversified, and individuals have become more personalized, so people have gradually become incomprehensible "others." How to deal with "others" has become an important issue of contemporary society. The "doctrine of loyalty and forgiveness" reminds us to have "agreement with others without being an echo," to accommodate each other, to protect ourselves, to avoid annexing each other, and to enhance each other so as to strike a balance between oneself and others. The doctrine reminds us further to optimize diversity and fulfill the ideal that "all living creatures grow together without harming each other and ways run parallel without interfering with one another" (*Doctrine of the Mean*).

In addition, the *Analects* reminds us to be "reasonable" and emphasize emotions. If one wants to enter into others' lives, one should eliminate emotional conflict and estrangement, be good at expressing and interpreting emotions, be close to each other emotionally, and be good at establishing emotional relationships. Moreover, in communicating with others, one should be good at entering the living circumstances of the other to construct the appropriate communication mode. Differences in values and culture usually result from differences in living circumstances. Only by entering into the circumstances of the other can one know the differences, their source as well as their value, so that one can really think from the other's perspectives and then find the optimal behavioral and communication model in consultation with others.

On the other hand, it is wisdom to face loneliness. In this more open and flexible era, when people have increasingly more rights to express and more ways to express them, more and more people feel a profound loneliness and find it hard to find partners of meaning. In the face of loneliness, the *Analects* first suggests that one should have the awareness of listening. It is not that the more sound the better or the bigger sound the better. In a noisy and impetuous environment, people need the wisdom of listening, to listen to one's own heart, and at the same time to listen to the meaning conveyed by others. Unable to listen, observe, or comprehend and unable to give up stubbornness, one will surely be imprisoned by loneliness. Therefore, the *Analects* says, "refuse to entertain conjectures or insist on certainty; refuse to be inflexible or to be egotistical" (Book 9), suggesting that we pay attention to observation.

Second, the *Analects* reminds us to have the wisdom of expression. Confucius does not fix meaning within language; instead, he tries to create opportunities and space for understanding meaning and for demonstrating meaning by various methods such as acts, rites, and music. This three-dimensional expression mode through the creation of circumstances is worthy of reference in the contemporary world.

Last, where the meaning of life is placed directly determines whether one is lonely. If the meaning of life is placed in the atomic self, in pure subjectivity, loneliness is inevitable, because others and the world are only of instrumental significance to the subject, in whose eyes there is only oneself. If the meaning of life can be placed in relationships and the meaning of one's own life is combined with that of the others, resonances in life will naturally increase and the sense of loneliness will diminish accordingly.

NOTES

1. An earlier version of this essay was published in the *Journal of International Communication* (Issue 6, 2014) under the title "Communicating Wisdom of the *Analects*: A Comparative Perspective." Shao Peiren of China Media Research has given permission for publication here.

2. The Master said, "if anyone can listen to me with unflagging attention, it is Hui, I suppose." The Master said, "I can speak to Hui all day without his disagreeing with me in any way. Thus he would seem to be stupid. However, when I take a closer look at what he does in private after he has withdrawn from my presence, I discover that it does, in fact, throw light on what I said. Hui is not stupid after all" (*Analects*, Book 2).

3. In Plato's early dialogues, Socrates expressed his own thoughts, while in the later dialogues, Plato's thoughts were expressed by the interlocutors in the name of Socrates. As the theme of this chapter is not to research Socrates' and Plato's communicative thoughts, we do not distinguish between the two here. All use of the name "Socrates" used in this essay refers to the interlocutors in the name of Socrates.

4. A significant distinction between "midwifery" and a rambling speech is whether a dialogue is about the same theme.

5. One feels absurd because beliefs contradict the intuition that we can withstand reflections in the social environment.

6. The original dialogue is abbreviated here to highlight the characteristics of Socrates' dialogues.

7. In specific aspects, Socrates, Plato, and Aristotle treat "dialogue" with different attitudes. Socrates discusses truth by way of dialogue. Plato uses dialogues a lot in his early literature, but in his later life, he chooses to express his ideas more in the form of monologues. Aristotle gives up the use of dialogic forms to express his ideas; his thoughts about dialogue are mainly reflected in his study of rhetoric.

8. Rulers of society are deemed similar to the rulers of a family, but the *Analects* does not directly compare the rulers of society to "father" nor propose to transfer filial piety to loyalty and to treat one's king as one's father. Instead, the *Analects* takes the emperor-subject relationship as a similar example to the relationship of friends, as is reflected in "to be importunate with one's lord will mean humiliation. To be importunate with one's friends will mean estrangement" (Book 4). An emperor and his subjects should enjoy a certain degree of independence and well-meaning advice should also be made appropriately, which is quite

different from the later idea of the subject making his remonstrance with his emperor by way of threatening to commit suicide. Please refer to Li, Zehou, *Reading the* Analects *Today* (2007, 1:87).

9. Ji Kang Zi asked, "How can one get the common people to be reverent, to do their utmost and to be filled with enthusiasm?" The Master said, "Rule over them with dignity and they will be reverent; treat them with kindness and they will do their utmost; raise the good and instruct those who are backward and they will be filled with enthusiasm" (*Analects*, Book 2).

10. Fan Chi asked about benevolence. The Master said, "Love your fellow men" (*Analects*, Book 12).

11. "Nowadays for a man to be filial means no more than that he is able to provide his parents with food. Every hound and horse are, in some way, provided with food. If a man shows no reverence, where is the difference?" (*Analects*, Book 2).

12. Zi-xia asked about being filial. The Master said, "What is difficult to manage is the expression on one's face. As for the young taking on the burden when there is work to be done or letting the old enjoy wine and food when these are available, that hardly deserves to be called filial" (*Analects*, Book 2).

13. Aristotle has made a detailed analysis of the emotions of "kindness," "anger," "charity," and "shame" in the *Rhetoric* but did not regard them as important factors in constructing relationships.

14. In the *Republic*, Plato even canceled the family and arranged the combination of man and woman and breeding of offspring purely with "rationality."

15. In *The Nicomachean Ethics*, the exchange not only refers to commercial transactions but also includes a variety of exchange activities with gain for one party and loss for another, such as theft, adultery, poisoning, pimping, luring away one's slave, assassinations, perjury, assault, robbery, abuse, insults, and so forth (1131a5–7).

16. In the eyes of Aristotle, friendship does not exist only in the relationship of friends, but also in the mutual attraction of people. Aristotle believes that there are three kinds of friendship, those based on happiness, usefulness, and virtue, respectively (1155b18–56b30).

17. In the *Politics*, Aristotle believes that music serves to entertain, to delight (being amused at an appropriate thing), and for improvement (cultivating rationality) (1339b13).

18. The Master said "of the *shao* that it was both perfectly beautiful and perfectly good and of the *wu* that it was perfectly beautiful but not perfectly good" (*Analects*, Book 3).

19. "While singing in the company of others, when the Master found a song attractive, he always asked to hear it again before joining in" (*Analects*, Book 7).

20. Confucius attaches importance to the combination of history with interaction, the inheriting and learning form the tradition, and dialogues with the tradition. I myself believe in the principle of "interpreting instead of creating" and often take historical events and figures (Yao, Shun Wen, Wu, Duke) as examples in my teaching.

21. While the *Analects* emphasizes applying history to enlightenment and to people in history, history has the least importance in Aristotle's works on how to build a city-state and cultivate a good citizen. For him, while ancestor worship is not crucial to cultivating citizens and building a city-state, rationality is the only blueprint for building the city-state and cultivating citizens.

22. One is able to hear about the Master's accomplishments, but one cannot get to hear his views on human nature and the Way of Heaven (*Analects*, Book 5). This is quite different from the construction of public life in the West, which starts from abstract humanity.

23. "The gentleman agrees with others without being an echo. The small man echoes without being in agreement" (*Analects*, Book 13).
24. In Aristotle's eyes, prudence differs from wisdom. Prudence is the rationality to tackle changeable matters without inevitability, while wisdom is the rationality to perceive unchangeable matters with inevitability (1138b19–1141b23).
25. Bravery of a soldier on the battlefield determines the life of the soldier's comrades and the survival of a city-state, so bravery involves the virtues of interpersonal interactions.
26. Here learning mainly refers to learning how to apply rationality based on outstanding people. They mainly demonstrate the ability of rationality, which is different from the demonstration of enlightenment.
27. Linguistically speaking, rationality itself connotes scale.
28. In discussing distributive justice, Aristotle indicates that justice in distribution should be based on some kind of desert (1131a27–29).
29. Although both Plato and Aristotle emphasize the role of rationality in practice, Aristotle notices the tensility between rationality and experience, between universality and particularity. He treats rationality with less absoluteness than Plato does, that is, with some effort to tone it down.

BIBLIOGRAPHY

An Lezhe & Luo Siwen. (2003). *A philosophical annotation of the Analects of Confucius: A comparative philosophical perspective.* Beijing: China Social Science Press.

Aristotle. (1997). *The complete works of Aristotle.* Ed. Barnes Jonathan. Princeton, NJ: Princeton University Press.

Bohm, D. (2004). *On dialogues.* Trans. Wang Songtao. Beijing: Education Science Press.

Cheng, C. (1987). Chinese philosophy and contemporary human communication theory. In D. L. Kincaid (Ed.), *Communication theory: Eastern and Western perspectives* (pp. 20–43). New York: Academic Press.

Confucius. (1980). *The Analects.* Annotated Yang Bojun. Beijing: Zhonghua Book Company.

Hegel, G. W. F. (1996). *Lectures on the history of philosophy: Lectures of 1825–1826.* Ed. Robert F. Brown. Trans. J. M. Stewart. Berkeley: University of California Press.

Li, Z. (2007). *Reading the* Analects *today.* Tianjin: Tianjin Social Science Press.

Mencius. (2005). *Mencius.* Annotated Yang Bojun. Beijing: Zhonghua Book Company.

Plato. (1997). *Complete works.* Ed. John M. Cooper. Indianapolis: Hackett Publishing.

Shao, P., & Yao, J. (2014a). Dialectical theory of communication: Dialectical communication ideas in the pre-Qin period and their transformation into modern theory. *Journal of Hangzhou Normal University* (Humanities and Social Sciences), *2*(3), 96–111.

Shao, P., & Yao, J. (2014b). On the mode of communication: Core communication mode of the *Analects* and Confucianism communication. *Journal of Zhejiang University* (Humanities and Social Sciences), *44*(4), 56–76.

Wu, Y. (1988). *The invisible network.* Beijing: International Cultural Press.

Xenophon. (1994). *Memorabilia.* Trans. A. L. Bonnette. Ithaca: Cornell University Press.

Zhu, C. (1988). *The Analects of communication in pre-Qin, Tang, Song, Ming and Qing Dynasty.* Taiwan: Commercial Press.

CHAPTER TWO

The Problem OF *Communitas* IN Western Moral Philosophy

CLIFFORD CHRISTIANS

Despite their conceptual differences rooted in various periods of intellectual history, classical Western philosophers make individual choice and accountability their centerpiece. Aristotle promoted self-realization, Kant's *Groundwork of the Metaphysic of Morals* is an argument for individual rationality, and the British philosopher John Stuart Mill's utilitarianism centered on personal autonomy. Ethics that depends on these historic approaches is formalistic, grounding reason in an apparatus of neutral standards outside of society and culture. The idea of *communitas*, which is fundamental to interculturalism, is undeveloped or since Locke cast into a dualism of individual and society.

However, for communication ethics that is multicultural, goodness and badness do not merely express solitary subjective attitudes but are judgments a community together believes to be true about the world. In these communal terms, the tradition of Counter-Enlightenment philosophy is needed for the West to contribute substantially to the intercultural era. The philosophers of language are of particular relevance, with Ernst Cassirer, Hans-Georg Gadamer, Charles Sanders Peirce, and Paul Ricoeur representative of those who define humans as dialogic beings. This onto-linguistic trajectory enables moral philosophy to develop community as a normative ideal.

There are two problems in media ethics that need to be overcome for multiculturalism to flourish: formal rules and ethical models built on the abstracted self. However, both issues are deeply entrenched in media ethics as a whole and warrant a systematic review so that the promise of this path-breaking book on the ethics of multiculturalism will be fulfilled.

RATIONAL CHOICE THEORY

Ethical thinking in the Western tradition is rooted in the individual decision maker, and for good reason. Persons involved in moral decisions must have the freedom to make choices, otherwise they cannot be held accountable for their behavior. From this focus on the decision maker, three prominent ethical systems have emerged: virtue, consequences, and duty. These moral philosophies produce formal principles and presume individuated choice.

Aristotle in Classical Greece

The Athenian Greeks first established rationalistic ethics. Since Parmenides, Greek philosophy assumed the identity of reason and being. Plato and Aristotle shared a common rationalism as identifying our essential humanness. "In the thought of Aristotle only the active *nous*, precisely the mind which is not involved in the soul, is immortal; and for Plato the immutability of ideas is regarded as proof of the immortality of the *nous*" (Niebuhr, 1941/1964, p. 7). In classical theory, the moral reasoning process begins with the individual, specifically the autonomous moral actor who is considered culpable for choices made. This view of human nature centers on the uniqueness of the rational faculties in the human species and places extraordinary emphasis on the human actor's capacity for rational thought. Philosophical ethics in this tradition is "based on the common principle" that we ought to "do the good which stands the test of reason" (Landmann, 1974, p. 110).

Aristotle stipulates that the proper function of the human being must be our defining characteristic as a species. Sensation or perception "seems to be common even to the horse, the ox, and every animal." What is distinctive, then, is "an active life of the soul (*psyche*) that follows a rational principle" (*Nicomachean Ethics*, 1098a4; cf. 1098a6). Aristotle identifies the capacity for thinking as the distinctive function of *Homo sapiens* among the activities of all living creatures. He is preoccupied with the way humans think, how they deliberate and choose, how they experience voluntary and coerced choices differently. In short, "Aristotle introduces a phenomenology of thinking. It is in the act of thinking itself—whether this be in the 'pure' form of contemplation or in the 'applied' form of practical reasoning—that we exercise our natural function and thus we obtain happiness or well-being" (Johnstone, 2002, p. 20).

In the *Categories, On Interpretation,* the *Prior* and *Posterior Analytics, On Sophistical Refutations,* and the *Topics,* Aristotle elaborates on the methods of logical inquiry and proof. Aristotle distinguishes two kinds of intellect: the "scientific" (*episteme*) and the "calculative" or "logistical" (*logistikon*). Scientific cognition concerns the eternal and immutable. Scientific knowledge is deductive reasoning from universal premises to conclusions that are invariably true.

The calculative mind makes sense of human action. *Logistikon* can be understood as everyday judgments. In the moral domain, Aristotle calls it *phronesis,* practical wisdom. *Phronesis* concerns the choice of specific actions that will promote the good. It is "a true and reasoned state of capacity to act with regard to the things that are good or bad" (*Nicomachean Ethics,* 1140b5–6). For *phronesis* to play an essential role in morality, one's desires or appetites must be conditioned by habit to be receptive to the directives of reason. The agent must act from "a firm and unchangeable character" (*Nicomachean Ethics,* 1105a31–34). The moral imperative for each of us is to develop the kind of character that will tend to make such choices as a result of habit or inclination.

Aristotle's ethical theory is built on the premise that the good life for a human being is one in which all one's actions imply or follow a rational principle.

> The important idea is that in the human soul (*psyche*) there is a rational principle whose proper activity is thinking, and an appetitive element that "is naturally opposed to the rational principle, [that] fights and resists this principle" (*Nicomachean Ethics,* 1102b13– 19). Nonetheless, in the self-controlled person the appetitive element is "submissive and obedient" to reason, and in the virtuous person it is "in complete harmony with the rational principle," to obey it "as one does one's father" (*Nicomachean Ethics,* 1102b35– 1103a3). (Johnstone, 2002, pp. 22, 26)

In Aristotle's rational choice theory, the idea of responsibility is linked to actions performed voluntarily. Aristotle's conception of virtue assumes "that individuals actually choose, or at least that they have the experience of choosing. To reject the idea of agency is to reject the possibility of ethics" (Johnstone, 2002, p. 29).

Aristotle's ethics of rational choice is rooted in a vision of human life that is fundamentally social and political. As Aristotle observes in his *Politics,* "the human being is by nature an animal intended to live in a *polis*" (1253a). He states it this way in his *Nicomachean Ethics*: "the human is a being meant for political association" (1097b). While moral action is finally a personal matter, Aristotle locates moral judgment in the context of our situatedness in communities. The responsible life includes both self-reflection and involvement in public life.

Kant and the Enlightenment Mind

Rational choice theory supposes that decisions are made by individuals who live with the consequences. In the Western Enlightenment of the 18th century, human beings were considered to be entities with discrete boundaries. Human personality was sovereign. Individuals were understood as ends in themselves, and self-determination became the highest good. Autonomy became the core of our humanness and the central ideal of life. The innermost self defined our humanity and must be protected from any outside force.

This version of rational being was established by Rene Descartes, who portrayed human subjects as "interiorized mental substances" (Schrag, 1997, p. 4). The essence of the self is *res cognitans*, a thinking substance. *Cogito ergo sum*, genuine knowledge, is testable and objectively true. It is as cognitively clean as mathematics, built in linear fashion from a neutral, noncontingent starting point. What was called thought in the 18th century was no longer the Platonic conception of ideas or Aristotle's integrative *logos*; rather, rationality was understood as analytic calculating that dissolves the world into quantitative particles that are to be mastered technically.

Descartes described this method of reasoning in his *Rules for the Direction of the Mind* (1638/1964):

> Reduce complex and obscure propositions step by step to simpler ones, and then try to advance by the same gradual process from the … very simplest to the knowledge of all the rest. … We should not examine what follows, but refrain from a useless task. (pp. 163, 172)

Descartes contended, in effect, that we can demonstrate the truth only of what we can measure. The realm of spirit was beyond such measurement, a matter of faith and intuition, not truth. The physical became the only legitimate domain of knowledge. The narrow calculation of science was accepted as the ideology by which modernity ought to live (cf. Descartes, 1641/1993).

The entire 18th century was captivated by Cartesian rationalism. Descartes expressed his delight "at the certitude" of mathematics, and the guiding idea of his entire work was to develop a philosophy of nature and a picture of the human person from a mathematical foundation (Descartes, 1637/1938). The scientific successes of the 17th century in astronomy and physics became the structural model for philosophy. The physical sciences suggested to the Enlightenment mind that even as the atom is the fundamental building block of all matter, discrete individuals are the essential unit of society. The astrophysical worldview of the 17th-century Age of Science provided an analogue for humans as irreducible, self-sufficient entities. The cosmos was understood to mirror in its mathematical and quantitative character the explicitly rational character of human thought. Thus the 18th century carries over Newtonian science and Cartesian mathematics into its conception of human nature as defined by the quantitative judgment we call "calculation." In the three-volume *Principia Mathematica* by Bertrand Russell and Alfred North Whitehead (1910–1913), mathematics is established as formal logic; the world is thought to contain clear and distinct facts and properties that are true if they correspond to reality. Social science should be ordered on statistical precision, on sophisticated procedures of induction and logic. Rational choice becomes the foundation of deontological and utilitarian ethics.

As the 18th century developed around Cartesian rationality, Immanuel Kant (1724–1804) was schooled in Descartes, mathematics, and Newtonian science. In his early years as lecturer in Königsberg, he taught mathematics, logic, and physics. In 1755, his first major book, *Universal Natural History and Theory of Heaven*, explained the structure of the universe in terms of Newtonian cosmology (Kant, 1755/2000). His physics is sophisticated enough to produce the Kant-Laplace theory of the origin of the universe.

Then, in the *Critique of Practical Reason* (1788) and *Groundwork of the Metaphysic of Morals* (1785), Kant assimilated ethics to logic. He demanded that moral laws be universally applicable and free from inner contradiction. Society was presumed to have a fundamental moral structure embedded in human nature as basic as atoms in physics, with the moral law the analog of the unchanging laws of gravity. Through the mental calculus of willing my action to be universalized, imperatives emerge unconditioned by circumstances. Someone wishes for everybody to keep their promises, for example, and through this formal test, moral absolutes are identified precisely in the rational way syllogisms are divided into valid and invalid.

Kant's deontological project is based on the belief that only through human reason can autonomous agents attain reliable knowledge for living well. In a context-free rationality, moral principles are derived from the essential structure of disembodied reason. This is a correspondence view of truth, with a constricted definition of what counts as morality. Instead of prizing care and reciprocity, for example, our moral understanding becomes prescriptivist and absolutist.

In this version of rational choice theory, the truth of all legitimate claims about moral obligation can be settled by formally examining their logical structure. Consistency requires that moral agents apply rules always and everywhere the same. Humans act against moral obligations only if they are willing to live with the irrationality of self-contradiction. The Enlightenment's confidence in the power of reason combined with the ancient emphasis on reason's universality to create ethical principles that are the same for all thinking subjects, all epochs, and every culture.

Mill's Autonomous Subjectivity

In John Stuart Mill, autonomous individuality is the supreme principle. Mill established social scientific inquiry on this concept, and it is the basic rationale for his political philosophy. The subject-object dichotomy in Mill becomes a dualism of means and ends. For Mill,

> Neutrality is necessary in order to promote autonomy. … A person cannot be forced to be good, and the state should not dictate the kind of life a citizen should lead; it would be better for citizens to choose badly than for them to be forced by the state to choose well. (Root, 1993, pp. 12–13)

Since we are autonomous beings, living our lives according to our own purposes is obvious and essential, as Mill insists in his *On Liberty* (1859/1975): "The free development of individuality is one of the principal ingredients of human happiness, and quite the chief ingredient of individual and social progress" (p. 50). The supremacy of individual autonomy is the foundational principle in Mill's *Utilitarianism* (1861/1979) and in *A System of Logic* (1843/1888). For Mill, the principle of utility requires that individuals be given full freedom, except when such liberty would harm others. In addition, through autonomous subjectivity, Mill delineated the foundations of empiricism as a social scientific method. In fact, this problem-solving methodology is powerful enough to replace Aristotelian logic.

According to Mill, syllogisms do not create new knowledge. If we conclude that because "all men are mortal," Sir William Hamilton is mortal by virtue of his male gender, then the conclusion does not advance the premise (see Mill, 1843/1888, II.3.2, p. 140). Such logic reorders concepts, but the crucial task is discriminating genuine knowledge from superstition, and syllogistic logic does not address it. Generalization and synthesis are necessary to advance from the known to the unknown, and, therefore, Mill works out the logic for inferring the unknown from the empirical (Mill, 1843/1888, III). Instead of focusing on formal rules for rigorous reasoning, Mill proposes an inductive science in which propositions are empirically derived and the content of our knowledge is based on experience.[1] In Book 6 of *A System of Logic*, Mill (1843/1888) described a social science that explains human behavior in terms of causal laws, but he warned against the arrogance of full predictability (VI.6.1, p. 6060). He drew the now obvious conclusion that empirical knowledge about human behavior has fewer exceptions, and therefore has greater predictive power, when it deals with collectivities instead of individual actors (see Mill, 1843/1888, VI.5.1, p. 596).

Mill's positivism is obvious throughout his work on experimental inquiry. Based on Auguste Comte's *Cours de Philosophie Positive* (1830), he defined matter as the "permanent possibility of sensation" (1865b, p. 198).[2] Social research is neutral, speaking to questions of means only. Ends are extraneous to its structure and rationale. In developing precise methods of induction and verification, Mill's establishing knowledge in empirical terms limits social investigation to the risks and benefits of possible courses of action (Mill,

1843/1888, II, Vol. 6, p. 181). With Comte, Mill insisted that only the facts of sense phenomena exist, and therefore metaphysical categories are not real. There is no essence behind sensations; therefore, Mill (1865/2005), following Comte (1848/1910), argued that social science should be limited to particular data as a factual source out of which experimentally valid laws can be derived. For both, this is the only kind of knowledge that yields tangible benefits to society (Mill, 1865, p. 242).[3]

Mill's utilitarian ethics is likewise based on his neutral scientific methodology that presumes autonomous individuals. Utilitarianism is grounded in a system of inductive reasoning that renders ethics inescapably into formalistic structures. Mill considered utility alone to be the final appeal on all ethical questions (Mill, 1861/1979, ch. 1). His utilitarianism is intellectually appealing in the same way scientific theories are—a single principle constitutes all moral judgments. Utility requires that only an action's consequences need to be assessed, not the actor's motives or character traits.

Utilitarianism presumes "that there is one set of considerations that determines what we ought morally to do" (Taylor, 1982, p. 132), and therefore equates moral reasoning with the process of calculating consequence. Empirical quantities replace metaphysical distinctions in utilitarian ethics, reflecting the inductive processes Mill delineated in his *System of Logic*. Utilitarians favor specific actions or policies based on evidence. They follow the procedural demand that if "the happiness of each agent counts for one ... the right course of action should be what satisfies all, or the largest number possible" (Taylor, 1982, p. 131).

The balance of pleasure over pain is a non-negotiable principle that resolves conflicts and ambiguities. Euthanasia, theft, and deceit are not wrong in themselves, but only if their consequences are less productive than their alternatives. Since individual liberty has priority, the most effective way to produce maximum happiness is by the freedom to develop one's personal preferences. Individuated selves have priority over the domain of the good, and in that sense, utilitarianism parallels the methodological features of empirical social science. Utilitarian ethics fits the canons of rational calculation as they were developed by the Enlightenment's intellectual culture in general and empiricism in particular.

Dialogic Interpretation

In terms of Western intellectual history, rational choice theory takes on its modern form as Kant's deontology and Mill's utilitarianism. For Alasdair MacIntyre (2007), it is the "Enlightenment Project After Virtue." Aristotle's morality of social action becomes decisively individuated. His living-in-a-*polis* is replaced by the embedded self. Descartes's rationalism was born at the time when science had introduced the laws of physics to explain nature. Philosophers constructed principles to explain human behavior and basically agreed that morality ought to be justified in terms of rational standards. Immanuel Kant and others in the Enlightenment Project such as John Stuart Mill were committed to constructing an ethics that moves from premises about human nature "to conclusions about the authority of moral rules and precepts" (MacIntyre, 2007, p. 52).

Consistent with the rational choice tradition in Western philosophy, the general trend in formalist morality entails an ethical rationalism that requires autonomous moral agents to apply rules consistently and self-consciously to every choice. Rational processes create basic norms that sovereign individuals must follow and against which all failures in moral duty can be measured. At the centerpiece of traditional media ethics is autonomous subjectivity, a theory of human nature presumed to be unproblematic. In mainstream professional ethics, an apparatus of neutral standards is constructed in terms of the major issues practitioners face in their everyday routines. The mainstream view disembeds the self and operates by procedures. This formulation is the premiere reason that multiculturalism has not received adequate attention to date in media ethics.

Rather than uncritically assume formalism or individualism and be trapped in the limitations of the mainstream view, we can make substantial progress in the morality of intercultural representation with a different philosophical foundation. For an ethics of diversity to be legitimate intellectually and possible practically, dialogic social philosophy is the only alternative. The social bondedness of the philosophy of language enables us to start over intellectually and establishes a credible ethics to understand the cultural images of diversity and act on them with integrity.

The philosophers of language developed the concept of "dialogic interactionism" to replace rational choice theory. People are born into a sociocultural universe where values and meanings are either presumed or negotiated. Linguistic systems precede their human occupants and endure after them. Therefore, morally appropriate action intends community. Contrary to the individual-and-society dualism in the rational choice tradition, people know themselves primarily as dialogic beings-in-relation. Fulfillment is never achieved in isolation, but only through the human bonding that results from our constructing and maintaining communities. Common moral values are intrinsic to a community's ongoing existence and identity. Moral agents need a context of social commitments and community ties for assessing what is valuable. What is worth preserving as a good cannot be determined in isolation; it can only be ascertained within specific social situations where human identity is nurtured. The public sphere is conceived as a mosaic of particular communities, a pluralism of ethnic identities and worldviews intersecting to form a social bond but each distinctive as well.

The communal, our commonness, *communitas*, is the context in which the nature of morality is understood correctly. As the philosophy of language documents, we are human primarily in dialogic relation and derivatively as thinkers withdrawn from action. Therefore, the the domain of the good is not extrinsic but socially derived.

PHILOSOPHY OF LANGUAGE

The Counter-Enlightenment

Philosophical opposition to the paradigm of linear rationality has persisted in the West through the centuries. But its contemporary manifestation traces its lineage to the Counter-Enlightenment of Giambattista Vico, professor of rhetoric at the University of Naples for 42 years (1699–1741). The main product of his study was an expansive work called *New Science* (1725/1948). His *Study Methods of Our Time* (1709/1965) is a testimony to his genius also, considered by some scholars the most brilliant defense of the humanities ever written. *New Science* was a detailed account of the history of language and cultural customs. He contended, contra Descartes, that philology ought to preoccupy philosophers because language was the central human activity. Mathematics, in his view, was a form of knowledge appropriate to the natural order, but not for animate reality.[4] The issue for Vico was the subject-object dichotomy of Cartesian epistemology—a dualism of subjective observer and objective nature that entails a correspondence view of truth. Rather than presuming this subject-object dichotomy and making adjustments in it for the social sciences, the Counter-Enlightenment tradition starts over intellectually by denying the validity of this dualism for the study of living, growing, organic human existence.

Wilhelm Dilthey continued the Counter-Enlightenment's holistic understanding of our humanness into the 19th century. Influential successor to Hegel at Berlin and a major thinker in his own right, Dilthey (1966) considered *New Science* "one of the greatest triumphs of modern thought" (vol. 14/1, p. 698). He believed that the nature of understanding (*Verstehen*) was the premiere issue in intellectual history for his century even as Vico had identified it as such in the 18th. Dilthey put *Verstehen* into the framework of lived experience (*Erlebnis*). *Erlebnis* becomes the ultimate basis of knowledge. *Erlebnis* is not an epiphenomenon for him but the irreplaceable grasp of meaning that underlies reflexive thought.

For Dilthey (1958), lived experience is an ever-flowing stream. The relations of life are historical in nature. Our forms of consciousness and expression are determined by history, he argued: "Life contains as the first categorical definition, fundamental to all others, being in time (*Zeitlichkeit*)" (vol. VI, p. 192). He defined the problem of understanding as recovering a consciousness of the human race's historicality (*Geschichtlichkeit*). Human experience he saw as intrinsically chronological, and therefore our understanding of the human domain must also be commensurately temporal.

Ernst Cassirer's Symbolic Forms

This Counter-Enlightenment philosophy of language is developed further in 19th-century Europe by Frederick Schleiermacher's *Hermeneutik* (1805–1833), August Schleicher's *Comparative Grammar* (1848), Jacob Burckhardt's *Civilization of the Renaissance in Italy* (1860), and Georg Simmel's *Problems of Philosophy of History* (1892). It establishes definitive form in the 20th century in an intellectual trajectory from Ferdinand De Saussure's *Cours de linguistique gènèral* (1916) to Ernst Cassirer's four-volume *Philosophy of Symbolic Forms* (1923–1929/1953–1957/1996). For Cassirer, symbolization is not merely the hallmark of human cognition; our representational capacity defines us anthropologically. Cassirer (1944) titled his monograph summarizing the four volumes *An Essay on Man*. He identified our unique capacity to generate symbolic structures as a radical alternative to the *animale rationale* of ancient Greece, Descartes's rational being, and Mill's British empiricism. *Animale symbolicum* is likewise radically different from the biological being of evolutionary naturalism. Arguing that the issues are fundamentally anthropological rather than epistemological per se, Cassirer's creative being is carved out against the reductionism of rational choice theories on one hand and a naturalistic neurophysiology and biochemistry on the other.[5]

In Cassirer's *Philosophy of Symbolic Forms*, humanity has no static nature in itself, only history. We know ourselves through our symbolic expressions. No inherent principle defines our metaphysical essence, nor is an inborn faculty or instinct ascertained by empirical observation. We cannot look through language to determine what really occurred but live at those points where meaning is created in language. Language does not merely reflect reality from the outside; recomposing events into a narrative ensures that humans can comprehend reality at all. Words derive their meaning from the interpretive, historical context humans themselves supply. Language is the matrix of humanity, and, therefore, is inescapably communal, the public agency through which human identity is realized. The social and personal dimensions of language are woven into a unified whole.

In this shift from rational being to cultural being, reason is reoriented and redefined, though it does not disappear. Charles Taylor (1985) sees the philosophy of language as displacing reason's center of gravity. When language is considered central to our humanness, rationality is situated in the "thought/ language complex" and is not isolated as a separate faculty. Language is not a vehicle of private meaning and subjectivism, as rational choice epistemology assumes, but belongs to the community where it is nurtured in reflection and action. As humans create worlds through language, this creation itself is permeated by ideas, analysis, and generalization. Cassirer (1944) collapsed the differences among human symbolic systems as merely variations of human thinking. Music, art, philosophical essays, oral discourse, mathematics, electronic entertainment, religious ritual, and Bacon's scientific method are placed on a level playing floor. Symbol is the critical concept. Cultures are interconnections of symbolic forms—those fundamental units of meaning expressed in words, gestures, and graphics. Realities called *cultures* are inherited and built from symbols that intermix our thoughts with sentiment, action, and identity.

In Cassirer's symbolization theory, symbols participate in the meaning of what they symbolize; they share the significance of that to which they point. Because the symbolic realm is intrinsic to the human species, humans alone of living creatures possess the creative mind, the irrevocable capacity to reconstruct the world typically called "culture." Symbol is the basic unit that carries meaning and thus anchors the communicative capacity, which in turn is central to our humanity, and humans are therefore culture builders. Language is the catalytic agent in cultural formation, and therefore the domain of intercultural understanding.

In Cassirer's philosophy of language, if cultures are sets of symbols that orient life and provide it significance, then cultural patterns are inherently normative. Assuming that culture is the container of our symbolic capacity, the constituent units of such containers are a society's values. As ordering relations for organizing reality, values direct the ends of societal practice and provide implicit standards for selecting courses of action. Communities are knit together linguistically, and because the lingual is not neutral but value laden, our social bonds are moral claims.

Gadamer's Ontological-Linguistic Paradigm

In the work of Hans-Georg Gadamer (1900–2002), the philosophy of language investigates the nature of dialogic interpretation, not as an epistemological question per se but an ontological one about human consciousness.[6] Rather than viewing language in terms of linguistic signs (as is typically the case outside Counter-Enlightenment philology), language is an active presence in the constitutive structure of existence.

Gadamer organizes his philosophy of language around the contradiction between objectivist dogmatism and subjectivist relativism. He seeks a conceptual pathway out of this dilemma:

> Gadamer's hermeneutics replaces the foundationalist conception of knowledge with the idea of understanding. The hermeneutical idea of understanding is very different from a scientistic formulation which is based on the logic of mathematics. ... Gadamer shows that human understanding must be viewed neither dogmatically nor relativistically, but rather dialogically. ... He develops hermeneutics into a grand philosophical project which aims to explicate understanding as the mode of human existence. (Shin, 1994, pp. 36, 41, 43)

The essence of understanding is not individualistic rationality but interactive dialogue through which humans engage each other's cultures and make collaboration possible. Subjectivity is not understood as Cartesian self-identity but our interpretation of a world already made meaningful to us. The language of experience is neither subjective nor objective but a refraction of our being-in-the-world.

The philosophy of language gives us a new conception of communication. Communication is no longer seen as an exchange of signs through which we attempt to communicate with others. It is not merely a tool for the production of a shared reality or relationship. It is not a bridge between two social entities that exist as political or economic domains outside it. Communication is the medium of human existence as intersubjectivity, that is, as our mode of belonging together with others in a community. It is "a living process in which a community of life is lived out" (Gadamer, 1989, p. 404). "Understanding," Gadamer argues, "is essentially an effective-historical relation" in which the accumulated history of meanings is a constituent element in our own interpretation (Gadamer, 1989, p. 266). Taking a cue from Dilthey's concern to make history central but radicalizing that notion, the world itself is seen as essentially historical. History is the medium within which people dwell, a precondition of all thought including critical reflection. That which appears to us in our understanding is also hidden from us behind the multifaceted givens of our culture. Knowledge is gained within this pregiven interpretive context.

The dialogic nature of the language experience and the multiplicity of languages do not, however, imply relativity. Instead, they only demonstrate that "our verbal experience of the world has the capacity to embrace the most varied relationships of life" (Gadamer, 1989, p. 448). Understanding is not, first of all, a human operation governed by rules and procedures, but the "basic structure of our experience of life." Our world orientation is a primordial givenness that we cannot reduce to anything simpler or more immediate (Gadamer, 1970, p. 87).

For Gadamer, language is all encompassing, a natural ability across the human race. Through our involvement in and our study of language, we disclose the fundamental conditions of our humanness. Language enables the entire arena of understanding. As with Heidegger, natural language, rather than the artificial language of logic and method, is the way of understanding for Gadamer (1989): "Language is not just one of man's possessions in the world; rather, on it depends the fact that we have a world at all. ... That language is originally human, means at the same time that man's being in the world is primordially linguistic" (p. 443). The ontological-linguistic paradigm opens a pathway through dialogic understanding for the universals of our humanity and the diversity of our indigeneity to be embedded in each other.

In rational choice theory since Descartes, the self is a "first-person singular ... disengaged from embodied agency and social embedding" (Taylor, 1995, p. 60). In this view, human agents use language to engage the world outside, with meaning understood as the way things are depicted. The subject is first of all a mind, "an inner space, capable of processing representations" (Taylor, 1995, p. 60). However, instead of separating human agents from the representational domain, words derive their meaning from the historical context humans themselves supply. Understanding is dialogic and therefore normative. The essence of the human order is interactive communication through which humans interpret other cultures and enable collaboration among themselves.

For Gadamer, understanding is the key concept for public communication within societies and between them. The concept "information" is technology centered—the data, facts, and reports made available by the electronic media. The idea of "knowledge" assumes a rational human being and has been shaped largely by the logic of mathematics and science. "Opinion" is generally seen as subjective and relativistic. For public life, Gadamer replaces these terms with the idea of understanding. Language is inescapably communal, the public agent through which people comprehend the world. Language is meaningful before it is spoken by anyone. That meaningfulness comes not from individual acts of rational speech and action but from our communal linguisticality. We should no longer assume that we possess some "pure" knowledge within our autonomous self, since individuated interpretations arise from the more basic lingual world in which we live. *Communitas*, not individual rationality, is primordial to the human order.

Ricoeur's Surplus of Meaning

As with Gadamer, Paul Ricoeur's philosophy of language is ontological, but Ricoeur's *Conflict of Interpretation* and *Interpretation Theory* are more explicit about the interpretive modality. The more generic concept "understanding" is given multilevel complexity as "interpretation." Interpretation is not inquiry for the sake of epistemic certainty but dialogue with human existence past and present. The definition of humans as beings-in-the-world assumes that understanding is based on a prior relationship of belongingness that can never become fully transparent to our awareness.

From this perspective, human existence is characterized chiefly by its finitude, by the fact that one's self-being is always limited by other-beings past and present: "The subject that interprets himself while interpreting signs is no longer the *cogito*; rather, he is a being who discovers by the exegesis of his own life, that he is placed in being before he places and possesses himself"; our manner of existence "remains from start to finish a being-interpreted" (Ricoeur, 1974, p. 11). Subjectivity is not to be understood as Cartesian individuated consciousness but as a moment in that structure of interpretation that is human existence. That is, we can no longer assume that we possess "pure" knowledge of our self nor that the self is autonomous, since self-understanding is only an interpretation of our historical situatedness. We understand ourselves as subjects and the world in which we live only through an interpretation of symbolic meanings within that world. Given that language recapitulates, symbols create what we view as reality. We cannot step outside language to determine what something really is or means but must intervene at the level of the lingual world in which we live.

For Ricoeur, whatever is intelligible is accessible to us in and through language, and all deployments of language require interpretation. The reality given by language is fundamentally different from the reality given by sense data. Humans do not live in a world of "sheer facticity in itself," as Ricoeur calls it, but in systems of thought and culture. Just as the astronomer's telescope and the biologist's microscope bring transformed realities into view, so languages represent conceptions of the world. There is a pregiven interpretive context, and the accumulated history of meanings is a constituent element in our own interpretations.

Ricoeur challenges classical rhetoric's understanding of metaphor. He notes that in traditional metaphor theory, the existence of multiple levels of signification presupposed a primary literal one and another secondary symbolic level. For Ricoeur, there are not two significations, one literal and the other symbolic, but rather a fluid movement in narrative that transfers humans from one level to another. Ricoeur does not deny the existence of primary and ancillary but directs inquiry to the movement of actors between levels, that is, to the context of viewer-reader-hearer.

Semiotician Charles Sanders Peirce (1839–1914) calls this phenomenon of human language retroduction. In Peirce's (1992) typology, scientific theories are inductive or deductive. In deduction, the conclusion is self-evidentiary, guaranteed by logical necessity from the premise. In inductive reasoning, generalizations are restricted to the data through the standards of internal and external validity. Retroduction is distinctive from both, interactive in character, dialectical between insight and application. We interpret discourse in light of its several parts and any particular in light of the whole (Peirce, 1958). We choose an interpretation by vindicating it against competing interpretations. For Peirce and Ricoeur, deduction does not increase human knowledge but reorganizes it. Induction potentially amplifies knowledge, but its novelty is circumscribed by the epistemological criteria of induction. Induction and deduction yield the abstractions of artifice; retroduction is the pathway of interpreting natural language.

Words are polysemic. Language contains within itself resources that allow it to be used creatively. Raymond Williams (1961) calls it "the long revolution." Ricoeur in *The Rule of Metaphor* (1977) defined surplus of meaning as the linguistic imagination that generates and regenerates meaning through the power of metaphor to state things in new ways. Language as a metaphorical resource can be used creatively to produce new meanings. The signs in a language system do not refer only to other signs but engage a world that both constructs and represents. Rather than limiting our understanding of discourse to its correspondence with facts or the author's intent or to one literal meaning, he sees discourse in terms of the "principle of plenitude": "a text means all that it can mean" (Ricoeur, 1981, p. 176). Meaning is limited by the dialectic of context, history of the narrative, and boundaries of lived experience (the codal "hot" will not be understood as "cold"), but the central feature of interpretation is the fecundity of meaning. The plentitude of symbolic systems defines them as a reservoir of meaning that can be used again and again.

Ricoeur's surplus of meaning has special relevance to the question of multiple realizability in ethics. "Multiple realization" is central to theories from natural science to the humanities. Phenomena can share in a fundamental meaning across a system, but its interpretations and elaborations are multiple. For Ricoeur (1960/1986), our spatiotemporal location and transcending the local are simultaneous. Humans are collective beings "in which the unity of destination and the differences of destinies are to be understood through each other" (p. 138). In ethics it means that basic concepts such as social responsibility carry enough commonness across cultures that journalists and media executives understand the basic idea, though they explain and apply it in various ways (Christians & Ward, 2013, pp. 82–84; cf. Ward, 2011). For the ethics of intercultural communication, one can plausibly argue that a protonorm such as human dignity can be both one and many, understood on the deep level of worldview, but constructed variously in different cultural contexts. As Ricoeur (2005) puts it, the unity that binds humans together is the common quest for esteem and recognition. The "constitutive disproportion" of worthiness in every person represents a combination of individual uniqueness and recognition of our mutual humanity.[7]

CONCLUSION

Suzanne Langer (1942) calls the philosophy of language tradition from Vico to Ricoeur *Philosophy in a New Key*. Symbolization is used to understand the human mind. Symbolic thought sets up a theory of communication called "dialogic interpretation" as an alternative to "rational choice theory." Langer argues that there is a new question at the centerpiece of philosophical inquiry: What is the nature of symbolic representation and how does it function, in its various transformations, in human existence? In *Feeling and Form* (1953), Langer analyzes the symbolic structures and functions of narrative, of painting, sculpture, music, dance, fiction, drama, and film. Meaning derives from an interpretive context of symbol, myth, and metaphor that humans themselves supply. In the philosophy of language, concepts are not isolated from their representations. Through the social nature of language, human beings integrate specific messages into the larger project of cultural formation. Symbolic transformation is the distinctive activity of the human species (Langer, 1967).

The philosophy of language contradicts the rational foundation on which Western media ethics is based. Social constructions replace formal law systems. Contextual values become the centerpiece instead of ethical prescriptions. In the dialogic model, morality is rooted in everyday experience and has multiple levels of complexity. From the *communitas* perspective, a formalist ethics of procedures fails to recognize that as lingual beings, humans forget and remember, struggle with the past and hope for the future, listen and speak, show remorse and make excuses. In Nel Noddings's (1984) terms, an ethics that concentrates on arranging principles hierarchically and that derives conclusions logically is "peripheral to or even alien to, many problems of moral action ... Moral decisions are, after all, made in real situations; they are qualitatively different from the solution of geometry problems" (pp. 2–3). In dialogic ethics rooted in *communitas*, moral experience is formed in terms of its origins, present concerns, and outcomes. Rational calculation and impartial reflection are secondary to an understanding of the good that is nurtured in community. The moral life develops through community formation and not in the obscure sanctums of isolated individuals. Moral values are situated in the social context rather than anchored by theoretical abstractions. Rather than individual rights as the integrating norm, our obligations to one another define our existence.

In the philosophy of language, communication is not external to human life but constitutive of it. There is no language and human being, but the one is ultimately inextricable from the other. This confronts us with a conundrum. How is it logically possible that humans who are themselves constituted by communication can fully explain the process by which they are enabled to do the explaining? It is an old paradox in new clothes: Can a theory of something contain itself? We confront a difficulty unique to the study of language and dialogic interpretation does not resolve it. However, the conundrum makes normativity transparent and inescapable. The manner in which we practice communication and study it becomes paramount.

Community is the home of dialogic interpretation, community understood as what Daniel Bell (2010) calls "a normative ideal." People's lives are bound up with the good of the community in which their identity is established. This excludes contingent swimming pool memberships that do not define and condition one's well-being. In their *Habits of the Heart*, Bellah and colleagues (1996) define communities as those "attachments one values," considering this definition applicable to communities worldwide where these valued forms of human life illustrate multiple diversity (p. 335). The various concepts, histories, and problematics of *communitas* are only dialects of the same language—pluralities that feed from and into one another, held together by a body of similar ideas. *Communitas* as a philosophical concept yields an ethics of intercultural communication that is centered on human dignity and stretches across the continents. In this formulation, research on the transnational and intercultural is accountable to the widely shared common good that orients the people-groups in which they operate and by which they are given meaning.[8]

NOTES

1. Although committed to what he called "the logic of the moral sciences" in delineating the canons or methods for induction, Mill shared with natural science a belief in the uniformity of nature and the presumption that all phenomena are subject to cause-and-effect relationships. His five principles of induction reflect a Newtonian/Enlightenment cosmology.

2. Mill's realism is most explicitly developed in his *Examination of Sir William Hamilton's Philosophy* (1865/2005). Our belief in a common external world, in his view, is rooted in the fact that our sensations of physical reality "belong as much to other human or sentient beings as to ourselves" (p. 196).

3. Mill credits Comte for his use of the inverse deductive or historical method: "This was an idea entirely new to me when I found it in Comte; and but for him I might not soon (if ever) have arrived at it" (Mill, 1861/1969, p. 126). He published two essays on Comte's influence in the *Westminster Review*, which were reprinted as *Auguste Comte and Positivism* (Mill, 1865; see also Mill, 1861/1969, p. 165).

4. For documentation that Vico was not merely anti-Descartes but was inspired by pre-Enlightenment traditions, see Janik (1983). For stimulating essays on Vico and the Counter-Enlightenment generally, see Cassirer (1960, pp. 3–38, 117–158) especially.
5. For understanding cultural beings in the context of the West's Enlightenment rationality, see Cassirer (1951). For a systematic treatment of the cultural sciences that emerge from his philosophy of language, see Cassirer (1960).
6. Gadamer succeeded Karl Jaspers at Heidelberg (1949–1968). Ricoeur was the chair of general philosophy at the Sorbonne (1956–1967) and on the faculty at the University of Paris at Nanterre (1967–1980). From 1967–1992, he also served as the successor to Paul Tillich at the University of Chicago.
7. Ricoeur (1967) describes his work, and the philosophy-of-language tradition he represents, as philosophical anthropology (Rasmussen, 1971). Philosophical anthropology examines "what characteristics (if any) are both common and unique to human beings as such," or, in other words, "what are the necessary and sufficient conditions of being a human being" (Schacht, 1990, p. 157; cf. Schacht, 1975). "Dialogic interpretation" is to be understood in these terms, with "rational choice theory" primarily epistemological in character.
8. Nancy Fraser (2014) labels this the transnationalizing of the public sphere. She calls us to move beyond Habermas, arguing that his *Communicative Ethics and Moral Consciousness* is not culturally constituted, and his public sphere needs to be transnationalized into alternative counter-publics. She critiques Habermas's nation-state procedural justice, recognizing that in today's decentralizing world, a community-based social justice is more compatible with the philosophy-of-language tradition.

BIBLIOGRAPHY

Aristotle. (1975). *Nicomachean ethics* (H. Rackham, Trans.). Loeb Classical Library. Cambridge, MA: Harvard University Press.

Bell, D. (2010). Communitarianism. *Stanford encyclopedia of philosophy.* Retrieved from http://plato.stanford.edu/entries/communitarianism/

Bellah, R., Madsen, R., Sullivan, W. M., Swindler, A., & Tipton, S. M. (1996). *Habits of the heart: Individualism and commitment in American life.* Berkeley: University of California Press.

Cassirer, E. (1944). *An essay on man: An introduction to the philosophy of human culture.* New Haven, CT: Yale University Press.

Cassirer, E. (1951). *The philosophy of the Enlightenment.* Princeton, NJ: Princeton University Press.

Cassirer, E. (1953–1957, 1996). *The philosophy of symbolic forms* (Vols. 1–4; R. Manheim & J. M. Krois, Trans.). New Haven, CT: Yale University Press. (Original work published 1923–1929)

Cassirer, E. (1960). *The logic of the humanities* (C. S. Howe, Trans.). New Haven, CT: Yale University Press.

Christians, C. G., & Ward, S. J. A. (2013). Anthropological realism for global media ethics. In N. Couldry, M. Madianou, & A. Pinchevski (Eds.), *Ethics of media* (pp. 72–88). Basingstoke, Hampshire, UK: Palgrave Macmillan.

Comte, A. (1910). *A general view of positivism* (J. H. Bridges, Trans.). London: George Routledge & Sons, Limited. (Original work published 1848)

Descartes, R. (1938). *Discourse on method.* Chicago: Open Court Publishing. (Original work published 1637)

Descartes, R. (1964). *Rules for the direction of mind.* In *Philosophical essays* (pp. 147–236; L. J. Lafleur, Trans.). Indianapolis: Bobbs-Merrill. (Original work published 1638)

Descartes, R. (1993). *Meditations on first philosophy: Second meditation* (S. Tweyman, Ed.). London: Routledge. (Original work published 1641)

Dilthey, W. (1914–1982). *Gesammelte shriften.* 19 vols. Leipzig & Berlin, Germany: Tuebner; Göttingen, Germany: Vadenhoeck & Ruprecht.

Fraser, N. (2014). *Transnationalizing the public sphere.* Cambridge, UK: Polity.

Gadamer, H.-G. (1967). Rhetorik, hermenutik und ideologiekritik. *Kleine Schriften* (Vol. l, pp. 113–130). Tübingen: J. C. B. Mohr.

Gadamer, H.-G. (1970). On the scope and function of hermeneutical reflection (G. B. Hess & R. E. Palmer, Trans.). *Continuum, 8,* 77–95.

Gadamer, H.-G. (1986). *The relevance of the beautiful and other essays.* Cambridge, UK: Cambridge University Press.

Gadamer, H.-G. (1989). *Truth and method [Wahrheit und methode: Grunzuge einer philosophischen hermeneutic]* (2nd ed.; J. Weinsheimer & D. G. Marshall, Trans.). New York: Seabury Press. (Original work published 1965)

Janik, L. G. (1983). A renaissance quarrel: The origins of Vico's anti-Cartesianism. In G. Tagliacozzo (Ed.), *New Vico studies* (pp. 39–50). Atlantic Highlands, NJ: Humanities.

Johnstone, C. L. (2002). Aristotle's ethical theory in the contemporary world. In S. B. Bracci & C. G. Christians (Eds.), *Moral engagement in public life: Theorists for contemporary ethics* (pp. 16–34). New York: Peter Lang.

Kant, I. (1997). *Critique of practical reason* (M. Gregor, Ed.). Cambridge, UK: Cambridge University Press. (Original work published 1788)

Kant, I. (1998). *Groundwork of the metaphysic of morals* (M. Gregor, Ed.). Cambridge, UK: Cambridge University Press. (Original work published 1785)

Kant, I. (2000). *Universal natural history and theory of heaven* (I. Johnston, Trans.). Arlington, VA: Richer Resources Publications. (Original work published 1755)

Landmann, M. (1974). *Philosophical anthropology* (D. J. Parent, Trans.). Philadelphia: Westminster Press.

Langer, S. K. (1942). *Philosophy in a new key: A study in the symbolism of reason, rite, and art.* Cambridge, MA: Harvard University Press.

Langer, S. K. (1953). *Feeling and form.* New York: Scribner's.

Langer, S. K. (1967). *Problems of art: Ten philosophical lectures.* New York: Scribner's.

MacIntyre, A. (2007). *After virtue: A study in moral theory.* Notre Dame, IN: Notre Dame University Press.

Mill, J. S. (1865). *Auguste Comte and positivism.* London.

Mill, J. S. (1888). *A system of logic, ratiocinative and inductive: Being a connected view of the principles of evidence and the methods of scientific investigation* (8th ed.). New York: Harper & Brothers. (Original work published 1843)

Mill, J. S. (1969). *Autobiography.* Boston: Houghton Mifflin. (Original work published 1861)

Mill, J. S. (1975). *On liberty.* New York: Norton. (Original work published 1859)

Mill, J. S. (1979). *Utilitarianism.* Indianapolis, IN: Hackett. (Original work published 1861)

Mill, J. S. (2005). *Examination of Sir William Hamilton's philosophy and of the principal philosophical questions discussed in his writings.* Ann Arbor: Michigan Historical Reprint Series. (Original work published 1865)

Niebuhr, R. (1964). *The nature and destiny of man. Vol. 1: Human nature.* New York: Scribner's. (Original work published 1941)

Noddings, N. (1984). *Caring: A feminine approach to ethics and moral education.* Berkeley: University of California Press.

Peirce, C. S. (1958). *Collected papers of C. S. Peirce.* 8 vols. Cambridge, MA: Harvard University Press.

Peirce, C. S. (1992). *Reasoning and the logic of things: Cambridge Conference lectures of 1898.* Cambridge, MA: Harvard University Press.

Rasmussen, D. M. (1971). *Mythic-symbolic language and philosophical anthropology: A constructive interpretation of the thought of Paul Ricoeur.* The Hague, Netherlands: Martinus Nijhoff.

Ricoeur, P. (1967). The antinomy of human reality and the problem of philosophical anthropology. In N. Lawrence & D. O'Connor (Eds.), *Readings in existential phenomenology* (pp. 390–401). Englewood Cliffs, NJ: Prentice-Hall.

Ricoeur, P. (1973, Summer). Ethics and culture: Habermas and Gadamer in dialogue. *Philosophy Today, 17*(2/4).

Ricoeur, P. (1974). *The conflict of interpretations: Essays in hermeneutics* (D. Ihde, Ed.). Evanston, IL: Northwestern University Press.

Ricoeur, P. (1976). *Interpretation theory: Discourse and the surplus of meaning.* Fort Worth: Texas Christian University Press.

Ricoeur, P. (1977). *The rule of metaphor: Multi-disciplinary studies in the creation of meaning in language [La métaphore vive]* (R. Czerny, Trans.). Toronto: University of Toronto Press.

Ricoeur, P. (1981). Metaphor and the central problem of hermeneutics. In J. B. Thompson (Ed.), *Hermeneutics and the human sciences: Essays on language, action and interpretation.* Cambridge, UK: Cambridge University Press.

Ricoeur, P. (1984, 1985, 1988). *Time and narrative.* 3 vols. (K. Blamey & D. Pellauer, Trans.). Chicago: University of Chicago Press.

Ricoeur, P. (1986). *Fallible man,* rev. ed. (C. A. Kelby, Trans.). New York: Fordham University Press. (Original work published 1960)

Ricoeur, P. (2005). *The course of recognition* (D. Pellauer, Trans.). Cambridge, MA: Harvard University Press.

Root, M. (1993). *Philosophy of social science: The methods, ideals, and politics of social inquiry.* Oxford, UK: Blackwell.

Schacht, R. (1975). *Existentialism, Existenz-philosophy, and philosophical anthropology* (pp. 228–253). Pittsburgh, PA: University of Pittsburgh Press.

Schacht, R. (1990, Fall). Philosophical anthropology: What, why, and how. *Philosophy and Phenomenological Research, 50,* 155–176.

Schrag, C. O. (1997). *The self after postmodernity.* New Haven, CT: Yale University Press.

Shin, K.-W. (1994). *A hermeneutic utopia: H.-G. Gadamer's philosophy of culture.* Toronto: Tea for Two Press.

Taylor, C. (1982). The diversity of goods. In A. Sen & B. Williams (Eds.), *Utilitarianism and beyond* (pp. 129–144). Cambridge, UK: Cambridge University Press.

Taylor, C. (1985). *Human agency and language: Philosophical papers,* vol. 1. Cambridge, UK: Cambridge University Press.

Taylor, C. (1989). *Sources of the self: The making of the modern identity.* Cambridge, MA: Harvard University Press.

Taylor, C. (1995). The dialogical self. In R. Goodman & W. Fisher (Eds.), *Rethinking knowledge: Reflections across the disciplines* (pp. 57–66). Albany: State University of New York Press.

Vico, G. (1948). *The new science of G. Vico* (T. G. Bergin & M. H. Fisch, Trans.). Ithaca, NY: Cornell University Press. (Original work published 1725)

Vico, G. (1965). *On the study methods of our time* (E. Ginaturco, Trans.). Indianapolis, IN: Bobbs-Merrill. (Original work published 1709)

Ward, S. J. A. (2011). *Ethics and the media: An introduction.* Cambridge, UK: Cambridge University Press.

Williams, R. (1961). *The long revolution.* London: Chatto & Windus.

Intercultural Conflicts AND Intercultural News Coverage

CHAPTER THREE

The Islamic Veil IN France

The Body That Communicates

HUGUES HOTIER

There are several reasons for incomprehension (even for conflict) between cultures, and one is particularly acute at the moment, namely the place of women in the religions that structure societies. The return in Islam to the founding texts deeply modifies the clothes of Muslim women who, in greater and greater numbers, adopt not only the hidjab hiding their hair but also the niqabor forms of dress that hide the body totally. Since 1905, France has been under secularism based on the separation of church and state. Indeed, this principle is written in the French constitution. Western women have become emancipated from religious prescription, particularly with regard to her body. And the relatively recent appearance of what is called the "Islamic veil" in public generates such a culture shock that the government has had to legislate. This chapter analyzes this antinomic attitude relative to the female body and confronts it with the culture of contemporary French society.

HISTORY OF THE VEIL

Islam did not invent the Islamic veil! This veil, with which many Muslim women cover their heads and at least part of their bodies, existed before Muhammad. The Bible says that Jewish women covered their heads with a veil.

If, as many non-Muslim Westerners think, this veil symbolizes the inferiority of women, and their subjection to men, then it is indeed in the Bible that we have to seek its origin. Judaism, Christianity, and Islam all admit that the

Book of Genesis, which opens the Bible, was transmitted by God to Moses. These three big religious movements all recognize the existence of a unique god, and all consider this first book of the Bible to be the foundation of their faiths, even if it has been completed by other books. This applies in particular to the Gospels, which relate the life and teachings of Christ, the son of God the Father for Christians, and for Muslims, to the Koran, which relates the life of the prophet Muhammad, the messenger of Allah through whom He passed on His teachings. These three major monotheistic movements are the so-called religions of the Book.

However, an attentive reading of the Bible, with its repetitions, its anachronisms, and its improbabilities, leads us to conclude that there were several authors over a wide period of time following the era evoked in the narratives. According to critics and historians, the Book of Genesis (the first book of the Hebrew Bible) is a compilation of texts that, in the course of centuries, aimed at passing on the foundations and traditions of the Jewish religion to its believers.

It seems advisable to indicate that two types of reading exist. Some consider the Bible to be an allegorical book, which it is necessary to interpret in order to understand the Word of God and adapt His principles to contemporary society. Others, such as fundamentalist evangelicals in the North American "Bible Belt,"[1] consider that the Word of God is timeless and is not to be interpreted. So, in spite of the contribution of science to knowledge, most fundamentalists[2] proclaim that "the only book of science that counts is the Bible," that the world really was created in 7 days some 6,000 years ago, that humanity results from a unique couple—Adam and Eve—and that Darwin's theory of evolution is an impostor.

Be that as it may, the Book of Genesis explains to us very well why woman has to submit to man:

At first, woman was created to help man, and not as an autonomous being: 2.8. *"And the Lord God said, It is not good that the man shall be alone; I will make him a help mate for him."*[3]

Then, seduced by the snake, she ate the fruit of the tree of knowledge and gave one to the man. This had been forbidden by God! It is worth noting that in the Book of Genesis, knowledge and life are alternative propositions: the consequence of eating the fruit of the tree of knowledge is to be deprived of the fruit of the tree of life; to have knowledge is to become mortal: 3.22. *"Then the LORD God said, See, the man has become like one of us, knowing good and evil; and now, he might reach out his hand and take also from the tree of life, and eat, and live forever."*

When they disobeyed God, man and woman—Adam and Eve—committed the first sin, the original sin, and were punished: 3.16. *"Unto the woman He said, I will greatly multiply thy sorrow and thy conception; in sorrow thou shalt bring forth children; and thy desire shall be to thy husband, and he shall rule over thee."*

So, the situation of inferiority known to contemporary women has a culture that is based on one of the religions of the Book, making it divine; it is God's prescribed punishment for a fault committed by the first woman. It is also necessary to specify that although in the Catholic religion—the largest Christian religion with 1.2 billion adherents[4]—women are not allowed to become priests and are confined to the base of the hierarchy,[5] the reformed Calvinist and Lutheran churches allow ministers of both sexes. On the other hand, North American evangelicals (who are spread throughout the world) refer to the apostle Paul in order to forbid women access to the clergy. This is what we find on the website www.pasteurweb.org: *"As a person, woman is completely identical to man; but in the hierarchy she must submit to man, who is the head. This is the way God established order and harmony. If we want this harmony, the woman has to accept submission and obedience to the order which God established. Because it is the Eternal who wanted it, and we want to please Him. To please Him, it is necessary to submit ourselves. In churches in which Paul exercised his apostle's ministry, women did not preach or teach, or carry out pastoral ministry."*

And in referring to Paul's very clear epistle on the access of women to the priesthood, see I Timothy 2.11–13: *"The woman has to educate herself silently with a whole submission. I do not allow a woman to teach, nor to take authority on a man, but she has to remain in silence. Because Adam was created first, and then Eve."*

In Judaism, the orthodox branch denies to women the possibility of becoming rabbis, although other branches admitted them recently.[6] It should be noted that if there are few female rabbis in Europe, this is not the case in the United States.

As for Islam, the explanation that we find on the website "House of Islam" (www.maison-islam.com) is very interesting. A woman is allowed to be in charge of prayer unless the prayer group contains men. Not because she would be lower than the men, the House of Islam tells us, but just as a question of decency.

"There is not in that 'a proof that Islam considers the woman lower than the man'. There is an obvious and sensible reason. The reason is simply that the imam— the person who manages the prayer in the group—out of necessity takes his place in front of the group. And the postures of Muslim prayer, such as prostration, make it totally unthinkable for a woman to pray in front of a man. That is also why the Prophet (peace be on Him) decided that in his mosque in Medina, the rows of women coming to prayer would be placed behind those of the men." ("Can a woman be an imam?" 18 June 2008)

However, as for the other religions of the Book, Islam states that woman is dominated by man. And, likewise, it is Genesis that explains the legitimacy of this situation at the same time, by the very nature of woman stemming from man rather than being created to be different, and also by divine punishment. God is not satisfied with half measures. It is the entire "lineage of Eve" that will be dominated by man until the end of our days, and the end of time. Thus, today, the Muslim who dominates his wife and imposes upon her the wearing of veils to hide her hair, her body, even her face, is only putting into practice the Word of God such as it is told to us in the Bible, and in accordance with the rules of the prophet Muhammad, who said: *"Tell the believers to lower their eyes and to keep their chastity. It is purer for them. Allah, of course, knows exactly what they do. And tell female believers to lower their eyes and to keep their chastity, and to show in their attire only what appears, and to pull down their veil on their breast; and to show their attire only to their husbands, to their fathers, or to the fathers of their husbands, or to their sons, or to the sons of their husbands, or to their brothers, or to the sons of their brothers, or to the sons of their sisters"* (Sura XXIV, verses 30, 31).

Or also: *"O Prophet! Say to your wives, to your daughters, and to the women of the believers to tighten their veils on them; it is for them the best." Tell the believers to lower their eyes and to keep their chastity. It is purer for them. Allah, it means to be known and not to offend"* (XXXIII, 59).

The meaning of "to tighten their veils on them" remains to be defined. Is the totality of the body to be hidden from male view, the face included? The understanding of the texts is not unanimous among the *ulemas* (doctors of the faith).

We understand that all religions of the Book draw from the same source the justification of the superiority of man over woman, who is the property of her husband, and, secondarily, in effect, a child of the men in her family. Obviously, if we believe that Genesis was dictated to Moses by God, we can only bow our heads and leave the woman with her subordinate fate. But if, according to the conclusions of critics and historians, we consider that the texts that constitute the Bible were written at different times by various authors, we can formulate the hypothesis that we are in the presence of a terribly male, chauvinistic book. We could, as well, consider the Book of Genesis as a mythological narrative, in the same way as those of other civilizations: Egypt, the Near East, Asia Minor. Be that as it may, this story of a woman who was seduced by a snake and drew her companion into her fall is a magnificent pretext to explain the misery of the human condition and to supply a scapegoat for men. Please forgive the present atheistic author for his reinterpretation of a story that is too good to be true, especially when used by societies who derive their culture and legislation from these texts in order to subjugate women.

It is time to examine the effects of that age-old curse. According to the title of this chapter, we shall limit our examination to the possible consequences if women are given the latitude to dress as they desire. This study will be limited to France, a secular country by law, where the question has arisen and continues to arise even now with great intensity.[7] Finally, it should be noted that Judaism and Christianity, as opposed to Islam, exert considerably less influence on the everyday life of their followers, which is particularly apparent in the dress code. Only Islam insists on the conspicuous display of religious identity, especially among women.

VARIETIES OF ISLAMIC VEILS

It seems useful to remind ourselves of the various kinds of Islamic veils. The names change from country to country, so we shall use the anglicized forms of the words used in France and limit ourselves to three types of veil, the **hijab,** the **chador** and its variants, and the **niqab** and its variants.

1. The **hijab,** also called the Islamic headscarf, hides hair, ears, and neck. The public sees only the oval of the face. Apart from its main function (the word *hijab* comes from the Arabic *hajaba*, which means "to mask the looks"), it can be worn as a fashion accessory.

What costs are there to those who are guilty of using the hijab as a scarf without emphasizing the oval of the face? They incur the wrath of the men of faith who proclaim themselves guardians of the modesty of Muslim women. *Men*, because it is always men who say what women have to do. It is enough to give two examples from the numerous websites that—sometimes contradictorily—specify the obligations of Muslim women.

- *"My sisters, if you wear the hijab in this way, know that you are in error. The veil should not be a finery in itself, and not an improvement. You really have to become aware of it"* (http://oumsoumaya2.over-blog.com/article-32040756.html).
- *"Question: What are male clothing requirements in Islam? Answer: We do not demand that Muslims living in their various countries subscribe to any specific type of garment or tunic that Islam made compulsory for them. We say, rather, that the members of every nation are allowed to wear what they wish, according to the word of the Prophet (peace and blessings of Allah on him); 'eat what you wish and wear what you wish, as long as you avoid waste and pride'"* (http://francais.islammessage.com/Article.aspxi?-2181).

2. The **chador**, a large shawl or veil, is intended to hide the body and head totally, leaving only the face visible. This effect can be obtained, also, by combining the hijab and the **abaya,** a long and ample dress that avoids accentuating the body. However, the elegance of the abaya is inacceptable to fundamentalists who dictate how women should dress.

3. The **niqab** or its variant, the **burqa**, follows the same principle: to hide the feminine body completely, face included. It is a complete veil. The niqab allows only a slit for the eyes, whereas the burqa contains a gauze netting in front of the eyes. To avoid any temptation to make it fashionable, the niqab is black most of the time. In Afghanistan, almost exclusively, the burqa is blue or brown by tradition.

Fundamentalist Muslims are right to distrust the takeover of the rules of Muhammad by the gurus of fashion. For example, the **burquini** or **burkini** was invented and put on sale in clothing stores to allow Muslim ladies to frequent swimming pools and beaches while protecting their honor. Muslim leaders have other solutions; they have requested that cities reserve certain time slots for women at municipal swimming pools, which is not a Western custom.

In fact, what Islam imposes is modesty. This is no different from other religions. But, as in all other religions, there are extreme interpretations of the texts. So when the ulemas (the theologians of Islam) say that a woman should not show to a man other than her husband "the part of the body between the navel and the knees," they add that there is an exception in the case of medical necessity. That does not prevent husbands, fathers, or brothers from threatening doctors, who sometimes have to call the police to enable them to treat Muslim women.

I add that for Westerners, modesty takes on another sense. There is no need to hide the body completely in order to be chaste. There is a middle ground between dissimulation and showing off the body. There are many occasions in which women dressed in Western style seem no less unchaste than the one who wears the niqab. At least, this is the point of view of a Western observer.

Christian societies are all aware of dresses that hide the female body, such as the habits worn by certain nuns—women who give up secular marriage in order to serve God. For example, nuns take the vows of celibacy and chastity and dedicate themselves to prayer and charity. They are teachers or nurses, and most of them help disabled, poor, deprived, and elderly people. Depending on the religious order to which they belong, they wear clothes more or less similar to those worn by the civil female population. Most of them only wear a discreet headscarf with city clothes. Occasionally—but more and more rarely now—a dress that resembles that of a Muslim woman is worn: an ample and long dress with a veil covering her hair and neck.

THE PROBLEM OF ISLAMIC VEILS IN FRANCE

So where is the problem in a contemporary French society that includes veiled Muslims and nuns who are also veiled? The problem does exist, and it has several dimensions. On the one hand, only nuns are dressed this way, and most of them wear a simple scarf that only partially hides their hair. From a quantitative point of view, they are less and less numerous in France, which is becoming more and more dechristianized—28,678 nuns living and working in small communities in 2010 as opposed to 48,412 in 2000. That is 2,000 fewer every year. Once more, let us remember that most nuns are discreetly dressed and distinguished only by a scarf and a small cross pinned on their civil attire, while Islam is displayed more and more obviously through the dresses worn by "ordinary" women who have "normal" lives as wives and mothers, students or workers, engineers or nurses. Muslim women are active in civil society, whereas the Christian nuns are on the fringe of society. According to a survey by the French Ministry of the Interior in 2009, approximately 2,000 women wear the niqab in France. Their visibility is all the stronger as most of them live in the suburbs of big cities, particularly Paris. Finally, in most of the countries of Europe where an economic crisis rages, the political parties that denounce immigration offer the unemployed population a simplistic solution and an easy-to-spot scapegoat. These parties are called "populist" because they flatter people by denouncing the elites who govern them and because they propose demagogic solutions to the problems that make them suffer. In France, the main one of these parties, the National Front ("Front National" in French), instigates the rejection of Islam by evoking systematically the "Christian roots of France," which are historically undeniable but which, it would seem, have little sense in as cosmopolitan a society as the one in which we live. If we were to examine how Christ's teachings are applied in the everyday life of the French people and of immigrants with a strong Christian heritage, we would see that they are generally not followed, even by those who claim to be Christian.

It is also necessary to remind ourselves that, unlike England, for example, France lives under a system of the separation of religion and state and has done so for more than a century. The 1st Article of the law of December 9, 1905, stipulated that "The Republic ensures freedom of conscience. It guarantees free exercise of worship under only the limitations promulgated below, in the interest of law and order." Article 2 states, "The Republic neither recognizes, nor puts on payroll, nor subsidizes any form of worship." France is a secular country, and those people who work for the state or who enter in the places devoted to a message of public service must not show signs of membership in any religion. So when I was a child brought up in the Catholic religion, in school I had to hide under the collar of my shirt the small cross or medallion that I wore. This I did without any trouble because that was the rule, and Christians did not oppose the law of the Republic, even though they had previously, before and during the adoption of the 1905 law on the separation between Church and State, at a time when the Vatican was speaking of France as "the elder daughter of the Church."

With the appearance—once again recent—of Islamic signs in the public space and the refusal of most of the offenders to comply with the law, the French parliament (on March 15, 2004) voted for a "law restricting under the principle of secularism, the bearing of signs or dress showing religious membership, in primary schools and public high schools." This law only contains two articles. The second defines the places of application, and the first says that, "In schools, middle schools and public high schools, the bearing of signs or dress by which pupils show an obvious religious membership is forbidden. School officials have to be aware that the implementation of a disciplinary procedure must be preceded by a dialogue with the pupil."

On September 9, 2013, a "Charter of secularism at school" was posted in all French state schools, as well as in the "private schools under contract." The latter are private schools that are state subsidized and in which the teachers are paid by the state, provided that they have the same qualifications as their colleagues in the state sector. Most such schools belong to a religious organization, Catholic more often than not. The charter has 15 articles and reminds us at first that "the secular Republic organizes the separation of religion and state" and that "secularism guarantees freedom of conscience to all: each is free to believe or not to believe." Finally, the last four articles deal with the application of the principle of secularism within a school. "No subject is *a priori* excluded from scientific or educational questioning; no pupil can call upon a religious or political conviction to dispute a teacher's right to address a question in the curriculum." Also, "nobody can take advantage of religious membership to refuse to conform to the rules applicable within a school of the Republic." As regards "the bearing of symbols or dresses showing an obvious membership of a religion," the charter does make a distinction between state schools and other schools under contract. However, it makes it explicitly clear that secularism guarantees the equality between girls and boys and "implies the rejection of all violence, and all discrimination."

Reference can be made to England. The wearing of the niqab does not pose a problem. In this country, every school has the right to authorize or to forbid the clothes that they want—among which is the niqab. Admittedly there has been such a debate within the population that the Secretary of State in charge of the fight against criminality intended publicly to forbid the bearing of the niqab for minors in schools and in public space.

The French situation needs to be examined further. A law "forbidding the dissimulation of the face in the public place" was adopted on October 11, 2010, and implemented on April 11, 2011. Its first article stipulates that "nobody can, in the public space, wear a dress intended to hide the face." Article 2 defines the public space: "For the application of the 1st article, the public space is constituted by public roads, as well as places open to the public, or allocated to public service. The ban planned in the 1st article does not apply if the dress is prescribed or authorized by legal or statutory measures, if it is justified by reasons of health or professional motives, or if it fits within the framework of sports practices, or festivals or traditional manifestations." In fact, it is a law that forbids the wearing of the burka and the niqab in the public space. But it is one that certain Muslims are reluctant to respect.

For example, at the time of writing, the newspaper *Ouest-France* (July 20, 2013) carries the headline, *"Trappes: A night of violence after the identity check of a veiled woman by the police"* (Trappes is a suburb of the city of Paris). More than 200 demonstrators spent the night of Friday/Saturday 19/20 (continuing into the next day) throwing stones at the police station and at police officers and setting fire to trash cans and cars because a man who opposed virulently the questioning by police of his niqab-wearing wife had been placed under custody. He had even tried to choke a police officer. And, maybe in solidarity, demonstrators continued through the next few nights, burning cars belonging to neighbors with whom they often shared the same religion and the same generally precarious social status.

Is it necessary to say that politicians and the extremist political parties were very quick to speak out? It is true that certain imams preach that the law of Allah is superior to the laws of the Republic. It is true as well that the former President of the Republic, Nicolas Sarkozy, had (on December 20, 2007, just a few months after his election) made a very surprising speech in the Vatican, saying that "the primary school teacher can never replace the priest or the minister in the transmission of values and in the learning of the difference between good and evil." These are hardly acceptable comments when they are pronounced by the guarantor of the institutions of a secular state.

On July 23, 2013, the anthropologist Dounia Bouzar reminded us on the *France Inter* radio station that, just as the Pentecostal churches of the United States were not a resurgence of Christianity in its initial purity, so the Salafists are not a return to the basics of Islam. In both cases, she says it is just sectarian abuse, which has no other object than to cut the followers from the society in which they live. She adds that instead of wondering if the police are checking correctly if a woman is wearing a complete veil, it would be better to wonder about the offence that such a veil represents as a violation of the law of the Republic.

On July 20, 2013, in accordance with the law of April 2011, 705 checks gave rise to 661 verbal warnings against 423 women. Most of them were less than 30 years old and were born in France. When the movements for the defence of Islam report that the young woman—a Frenchwoman married to a Frenchman—whose identity check gave rise to the violent riots in Trappes always complies with the requests of the police, and shows her face at the same time as her ID card, the problem seems badly defined. We should wonder why she wears the niqab in contradiction to the law of her country. We cannot help but think that she too considers the laws of Allah to be superior to the laws of the secular Republic. That is not acceptable to the atheistic, Jewish, or Christian citizens, other than the fundamentalist sects of these last two families of religion, nor is it acceptable to the vast majority of the French people, Muslims included.

Even in other European countries, people wonder about the events that are taking place in France. As the British journalist of Arabic origin, Ahlam Akram, writes in the online daily paper *Elaph:* "*Does not this kind of behavior give the right to Western countries to revise their rules of attribution of nationality? Nationality confers citizen's rights to people who do not believe in it, because they feel a belonging to an 'Islamic nation' which is a 'homeland, for them, and gives them the 'right' to proselytise all around the world.*"[8]

But for Hicham Benaissa, researcher for the Research Group on societies, religion, secularism of the National Centre for Scientific Research (CNRS), "*the error would be in reducing this event to its religious character. ... Religion plays here the role of a unifying structure, but the malaise is deeper.*"[9] For him, the police check is only a pretext, and the heart of the problem is in the exasperation of a community convinced that racial victimization has become commonplace and the media ignore it, and in feeling marginalized in districts where high unemployment goes hand in hand with unbearable crime.

The strength of this explanation is seen in the behavior of the young people of the Parisian suburb of Bretigny-sur-Orge, where, on July 12, 2013, a train went off the rails, bringing about the deaths of six passengers, as well as causing numerous casualties. When the emergency services arrived, they were pelted with stones. The coaches were plundered, a doctor was molested, and his mobile phone was stolen. Does social precariousness excuse everything?

As for police checks, Dounia Bouzar undoubtedly speaks best about them by asserting that they are necessary, but often awkward, to say the least. "*These checks are difficult, but at the same time it was necessary to stress the obligation of having a bare face, because otherwise this behavior would be validated as freedom of conscience and as religion. We were obliged to do something symbolic to say, 'we know that it is not freedom of conscience; we know that it is not a matter of religion to put a sheet on your head. We know that there is an individual dysfunction'. ... Are the police equipped to apply the law without slipping into a hotchpotch of systematisations? If you slip just a little, you are no longer credible. Then this institution, the State, is no longer credible to these people.*"[10]

In other words, for all French people, and all the people who live in France or who come there as visitors, the rule is clear, even if it is not always easy to apply: freedom of religion in private space, secularism in public space. France rejects communitarianism, and the doctrine which prevails is that of integration. Those who want to live in France must (at least in public) live "French-style" and not according to the habits and customs of their country of origin. And he or she must respect the laws of the Republic when they seem restrictive, just as he or she does when they are beneficial to him or her. The vast majority of French people agree with this doctrine, even if one notices every day that it is being challenged by the resistance of some communities. In brief, the doctrine that prevails in France advocates integration and excludes communitarianism. *"That integration consists of welcoming populations originally from diverse countries, who come to France of their own free will, to become established there, work there, start a family there, stay by becoming French citizens if they wish, and see their children declared French by the fact that they were born on French soil."*[11] To become integrated, or to be integrated, means to adopt the French way of life; to live French-style in France, although it is not forbidden to keep lifestyles inherited from the country of origin in private, so long as they are not in contradiction with French law. Eating, drinking, dressing, and furnishing one's home are obviously in the domain of personal choice and constitute domains that the immigrant can enjoy freely.

On the other hand, communitarianism means that immigrants group together by communities according to their geographical or religious origins and try to impose their former habits and customs on the society that welcomes them. It begins with food practices, and we see Jews and Muslims demanding, sometimes vehemently, that the menus of school canteens be in accordance with their religious practices. In the extreme, members of the African communities that practice excision do not understand that the French state sues them and that justice condemns them for barbaric trespassing and practices in violation of human rights. These community practices are not only a matter of ethnic origin. Most of the time, they stem from a fundamentalist conception of religion.

In an article published by the Israeli newspaper *Ha'Aretz,* Ze'ev Sternhell denounced the threats that the Orthodox Jews make to the state of Israel in view of the fact that Jews living in the United States and in Europe are protected by *"their adherence to liberal and democratic values: the appearance of all kinds of fanaticism in Israel—of which the humiliation of women in the army (by the more religious soldiers), and, very soon, in higher education (the existence of a bill to create men-only classes, to please members of a religious order), the refusal to grant equality of rights to non-Jewish citizens, and the segmentation of the population by ethnic origin—can all be perceived as striking a blow at the image of Jews in their respective countries."*[12]

The refusal to comply with the law can cause a scandal. For example, in December 2010, the court of Nantes cancelled a fine imposed by a police officer on a woman who drove her car while wearing a niqab. The motive for the fine was sufficient safety standards were not met. It was not long before indignant comments appeared on blogs! The vote for the law of 2011 deals with situations of this kind.

Here is another example of a case that shows, at the same time, the legal complexity and the sense of injustice felt by the population—*all* the population, both Muslim and non-Muslim, albeit for different reasons.

In 2008, after taking maternity leave for 5 years, the (female) deputy director of an independently run crèche in the Paris area returned to work. The crèche is called "Baby Loup," an affectionate name for children. The nursery is based on feminist philosophy and, as such, is open 24 hours a day, 7 days a week, to allow the mothers to take up any sort of employment. The internal rules (accepted and signed by all parties) of the association that manages the nursery stipulate that *"the principle of freedom of conscience and religion of each member of the staff cannot oppose the respect for the principle of secularism and neutrality which applies to all the activities developed by Baby Loup."*

Yet during her maternity leave, the young woman changed her appearance. On her return, she wore the hijab. The manager (also a woman) asked her to remove it when she was present at the nursery, in accordance with the internal rules. Because she refused, she was dismissed.

The case went before a labor relations tribunal, which deals with work-related conflicts, and ruled in favor of the employer in December 2010. This ruling was confirmed by the Court of Appeal of Versailles on March 19, 2012. But the Court of Cassation (the highest judicial authority) overturned this judgment on March 19, 2013. The Court of Cassation does not say if a decision is just; it says if the decision is in compliance with the law. In this case, it ruled that the nursery Baby Loup falls within private law and that the laws quoted do not apply to private enterprises. So the manager of the nursery would have doubtless won if she had shown that the veil hindered professional exercise rather than pleading the necessity of conforming to secularism according to internal rules.

The anthropologist Dounia Bouzar says that *"instead of citing the employee's obligation to follow the nursery's regulation on secularism, the lawyer for the nursery should have shown that her large scarf* 'hinders her capacities in her professional mission', *which means, for the deputy director of a nursery, an obligation to treat children equally, whether they come from an atheistic, Christian, Jewish or Muslim family."* And she adds: *"a principle remains; as soon as it hinders the mission, religion does not override the law. A sales manager who refuses to shake hands with women; the cook who refuses to touch pork, can be dismissed without it being discriminatory, even if they justify their behavior by their freedom of conscience!"*[13] As a conclusion to this appalling affair, *Le Monde* published on September 29–30, 2013, an article titled *"Community divisions and bullying defeat the Yvelines nursery, which closes its doors. The end of Crèche Baby-Loup."*

Natalia Baleato, who was born in Santiago, Chile, in 1955, founded the nursery in 1991 and has run it ever since, explains thus her decision to close down her establishment. After the decision of the Court of Appeal, *"the opposition took on a new look, emboldened by the assurance of legitimacy. After outside and anonymous hostilities there followed altercations on our premises, involving parents with whom we had been working for years without problems and in a climate of confidence, and who had suddenly become the ardent defenders of singular demands which we were now forced to implement 'by law'. If they were to be taken seriously, these demands would entail the separation of children according to lifestyles chosen by their parents, the exclusion of some of them from games or festivals considered inappropriate by this or that religion, the isolation of others at meal time to prevent them from tasting (and even touching) forbidden foods, the regulation of sleep patterns according to various arbitrary customs ... all this in the face of needs and wants considered important in child psychiatry."*

When they are angry, fanatics burn cars belonging to neighbors who are just as needy as they are. They discourage goodwill until the structures built on it, for them, have been destroyed. It is easy to see what type of society they are destroying, but one has to wonder what type of society they are building. My God, Islam was so peaceful and tolerant before the Salafists!

Be that as it may, affairs of this type are all grist to the mill for extremists, who find it easy to say that if the Spaniards, the Italians, and the Poles who came to work in France previously merged with the French population, it is because they had the same Christian roots as the French people, and that the integration of Muslims is almost impossible. In fact, history teaches us that these European immigrants were despised and rejected just as much, in spite of claimed Christian roots. These cases are all the more grist to the mill of ill will as the media use a unique and ambiguous term to name the hijab, the niqab, or the burka—the Islamic veil. We always and imprecisely speak about "veil." The difference is big between the scarf that hides hair and the fenced dress that hides the body and the face and that is now outlawed.

If these extremists can amplify the malaise, it is because the arrival of the niqab in France seemed to be a break with the Islam that the French people knew; a regression with regard to what was essentially the Islam of the Maghreb, because the immigrant populations of Muslim faith were almost exclusively Algerian, Moroccan, and Tunisian, for historic reasons. These countries being French colonies, their inhabitants came to work in France. Samir Amghar, a researcher in sociology at the French Research Centre in Social Sciences (EHESS), Institute of Studies of Islam and Muslim Societies, says quite rightly: *"In France, the wearing of the niqab is connected to the development of the Salafiste movement.*[14] *Appearing at the start of the 90s, this movement became established in France following the preaching of some young French Muslims who studied at the University of Medina in Jordan or in Yemen. It also results from contacts established over borders, in particular by the Internet, with leading Salafis who came to France to speak at conferences."*[15]

What all the fundamentalists have in common is to refuse evolution, adaptation, and modernization. Jewish, Christian, or Muslim, they profess that the sacred texts are the only expression of the truth, that they are to be taken literally, and that they must not be interpreted in the light of history or of science. This is how Muslim fundamentalists can refuse any emancipation of women and, in fact, any philosophy based on sexual equality. And they impose a literal reading of the texts today, as they always have, suggesting that women must be submissive and must hide their body.

In an article published in the magazine *Esprit* and titled "*Our Responsibilities for Islam*," the Muslim philosopher Abdennour Bidar recommends that we ensure that "*Islam gets free of its ritualistic and dogmatic strait jacket.*"[16] However, we must not believe that the wearing of the veil is always imposed on Muslim women by an indisputable order of their male superior. There are certainly women who decide for themselves to veil their bodies. On the one hand, they live in a strongly inductive environment: their readings, the comments they hear, the consultation of websites lauding the wearing of the veil in one form or another. All this generates a pressure to conform that is difficult to resist. On the other hand, they are often young women who express both the rejection of the French social model and the Islam of their parents.

Samir Amghar explains it very well: "*However surprising it may appear, the complete veil is claimed by these women. They get a very big pride from the niqab; a symbol of respectability, the niqab ensures that they belong to a community of their own choosing. Because they feel excluded by a society with racist overtones, they decide, by their garment, to exclude those who are at the root of the discrimination. Convinced that they embody the way to salvation required by Allah, they believe they are the only ones to dispense the religious truth in front of their co-religionists who do not belong to their movement, and just wear a 'simple veil'.*"[17]

We are facing a religion of "fight," often aggressive in its attitudes and its comments, just as much as in its dress code, which demonstrates both the difference with and superiority over non-believers and "ordinary" Muslims. The Western world tends to confuse this very visible Islamic minority with moderate Islam, which is practised by the vast majority of believers. The Western world tends to confuse Islam and Islamism.

If we want to be cautious in our interpretation, we must remember that Islam is not monolithic. The Salafists are not representative of the whole of Islam. Let us not confuse Islam with Islamism. Again the hijab—the widespread headscarf—is actually generally accepted by non-Muslim French people. It is the niqab that shocks, probably because it hides entirely the body of the woman who wears it, face included. Even when the wearing of the garment results from the voluntary choice of the woman concerned, it appears to French people not so much as a sign of membership in a religion but as a patently obvious symbol of alienation. It is like seeing a woman in handcuffs and chains. We see images of these Arabic monarchies where a woman is not allowed to drive a car or walk in the streets without being accompanied by a male member of her family. The niqab and similar dresses work as vectors of communication, encouraging memories and fantasies that constitute a rough and often unfounded representation of the Muslim faith.

Not that this established fact is specific to France. In its issue of July 9, 2013, the British newspaper *The Independent* (quoted by the French *Courrier International*)[18] stated that a study led by the Royal Statistical Society showed how, from a strictly statistical point of view, British opinion differs from reality. To stay on topic, "*Citizens think that 24% of the British population is Muslim. The actual figure is 5%!*" Be that as it may, whether Femen strip off in the Islamic country of Tunisia or Muslim women wear a complete veil in France—a secular country—the symbolism is the same, and the culture shock is comparable.

CONCLUDING REFLECTIONS

As a researcher, I cannot totally distance myself from my own culture. The researcher tries hard to do so when he inventories, examines, and analyzes the facts. But it would be hypocritical to claim that he does so when he gives a final look at the matter he has analyzed. He has to be as objective as possible during the research itself, but he is allowed to give his personal opinion when his work is finished. That is why I shall end by saying that I adhere totally to the comment of anthropologist Dounia Bouzar, who specializes in religion. I quote her once again: "*As for religious visibility, it depends on the look and the function. Rather than perceiving straight away 'a Catholic', 'a Jew', 'a Muslim', we prefer to identify 'a nurse', 'a secretary', 'a manager'. This notion should be passed on to all. And remember that if we are allowed to be atheistic, Jewish or Muslim in France, and not only Christian, even though the history of the country is Christian, it is precisely thanks to secularism. It is enough to look at the situation in non-secular countries to strive to protect our system, and to educate about secularism.*"

The moment must come when researchers believe they can put an end to the presentation of the results of their research. That moment comes when it is necessary, whatever happens, to switch off the computer and finish the report. I do not doubt that new events could happen, which would deserve to be examined, but which will or will not merit new, even deeper research. However, in its edition of August 31, the French newspaper *Le Monde* tells of a debate occurring in Canada, in the province of Quebec. The head of government of Quebec is preparing to submit to the Provincial parliament a "Charter of Values of Quebec," the subject of which is "to reaffirm the religious neutrality of the state by refusing to allow state employees and employees of semi-public organisations to bear religious symbols." In 2008, the government had asked philosopher Charles Taylor and historian and sociologist Roger Bouchard to write a report on "the practices of accommodation linked to cultural differences." The object of this report was to recommend ways to reconcile the laws and regulations of Quebec (a secular state) with freedom of religion and rights for equality in a country where it seems that the word *discrimination* is the worst that can be used and which evokes the most formidable of offences. In what the French call "a game of balance" that opened between secularism and freedom of religion, the report recommended, in the name of impartiality, that certain officials (magistrates, police officers, prison guards) be forbidden to bear religious symbols but considered that, in the name of respect for individual rights, other state employees (teachers, doctors, nurses) should be free to wear them. The presentation of the Charter of Values to the legislative assembly of Quebec occurs under a jurisprudence established over the years. A jurisprudence which, for example, forbids the Islamic courts to judge family affairs but allows orthodox Sikh policemen to wear the turban or the children of that same religion to have a small dagger in their belts, or Muslim girls to hide their hair under the hijab at school.

On these points, the Supreme Court of Canada judges according to criteria opposite to those of the French courts, including the Court of Cassation, which is the Supreme Court of the French judicial system. In France, we conclude that a child of school age must give up his religious symbols in order to be allowed to attend a state school. But the Canadian Supreme Court, conversely, says that if we forbid a Muslim girl to wear the hijab or a young Sikh to carry a dagger, we deprive that child of access to a state school. Two cultures that would seem close thus produce different decisions, based on opposite ideological presuppositions. If the Islamic sphere of influence was able to try to obtain the recognition of Islamic courts by the Canadian provincial governments—as indicated in Mounia Chadi's article—it is because there are two concurrent notions in Canada. The first is communitarianism, the second the fear of discrimination. In France, though, the secular ideology is based on integration and on the distinction between public and private spaces. Neither must encroach on the other. However, as Christian Rioux points out, correspondent in Paris for the Quebec newspaper *Le Devoir*: "*France remains a model for the whole world regarding secularism, though its experience is obviously never entirely transposable. Quebec is the only place in North America where we understand more or less what the word 'laïcité' (secularism) means, besides being practically untranslatable in English. An extraordinary courage is needed to dare to propose such a charter in the Canadian context, where multiculturalism became the national religion. Remember yourselves that, without the international opposition aroused by Quebec, the neighbouring province (Ontario) would have Islamic courts today.*"[19]

I shall finish by quoting from a private conversation with my friend Professor Alain Thomas. A Frenchman by origin, he has lived and taught in Ontario for more than 40 years and knows the two cultures well: "*I see a new illustration of a fundamental difference between the French and Canadian priorities there. The French are eager to defend principles—freedom, equality, brotherhood, secularism—without worrying too much about abuses in their application. In Canada, and especially in English-speaking Canada, we are more pragmatic: we wonder where is the real danger in the practices that may be banned, before we attack the symbols. I think that Quebec lies somewhere between the two.*"

One might well conclude that the notion of secularism is relative and submits to national cultures, whereas religion as conceived by the Salafists seems to suffer no adaptation, and leads to an intransigence that is well summarized by the following basic principle: the law of Allah is above the law of men. They may be activists and cause a lot of people to speak about them because of this intransigence. We should not lose sight of the fact that it is at this moment that hostile reactions appear in Western countries. It is at the moment that the situation becomes intolerable for the concerned populations. Doubtless because enough is enough. But, at least for the time being, the Salafists are a minority group. Thank God!

NOTES

A different version of this chapter, with photos and a section on the Femen, will be published in *Cultural Conflicts and Intercultural Communication*, Social Sciences Academic Press, Beijing (2015), with the title, "From the Islamic Veil to the Femen: The Body That Communicates." Mr. Zhu Debin, Director, Division of Global and Regional Studies, grants permission to publish chapter 3.

1. This expression refers to the heavily evangelical part of the United States. Nineteen states constitute this region, all in the South of the country.
2. Most belong to the Baptist branch of Protestantism, which includes 125 million believers in the world, among which 36 million live in the United States.
3. 2.18 means Chapter 2 verse 18. The same reference system is used for the Koran.
4. This is the number of baptized. Since baptism takes place in early childhood, the number of adult Catholics is lower and that of practicing Catholics even lower (cf. *Pontifical Yearbook*, 2004); Carol Glatz, "Vatican Statistics: Church Growth Remains Steady Worldwide," *The Catholic Herald*, May 5, 2014.
5. On July 29, 2013, in the aircraft returning him from Rio de Janeiro, the Pope said to the journalists who questioned him: "for the ordination of women, the Church said no; Pope John-Paul II said it in a definitive way, this door is closed."
6. The reformist branch admitted them into the rabbinate in 1922. Other branches admitted them respectively in 1968 and 1983. Cf. Renee Ghert-Zand, "Female Rabbis Crack the Stained Glass Ceiling," *The Times of Israel*, Sept. 1, 2014.

7. For background comparing France to Germany and the UK, see C. Joppke, *The Veil: Mirror of Identity*. Cambridge, UK: Polity, 2009.

8. *Elaph*, London, 21-7-2013 and *Courrier International Paris*, no. 1186 25/31-7-2013.

9. *La Monde*, 23-7-2013.

10. *France Inter*, Radio France, 22-7-2013.

11. http://www.agoravox.fr/actualities/integration-et-communautarisme-79447

12. *Ha'Aretz*, 5-7-2013, and *Courrier International*, no. 1186 25/31-7-2013.

13. "Crèche Baby Loup, what says the law on secularism?" Interview by Stéphanie Combe, *La vie*, 26-3-2013. (*La vie* is a weekly magazine published by a Catholic publishing house.)

14. The Salafiste movement recognizes only the Koran and the Sunna, that is, all the *hadiths* or the words pronounced by Muhammad and his companions (hence "Sunni"). It demands a literal reading of the texts, not an interpretive one. It is multiform and takes, according to the different currents, different positions that go from jihad (or holy war) to the rejection of attacks and suicide attacks, even to the refusal of political action for believers. Quietist Salafism, the one which refuses the holy war, is close to Saudi Arabia.

15. "Le niqâb pour s'affirmer?" *Projets*, Ceras, no. 314, January, 2010.

16. "Nos responabilités pour l'islam." *Esprit*, March–April, 2007. Abdennour Bidar, "Je suis convaincu qu'existe un universel humaniste." *Télérama.fr*, 25-01-2015.

17. Op. cit.

18. *Courier International*, no. 1185, 18/24 July 7, 2013.

REFERENCES

SACRED TEXTS

Osty, E. *La Bible*. (1973 dition). Paris: Le Seuil.

Le Coran. (1980). *Essai d'interprétation du Coran inimitable, traduction par D. Masson revue par Sobih El-Saleh*. Paris: Editions Gallimard.

BOOKS AND ARTICLES

Abdul, S. (2013). Trappes, le récit d'un week-end sous tension. *Le Monde*, 23-7-2013.

Abdul, S., & Borredon, L. (2013). Le djihad s'apprend tout seul sur Internet. *Le Monde*, 31-7-2013.

Akram, A. (2013). L'erreur des musulmans de Trappes, in *Courrier International*, no. 118625/31-7-2013, translation of an article published in *Elaph*, London, 21-7-2013.

Ali, L. (2010). Behind the Veil. *New York Times*, 31-6-2010.

Al-Gharbi, I. (2007). Ce que dit vraiment le Coran. File of the main themes treated by the Koran, in particular "Women." *Le Monde des religions*, Sept.–Oct., 2007.

Barry, E. (2013). Local Russian hijab ban puts Muslims in squeeze. *New York Times*, 19-3-2013.

Beji, H. (2013). La revolution tunisienne sombre dans la confusion, seule une jeune femine dénudée incarne le voie de la raison. Amina, l'historie en marche. *Le Monde*, 16/17-6-2013.

Benaissa, H., & Crepon, S. (2013). L'entreprise et son tabou religieux. *Le Monde*, 6-8-2013.

Bianco, J-L. (2013). Chairman of Observatoire de la laïcité, La France n'a pas de problème avec sa laïcité. Interview by Stéphanie Le Bars. *Le Monde*, 26-6-2013.

Bidar, A. (2004). *Un islam pour notre temps*. Paris: Le Seuil.

Bidar, A. (2006). *Self Islam*. Paris: Le Seuil.

Bidar, A. (2007). Nos responsabilités pour l'Islam. In revue *Esprit,* March–April 2007.

Bidar, A. (2015). Je sius convaincu qu'existe un universel humaniste. *Télérma.fr,* January 25.

Bielefeldt, H. (2007). La liberté religieuse: le critère ultime. In revue *Esprit,* March–April, 2007.

Borghee, M. (2012). *Voile integral en France, sociologie d'un paradoxe.* Paris: Editions Michalon.

Bouchard, G. (1998). *Christianisme.* Rome: Editions Liana Levi; Paris: Editions France-Loisirs for the French Translation.

Brantl, G. (1961). *Christianity: Catholicism.* New York: George Braziller.

Chebel, M. (2004). *Manifeste pour un islam des Lumières, 27 propositions pour reformer l'islam.* Paris: Hachette Littératures.

Clarke, P. B. (1995). *Le grand livre des religions du monde.* Paris: Solar.

Dhumieres, M. (2013). Why is the right of Muslim women to wear the veil still so controversial in France? *The Independent,* 16-4-2013.

Donegani, J. M., Duchesne, S., & Haegel, F. (Eds.). (2002). *Aux frontiers des attitudes: entre le politque et le religieux.* Paris: L'harmattan.

Dunstan, J. L. (1962). *Christianity: Protestantism.* New York: George Braziller Inc.

Erlanger, S. (2009). Burqa furor scrambles French politics. *New York Times,* January 9.

Erlanger, S. (2013a). France: Court says head scarf is not grounds for firing. *New York Times,* March 20.

Erlanger, S. (2013b). Muslim woman suffers miscarriage after attack in France. *New York Times,* June 19.

Erlanger, S. (2015). France's ideals, forged in revolution, face a modern test. *New York Times,* February 2.

Ghazal, R. J., & Bartowski, J. P. (2000). To veil or not to veil? A case study of identity negotiation among Muslim women in Austin, Texas. *Gender and Society, 14*(3), June, 395–417.

Ghert-Zand, Renee. (2014). Female rabbis crack the stained glass ceiling. *The Times of Israel,* Sept. 1.

Glatz, Carol. (2014). Vatican statistics: Church growth remains steady worldwide. *The Catholic Herald,* May 5.

Gurwith, J. (1987). *Les Judéo-chrétiens aujourd'hui.* Paris: Editions du cerf.

Hertzberg, A. (1962). *Judaism,* 3rd ed. New York: George Braziller, Inc.

Joppke, C. (2009). *The veil: Mirror of identity.* Cambridge, UK: Polity.

Kepel, G. (1997). *Allah in the West: Islamic movements in America and Europe.* Paris: Editions Lavoisier.

Le Bars, S. (2013a). Les associations musulmanes s'inquiètent d'un "climat islamophobe." *Le Mos/ nde,* 21/22-7-2013.

Le Bars, S. (2013b). Le pape prône l'ouverture à l'égard des homosexuels—"Pour l'ordination des femmes, l'Eglise a dit non (…) Cette porte est fermée." *Le Monde,* 31-7-2013.

Le Bars, S. (2013c). Le droit de porer le voile à la fac remis en question, "J'enlève mon voile aux toilettes quand j'arrive à l'hôpital; j'ai l'impression d'être nue." *Le Monde,* 6-8-2013.

Maillard de, J. (2013). Le voile révèle les failles du pacte républicain. *Le Monde,* 25-7-2013.

Marian, M., & Roy, O. (2007). La difficule acclimatation de l'islam. In revue *Esprit,* March–April, 2007.

Pélouas, A. (2013). Polémique sur la laïcité au Québec. *Le Monde,* 31-8-2013.

Poupard, R. (1987). *Les religions.* Paris: PUF, coll. Que sais-je.

Rheims, B. (2013). Troublante militante. *Le Monde,* 27-7-2013.

Roy, O. (2007). Le découplage de la religion et de la culture: une exception musulmane. In revue *Esprit,* March–April, 2007.

Rubin, A. (2013). A French town bridges the gap between Muslims and non-Muslims. *New York Times*, August 6.

Sciolino, E. (2011). The French, the veil and the look. *New York Times*, April 17.

Seniguer, H. (2013). Contre l'islamophobie, des collectifs en "concurrence." Interview by Elise Vincent, *Le Monde*, 17-8-2013.

Tawfik, Y. (1997). *Islam.* Rome: Editions Liana Levi; Paris: Editions France-Loisirs for the French translation (1998).

Vincent, E. (2013). Retour à Trappes, les raisons d'une émeute. *Le Monde*, 17-8-2013.

Willaime, J-P. (2007). Reconfigurations ultramodernes. In revue *Esprit*, March-April, 2007.

Williams, J. A. (2012). *Islam.* New York: George Braziller, Inc.

ONLINE

1. About the clothes

"Iran en terre perse." Traveller's blog. artizenvelo.org/blog/ (June 2010)

"Le vêtement de la femme musulmane." http://oumsoumaya2.over-blog.com/article-32040756.html (undated)

"Le vêtement de la femme musulmane dans le Qu'ran et la Sunna." http: www.zaynab.fr/le-vetement-de-la-femme-musulmane/ (undated)

"Les conditions de la tenue vestimentaire du musulman." http://francais.islammessage.com/Article.aspx?i=2181 (undated)

"Quelles limites à l'action des regards? Pourquoi?" http://www.maison-islam.com/articles/?p=22 (undated)

2. About the crèche Baby Loup

"Baby Loup: une crèche peut interdire le port de signes religieux." *liberation.fr* (27-10-2011).

"Les dits et les non-dits de la crèche Baby Loup." *slate.fr* (21-3-2013).

"Crèche Baby Loup: que dit la loi sur la laïcité?" Interview of Dounia Bouzar, *lavie.fr* (26-3-2013).

"Baby Loup: la Cour de cassation confirme le licenciement de la salariée voilée." *Le Figaro.fr* (25/06/2014).

3. About other subjects

"Statistiques sur l'Eglise catholique dans le monde." http:/www.eglise.catholique.fr/ressources-annuaires/guide-de-l-eglise/statistiques-de-l-eglise/statistiques-sur-l-eglise-catholique-dans-le-monde.html (2013).

"La laïcité à l'usage des éducateurs. Trouvez des responses à vos questions." http://www.laicite-educateurs.org/rubrique.php3?id_rubrique=5 (undated).

"Des tribunaux islamiques au Canada?" *Mounia Chadi,* http://www.syfia.info (7-12-2012).

CHAPTER FOUR

Derailed News Frames AND Dynamic Cultural Hegemony

A Textual Analysis of 9/11 10th-Anniversary Reports

JIAMEI TANG AND BO SHAN

Through content analysis of 9/11 10th-anniversary reports by major Western newspapers, this chapter aims to explain the news frames on macro, medium, and micro levels and the "derailment" of its narrative pattern. The evolution of 9/11 news frames during the past 10 years also reveals the interaction between news production and cultural hegemony, and the nature of cultural centrism behind the current hegemony.

Publicness or the public sphere is the imagined "rail" of the news media on which public discussions are constructed. On this rail, public topics and opinions are represented; interactive political, religious, or cultural negotiations and dialogues are carried out for prompting the public power to solve public problems. However, in reality, the news media have always "derailed" into the control of a certain cultural hegemony. This "derailment" starts, at a micro perspective, during the news production process of event selecting, source structuring, story framing, and meaning interpretation. Restrained by social context, news therefore seems to run off the rail of the essential meanings of news events, the interactive discussions, negotiations, and dialogues. In the end, news outputs are the products of the mainstream process of social reproduction.

In 2011, the 10th-anniversary memorials of 9/11 were covered by the global media, becoming a typical media event of fighting terrorism and evoking fundamental social values to defuse conflicts. Opposing war and striving for peace appear to be a "consensual script" agreed by memorial organizers, media organizations, and public audiences. Would the news media be able to follow and further develop the "consensual" meaning sphere to make sure this media event is produced on the negotiated public rail? To answer this question, this chapter, through textual analysis of 9/11 10th-anniversary reports of major Western newspapers, examines the interactivity between news production and cultural hegemony. It discusses the impact and significance of news construction and the hegemony behind the conflicts of different races, religions, and cultures.

RESEARCH QUESTIONS AND THEORETICAL FRAMEWORK

The first research question is what kind of frames the mainstream Western news media presented for 9/11 10th-anniversary reports. Framing theory is adopted to look into this question. Framing is not only a tool to perceive and interpret social and life experiences but also a means to select and structure meaning during the process of construction and production. Media frames play four major functions: problem definition, causal interpretation, moral evaluation, and/or treatment recommendation. The framing strategies used are salience or neglect, setting agendas, and rhetoric and standpoint (Entman, 1993, pp. 51–58; Gamson, 1989, pp. 157–161; Gitlin, 1980; Goffman, 1974; Pan, 1993, pp. 55–75; Scheufele, 1999, pp. 103–122). News frames are influenced by micro, mid-scale, and macro factors of news practitioners, organizational routines, media systems, and social cultures. Operating within these factors, ideology and cultural hegemony affect news frames most significantly (Durham & Carpenter, 2014; Melki, 2014, pp. 165–186; Preston, 2009; Shoemaker & Reese, 1996). News frames are divided into higher, medium, and lower levels. The higher level of news frames, represented through headlines and leads, defines the themes and topics of particular events. The medium-level frame explains major events, their histories, consequences, influences, attributions, and evaluations. The lower level represented by words and phrases interprets rhetoric and style (Zhang, 1999, pp. 32–34).

The second question is whether the 9/11 10th-anniversary reports "derail" from the consensual script. If so, how should this derailment be understood and interpreted? "Derailment" is a concept proposed by Dayan and Katz (1992) in their research of media events. Media events on satellite TV, according to them, are "the live broadcasting of history," and "Contest, Conquest, Coronation" are three major types of media events. In 2008, Dayan developed a new model of media events as "Disenchantment, Derailment, Disruption." In his chapter "Beyond Media Events," Dayan explained that "Contest, Conquest, Coronation" represent integrations and consensuses, while "Disenchantment, Derailment, Disruption" produce differentiations (pp. 391–402). In studying the complexity of media events, the consensual media event can be mingled with differentiation and dissent. What researchers using this model need to examine is the extent to which these integrations, consensuses, differentiations, and dissents are restrained by social context and are shaped during the process of social reproduction.

To answer this second question about derailment, the theoretical framework of cultural hegemony needs to be drawn upon to further analyze the confining forces behind news frames. Gitlin (1980) applied Gramsci's cultural hegemony to explain news production and to reveal the restrained and interactive relations between cultural hegemony and the news industry. He pointed out that operational routines significantly affect news production, and its formation embodies social hegemony that at the same time has always been dynamically developed and shaped by both the power class and the ruled. Hegemony and media have similar core interests in stabilizing free capitalist social orders. Media frames therefore adjust and change correspondingly as hegemony adapts to social change. Frames even question or challenge an old hegemony to together create a new one in accordance with the dominant interests. Cultural hegemony has also been imported into cultural studies to analyze the media as a major representation of hegemony. The hegemonic perspective holds that media representations can win, ensure, and maintain the ideological consent of audiences. Moreover, this process, as a factor in changing historical progress, preserves the ruling class's interests through reconstructing social values and beliefs (Taylor & Willis, 2005).

THREE LEVELS OF NEWS FRAMES FOR 9/11 10TH-ANNIVERSARY REPORTS

Key words and phrases were searched—*9/11, 9/11 10th anniversary, World Trade Center, terrorist attacks, anti-terrorism/anti-terrorism war, war on terror/ war on terrorism, war against terror/war against terrorism*—in the databases of Lexis-Nexis for English language news on September 11, 2011. We collected and analyzed 133 full-text news reports of the major American, British, Australian, and Canadian newspapers as research samples. Among these samples were 60 American news items from the *New York Times, Washington Post, Los Angeles Times, Christian Science Monitor, Philadelphia Inquirer,* and so forth. There were 40 British items from the *Times, Daily Telegraph, Observer, Mail,* and the *Mirror;* 28 Australian news reports from the *Sun Herald* and the *Age;* and 5 Canadian news reports from the *Toronto Star.* News frames can be discerned through the qualitative textual analysis of a close reading of news items. This close reading elaborates on the construction of meaning by analyzing the use of narrative structures and language choices. The textual analysis of this study is supplemented with the quantitative analysis of key words and high-frequency words and phrases, to analyze the macro, medium, and micro news frames of these sample stories.

Macro Level of News Frames

The macro level of frames concerns core agendas of news stories, represented mainly by headlines and leads. Seven news frames including human interest, attribution of responsibility, morality, economic consequences, and conflicts provide a useful frame structure for the macro level of news frames (Zhou, 2008, pp. 117–136). The core agendas of 9/11 10th-anniversary reports are commemoration and introspection, representing the human interest frame and morality frame, respectively. The human interest frame is represented by news stories from personal and sensational perspectives, while the morality frame interprets and evaluates media events from an ethical perspective. Those stories recalling the attack, depicting commemorative activities, telling life stories of involved individuals including families of the victims, witnesses of the attack, soldiers and their families, Muslims, and so forth, all compose the macro level of the commemoration frame from a human interest perspective. The other major type of reports includes the evaluations of wars; reflections toward cultural, racial, and religious differences and conflicts; and analysis of domestic and international status quo. This type of report tries to interpret and evaluate the above issues with consensual social values and moral principles, therefore composing the macro level of introspection. Table 4.1 lists the macro-level news frames and some of their representative news headlines.

Table 4.1. Macro Level of News Frames for 9/11 10th-Anniversary Reports.

Commemoration frame	Recalling the attack	"September 11th: What Happened?" (*Washington Post*)
	Depicting commemorative activities	"9.11 Anniversary: Around the Country, Americans Pause to Remember" (*Christian Science Monitor*)
	Telling life stories of the involved	"Small Leaps of Faith" (*New York Times*)
	Telling life stories of ordinary people	"9.11. Ten Years After/Readers Remember; Nothing Would Be the Same" (*Los Angeles Times*)
Introspection frame	Evaluation of wars	"Worldview: War on Terrorism a Phantom" (*Philadelphia Inquirer*)
	Reflection of religious and cultural conflicts	"This Is a Day to Remember What We Stand For" (*Australian Times*) "The War on Terror's Missing Battle" (*Toronto Star*)
	Analysis of domestic and international status quo	"Civil Liberties Today" (*New York Times*) "Ten Years Later, and the World Is Still in Flux" (*Times*)

Medium Level of News Frames

The medium level of news frames concerns major topics of the reports and their overall reviews and contexts through representing the histories, attributions, consequences, and evaluations of the relevant stories. Medium-level frames incarnate the functions of news frames in problem definition, causal interpretation, moral evaluation, and/or treatment recommendations. This level reflects what Entman (1993) describes as constructing realities through the salience of frames (pp. 51–58). Through careful readings of sample news reports, it has been revealed that the medium-level frames are actually extended sub-agendas of the macro frames. By inspecting the commemoration of 9/11, four medium-level news frames emerged: the high cost of anti-terror wars, security policies and the deterioration of democracy and liberty, rational attitudes toward Islam and Muslims, and a soft power strategy for winning the battle of ideas.

News Frame One: High Cost of Wars on Terror

Ten years after 9/11, the mainstream Western media began reporting that America's wars in Afghanistan and Iraq were an overreactive mistake for which America had to pay not only a heavy economic price but also a large number of soldiers and civilians lost their lives. The ground for the Iraq war, alleged by some media, is now considered inadequate:

- "The emotional response to 9/11 connected at an intellectual level to a narrative fed both by Al Qaeda and by some outspoken American commentators: that the two sides were engaged in nothing less than a clash of civilizations, a fight to the death over life and liberty. This jihadist narrative magnified any harebrained scheme it touched" ("Al Qaeda's Outsize Shadow," *New York Times*).
- "Based on false pretexts, we were drawn into a misdirected war that has exacted enormous costs in lives and money" ("Loss and Hope," *New York Times*).
- "More than two million sent to Iraq or Afghanistan. More than 6,000 killed. About 44,000 wounded in action. One in five returning with post-traumatic stress, major depression or traumatic brain injury. More than 1,000 missing a limb" ("They Signed Up to Fight," *New York Times*).

After interviewing a number of American elites and opinion leaders who had expressed their views on the attack 10 years ago, the *Los Angeles Times* presented the comment of Jonathan Turley, a law professor at George Washington University, on a false reason of war: "Bush decided to invoke the heightened constitutional powers of a wartime president by declaring war on what was a category of crime" ("9/11 Ten Years After: Perspectives"). The *Los Angeles Times* pointed out the cost and casualties of war by quoting a government worker in Afghanistan: "People couldn't imagine that their houses would be raided in the night and their children killed by those who came in the name of international peacekeeping" ("9/11 Ten Years After: War's Toll").

The American government's support of the war on terror is opposed by satirizing the president: "In his 32 months as President, Obama—a Nobel Peace Prize winner—has embraced the role of commander in chief of the most powerful military in human history" ("How 9/11 Made Barack Obama a War President," *Christian Science Monitor*). The *Philadelphia Inquirer* commented in its op-ed that "More than 6,000 Americans have died on two different battlefronts, most of them in a war fought on false pretenses in a country that had nothing to do with the attacks" ("Editorial: 10 Years Later, a Different Country"). The *Dallas Morning News* also criticized the excessively high cost of the Iraq war: "Ten years after 9/11, we can all look back on the trajectory of President George W. Bush's war on terrorism and see how wrongheaded rationale by top decision makers put America on a skewed path that made defeating al-Qaeda more costly than it had to be. We can't ignore the catastrophic blunder of invading Iraq in 2003 … Their mistake bled our economy and destroyed the lives of thousands of American service members and their families, not to mention millions of Iraqis. All in the name of fighting terrorism in a place where al-Qaeda didn't exist before March 2003" ("U.S. vs. al-Qaeda: Who Won?").

The British, Australian, and Canadian press shared similar reflections toward wars on terror. *The Observer* (England) published the well-known American political scholar Francis Fukuyama's article depicting Bush's war on terror as invasion: "The Bush administration did much the opposite, elevating the 'war on terrorism' to the level of 20th-century struggles against fascism and communism, and justifying its invasion of Iraq on these grounds" ("Comment: 9/11 Special, The Legacy of That Terrible Time Will Be Less Significant Than We Then Feared"). In the *Sunday Mail*'s analysis, "The invasions of Iraq and Afghanistan have proved to be catastrophic military errors. For most of the time during the war on terror, we were fighting an enemy who was never really there" ("Evil Lost, 9/11 Ten Years On"). The Australian newspaper *Sunday Age* also pointed out the negative consequences of America's wars: "Terrorism specialist Peter Bergen says 'bin Ladenism' would never enjoy the mass appeal of other destructive ideologies, such as communism, but does that mean that the West overreacted? The answer 10 years on would be 'no … and yes.' No, in terms of assessing the threat from al-Qaeda, but yes in the botched handling of two wars that made the counterterrorism challenge so much more difficult and complex than it had to be" ("Revisiting Ground Zero: Ten Years On").

News Frame Two: Security Policies and Deterioration of Democracy and Liberty

The second frame for 9/11 10th-anniversary reports is critique and introspection of how soaring patriotism after 9/11 and the ensuing policies, behaviors, and perceptions have damaged democracy, justice, and freedom. The reflections in this category focus on patriotism and rationality, national security and liberty, the media's internalizing of the government's agenda, and prisoner abuse. Xenophobia after 9/11 and its negative implications have been pointed out in this form: "Our civic life is tainted by a rise in xenophobia that betrays our best ideals. As we prepared for a war on terrorism, we gave in to a weakening of the civil liberties that have been the foundation of our culture" ("Loss and Hope," *New York Times*). Other possible damages from fighting terrorism were also stated this way: "Opinions vary about whether efforts to fight terrorism in the United States have inflicted collateral damage on political dissent, religious liberty and the freedom of association" ("Civil Liberties Today," *New York Times*).

As for the widespread criticism that the media internalized the government's agenda, the chief editor of the *New York Times* responded this way: "The remedy for bad journalism is more and better journalism. Reporters at *The Times* made amends for the credulous prewar stories with investigations of the bad intelligence and with brave, relentless and illuminating coverage of the war and occupation" ("My Unfinished 9/11 Business"). The perception of Islam and Muslims after 9/11 has been full of stereotyping, misunderstanding, and even hatred, leading the *Philadelphia Inquirer* to point out that "our open society, one that prospered by welcoming the contributions of those from other lands, has become less free and more hostile to immigrants" ("Editorial: 10 Years Later, a Different Country"). The *St. Petersburg Times* quoted people's worry on the unfair treatment of Muslims: "With the destruction of the twin towers and murder of thousands of people by Muslim terrorists, my chief civil liberties concern was the potential for unfair treatment of Arabs and Muslims in the United States" ("Where Is the Liberty for All?"). The British newspaper *The Observer* criticized America's prisoner abuse: "By neglecting Afghanistan and occupying Iraq, it turned both countries into magnets for new terrorist recruitment, diminished its own moral stature through prisoner abuse, and tarnished the name of democracy promotion" ("Comment: 9/11 Special").

News Frame Three: A Rational Attitude Toward Islam and Muslims

The media's coverage of Islam and Muslims after 9/11 has become a major factor in stereotyping and demonizing Islamic culture and the Muslim image (Adnan, 1989, pp. 63–70; Lueg, 1995; Said, 1981; Sheikh, Price, & Oshagan,

1995, pp. 139–154). On the 10th anniversary of 9/11, the Western media started to appeal to treating Islam and Muslims more fairly and representing Islam and Muslims more objectively by avoiding blind xenophobia and stereotypes. The *Sunday Mirror* depicted the unfair treatment of Muslims in this way: "America suddenly became a land of fear—fearful of foreign attackers, fearful of it happening again, fearful of Muslims and even of men with beards. Bizarrely, some American Sikhs were attacked by those who thought their turbans and beards linked them to Islamic fundamentalism and Al Qaeda. But opinion polls show that the Muslim world and the West regard each other with mutual suspicion and fear" ("10 Years After 9/11: Out of the Dust"). The hatred aroused by military actions and prejudiced attitudes toward Muslims was reviewed in this account: "Every time U.S. airline pilots kicked Muslims off their flights for praying in airports or wearing traditional garb, every time U.S. security contractors shot up traffic intersections in Baghdad, every time our troops kicked in doors and ransacked noncombatants' houses, we turned supporters against us and handed a powerful recruitment tool to the enemy" ("U.S. vs. al-Qaeda: Who Won?" *Dallas Morning News*). As a consequence, "In Western countries, distrust of Muslims has grown since 9/11. It will make the already difficult integration of immigrant communities much more difficult to accomplish" ("Comment: 9/11 Special," *The Observer*).

Efforts to improve the relations of Muslims and other ethnic groups were covered to show how to tackle the problem of prejudice and stereotype. The *Washington Post* tried to educate its readers in this manner: "The popular uprisings that have swept the Arabic-speaking Middle East from North Africa and the Levant to the Persian Gulf are in the context of a larger movement: counter-jihad. Muslims around the world, … are increasingly rejecting extremism, Muslims turning not toward extremism but moderation … What's now required of Americans and their elected officials is moving beyond fear as the most influential factor in decisions. And that means more exposure to Muslims or education about Islam" ("The Fading Lure of Jihad"). Efforts to fight against the phenomenon of Islamophobia in American communities were depicted by a *New York Times* report that "in Syracuse, as in countless other communities, 9/11 set off a phenomenon that may seem counterintuitive in an era of increasingly vocal Islamophobia. A terrorist attack that provoked widespread distrust and hostility toward Muslims also brought Muslims in from the margins of American religious life—into living rooms, churches, synagogues and offices where they had never set foot before" ("Small Leaps of Faith"). The positive efforts of Muslims to improve relations with other ethnic groups were reported by *Newsday* (New York): "Muslims invite all, in a gesture of religious unity … Such unity was the best response to terrorists who hurt and divide … Our very presence here, today, is testimony to the terrorists' failure … We cherish diversity of belief" ("Muslims Invite All in Gesture of Religious Unity").

Multicultural representations of Muslims and other ethnic groups in the media have already been improved in Australia 10 years after 9/11. The *Sunday Age* claimed that Australian TV soap operas have been "creating an irresistible Muslim detective in the lead role and continuing to probe the complexities of multicultural Australia after September 11, 2001. Most people are cognizant of the fact that casting all Arabs and all Muslims as bogeymen is not helping anyone" ("This Week: Terror and the Telly"). This conclusion is representative: "We need to dismantle the structures of isolation which have been built up in the name of multiculturalism" and "to encourage mobility and engagement across religious and communal divides" ("Ten Years On, the Terrorist Threat Remains," *Sunday Telegraph*).

News Frame Four: Soft Power Strategy for Winning the Battle of Opinion

Ten years after 9/11, the media presented a consensus that the cost of promoting democracy and liberty in Islamic countries through the hard power of wars on terror is too heavy. Instead, a battle of cultures, ideologies, and ideas should be started to instill freedom and democracy among Arabs through the soft power of propaganda, psychological warfare, public and cultural diplomacies, and so forth. The *New York Times* included this quotation from George W. Bush: "The attack was on our values, and the war against terror was a war of ideas meant to advance the idea of freedom … We should try to demonstrate the falsity of horrendous ideas—e.g., the false nature of Islamism. Islamism is not 'the solution' as it claims to be. We should try to expose the nature of these doctrines" ("My God, Man!"). As the *Philadelphia Inquirer* put it, the nature of the "war on terrorism" is actually a "battle of ideas": "We know now (and many knew at the start) that there never was a 'war on terrorism.' The Bush administration used that term to rally the country at a terrible time, but it was badly misleading. It misdiagnosed the nature of the struggle. At the broader level, it was a battle of ideas that would take decades to play out" ("Worldview: War on Terrorism a Phantom").

How 9/11 triggered America's policy change in Arab countries was explained by a *Times* story in these terms: "For 60 years America's desire for stability in the Middle East was more important than pushing for democratic reforms. But 9/11 changed all that. It led to the Bush administration's 'freedom agenda', which stated that the United States should advance liberty and hope as an antidote to the enemy's ideology of repression and fear" ("Iraq Was a Good War—It Sparked the Arab Spring"). The same story also depicted the soft power strategy that America has adopted: "America has been quietly pushing democratization in the Middle East through the use of what she describes as 'government-to-people aid', with an emphasis on strengthening civil society, good governance, media reform and enfranchising women. The jazz-and-jeans approach to popular diplomacy that was used during the cold war was shifted to harness the 21st-century power of the Internet and mobile phones" ("Iraq Was a Good War—It Sparked the Arab Spring").

Then-British Prime Minister Tony Blair's consensual view on how to wage a better ideological battle was quoted by the *Sunday Mail:* "A Middle East peace envoy, warned the threat would only end when we defeat the ideology ... The way to defeat it ultimately is by a better idea. We have it—a way of life based on openness, democracy, freedom and the rule of law" ("Blair: Iraq War Didn't Fuel Terror"). The *Sunday Telegraph* explained Blair's kind of thinking further: "The war that was ignited by the planes that crashed into the World Trade Center is a war between Western values of democracy, liberty and equality, and the narrow, dogmatic, and hate-filled bigotry of Islamist fanaticism" ("Ten Years On, the Terrorist Threat Remains") and "in the battle of ideas, the West has prevailed over Islamism and the Arab Spring has unleashed democratic forces more powerful than al-Qaeda" ("Suddenly, We Would Never Be the Same").

Australia's media also presented a shared consensus about the inevitable clashes and combat of cultures and values by alleging that "the ideology which drove the middle-class Arab terrorists to hijack aircraft for the sole purpose of murdering as many Western civilians as possible, and to strike at the heart of the American culture, is still being preached in mosques and madrasahs across the Middle East and South-East Asia ... We must not lose sight of the enormity of what happened on that most terrible of days and we must not let those who wish to erase our memory destroy our culture and its values" ("Do Mention the War," *Sunday Telegraph Australia*). Huntington's clash of civilizations appeared again as the theoretical support for the "battle of ideas" thinking: "Language had been brewing for quite some time in Europe where the 'Eurabia' thesis had emerged to complement the clash of civilizations. Indeed, terrorism itself was being conscripted into a broader war of culture, much in the way Huntington might have predicted" ("Sifting Through the Debris for Real Legacy of Attacks; 9/11 the Day That Changed the World," *Sun Herald*). The former Australian Prime Minister John Howard's opinion of defending Western values was also quoted in the *Sunday Age*: "I saw this as an attack on our common values. And they are not just the values of Australia and America; they are values of democracy and freedom and religious tolerance, of equality between men and women ... These are precious values that the terrorists despised. The September 11 atrocities were a wake-up call for many—a reminder these values are fragile and worth defending" ("This Is a Day to Remember What We Stand for: September 11, Ten Years on"). This newspaper then proposed how to win in the battle of ideas by quoting American political scholar Joseph Nyre, who is the original researcher of soft power: "A key lesson of 9/11 is that hard military power is essential in countering terrorism by the likes of bin Laden, but that the soft power of ideas and legitimacy is essential for winning the hearts and minds of the mainstream Muslim populations from whom al-Qaeda would like to recruit" ("Revisiting Ground Zero; Ten Years On").

The frame of soft power has also been presented in Canadian media, as this quotation from the *Toronto Star* indicates: "Ten years after 9/11, the United States has a new window of opportunity to regain the initiative in the 'missing battle' of the campaign against terrorism. That is, a sustained soft power effort to win the battle for hearts and minds in predominantly Muslim countries" ("The War on Terror's Missing Battle").

MICRO LEVEL OF NEWS FRAMES

The micro level of news frames is represented by the rhetoric and style of news stories. Words and phrases appearing frequently in news stories were collected and counted by ROST, a language statistic software, and then analyzed for semantic frames. This follows Entman's (1993) method of defining news frames through key words, frequent phrases, and constant images (pp. 51–58). (See Table 4.2.)

Table 4.2. Key Words, High-Frequency Words, and Phrases of 9/11 10th-Anniversary Reports.

commemoration	attack (663 times); terrorist (325 times); terrorism (247 times); victims (108 times); remember (145 times); memorial (141 times); honor (33 times)
Wars	war (736 times); Iraq (305 times); Afghanistan (263 times); killed (228 times); died (110 times); cost (88 times); war on terror (51 times); invasion+invading (47 times); war in (against) Iraq (19 times); war in Afghanistan (8 times)
security and civil rights	security (345 times); freedom (66 times); democracy (63 times); patriotism + patriot (60 times); moral (47 times); surveillance (24 times); liberty (22 times); suspicion (21 times); civil rights (9 times)
Islam and Muslims	Muslim (307 times); Islam (213 times); threat (181 times); fear (112 times); religion (44 times); hate (46 times); extremist (39 times); multi-cultural (12 times); tolerance (11 times)
battle of ideas	idea (82 times); value (46 times); culture (40 times); ideology (18 times); soft power (8 times); hearts and minds (8 times); battle of ideas (5 times); clash of civilizations (4 times); missing battle (4 times)

The statistics of key and high-frequency words and phrases echo the news frames of the macro and medium levels. The most frequently quoted words *wars* and *attacks* actually present the core themes of the relevant media stories: anti-war and commemoration. The high-frequency words *cost, killed,* and *died,* together with the replacement of the phrase *war on terror* with *war in (against) Iraq,* also represent the evolvement of the war frame. The frequent appearance of the words *surveillance* and *suspicion* in the reports reflects the Western media's concern and cautiousness toward the negative influences of patriotism and security policies on democracy and liberty. The high frequency of words such as *threat, hate, multi-cultural,* and *tolerance* expose the unfair attitudes toward Muslims after 9/11. At the same time, these words express the media's criticism of racial, ethnic, and cultural exclusionism that present the "moral evaluation" function of news frames. Key words such as *values, soft power,* and *battle of ideas* represent the "treatment recommendation" function of news frames, indicating a direction for the West on how to win the clash of civilizations and the battle of ideas.

ANALYSIS AND FINDINGS

Figure 4.1 displays the above textual analysis and analytical rationale for news frames of the Western media's 9/11 10th-anniversary reports.

During the 10 years after 9/11, the mainstream Western media adjusted the news frames in accordance with the changes in the United States and the world. The frames have evolved from "pro-war" to "anti-war," from "echoing government" to "criticizing and introspecting," from "stereotyped representations of the Other" to "diversified representations of the Other," and from the "clash of civilizations" to the "battle of ideas."

Indicating that Bush's war policy was supported after 9/11, research comparing the photos of 9/11 and Afghanistan war on Western and Arabic newspapers found that the visual narrations of 9/11 victims and the neglect of war casualties by Western newspapers reflected a pro-war frame (Fahmy, 2010, pp. 695–717). Another study of textual analysis examined how the American news media internalized the government's anti-terrorist war agendas into the media's agenda. It concluded that after 9/11, the American news media presented the government's anti-terror war discourse and promoted it as public discourse without any critique (Reese & Lewis, 2009, pp. 777–797). Overall, U.S. media supported and propagated the government's war policies after 9/11 so that "many Americans described when recalling that period of time that American news reports were like the government's advertisements" (Shan & Xiao, 2003, pp. 14–18). Ten years later, although a few media are still defending the wars, most of them have tended to an anti-war stance and news frame. Having gone through his own reflecting and introspection, the *New York Times* chief editor concluded that the "media should learn a lesson

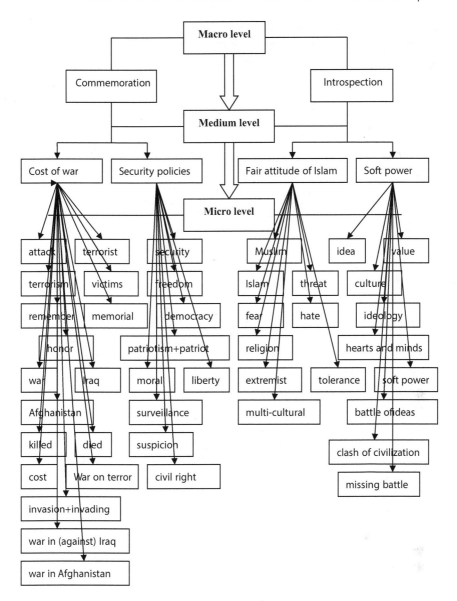

Figure 4.1. Western Media's Framing Structure of 9/11 10th-Anniversary Reports.

not to involve itself blindly into a dramatic plot that we do not understand completely" ("My Unfinished 9/11 Business").

The media have also started to challenge the possible damages brought by the government in the name of patriotism and national security to citizens—especially Muslim groups—and to the values of democracy and liberty. The view of the clash of civilizations, once providing a theoretical and ideological foundation for pro-war policies, has been a dominant opinion supported by the American government and media ever since the attack of 9/11. As with introspection on wars, social cultural values, and international context, this long-standing dominant ideological view has gradually been replaced by another view of non-military soft power that is now regarded as a better strategy to win "the battle of ideas."

The evolving news frames, however, have not essentially been extended on the rail of anti-war and peace. According to Dayan and Katz's (1992) three types of ritual media events, the 10th anniversary of 9/11 would be classified as "Coronation." The most significant difference between "Coronation" and "Contest"/"Conquest" lies in their correlations with conflict management, that is, "Contest" constructs conflict, "Conquest" conquers conflict, while "Coronation" tries to break off conflict by arousing fundamental social values and reasserting social cultural traditions. This frame analysis indicates that the media event of 9/11's 10th anniversary has also tried to seek a solution for dispelling terrorism and conflicts through reasserting America's basic values of democracy and freedom, reflecting its war policies, the introspection of "Islamophobia" and xenophobia, and commemorating 9/11. Out of these various trajectories, the view of anti-war and pro-peace has become the consensual script, agreed by anniversary commemoration organizers, the media, and the public. Therefore, the news can be produced along this negotiated rail of all parties.

However, a further analysis of the 9/11 10th-anniversary news frames reveals the parallel contradictory narratives of appealing to cultural pluralism and to rational attitudes toward Islam and Muslims, on one hand, and highlighting "our" culture, values, and lifestyles as better than "theirs" on the other. Within this contradiction, promoting Western democracy and liberty in the Middle East is seen as conquering the religious and cultural obstacles. Another inconsistent narrative is to oppose the cruelty of military wars but to advocate the soft power of winning the "battle of ideas" and "hearts and minds" of the others. This Orientalist binary thinking of subject and object behind these contradictory narratives, the cultural majoritarianism of "us" better than "them" hidden under the veil of cultural pluralism, and the substance of soft power and the battle of ideas are leading in a direction away from peace.

These contradictions indeed corroborate the evolving media event models of Disenchantment, Derailment, and Disruption (Dayan, 2008, pp. 391–402). In his analysis of the Beijing Olympics, Dayan and Chen (2009) pointed out that the Olympics was a "disenchantment" to European audiences after they realized it was merely a political event. The event became a "derailment" from a celebration in China to a protest of China's role in Tibet. And the involved parties had to take measures to prevent possible "disruption" (pp. 1–18). Similarly, the 9/11 10th anniversary is a "disenchantment" to people who expect true cultural pluralism, because behind the plural narratives of the news reports still is cultural centrism. The event became a "derailment" from maintaining the consensus of commemoration, anti-war, and pro-peace views, to the different position of winning the battle of ideas. Thus, this binary opposition in thinking of subject and object, and the dominant ideology and value of mainstream culture, will surely lead to more "disruptions" because the culturally underprivileged minorities will instinctively resort to conflicts and violence as their resistance. It will be further away from understanding differentiations and from the cultural interactivity of mutually reciprocal understanding through dialogue (Shan, 2010).

How media produce and reproduce hegemony offers a theoretical framework to explain the change and the derailment in news frames for 9/11 10th-anniversary reports. The news media participate in the process of producing consensus for cultural hegemony by constructing the image of "the others" in terms of the overseas political and economic interests of a certain country (Said, 1981). News production accords with power networks and mainstream ideology to maintain established social orders and serve the dominant class, race, and gender (Gitlin, 1980). When an old consensus is disrupted, the media start to represent disagreements of diversified opinions and participate in constructing a new hegemony and consensus but not in challenging established social orders (Schlesinger, 1979, pp. 295–309; Tuchman, 1978). Therefore, news frames and cultural hegemony have an interactive relation for which news production represents cultural hegemony, while hegemony affects news production at the same time.

Furthermore, the construction of cultural hegemony is a dynamic process during which news production involves the challenging of the old hegemony and framing hegemonic development and transformation. In that sense, the news frame changes 10 years after 9/11 from pro-war to anti-war and from hard power to soft power actually represent the dynamic changes of challenging the old hegemony and evolving to the new one. The "derailment" of 9/11 10th-anniversary reports reveals that the new cultural hegemony and dominant ideology are indeed not to oppose wars but overpriced military actions. And the "derailed" news frames also participate in constructing the new hegemony that has gradually come to dominate the social culture.

In the end, through the "derailment" of news frames, the public's anti-war and pro-peace proposition has been "disenchanted" because the nature of the new hegemony is to transfer from traditional battles to a battle of ideas. The advocacy of the battle of ideas and soft power actually reflect the differences and oppositions of "us" and "them" hidden behind the new hegemony and also a cultural centrism behind this new dominant ideology. A pessimistic prediction is that the battle of ideas will trigger new "disruptions" and the ideal of peaceful coexistence of different races, religions, and cultures will hardly be realized in reality.

More importantly, though the crisis of 9/11 has been defused, the representation of 9/11 is facing a new crisis. The publicness of news has become a distorted public sphere of discussion, negotiation, and contention, where the understanding and communication of people from different cultural backgrounds have been excluded.

BIBLIOGRAPHY

Adnan, M. (1989). Mass media and reporting Islamic affairs. *Media Asia, 16*, 63–70.

Dayan, D. (2008). Beyond media events: Disenchantment, derailment, disruption. In M. Price & D. Dayan (Eds.), *Owning the Olympics: Narratives of the new China* (pp. 391–402). Ann Arbor: University of Michigan Press.

Dayan, D., & Katz, E. (1992). *Media events: The live broadcasting of history.* Cambridge, MA: Harvard University Press.

Dayan, D., Qiu, L. C., & Chen, T. W. (2009). The evolution of the concept of media events. *Communication and Society, 9*, 1–18.

Durham, F. D., & Carpenter, J. C. (2014). The face of multiculturalism in Korea: Media ritual as framing in news coverage of Jasmine Lee. *Journalism*, September 23, 1464884914550137.

Entman, R. M. (1993). Framing: Toward clarification of a fractured paradigm. *Journal of Communication, 43*(4), 51–58.

Fahmy, S. (2010). Contrasting visual fames in our times: A framing analysis of English- and Arabic-language press coverage of war and terrorism. *International Communication Gazette, 72*, 695–717.

Gamson, W. A. (1989). News as framing. *American Behavioral Scientist, 32*(2), 157–161.

Gitlin, T. (1980). *The whole world is watching: Mass media in the making and unmaking of the New Left.* Berkeley: University of California Press.

Goffman, E. (1974). *Framing analysis: An essay on the organization of experience.* New York: Longman.

Lueg, A. (1995). The perception of Islam in Western debate. In J. Hippler & A. Lueg (Eds.), *The next threat: Western perceptions of Islam* (pp. 7–31). Boulder, CO: Pluto Press.

Melki, J. (2014). The interplay of politics, economics and culture in news framing of Middle East wars. *Media, War & Conflict, 7*(2), 165–186.

Pan., Z., & Kosicki, G. M. (1993). Framing analysis: An approach to news discourse. *Political Communication, 10*, 55–75.

Preston, P. (2009). *Making the news: Journalism and news cultures in Europe.* London: Routledge.

Reese, S. D., & Lewis, S. C. (2009). Framing the war on terror: The internalization of policy in the U.S. press. *Journalism, 10*, 777–797.

Said, E. (1981). *Covering Islam: How the media and the experts determine how we see the rest of the world.* London: Vintage.

Scheufele, D. A. (1999). Framing as a theory of media effects. *Journal of Communication, 49*, 103–122.

Schlesinger, P. (1979). *Putting "reality" together: BBC News.* London: Constable. Cited from C. C. Lee, J. M. Chan, Z. Pan, & C. Y. K. So. (2000). National prisms of a global media event. In J. Curran & M. Gurevitch (Eds.), *Mass media and society* (pp. 295–309). London: Arnold.

Shan, B. (2010). *Problems and possibilities of cross-cultural communication.* Wuhan: Wuhan University Press.

Shan, B., & Xiao, J. (2003). American media's selling points of wars and humanistic reflections. *Modern Communication, 3,* 14–18.

Sheikh, K., Price, V., & Oshagan, H. (1995). Press treatment of Islam: What kind of picture do the media paint? *Gazette, 56,* 139–154.

Shoemaker, P. J., & Reese, S. D. (1996). *Mediating the message: Theories of influences on mass media content.* New York: Longman.

Taylor, L., & Willis, A. (2005). *Media studies: Texts, institutions and audiences* (J. Wu & P. Huang, Trans.). Beijing: Beijing University Press.

Tuchman, G. (1978). *Making news: A study in the construction of reality.* New York: Free Press.

Zhang, G. Z. (1999). *News media and news sources: On media frames and reality construction* (pp. 32–34). Taipei: Sanmin Publishing House.

Zhou, X. (2008). Cultural dimensions and framing the Internet in China. *International Communication Gazette, 70,* 117–136.

CHAPTER FIVE

Framing White Privilege

Eliminating Ethnic Studies from Arizona Schools

HEMANT SHAH

In recent years, the state of Arizona has become a lightning rod for interracial and interethnic tension. For example, Maricopa County Sheriff Joe Arpaio's department has earned a reputation for systematically violating the constitutional rights of Latinos. In April 2010, Governor Jan Brewer signed into law Senate Bill 1070, which, among other things, empowered law enforcement officials to detain people the officers deemed to be undocumented. (The U.S. Supreme Court upheld that part of the law in a ruling in 2012.) And in May 2010, Governor Brewer signed into law HB2281, which outlawed teaching ethnic studies in Arizona schools.

This chapter examines the ways mainstream and ethnic minority news media reported on Arizona's law forbidding the teaching of "ethnic studies" in K–12 classrooms. In the U.S. context, mainstream news media is defined as those news organizations that are owned and operated primarily by white Americans and try to reach as wide an audience as possible. Ethnic minority new media are those that are owned and operated by members of non-white ethnic minority groups and tailor content for an ethnic minority audience (see Matsaganis, Katz, & Ball-Rokeach, 2011). The research reported in this chapter investigates the extent to which and the ways in which mainstream and ethnic minority news media depicted the Arizona ethnic studies ban through concepts and narratives consistent with the idea of white privilege, the idea that people designated as "white" enjoy unearned social and cultural advantages merely by belonging to this category. I am interested in the debate over ethnic studies in Arizona schools because it has forced news media and the public at large to once again confront the implication that the history and culture of *white* Americans is the norm under which other histories and cultures ought to be subsumed and understood.

On May 11, 2010, Governor Jan Brewer signed into law HB2281, which outlawed teaching ethnic studies in Arizona schools. The law reads:

A school district or charter school in this state shall not include in its program of instruction any courses or classes that include any of the following:

1. Promote the overthrow of the United States government.
2. Promote resentment toward a race or class of people.
3. Are designed primarily for pupils of a particular ethnic group.
4. Advocate ethnic solidarity instead of the treatment of pupils as individuals.

The law took effect on December 31, 2010. On January 3, Tom Horne, Superintendent of Public Instruction, declared the Mexican American Studies program in the Tucson Unified School District to be out of compliance with the new law. The District had to bring the course into compliance or face the loss of nearly $10 million in funding. Arizona legislators and residents who supported the elimination of ethnic studies courses from schools believed that the teaching of ethnic studies promotes ethnic chauvinism and prevents national unity. They believed generic classes on American history and culture sufficiently cover non-white ethnic groups and wanted a curriculum that excluded material acknowledging the unique role and distinct place of non-white ethnics in American history. This position is an assertion of white privilege to the extent that it situates the experience of whites as applicable to all, thereby equating whiteness with "American-ness" and using the rhetoric of progress and civilization to justify white superiority.

Opponents of the legislation argued that the law reflects racial anxiety among many whites bent on eliminating the heritage of non-white groups in the state. They said that oppression of racial and ethnic minorities by the white majority is a part of U.S. history and not teaching that perspective is akin to "ethnic-studies cleansing." The opponents of the legislation also pointed out that students participating in the Mexican American Studies program tended to graduate on time and attend college.

The conflict over ethnic studies classes in Arizona schools began in April 2007. Chicano activist Delores Huerta, cofounder of the United Farm Workers, delivered a speech at Tucson High School in which she said, "Republicans hate Latinos." Horne objected and sent his deputy, Margaret Garcia Dugan, to provide a counterpoint to Huerta. A number of students walked out of the speech. Horne responded by accusing the Mexican American Studies courses of using books that painted the United States in unflattering ways and fostering resentment against whites. Horne crafted legislation to eliminate ethnic studies and pushed for its passage. After several failed attempts, Arizona's Republican-controlled legislature passed HB2281 in May 2010. Horne was elected as Arizona's Attorney General in November 2010. On January 3, 2011, his last day as Superintendent of Public Instruction, he found the Mexican American Studies program out of compliance with the new law on teaching ethnic studies. Horne left the enforcement of the law up to his successor, John Huppenthal.

The debate over ethnic studies in Arizona schools was about more than the content of ethnic studies courses. More broadly, in the wake of previous Arizona legislation that institutionalized racial profiling of non-white residents deemed illegal immigrants by law enforcement personnel, and an attempt by some Arizona school boards to monitor the classrooms of teachers who spoke with "accents," the debate over ethnic studies curricula in Arizona was also a struggle over not only the content of "American" culture and history but also a struggle to define who belongs in America and who does not.

WHITE PRIVILEGE AND THE NEWS

In many parts of the world, "whiteness" is often accepted as the norm against which people are measured and judged. Whiteness as a category of skin hue is arbitrarily associated with positive characteristics and with social, political, and cultural privilege, whereas being non-white is to lack positive characteristics and privilege. In this racial logic, white privilege is created, in part, by a flexible set of criteria for inclusion and exclusion of groups, communities, and nations. This flexibility is the basis for the power of whiteness: the elasticity of its boundaries allows easy policing of who will and who will not be considered white and thereby enjoy the power and privilege associated with being so designated (Dyer, 1997; Frankenberg, 1993; Goldberg, 1993; MacIntosh, 1998; Nakayama & Martin, 1999; Shome, 2000). But class, nationality, and color status can complicate this racial logic, as the following examples point out. In the mid-19th-century United States, the Irish were not always considered "white." Poor Irish immigrants and poor blacks often lived and worked side by side. They intermarried and were the targets of race-based discrimination that viewed the two groups as racially inferior to whites. But gradually, the Irish recognized that they could have upward social and economic mobility if they joined whites in oppressing blacks. The Irish segregated themselves from blacks, embraced anti-black rhetoric, and asserted their status as whites with attendant white privilege (see Ignatiev, 1995).

In another episode of policing the boundaries of whiteness, the U.S. Supreme Court in the 1923 *Ozawa* case said that Japanese Americans, even if they had been raised in the United States and embraced American values, could not become naturalized citizens because they were not Caucasian. A few months after the *Ozawa* ruling, an Indian American named Bhagat Singh Thind applied for U.S. citizenship arguing that since he was Caucasian (according to accepted scientific knowledge at the time), he should be allowed to become a naturalized citizen. However, the Supreme Court ruled in this case that even though Indian Americans were Caucasian, they could not be citizens because they were not white in complexion (Shah, 1999).

In yet another illustrative case, Susie Guillory Phipps grew up in the state of Louisiana believing she was a white. She was devastated when she discovered in 1977 that her birth certificate listed her race as "colored"—indicating a mixed-race background. The state law said that anyone with 1/32 African American heritage must be designated as "colored." Phipps must have sensed, living in a deep-South state, that she might lose certain race-based privileges if her racial designation was something other than white. Thus, she fought in the courts of Louisiana to have her racial designation changed to white. She insisted that the state had made a mistake and demanded that her racial designation be changed to "white." However, state officials refused to make the change, and in 1981, Phipps filed a lawsuit asking officials to rescind the law and change her racial designation. At trial, the state attorneys presented evidence showing that Phipps was, in fact, 3/32 African American and, therefore, colored under the laws of Louisiana. Phipps appealed to the Louisiana Supreme Court, which refused to hear the case. (See Haney-Lopez, 1996, for a detailed summary of the case.)

As these examples demonstrate, in the Anglo-European West, discourses about race and nation assert whiteness as the norm. Whiteness and white privilege become naturalized to the extent that they need not be named or discussed because it's taken to be common sense. Discourses about race and nation often help create a national identity based on racial hierarchy that renders whiteness a sign of superiority and inclusion while relegating "people of color" to an inferior status that excludes them from the social, cultural, and political life of the nation. Throughout history, white nations have desired immigrants of color for their labor or, less often, their intellect. But these nations often were not as welcoming of immigrants' culture, language, and values (Hage, 1998; Prasad, 2001). Even for those immigrants of color granted "honorary white" status—West Indians and South Asians, for example—facing race-based discrimination and disadvantage is a fact of life (Bonilla-Silva, 2013).

The news media, as a major source of cultural production, sometimes play a key role in the process of constructing meaning for the role of whiteness in the articulation of race and nation. Journalists select certain issues, events, actors, and sources for coverage and emphasis over others and transform their selections into finished news items by identifying and contextualizing them into recognizable frames of reference. As a result, news stories are often imbued with meanings of whiteness that help establish and maintain geopolitical and cultural boundaries of the nation and the racial criteria by which people are considered a part of or apart from the nation (see Heider, 2000; Shah, 1999).

RESEARCH METHODS

The purpose of this research was to examine the ways mainstream and ethnic minority news media covered the Arizona ethnic studies legislation. For this research, I analyzed how the debate is framed by news organizations to determine what the framing reveals about perspectives on white privilege in America and consider the extent to which mainstream and minority news organizations convey competing visions of "America." Framing is the journalistic process of selecting, emphasizing, excluding, and elaborating certain aspects of an event or issue in a way that promotes particular ways of understanding. Framing comprises two elements—the selection of an organizing idea and the reasoning behind that selection. The organizing ideas are typically depicted through the use of metaphors, exemplars, and catchphrases. The reasoning devices include discussion of causes, speculations about consequences, and appeals to principle. Specific framing techniques might include using vivid language, making historical comparisons, presenting juxtapositions, making disdainful references, suggesting connections between unrelated ideas, and so forth. The framing process also typically develops a regular vocabulary that becomes a kind of terminological shorthand that refers to the actors, actions, and issues involved. The outcome of the framing process is a network of organizing ideas and their attendant reasoning devices that give the overall news story a measure of narrative coherence. In these ways, news frames provide guidance and closure to the ways news consumers interpret contemporary events and issues. Through framing, the news media has a certain amount of power, therefore, to influence the formation of public opinion and the process of political decision-making (see Entman, 1993; Goffman, 1974; Iyengar, 1991).

All unique news items about the battle over ethnic studies courses in the Arizona schools appearing between May 2010 and January 2012 and archived in the electronic databases Lexis-Nexis and Ethnic Newswatch were analyzed. I searched for the items with the search terms "ethnic studies AND Arizona." I also searched ProQuest and Factiva for additional news media discussions of the issue during the same time frame. The search yielded 29 articles from the mainstream news media and 21 articles from the ethnic minority media. By reading these news stories closely, I examined the ways language, sourcing, and rhetorical and metaphorical strategies contributed to news narratives about whiteness, race, and nation in relation to the debate over teaching ethnic studies in Arizona schools and considered the meaning and significance of white privilege in Arizona officials' efforts to ban ethnic studies in schools.

RESULTS

There were some clear distinctions between the mainstream and ethnic minority news about the ethnic studies law. In general, the ethnic minority items were almost exclusively op-ed pieces and were likely to frame the issue in ways that more readily revealed the operation of white privilege at work. The mainstream press published both news and op-ed pieces. In *news* items, the mainstream press tended to emphasize the policy and procedure of lawmaking with little reference to the idea of white privilege. In the mainstream media *op-ed pieces*, the publications took explicit positions for and against the ethnic studies law. Not surprisingly, those supporting the ban on ethnic studies were conservative in their orientation, endorsing 2012 presidential candidate Mitt Romney or consistently endorsing his policies, and those opposing the ban endorsed Barack Obama and his policies. Table 5.1 is the breakdown of publications examined and the number of items in each.

Table 5.1. Publications examined and number of items in each.

Endorsing Obama	Endorsing Romney	Ethnic Minority
New York Times = 5	Arizona Republic = 5	La Prensa San Diego = 8
Christian Science Monitor = 4	Wall Street Journal = 3	Philadelphia Tribune = 2
Los Angeles Times = 4	Washington Times = 2	Los Angeles Sentinel = 2
Buffalo News = 2	National Review Online = 1	Amsterdam News = 2
Philadelphia Inquirer = 1	US News & World Report = 1	Jewish News = 1
Daily Bulletin (Ontario, CA) = 1		Tennessee Tribune = 1
Washington Post = 1		Westside (Fla.) Gazette = 1
		Navajo Times = 1
		Sacramento Observer = 1
		Indian Country Today = 1
		The Skanner = 1

The sections below review main themes appearing in these three categories of publications. The first section covers the mainstream press, divided by Romney-endorsing and Obama-endorsing publications. The second section covers the ethnic minority press.

THEMES IN ROMNEY-ENDORSING PUBLICATIONS

De-legitimation of Ethnic Studies

Early denunciation of the ethnic studies program of the school district appeared in the state's leading daily newspaper, the *Arizona Republic*. Writers for the newspaper said that "ethnic studies spew hatred for America," and a history of the state that gives voice to a Latino perspective is "propaganda" and "a victimization siren song" (MacEachern, 2010). The writer never acknowledges, or perhaps does not even see, that history told only from the perspective of privilege might also be seen as propaganda. Elsewhere in the newspaper, the editors wrote that ethnic studies courses represent a "vile program" and that the teachers "never were especially good at teaching academically credible history" ("Light Is Shed on a Vile Program," 2011). The teachers, the paper editorialized, were "very good at one thing: waging vicious war on anyone who dared to criticize the program" ("Light Is Shed on a Vile Program," 2011). It is somewhat ironic that among the goals of the ethnic studies program was one to reveal the vicious war waged against the Mexican and indigenous populations of the region.

Other writers questioned the legitimacy of the debate itself. For one writer, the debate over HB2281 was "a reenactment of the tired old pantomime about multiculturalism and its discontents" (Galupo, 2010). The assumption here seems to be that there are some ethnic malcontents who have the nerve to want equal standing in historical accounts of the Southwest. In another piece, the writer claims that "critics say the ethnic studies program unfairly demean white people" and promotes "ethnic chauvinism" (Richardson, 2010). For this writer, demeaning brown people for hundreds of years and attempting to tell telling a more comprehensive history of the state is apparently unfair.

In a third example, the ethnic studies program is framed as "grievance and distortion" (Julian, 2008). A case could be made, the writer continues, that "teaching students history and literature through some concocted ethnic perspective is balderdash." It is a "profound disservice" to have Hispanic youngsters "skip the great works of literature and read only tracts, say, by Mexican authors" (Julian, 2008). In this article, the author suggests that distortion of history can be claimed only by whites who fear the browning of America. The writer does not acknowledge the distortion represented by history books that ignore the views of Latinos and put white experience at the center. The writer further delegitimizes ethnic studies by saying that an "ethnic perspective" is "concocted" or made up from whole cloth. Finally, one might argue that it is ethnically chauvinistic to make a distinction between "great works of literature" and work by "Mexican authors" who apparently only write "tracts."

Legitimation of Tom Horne's Political Strategy and Tactics

Horne was painted as a reasonable politician and implied as having liberal credentials: "Tom Horne has two degrees from Harvard University. He participated in Martin Luther King's 1963 March on Washington. He's Arizona's superintendent of public instruction. In other words, he's not the kind of guy you expect to find at the forefront of a movement to eliminate a politically sensitive program such as ethnic studies" (Richardson, 2009). This story serves the purpose of legitimizing the politics of HB2281 by essentially saying that since a liberal (linked to Harvard and Martin Luther King Jr.) is concerned about ethnic studies, liberals ought not be so critical of the legislation. Further, the writer implies, a liberal, such as Horne, would never resort to racist tactics. In a later story, the reporter quotes Horne without rebuttal: HB2281 "is the opposite of racism" (Richardson, 2010). In fact, said another writer, "most conservatives are not interested in white washing history" (Galupo, 2010).

Horne was consistently depicted as a proponent of U.S. individualism and a protector of American history. In one editorial, Horne is quoted without comment as objecting to dividing schoolchildren by race: "We should be teaching kids that they're individuals, not exemplars of racial groups" (Richardson, 2009). In another piece, he said that "these kids should be taking an American history course and getting American history in depth. Instead, they're getting propaganda and an ideology that teaches them to resent the United States" (Gersema, 2010). These excerpts show the ways that the publications in this category depicted Horne as a true American, thus legitimizing his attacks on ethnic studies programs that supposedly were ideological and, therefore, illegitimate.

THEMES IN OBAMA-ENDORSING MEDIA

Critique of HB2281 and Its Logic

The Obama-endorsing publications tended to criticize the legislation and the logic behind it. The *New York Times* argued in an editorial that HB2281 unnecessarily "injects nativist fears directly into the public school classroom" and that "Arizona's public leaders shame themselves" by passing the legislation ("Arizona, in the Classroom," 2011). When the legislation became law in January 2012, the paper called it "a blunt-force victory" for opponents of ethnic studies ("Rejected in Tucson," 2012). By pointing out that shame of 21st-century nativism, the *Times* was clearly a tough critic of HB2281. A columnist for the *Inland Valley Daily Bulletin* wrote that the law "demonstrates Arizona policymakers' lack of understanding about these programs" and that "the HB 2281 directive makes advocating ethnic solidarity illegal, in favor of treating students as individuals is entirely nonsensical" (Bonacorsi, 2011). For this writer, the legislation was another in a long line of attacks on U.S. Latinos living in the Southwest.

A Nod to White Privilege

Other publications in this category were even more critical. *Los Angeles Times* columnist Gregory Rodriguez (2012) pointedly observed, "Surely one doesn't have to believe in the infallibility of white people to be pro-American" and argued that whatever faults there were with the ethnic studies curricula in Arizona schools, "the program was not anywhere as dangerous as the white majority that simultaneously fights to protect its power and the purity of its reputation." The columnist challenges the tenets of white privilege by clearly pointing out the arbitrary connection between patriotism and embracing whiteness and the effort by whites to preserve racial hierarchy that attempts to subordinate non-whites. Another writer refers to Arizona as the "new South"—an allusion to the Arizona history of legislation aimed at controlling and monitoring non-whites as in the Jim Crow South (Medrano, 2010).

Ethnic Studies Is *U.S.* History

The *Philadelphia Inquirer* editorialized that ethnic studies *is* U.S. history. It is reported that Horne's assistant said, "The [argument] that bothers me the most is that they give credits to students for U.S. history for these [ethnic studies] courses." The newspaper then pointed out that "detractors ignore the fact that Mexican Americans also contributed to U.S. history" ("Class Politics," 2010). Turning to the accusation by Horne and others that the ethnic studies program in Tucson schools is a form of ethnic chauvinism, the *Christian Science Monitor* asked, "Since when is it bad to learn about different cultures? The only ethnic chauvinism in play here seems to be the idea that children don't need the opportunity to better understand minority history" ("The Other Arizona Battle," 2010).

THEMES IN THE ETHNIC MINORITY PRESS

Denying Historical Reality

One of the common themes in the ethnic minority press was highlighting the difference between history and nature. One writer pointed out that what HB2281 proponents consistently meant by American "history" was actually a set of "foundational myths and legends that defines the United States as the New Promised Land" (Rodriguez, 2009). History is something that can be argued over in good faith. History takes into account the ebbs and flows of power, explains the ways people are included in and excluded from the body politic. Nature assumes the order of things is an obvious, taken-for-granted truth. The ethnic minority press made a point of showing how HB2281 proponents such as Tom Horne turned history *into* nature. For example, several articles reproduced the following statement from Horne: "We're not trying to prevent the teaching of history. But they [students] shouldn't be taught they're oppressed. We're trying to prevent the promotion of victimology" ("Arizona Lawmakers Target Ethnic Studies Program," 2010). Many writers in the ethnic minority press stated that revealing the process of oppression and resistance is precisely what history should be about. But Horne asserts that this sort of knowledge breeds resentment toward whites and therefore should not be taught in school. In response, one ethnic minority newspaper editorialized: "Someone should tell Horne that it isn't ethnic studies that cause people of color to be wary of white people. It's racial history and how America has marginalized minorities since its inception to benefit white people" ("Arizona Gets Ethnic History Backward," 2010).

Exposing Racial Hierarchy

Another related theme in the ethnic minority press was pointing out that the racial anxiety experienced by whites was linked to a fear of losing dominant position in the state's racial hierarchy. Demographic shifts in Arizona have already placed the whites' numerical majority at risk. And the teaching of ethnic studies in Arizona schools—which has been in place since the 1970s in one form or another—represents a threat to white cultural dominance. In one article, the writer was blunt: "HB2281 is law motivated by the fear of an educated [white] citizenry" (Bow, 2011). For Horne and other supporters of the law, ideas with which they do not agree are frightening. Why? Because ethnic studies "as a discipline goes to the heart of how we narrate ourselves as being Americans. It asks us to consider foundational beliefs about democracy, meritocracy and colorblindness" (Bow, 2011). The ethnic minority press points out that ethnic studies puts into question the ideas HB2281 supporters believe are sacrosanct. Teaching ethnic studies creates racial anxiety among whites in the sense that many feel that their cultural identity is under attack.

Exnomination of Whiteness

A third related theme was what we might understand as the exnomination of whiteness. Part of white privilege is that whiteness is assumed to be the norm.

Whiteness not only is equivalent to being normal but also to being obviously more rational and moral than other racial subjectivities. Not only that, this self-perceived superiority is considered to be common sense, not something that has to be debated or named (exnominated). Horne's publicly stated rationale for pushing HB2281 was that he was "trying to get the schools to treat students as individuals and not as exemplars of the race they were born into" (Susser, 2010). Writers in the ethnic minority press pointed out that Horne's position assumes an either/or choice for minorities: One is either an individual or a member of a racial group. Horne's position only makes sense if the group one belongs to is exnominated. In other words, Horne's position makes sense since he is a white male. For him, whiteness as a group is so normalized that it does not even exist. Therefore, individualism is the only option for him. And further, Horne and his supporters believe it should be the only option for everyone—if it's good enough for whites, it should be good enough for all. Many writers in the ethnic minority press take Horne's position to task. Representative of the criticism is the following:

> HB2281 is a crude racist attempt to outlaw ethnic studies, and delegitimize positive ethnic solidarity and critical cultural consciousness under the pretense that the critique of white domination is racial resentment rather than an essential process of critical and ethical reasoning about life in this country. (Karenga, 2010)

This writer brings sharply into focus that Horne's view is hypocritical on two counts: only non-whites' group membership is considered a problem (not white group membership), and only the racial resentment of non-whites is considered a problem, not the racial resentment (and anxiety) of whites.

CONCLUSIONS

In mainstream *news pages*, all publications reported the story mainly as a procedural drama—the characters, plot, proceedings, climax, and outcome. In the *op-ed sections*, however, while there was almost no explicit analysis of white privilege, the Obama-endorsing publications raised important questions about the meaning of U.S. history, the value of multicultural perspectives, the hypocrisy and ignorance of HB2281 supporters, and so on. In the Obama-endorsing publications, there was sympathy for the idea of ethnic studies taught along the lines of multiculturalism where all cultural groups have equal standing. But only rarely did these publications delve into racial inequity borne of socioeconomic gains accruing to whites as a result *only* of racial status. Revealing the unearned advantages that have accrued in the hands of whites generation after generation was apparently not imaginable to an otherwise sympathetic nonpartisan mainstream press. There was a limit to the criticism of HB2281 in that it did not point out that ethnic studies means educating students in a way that teaches them to articulate reasons and motivations for demanding social justice in ways that end white privilege related to history, race, and class.

The Romney-endorsing publications within the mainstream press also reported the procedural drama but with occasional political jibes or word choices that revealed a conservative political position. There was no discussion of white privilege. In the *op-ed section* of these publications, the idea of ethnic studies was dismissed with derision, while the advocate of dismantling ethnic studies was praised as a loyal American fighting against divisiveness and ped-agogical incompetence. The Romney-endorsing publications did not deal at all with the question of white privilege. Instead, the writers labeled supporters of ethnic studies un-American and painted Tom Horne as a hero.

Content in the ethnic press invariably provided a deeper sense of the history, context, and knowledge of racial inequity and oppression. Writers engaged in a sophisticated analysis of white privilege and how it informed the ways HB2281 supporters thought about history, oppression, and whiteness itself.

Why was there relatively little discussion of white privilege in the mainstream press? Perhaps it is because ethnic history produces fear for some sectors of the white majority while empowering for ethnic minorities. Why is ethnic empowerment scary? Perhaps because it threatens to shake up the edifice of racial hierarchy that has Latinos (and blacks) at or near the bottom, where they are the load-bearing beams for white self-identity. If ethnic studies courses teach empowerment to ethnic minorities and the students no longer are willing to be subjugated for the benefit of white privilege, then white self-perception as the naturally superior group is undermined. When the load-bearing beams refuse to bear the burden of propping up white superiority, whites experience racial anxiety and fear. The result of this anxiety and fear is efforts to shore up the edifice of racial hierarchy by, for example, passing laws that keep non-whites "in line"—not only in the streets with legislation such as SB1070 but also in the classroom with HB2281 and monitoring the "accents" of public school teachers.

BIBLIOGRAPHY

Arizona gets ethnic history backward. (2010, May 16). *Philadelphia Tribune*, p. 10A.

Arizona, in the classroom. (2011, January 17). *New York Times*, p. A22.

Arizona lawmakers target ethnic studies program. (2010, May 13). *Tennessee Tribune*, p. A6.

Bonacorsi, B. (2011, May 2). Suppressing valuable education. *Inland Valley Daily Bulletin* (Ontario, CA), p. 18.

Bonilla-Silva, E. (2013). *Racism without racists: Color-blind racism and the persistence of racial inequality in the United States* (4th ed.). Lanham, MD: Rowman & Littlefield.

Bow, L. (2011, January 14). The assault on ethnic studies is unwise and undemocratic. *La Prensa*, p. 7.

Class politics. (2010, August 14). *Philadelphia Inquirer*, p. 6.

Dyer, R. (1997). *White*. London: Routledge.

Entman, R. (1993). Framing: Toward the clarification of a fractured paradigm. *Journal of Communication, 41*, 6–27.

Frankenberg, R. (1993). *White women, race matters: The social construction of whiteness*. Minneapolis: University of Minnesota Press.

Galupo, S. (2010, May 12). Arizona's ethnic studies fight is about defining American history. *U.S. News and World Report*. Retrieved from http://bit.ly/1uPdQ8X

Gersema, E. (2010, May 19). Ethnic studies ban reignites discrimination battle. *The Arizona Republic*. Retrieved from http://bit.ly/1zMYIsQ

Goffman, E. (1974). *Frame analysis*. Boston: Northeastern University Press.

Goldberg, D. T. (1993). *Racist culture: The philosophy and politics of meaning*. Oxford, UK: Blackwell.

Hage, G. (1998). *White nation: Fantasies of white supremacy in a multicultural society*. London: Pluto Press.

Haney-Lopez, I. (1996). *White by law: The legal construction of race*. New York: New York University Press.

Heider, D. (2000). *White news: Why local news programs don't cover people of color*. Mahwah, NJ: Erlbaum.

Ignatiev, N. (1995). *How the Irish became white*. New York: Routledge.

Iyengar, S. (1991). *Is anyone responsible?* Chicago: University of Chicago Press.

Julian, L. (2008, July 2). Come study la raza. *National Review*. Retrieved from http://bit.ly/1zMYRMU

Karenga, M. (2010, May 20). Remembering Malcolm, resisting Arizona: A call to common struggle. *Sentinel* (Los Angeles), p. 7.

Light is shed on a vile program. (2011, December 31). *Arizona Republic*. Retrieved from http://bit.ly/1FdnVh6

MacEachern, D. (2010, June 19). Tucson ethnic studies spews hatred for America. Retrieved from http://bit.ly/1uoYLpq

Matsaganis, M., Katz, V., & Ball-Rokeach, S. (2011). *Media*. Newbury Park, CA: Sage.

MacIntosh, P. (1998). White privilege, male privilege. Retrieved from http://bit.ly/U41MRM

Medrano, L. (2010, December 31). Ethnic studies classes illegal in Arizona public schools. *Christian Science Monitor*. Retrieved from http://bit.ly/1za3I9O

Nakayama, T., & Martin, J. (1999). *Whiteness: The communication of social identity*. Newbury Park, CA: Sage.

Prasad, V. (2001). *The karma of brown folk*. Minneapolis: University of Minnesota Press.

Rejected in Tucson. (2012, January 12). *New York Times*, p. A12.

Richardson, V. (2009, July 28). School head fights "ethnic chauvinism." *Washington Times*, p. B1.

Richardson, V. (2010, May 13). Arizona governor now targeting ethnic studies. *Washington Times*, p. 1.

Rodriguez, G. (2012, February 20). Why Arizona banned ethnic studies. *Los Angeles Times*. Retrieved from http://lat.ms/1v9rpQA

Rodriguez, R. (2009, June 26). Tom Horne to ethnic studies: Drop dead. *La Prensa*, p. 3.

Shah, H. (1999). Race, nation, and citizenship: Asian Indians and the idea of whiteness in the US press, 1906–1923. *Howard Journal of Communication, 10*, 249–269.

Shome, R. (2000). Outing whiteness. *Critical Studies in Media Communication, 17*(3), 366–371.

Susser, D. (2010, May 7). Studies ban debated. *Jewish News of Greater Phoenix*, pp. 1, 7.

The other Arizona battle (2010, June 4). *Christian Science Monitor*. Retrieved from http://bit.ly/1HAcoN3

Woolley J., & Peters, G. (2014). 2012 general election editorial endorsements by major newspapers. The American Presidency Project. Retrieved from http://bit.ly/1yEBmEX

Moral Indifference OR Unwillingness IN Public Affairs? Comparing Chinese AND Western News Discourse IN Reporting Moral Issues

XINYA LIU

Both the Xiao Yueyue incident, which happened in China in 2011, and the Hugo Alfredo Tale-Yax incident, which took place in the United States in 2010, were accidental and sudden events. The Chinese and Western media's strategies in reporting the two events were obviously different. Both sides used critical discourse and occupied the commanding height of morality. But the Chinese media applied a framework regarding the moral indifference of individuality, while Western media preferred a framework regarding the moral indifference of collectivity. When reporting the Tale-Yax incident, the Western media used a perspective that could be called "the diffusion of responsibility." This perspective regarded the incident as only an accidental moral lapse and used justification-discourse for the behavior of the passersby. Behind this media phenomenon, the media defended the passersby as merely unwilling or unable to trust each other or take part in public affairs.

Two-year-old girl Wang Yue, known as Xiao Yueyue, was struck and rolled to the side of the street by a minibus in Canton, China, on October 13, 2011. She lay on the street while 18 pedestrians passed by without assisting her. She was then helped by the 19th passerby, Chen Xianmei, but it was too late. Two days later, the little girl died; her death shocked the world. Just 18 months before, a homeless man named Hugo Alfredo Tale-Yax received deadly wounds from a gangster while saving a woman from a criminal's knife in New York City. During the one hour when he was lying bleeding profusely on the street, 25 passersby did not take any action to help him. The character of these two incidents is similar, but media reports on them were quite different. This difference also led to different media effects and social influence.

This chapter selects news from media in the United States and United Kingdom to compare the Chinese and Western media discourse strategies— *ABC News, Associated Press, BBC News, New York Times, New York Post, The Guardian,* and *The Telegraph*—as well as from Chinese media—*China Youth Daily, Guangzhou Daily, Oriental Morning, Phoenix New Media, Southern Weekly, Xinhua News Agency,* and *Yangcheng Evening News.* All selected news stories (47) were published in the week following the two events. Using content analysis and discourse analysis on the news texts of the above-mentioned media, this chapter then analyzes the different news meanings that the media tried to convey to their audiences.

COMPARISON OF DISCOURSE ORIENTATIONS

As a kind of discourse, news texts usually embed specific core values, beliefs, and positions toward specific news events. Early research suggested that framing is a way to construct the facts with salience (Entman, 1993). William Gamson (1988) divided the forming of public discourse into three elements: the *frame* (for making sense of relevant core events), which implies *a range of positions*; and the *condensing symbols,* which make it possible to display the discourse with deft metaphor, catch-phrase, or other symbolic devices. He believed that these three main elements could build a concrete form of public discourse, which he called a *discursive package.* Framing sets the topic or core idea of the issue and prescribes a limit to the expressive methods of meaning, such as metaphor, paradigm, symbols, portrayal, and signature devices of visual image (Pan, 2006). By using these discursive tools, speakers can start their logical deduction of seeking support for their positions and finally reconstruct the meaning of news texts by appealing to principles, implying results and finding roots (Entman, 1993). With the help of a framing perspective that analyzes news texts according to their core positions, metaphors, catch phrases, attributions of responsibility for problems, implied solutions, and core values (Siegel & Lotenberg, 2007, p. 255), researchers are able to examine the logical relationship between news texts and their social context.

Regarding methodology, this chapter applies framing analysis and discourse analysis to explore the strategy of Chinese and Western media discourse in reporting moral issues such as those concerning Xiao Yueyue and Hugo Alfredo Tale-Yax. Figure 6.1 displays the framing memos of Chinese and Western media reports on the two incidents.

	Xiao Yueyue (China)	Xiao Yueyue (Western)	Hugo Alfredo Tale-Yax (Western)
Core Position	The moral lapse of pedestrians, a heart-breaking accident	Chinese moral decline, lack of belief	Passersby can be excused for the diffusion of responsibility; Hugo Alfredo is a drunk
Metaphor	Passersby: cold-blooded individuals; Chen Xianmei (saver): garbage woman; Driver (perpetrator): guilty but he himself doesn't think so	Passersby: indifferent collectivity; Chen Xianmei (savior): Good Samaritan	Passersby: bystander; Hugo Alfredo (victim): Good Samaritan, drunk, homeless
Catch phrases	cold and detached; indifferent; do nothing to save Xiao Yueyue from ruin; moral lapse	cold and detached; indifferent; systematic problem; lack of belief; moral decline; Good Samaritan; the case of Peng Yu	bystanders; Good Samaritan; homeless; drunk
Attribution of responsibility for problem	social moral lapse; moral indifference of individuality; bystander effect; carelessness of Yueyue's parents	social moral decline; Good Samaritans have been punished; Chinese people's lack of belief and neglect of moral civilization	Culture's desensitization to violence from media; law of "imitation of others' behavior"; bystander effect and diffusion of responsibility; people are used to homeless alcoholics lying on the ground
Implied solution	Establish a social mechanism to encourage people to do good; enact related legislative regulation for parents	Improve laws and regulations; enhance education on morality and belief	Cultivate compassion through community service; professional education about saving others
Core values	Passersby are morally indifferent	Chinese are morally indifferent	Passersby responsibilities are diffused; as a homeless drunk, Tale-Yax's identity prevents people from helping

Figure 6.1. Framing Memos of Chinese and Western Media Reports.

Chinese Reports on Xiao Yueyue: The Moral Indifference of Individuality

When defining the actions of pedestrians, the Chinese media's main vocabulary was to form a frame of moral indifference. They set their report position as "morally indifferent; the loss of human nature; disappointed." For instance, more than three reports started with "How cold-blooded human nature is!"

to intensify the cold image of passersby. For one thing, the 18 passersby were described as "cold-blooded" and were reported as individuals. Most reports analyzed their action one by one through the security camera video. On the front page of the *Phoenix New Media*, every passerby was analyzed one after another in a specific column titled, "Look at These Indifferent People." Titles of articles in this column are all speeches or actions of the 18 passersby or witnesses, such as "mother and daughter who passed by: other people don't dare to touch her, how dare I do?"; "Plumbing shop owner: I didn't see it, if I lie, I'd die for you!" For another thing, the Chinese media emphasized the social identity of the 19th person, Chen Xianmei, who finally saved Xiao Yueyue. Chen is an old lady and lives her life by collecting garbage. Almost all media gave priority to Chen's social identity and compared her lower social class as a "garbage woman" with her noble morality. Her speech "Someone Should Help Anyway" was frequently quoted and used as the title of news stories. A report in *China Youth News* on October 25 started with the title, "At last, it was a garbage woman who stood out. Isn't it ironic?"

When telling the full story of the incident, the Chinese media preferred to take explicitly negative discourse as their vocabulary strategy. Their vocabularies or phrases are divided into three categories: description, speculation, evaluation. Description can be seen in depicting the action of passersby (most descriptions were directly summarized from security video). Speculation is mainly used to explain the reason for their action or to conjecture the actions that cannot be discerned directly from the monitor picture. Evaluation refers to the media's opinion of their action or of the whole story.

In the Chinese media, all three categories of their vocabulary strategy explicitly criticized the passersbys' actions. Take the reports on October 27 as an example:

Description: "nobody lent her a hand"; "directly passed the feet of Xiao Yueyue"; "ignored her even though she was only two meters away"; "looked at her without stopping"

Speculation: "seemed busy without coming out"; "pretended as if they've never seen it"; "bypassed her with possible special intention"; "indifferently went away as though nothing happened"

Evaluation: "take a deep look at these indifferent people"; "they just fold their hands and see her die"; "cold-blooded Chinese"; "how can they be so cold"

After calculating the frequency of these three categories, we found that the Chinese media gave the least proportion to objective description and the most to evaluation. And almost all evaluations were expressed with direct, explicitly critical words or phrases. Also, the Chinese media preferred to use some words similar to the literature of evaluation: "They bypassed both Xiao Yueyue and the moral bottom line silently, what the eighteen passers-by did runs over the hearts of human beings like vehicle wheels ran over Xiao Yueyue's body." This kind of literary expression carries a strong meaning of critique and sarcasm.

In analyzing the reasons—at the same time as critiquing the moral lapse of society—the Chinese media pointed out that these passersby only represented themselves. They were indifferent individuals, and it should not be seen as a common phenomenon in China. The passersby did not help the little girl, but there are kindhearted people anyway, like Chen Xianmei. In addition, the Chinese media explained the moral indifference with social theories such as "the bystander effect" and "the urban ecology of the incident" (a place full of strangers and social mobility). They also put more blame on the carelessness of Xiao Yueyue's parents. With these critiques, the Chinese media gave advice about adopting possible legal solutions: (1) to build up and enhance a social system that praises virtue and punishes vice; (2) to improve laws for protecting children's security and better regulating parents. Basically, the Chinese media placed extra emphasis on the moral level of this incident. They directly defined this incident as "the moral indifference of the individual passerby" and centered on reflection and finding solutions instead of paying much attention as to why passersby were so indifferent.

Western Reports on Xiao Yueyue: The Moral Indifference of Collectivity

Although Western media also applied a framework of criticizing passersby on their moral indifference, they tended to believe that this is a universal moral phenomenon in China. They framed the Xiao Yueyue incident this way: "It illustrated that the Chinese are lacking a sense of morality and belief." Under this frame, they did not analyze the 18 passersbys' actions one-by-one like the Chinese media did; instead, they briefly generalized them as a collectivity who "walked by, rode by, or drove by." The most specific character of Western media strategy is that they shaped another collectivity: Chinese netizens who were discussing vividly the incident. The two Chinese collectivities became heroes in the Western story. The savior, Chen Xianmei, was referred to as a "Good Samaritan" while 18 passersby stood for a symbol of "an almost Hobbesian state of struggle," with news reporters repeatedly saying that "Good Samaritans have been punished in the past for intervening in such episodes."

In the framework of the moral indifference of collectivity, the Western media also used explicitly negative discourse as their vocabulary, but their objective was the collective Chinese people. This study divided their vocabularies or phrases into description, speculation, and evaluation. When describing the passersby's action, the Western media used more neutral words to make objective expressions, such as "drove away," "ignored," "ran over." But when journalists attempted to speculate on the reasons for the actions of passersby, they gave priority to words with explicitly negative meanings such as "callousness," "lack compassion," "unwillingness to give help to others," and "lacking conscience." The same strategy can be seen in their opinions of the incident. Overall, the proportion of objective description is the least, even lesser than in Chinese media, while critical comments of passersby are the most frequent in the Western media. What is different from the Chinese media is that these negative critiques are extended to the higher level of the whole country.

Unlike the Chinese media, the Western media highlighted the big discussion among Chinese netizens. They attributed moral decline to integral problems in China's system and society by quoting netizens of *Sina Weibo*, China's biggest website for micro-blogs: (1) Chinese social environment is terrible: "This society is seriously ill." (2) China's economic development makes people cynical: The case, fueled by a security camera video of the incident, sparked soul searching in China over whether the nation's morals declined as the country chased economic growth (James, Yiu, & Dolak, 2011). (3) China does not have a Good Samaritan law and good people are thus afraid to be punished in the past cases: "There have been so many cases where people have been treated unjustly after doing good things; … we are all poor grassroots people." And another said, "If we get caught in a scam, this is it" (BBC News, 2011). (4) The problem of the Chinese social system: "It doesn't matter if an individual's nature is good or bad, it's the system that has made us deteriorate" (Wines, 2011). "In fact, it was all because of poor communication in the past that such incidents were not revealed; … China' s political environment had 'no tolerance' for people with a social conscience" (Yip, 2011).

Western Reports on Hugo Alfredo Tale-Yax: Diffusion of Responsibility

In the Tale-Yax incident, the Western media applied a "diffusion of responsibility" framework. This means they defended passersby by saying that since they had discrete individualities, their responsibility to save Tale-Yax was diffused. As the Chinese media did in the Xiao Yueyue incident, the Western media saw the passersby as 23 separate individuals and explained their actions one by one by following the security video. In Western news discourse, the passersby were defined as bystanders who should not be blamed too much because of the diffusion of their responsibilities. They were just "individuals rather than part of a group, so their responsibility was not diffused in the same way." Meanwhile, the Western media shaped the image of Tale-Yax as a homeless drunk who was categorized "as the kind of person that we pass by and don't help; we do this every day in New York City. It becomes business as usual" (Hutchison, 2010).

In the expressive strategy of specific vocabularies and phrases, the Western media seemed more neutral in their descriptive expressions of passerby action. However, they tended to use implicitly negative expressions of speculation and evaluation, such as "seem to notice and fail to help," "seem to see blood but then walk away," "gawk at," "vigorously shook," and "ignore." "Implicit" means that the negative meaning or critical thoughts of these words only appear in contexts. The vocabulary itself does not say anything. The mass usage of "seem to" weakens the explicitly negative meaning that the words might convey. What is more, all negative critiques were mainly focused on the specific action itself and were not extended to a higher level like the moral decline of society. While doing evaluation, most media aimed to find social reasons to excuse the passersby. Those defensive discourses in evaluation were also implicit, which, in the process, clear up the negative effect of description or speculation.

Instead of directly quoting netizens as they did in the Xiao Yueyue incident, the Western media interviewed a great number of psychologists and social workers and used their explanations as the media's discovery of social reasons: (1) the mass media have delivered too much violence to audiences for so long that American culture has been desensitized "to violence from so much exposure in movies, video games and music"; (2) the law of imitation in anonymous groups: "people tend to copy the behavior of others, so if one person ignored the injured man, then others were likely to do the same thing" (Davis, Milberger, & Santichen, 2010); (3) bystander effect and diffusion of responsibility: "the more people are around, the less likely it is for persons in trouble to get help" (CBC News, 2010); and most frequently, (4) the social identity of Tale-Yax as a homeless drunk: "There are a lot of alcoholics who drink and then fall down and they're lying on the ground. People say to each other: 'I don't know them so I won't get involved'" (Sulzberger & Meenan, 2010).

NEWS SOURCES AND DISCOURSE TENDENCIES

The choice of news sources is a major strategy for the media's construction of their discourse system. In making news discourse, the news source is the "consigner" of the actual speakers, while the journalist plays the role of "consignee" (Zeng, 2005, p. 18). News reporters can quote discourses from news resources with all kinds of citations and transfer them into news discourses. Reporters are not the master of news discourse, but they can speak their opinion by skillfully recombining the original discourse; usually the news media put a premium on language that is brief, topical, and easy to express (Woods, 2014, p. 67), which, in other words, means to choose, modify, and adjust news events to news discourse. The following figures display the news sources that Chinese and Western journalists used in reporting the Xiao Yueyue incident and Tale-Yax issue and how their voices were used and transferred.

Core and Authorized News Sources in Chinese Reports of Xiao Yueyue

In Chinese media coverage of the Xiao Yueyue incident, the main news sources were from doctors, police, relatives, and friends of Xiao Yueyue and the saver, Xianmei Chen. These were basically the core people of the incident and could offer the most timely and important details. Messages provided by them were mainly around (1) Yueyue's injury; (2) the driver who had caused the accident; (3) the course of the whole story; (4) Yueyue's daily activities before the incident; (5) living condition of Yueyue's family and their neighborhood; (6) later legislative measures taken by Yueyue's parents; and (7) the saver's explanation for her rescue action. Scholars and officials were listed as peripheral but authorized sources who may not have understood the full story but could provide professional analysis of human behavior or social systems. In the incident, messages provided by core sources were used far more than those offered by peripheral sources in a ratio of 34:7, and most of the discourses of core sources were narrative. There usually exists a positive correlation between the specificity of news discourse and the concreteness of news sources; the closer and more concrete a news source is to the event, the more persuasive the news will be. This is true because closer and concrete news sources give detailed information and can bring audiences back to the "theater" of the incident and thus make the cognitive pattern as similar as the actual parties concerned.

In addition, the social hierarchy of the news source will also influence the reliability of news contexts (van Dijk, 2013). Those who have specific social authority will be more reliable than ordinary people. In the Xiao Yueyue incident, therefore, core sources such as family members and friends of Xiao Yueyue and authorized sources such as police and doctors seemed more convincing than peripheral sources such as scholars or officials, and far more than ordinary netizens. The Chinese media have a clear order of news sources: (a) core sources with specific authority (police officers, hospital officials, doctors); (b) core sources (parents of Xiao Yueyue, the savior, witnesses); and (c) specific authority but peripheral sources (scholars, government officials, lawyers).

Basically, the Chinese media did not quote those who were neither core sources or authorized sources. Quotations from the chosen core and/or authorized sources were almost all negative and concrete discourses, while peripheral sources were mainly scholars, officials, media reports and journalists, and social celebrities, whose discourses were negative and abstract and were cited as comments on the actions of the passersby. The abstract evaluations supported the idea of moral indifference, but their moral denunciation was only aimed at individual passersby.

News Sources in Western Reports of Xiao Yueyue: Peripheral and Ordinary Netizens

In Western media reports of Xiao Yueyue, up to 28 sources were from the Internet, including *Sina Weibo* (a Chinese website similar to Twitter), online Chinese news stories, and the public intellectuals' online blog or *Weibo*. Their preference of news source was in contrast to the Chinese media: the peripheral source to core source ratio is 10 to 1. The order of the sources for the Western media is this: (a) peripheral sources with nonspecific authority; (b) peripheral sources with specific authority; and (c) core sources.

Most Western media sources were vague and came from netizens, some of whom were even anonymous. Their discourses were generally critical and did not have a concrete or individual dimension to them. For the most part, Internet sources quoted previous events to build a relationship between the Xiao Yueyue incident and many other former events and explained the reason of moral decline using this constructed causal relationship. The frequency of derogatory terms was the highest among vocabularies or phrases by customarily abstracting out a negative meaning toward all Chinese. Main participants in the construction of such discourses were netizens, and their main discourses referred to the moral indifference in Chinese society. In fact, the American academic field has discussed whether the press should use netizen sayings as a kind of news source. One of the most common ideas is that journalists should shut down their reliance on netizens as much as possible, for their authenticity and objectivity are in question due to their anonymous and spontaneous characteristics and their often remote distance from the incident. Researchers also show that in terms of discourse and linguistic properties, the identity of online discussion commentators is treated as an emerging construct (Lewandowska-Tmaszczyk, 2014, p. 85). Who can speak out in media and how their voices are presented as a discourse strategy illustrate the recognized differences of diverse media. In addition, overreliance on websites drives journalists away from the site and lower their interests in better understanding the cause and effect of the whole story. As can be seen from the Xiao Yueyue incident, all news sources were far from the core site of the event, and most of them were not as detailed as core sources provided to the Chinese media.

Core and Authorized News Sources in Western Reports of Hugo Alfredo Tale-Yax

When Western media covered the Tale-Yax incident, their sources were similar to the Chinese media in reports of Xiao Yueyue. This means that most of the information was offered by concrete and core people who had clear specifics and spoke mainly in narrative sentences. The amount of core sources and peripheral sources were almost equal and could be found in this order:

(a) core sources, (b) peripheral sources with specific authority, and then (c) peripheral sources.

More than half of the stories were by scholars and families and friends of Hugo Alfredo Tale-Yax. But the difference is that their voice was a defense of passersby rather than a critique of them. By quoting similar or the same information from different sources, the media used the frame emphasizing that the society is healthy, blaming social psychological mechanisms and, as noted before, the identity of Tale-Yax as a homeless alcoholic. Although the Western media contained many negative words in their discourses, the words mainly were directed to concrete objectivity or specific action of a passerby without abstracting the symbolic meaning. Normal citizens were more critical, but their voices could be heard in only one report and lacking in other supportive discourses. Even the most negative words were limited by uncertain symbols such as "appear to," "seem to," and so forth. All these news sources persuade their readers to believe that passersby were not morally indifferent; instead, they were just trying to avoid involvement in public affairs. Figure 6.2 shows the difference between the Chinese and Western media in their choice of news sources and quotation of main discourses in the Xiao Yueyue and Hugo Alfredo Tale-Yax's reports.

Incident	Sources (frequency)	Character of Sources	Main Discourses
Xiao Yueyue (China)	Doctors (12)	Specific authority Core sources	The situation of Xiao Yueyue's injury and death.
	Police (9)	Specific authority Core sources	The driver who hit Xiao Yueyue was captured; he privately said he would pay for Xiao Yueyue but never confessed his crime.
	Xiao Yueyue's parents (6)	Core sources	During course of incident and Xiao Yueyue's injury; they would give up civil compensation to make sure the driver would be punished.
	Chen Xianmei (4)	Core sources	The rescue is by instinct.
	Scholars (3)	Specific authority Peripheral sources	Bystander effect; urban biology in sites of the incident: high mobility, a society of strangers, weak relationship built by money and interests; social crisis of confidence.
	Merchants near the site (3)	Secondary core sources	Merchants come from all corners of the country and are busy with own business; lacking communication and the milk of human kindness; refused to be described as morally indifferent, said they were too busy to notice what happened.
	Officials (2)	Specific authority Peripheral sources	Xiao Yueyue incident reflected the malpractice of social development.
	Lawyers (2)	Specific authority Peripheral sources	Opposed to legally force people not to fold their hands and see people die.

Incident	Sources (frequency)	Character of Sources	Main Discourses
Xiao Yueyue (West)	Netizens (13)	Anonymous Peripheral sources	Chinese social morality is declining; social problems emerge in China, the Chinese society only sees money in its eyes; Peng Yu case and other previous events stimulated people's worry about fraud; Chen Xianmei saves people and becomes famous; feel ashamed and indignant for indifferent Chinese; Xiao Yueyue's parents should be responsible for their carelessness; proposed that everyone change his or her own behavior to change Chinese image; someone opened up a fake Weibo in the name of Xiao Yueyue's parents.
	Chinese media (10)	Specific authority Peripheral sources	Administration is thinking about making legal efforts to force people to help others in danger; most netizens are opposed to aforementioned proposition; previous events like Peng Yu case make people worry and doubt about helping strangers; Good Samaritans must be protected though it's difficult in reality; profit and materialism are perceived to be affecting society's values; there is no religion or faith, there are no role models.
	Chinese celebrities (5)	Peripheral sources	Apathy was deeply-rooted in society; in fact, it was all because of poor communication in the past that such incidents were not revealed; China's political environment has "no tolerance" for people with a social conscience; worry over liability should not be an excuse for not helping, and this case exposes the decline of humanity in Chinese society.
	Merchants near the site (2)	Secondary core sources	It's a shame not to save Xiao Yueyue; it was raining heavily that night and the sound of rainfall covered all other noises.
	Cantonese government (2)	Specific authority Peripheral sources	The provincial government's political and legal affairs committee is using its micro-blog site to gather opinions about how to "guide brave acts for just causes" and promote "socialist morals."
	Doctors (1)	Specific authority Core sources	Xiao Yueyue's injury situation

Incident	Sources (frequency)	Character of Sources	Main Discourses
Hugo Alfredo Tale-Yax (West)	Scholars (8)	Specific authority Peripheral sources	Being exposed to violence in mass media too long to distinguish between real violence and cyberviolence makes people not react to violence and pain; law of imitation of others' behavior; the cycle of apathy can be broken starting by teaching children to grow up to be compassionate adults; passersby were not sure about what was going on; the failure to help is tied less to acceptance of life on the streets and more to disdain for homeless people; the passersby were individuals rather than part of a group, so their responsibility was not diffused in the same way; there is no legal obligation for a bystander to help someone in distress in New York.
	Families and Friends of Tale-Yax (6)	Core sources	Tale-Yax had the problem of alcohol abuse and sometimes alcohol made him angry; Tale-Yax was currently unemployed and had been homeless for a long time; Tale-Yax held his head low while walking and always lays on the street; Tale-Yax's family has a hard life in Guatemala.
	People working nearby (3)	Secondary core sources	Many alcoholics lay on the street nearby the site; it becomes business as usual for people to pass and not help the homeless in New York city; some passersby may be illegal immigrants.
	Police (2)	Specific authority Core sources	The police responded to three 911 calls; expect someone to call 911 and, if possible, to stay with the victim until help arrives.
	Officials of Guatemala (2)	Specific authority Peripheral sources	Preparations were being made to fly the body of Mr. Tale-Yax back to Guatemala for burial.
	Media (2)	Specific authority Peripheral sources	It is not unusual to see individuals passed out or sleeping in public in New York.

Figure 6.2. News Sources and Their Main Discourses.

DISCOURSE ANALYSIS: HOW TO FORM NEWS CONTEXTS

As a literary form, news discourse has its own specific structure. In the texts of news reports, the way in which different elements are arranged implicitly decides how important they should be. Basically, a news schema should include peculiar elements such as Episode (including Main Events, Previous Events, Consequences), Background (including Context and History), and Comments (including Evaluation and Expectation) (van Dijk, 2013, p. 78). With discourse analysis of news schema, we can make salient the microstructure and the superstructure of news contexts and the discourse meaning that lies in the background of news texts. In this study, we chose two reports in the *New York Times*, one on the Xiao Yueyue incident and another on the Tale-Yax incident. One is titled "Chinese Debate Aiding Strangers After Toddler's Critical Injury" and the other is "Questions Surround a Delay in Help for a Dying Man." Another research sample is the Chinese *Yangcheng Evening*'s reports on the Xiao Yueyue incident titled "18 Cold Pedestrians Passed by after Two Vehicles Ran Over Two-year-old Toddler." The three reports were the earliest news stories after each incident had taken place.

After encoding and decoding the three stories, their respective microstructure and their preference of related information can be summarized. The code index "Relevance" means to what extent the information has direct relevance with the main event. A 0 means that the information is directly related to the event; -1 to -5 refers to the declining trend of the relevance and -5 means this information is the least related to main events.

The Moral Indifference of Individuality: Details Determine Discourse Trends

In *Yangcheng Evening*'s report, there are three main events: (1) No passerby ever stopped to help the injured toddler; they were morally indifferent. (2) It would be difficult for the little girl to survive. (3) The driver who caused the accident ought to pay compensation for it, and he escaped rather than voluntarily surrendering himself. The core person is the little girl Xiao Yueyue, about whom core sources were interviewed, including her parents, her doctors, the police responsible for the case, and the driver.

The microstructure of the news story could be illustrated in these terms: Criticizing the moral indifference of passersby set the tone (P1/S1).[1] Recovering the accident scene and retelling the details including two parts, how Xiao Yueyue was neglected by 18 passersby in one part and how the garbage woman Chen Xianmei saved her in another (P1/P2/P3). Telling the truth of how difficult it is for Xiao Yueyue to survive (P4/P5/P6/P7). Criticize passersby by reproducing their actions (P8). Consequences: the driver would make compensation but not give himself up to the law (P9/P10/P11/P12). Comment 1: how cold-blooded the passersby are (P13). Comment 2: Xiao Yueyue's parents should pay for their carelessness though they are sad about her death (P14/P15). Figure 6.3 illustrates how this report constructs its discursive structure in the narrative of Xiao Yueyue.

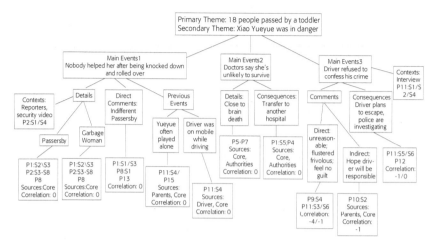

Figure 6.3. Discursive Structure of *Yangcheng Evening* on Xiao Yueyue.

In *Yangcheng Evening*'s report, the correlation of episode discourses to main events is very high (80%), and all discourses surround the core person Xiao Yueyue. The large number of details portray people as cold and indifferent passersby who left Xiao Yueyue unaided, center on the garbage woman who saved Xiao Yueyue, highlight sad relatives and families, quote doctors saying there is little hope for the treatment of Xiao Yueyue, describe the driver who hit Yueyue with no remorse, and include the police hunting for the driver. What should be given particular attention is the use of numbers in the text. It was repeatedly stressed that there were "18" indifferent passersby, cold individuals. Enhancing this digital rhetoric in the news, for readers, is a kind of hyperbole. If the number of passersby was not emphasized again and again, or if passersby were only reported as "some pedestrians" as an overall statement, then the visual impact would be completely inferior to pointing out this number 18, as well as magnifying the passersby's moral indifference by repeating the details of their actions over and over. What is interspersed together with detailed descriptions of the passersby is the direct use of comments that carry dominant and direct negative discourses, such as "how inconsistent human nature is," "it's incomprehensible for more than a dozen passers-by to sit on their hands," "look at these cold men," and so forth.

Another party in this case constructed by direct or indirect use of dominant and negative comments is the driver. Phrases such as "unreasonable demands," "flustered tone, frivolous intonation," and "in four times of dialogue (with journalists), the driver refused to reveal any obvious remorse for his atrocities" are good examples. Meanwhile, a reporter uncovered a detail that the driver had been using his cell phone while driving and attributed the cause of the accident to this.

Discourses about Xiao Yueyue's parents are sympathetic on the one side while blameful on the other. Words such as "crying their tears dry" were used to describe their sadness while details like "little Yueyue had usually played alone on the street where the tragedy took place" imply that the second reason causing the tragedy is the absence of parental protection.

According to Tuchman (1972), there are many effective discourse strategies for invoking journalists' news judgment that influence effects:

(1) present conflicting possibilities related to truth-claims;
(2) present supplementary evidence to support a "fact";
(3) use quotation marks to indicate that the reporter is not making a truth-claim;
(4) present the most "material facts" first;
(5) carefully distinguish "facts" from opinions by using the label "analysis" (pp. 660–679).

Generally, to emphasize the authenticity of a news event, reporters will directly describe the course of events, choose the core sources and the specific authority of their messages by trial and error, strengthen the details, and provide a sufficient amount of data. And if reporters want the audience to accept their point of view unreservedly, they usually arrange previous events as a reason or condition to imply the consequences that have occurred. Such organization of the news report will make previous events seem "objective" but full of deep connection with main events and later consequences, as noted in the analysis of the Xiao Yueyue incident. The "driver was on a cell phone while driving" and "her parents let little Yueyue play alone" are two previous events in this case and are inserted into a context that readers are already familiar with. Thereby the news story will strengthen the causal association between the previous events and the main event.

The Moral Indifference of Collectivity: Building Relevance Between Previous Events and Consequences

In the report of the *New York Times*, "Chinese Debate Aiding Strangers after Toddler's Critical Injury," we observe the aforementioned rhetorical and discursive strategies once again. The article downplays the course of the incident and details of Xiao Yueyue (even the name of the little girl was not mentioned until the tenth paragraph). By putting its focus directly on the consequences of the Xiao Yueyue incident—the heated debate on morality—the report mainly forms two categories of comments and leads to two main points: (a) Chinese society is sick, and (b) Chinese morality is declining and good Samaritans have no legal protection. Note that because this is a news story, these two main views are not expressed directly. Journalists set many previous events as reasons or conditions to suggest that they should be responsible for what happened in the Xiao Yueyue incident. Figure 6.4 describes the detailed discursive structure in the report of the *New York Times*.

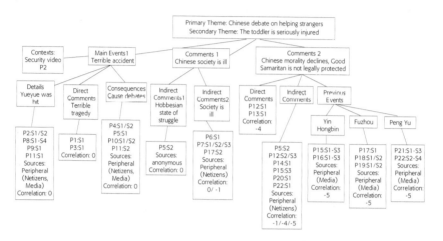

Figure 6.4. Discursive Structure of *New York Times* on Xiao Yueyue.

Those cases that were cited at length by the *New York Times* as previous events, but hardly had any direct relation with Xiao Yueyue, include the Yin Hongbin case, the Fuzhou case, and the Peng Yu case of 2006.[2] Similarly, some of the figures and details are amplified when reporting on these previous events, such as the age of the elderly person, the year when these cases occurred, the number of onlookers, as well as details such as the verdict saying that "'according to common sense,' it was highly possible that the defendant had bumped into the old woman, given that he was the first person to get off the bus when the old woman was pushed down in front of the bus door." This implies that in China, Good Samaritans have not been legally protected for a long time. In the reporting process, a large number of people from different backgrounds spoke their views of the incident to the media, and the ones presented are essentially similar to or the same as the reporter's point of view. For instance, the *Times* quoted netizen comments such as these: "this just shows how abnormal the moral situation is in this society"; and "the Xinhua news agency linked the episode to a perception of declining morals 'as profit and materialism are perceived to be affecting society's values.'"

Rhetorical studies have repeatedly confirmed that the use of direct and indirect quoted text in making news will help increase credibility more than the reporters' direct truth claim. To fulfill this aim, the *New York Times* discussion took three steps: (1) The reporter centered his framework on the consequences of main events from the outset; this immediately directed the main point of the Xiao Yueyue incident to the wrangle among Chinese netizens. (2) Netizens and the Chinese media who were originally in the periphery of the incident then became direct participants and core sources of the consequences. It does not matter to what extent they understood the ins and outs of the Xiao Yueyue incident, nor does it matter whether their speeches are true, correct, or objective. The only thing that counts is that they play the role of press spokespeople, and with quotation marks, their words become supplementary evidence to enhance the authenticity of news facts by achieving their rhetorical function and effect. (3) On the basis of quoted comments from netizens and the media, the report integrates previous events to establish their contact with the main events in specific circumstances, though these previous events may be totally unrelated to the Xiao Yueyue incident. But with indirect comments quoted in the first two steps, it seems to find exact social and legal evidence in the rebuilt rhetoric of authenticity to prove that aspersions such as "this is not the first time the Chinese people failed to trust the Good Samaritan" did not come from an empty cave.

Diffusion of Responsibility: Quotations Form Defensive Discourses for Passersby

The *New York Times* report on the Tale-Yax case mainly revolves around the question of "why passersby would ignore Hugo Alfredo Tale-Yax." Almost all of the component texts are highly correlated with the main event itself. Its discourses could be divided into two main levels. The first level of rhetorical structure is similar to the first step of *New York Times* coverage of the Xiao Yueyue incident, that is, it placed its focus on the analysis of whether passersby ignored Tale-Yax without dwelling on the event itself too much. In the Tale-Yax event, the news story first raised the question of how many people realized that Hugo Alfredo Tale-Yax was dying. Reflecting this train of thought, the news story distinguished one kind of passersby's acts from another based on different sources. Following the surveillance video—in which the rhetoric was similar to the Chinese media rhetoric of the Xiao Yueyue incident—the news reporter describes the individual behavior of every passersby in detail. Another kind of passersby are those who informed the police. From this story, people learned that there were indeed many Good Samaritans who did not neglect the tragedy on the street. Meanwhile, the victim, Hugo Alfredo Tale-Yax, is constructed differently than Xiao Yueyue. While the latter is portrayed as sadly as possible, the former is given more details: Hugo Alfredo was currently unemployed and homeless; he usually had the problem of alcohol abuse and often was drunk and slept in New York parks or on the streets. All this information was offered by core sources like Tale-Yax's friends and family. As a result, the fact that "passersby do not realize that Hugo Alfredo will die" may prove to have logical possibility. With this keynote, the news report quoted full indirect comments with quotation marks—as the *New York Times* did in the Xiao Yueyue incident—to answer why passersby were indifferent. Figure 6.5 shows how the *New York Times* built up its discursive structure.

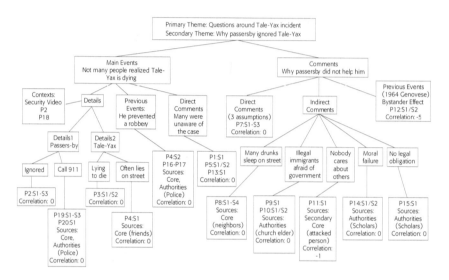

Figure 6.5. Discursive Structure of *New York Times* on Hugo Alfredo Tale-Yax.

Unlike its report on Xiao Yueyue, the *New York Times* applies a discursive strategy similar to the Chinese media in its selection of news sources. This means it finds parties as closely related to the event as possible and specific authorities to provide core information. It chose little information from peripheral and non-authoritative outsiders, and there are no anonymous news sources. The *New York Times* reconstructs the reasons for the Tale-Yax incident by messages from sources with relatively high credibility.

First, the news story directly assumed the following: (1) Perhaps the passersby thought he was just drunk. (2) Perhaps they were illegal immigrants themselves, too nervous to contact the authorities. Or (3) perhaps they had just learned a lesson that Mr. Tale-Yax so clearly had not: it is better to keep to oneself than to risk the trouble that comes from extending a helping hand. Then the story proved that all these three assumptions were right by ingeniously refitting the word order and the sentence pattern of discourses from authoritative news sources and core sources. Tale-Yax's relatives said he always slept on the street under the effects of alcohol. The superintendent of two buildings on the block where the stabbing occurred said that there were a lot of alcoholics who fall down and lie on the ground, and people do not get involved. These facts with quotation marks support the first assumption. A nearby church elder's believing that the inaction might have stemmed from illegal immigrants' trying to escape detection confirms the second assumption. And the church elder's word order is not simple and straightforward; instead, it was changed with a pause: "So they're going to be very afraid to call the authorities if they see something," he said. "It's not that people don't care."

The emphasis then falls on the last phrase, "It's not that people don't care." As for the third assumption, several victims of assault, psychologists, and law experts have proved that not only is it true that people want to keep themselves away from trouble, but it is also reasonable for them to do so. For example, there is no legal obligation for a bystander to help someone in distress in New York. At the same time, similar to what the news reporter did in reporting Xiao Yueyue, this news report selected specifics from a previous event—the 1964 Genovese case—as one of the reasons for pedestrians to take action. To conceal the original weak relevance between Genovese and Tale-Yax, the reporter put the 1964 case in the middle of those mentioned reasons to reconstruct its relevance as the bystander effect with Tale-Yax. "Moral decline"—which had been excessively emphasized in the Xiao Yueyue incident—is listed only as the fourth reason in the Tale-Yax incident and is placed in a discursive structure this way:

P12:S1:	*Regardless of the explanation, the death has become another unfortunate case study in bystander behavior in emergencies, a psychological field that developed after the notorious 1964 killing of Kitty Genovese. (Previous Event)*
P12:S2:	*She was stabbed to death at an apartment building in Kew Gardens, Queens, where a large number of neighbors heard her screams but did not call the police. (Previous Event)*
P13:S1:	*The death of Mr. Tale-Yax is all the more dramatic because police say that he was stabbed as a result of his apparently trying to help a stranger. (Direct Comments)*
P13:S2:	*"I'm afraid what we've got here is a situation of people failing to help, and the failure appears to be a moral failure." (Indirect Comments)*
P13:S3:	*said John Darley, a professor of psychology at Princeton University who has written about bystander response to emergencies. (Source)*
P13:S4:	*"He did what you're supposed to do, and we let the person, who did what he was supposed to do, die." (Indirect Comments)*
P14:	*In New York, as in most other states, there is no legal obligation for a bystander to help someone in distress, said Harold Takooshian, a psychology professor at Fordham University who has also studied the subject.*

First, this discursive structure cites the 1964 Genovese case, with which audiences are quite familiar. In this case, many scholars pointed out that the reason for pedestrians to stand by is due to the effect of being a bystander; the responsibilities of passersby were diffused. By this means, the Tale-Yax incident is incorporated into the common frame of normal crime news, which regards this incident as typical of other criminal cases in daily life. And the most intriguing and surprising point of Tale-Yax—the reasons passersby were apathetic—have been hinted at by previous events. Second, to stress the subjectivity of the speaker in direct speech implies a symbolic significance that the reporter is only a "recorder" of speakers' views who represent their private opinions. This suggests that *"the failure appears to be a moral failure"* is the personal worry of the psychologist. Then what follows, *"He did what you're supposed to do, and we let the person, who did what he was supposed to do, die,"* is indirect speech from another psychologist saying *"In New York, as in most other states, there is no legal obligation for a bystander to help someone in distress."* After removing quotation marks, the discourse power is returned to the reporter, who seems to offer an explanation by using indirect speech for the phenomenon of letting good people die that the first psychologist noticed. With these two reasons appearing in tandem, the potential rhetorical presentation lowers the extent of "moral failure" by using the fact of "no legal obligation" and still enhances the people's cognitive pattern of defensive discourse: "passersby responsibilities are diffused."

CONCLUSION: MORAL NARRATIVE OR THE POSITIVIST PRINCIPLE IN NEWS REPORTS

Both the Xiao Yueyue incident and the Tale-Yax events can be regarded as an emergency in social life. But different strategies adopted by Western and Chinese media of the two events allow us to see the discursive difference between moral narrative and empirical news reports. In the Xiao Yueyue incident, although the Chinese media attempted to be objective by using a large amount of detail and interviews with core sources, they finally present a critical tendency toward morality and focus on criticizing the behavior of passersby and the driver. In such reports, the Chinese media explicitly stand on the commanding height of morality to criticize humanity and moral decline. They tend to blame passersby for their absence of public spirit and take fewer situational factors, social factors, and social consequences into account.

On the contrary, the Western media tend to make a big fuss about the "collective moral indifference" of pedestrians in the Xiao Yueyue reports. This strategy, for one thing, reflects their ethical concept that individuals should bear public responsibility to promote the rule "love your neighbor as yourself." Therefore, they believe that the Chinese people think highly of private morality but, from their own point of view, think that the Chinese people look down on public morality. For another thing, and more importantly, objective limits on interview conditions and geopolitical factors force them to turn to the Chinese social network. Thus normal netizens, public intellectuals, opinion leaders, or online celebrities' voices are all absorbed and extracted in Western reports as representatives of social ideas to express their criticism of Chinese society as a whole.

But whether it is a framework of the moral indifference of individuality or a framework of collectivity, both the Chinese and Western media invariably see the Xiao Yueyue incident as a deplorable event. The two sides have adopted critical discourse as their media strategy, standing on the moral high ground to criticize the fall of human nature. In their discourse, the way passersby behaved in the Xiao Yueyue incident should be considered contradictory to normal social morality and social ethics and as seriously deviant behavior in the process of social development.

When reviewing Western media coverage of Tale-Yax, we find that the Western media do not generally criticize in moral terms. Like the Chinese media, they use positivistic methods to abstract deep meaning from large numbers of empirical materials. The media put the victim into a particular social position with the emphasis on his social identity and on the social structure of New York City. Passersby are considered social actors; thereby the moral conflict of their behavior is dispelled by its social meaning. The media fully take into consideration the social consequences that may arise, so their discourse strategy is to bring the occasional extreme event into the normal reporting frame of processing a common social crisis in daily life.

This difference in strategy has produced completely different discursive tendencies in reporting these two similar events. As can be seen, both sides have undertaken moral critiques of such kinds of sudden events, but the Western media tend more to find reasonable explanations for the cause of similar events happening in their own country. They utilize a defensive discourse strategy to incorporate occasional emergencies into the ordinary processing mode of finding social reasons to explain the current social crisis; the news is shaped by secular legal authority and psychological theory. In this discourse, all such kinds of events are normal social phenomena. Events like Tale-Yax are just occasional, seldom, and temporary social anomie or a type of social expression that will eventually return to a normal framework of social norms.

NOTES

1. This figure describes the detailed encoding and decoding steps of discourse analysis. Code P refers to the serial number of paragraphs and S refers to the numerical order of sentences;

for example, P1:S1 refers to the first sentence in the first paragraph. Category Coding divides the information provided by each sentence into the Title, Events (including Main Events, Previous Events), Consequences (the judgment of "Previous Events" and "Consequences" is based on their time order, according to which the events took place in reality, with Main Events), Details, Cause and/or Effect, Comments (including Direct Comments and Indirect Comments, the latter mainly refers to opinions expressed by quoting news sources), and Contexts (introduction of how and under which condition the information was obtained). Correlation Coding uses numbers to describe to what extent the information is directly related with Events. A 0 means the information is directly related with the event, -1 to -5 illustrates the reducing tendency of direct correlation, and code -5 means this information is in toto indirectly related to the Events.

2. Yin Hongbin case: a bus driver, Yin Hongbin, was falsely accused of knocking down an 81-year-old woman in Nantong city after he stopped to help the woman, who was lying on the ground. Fuzhou case: An 83-year-old man fell to the ground alone, but during half an hour, nobody ever dared to help him until he died. Pengyu case in 2006: a 65-year-old woman fell to the ground when she stepped off a bus in Nanjing, and a 26-year-old student, Peng Yu, who was just behind her, helped the woman to the hospital immediately. But then Peng was accused of knocking her down in the first place. Without other witnesses, Peng was ordered to pay 45,877 yuan. This case ricocheted around the Chinese press. However, almost five years later, the "good Samaritan" Peng Yu admitted to knocking over the old lady, and he begged the media and online forum operators to keep it a secret with financial bribes.

BIBLIOGRAPHY

BBC News. (2011, October 17). Outcry in China over hit-and-run toddler left in street. *BBC News*. Retrieved from http://www.bbc.co.uk/news/world-asia-pacific-15331773

CBC News. (2010, April 26). New Yorkers grapple with stabbing death. *CBC News*. Retrieved from http://www.cbc.ca/news/world/new-yorkers-grapple-with-stabbing-death-1.965750

Davis, L., Milberger, M., & Santichen, K. (2010, April 25). Good Samaritan left for dead on city sidewalk. *ABC News*. Retrieved from http://abcnews.go.com/GMA/Weekend/dying-homeless-man-stopped-mugging-sidewalk/story?id=10471047

Entman, R. M. (1993). Framing: Toward clarification of a fractured paradigm. *Journal of Communication, 43*(4), 51–58.

Gamson, W. A. (1988). A constructionist approach to mass media and public opinion. *Journal of Communication, 43*(4), 161–174.

Hutchison, C. (2010, April 28). Why homeless hero Hugo Alfredo Tale-Yax died on NYC street. *ABC News Medical Unit*. Retrieved from http://abcnews.go.com/Health/Wellness/dying-homeless-man-stopped-mugging-sidewalk/story?id=10471047

James, M. S., Yiu, K., & Dolan, K. (2011, October 20). YueYue, Chinese toddler run over in street and ignored, dies. *ABC News*.

Lewandowska-Tmaszczyk, B. (2014). Emergent group identity construal in online discussions: A linguistic perspective. In F. Zeller, C. Ponte, & B. O'Neill (Eds.), *Revitalising audience research: Innovations in European audience research* (pp. 80–105). New York: Routledge.

Pan, Z. (2006). Framing analysis: Toward an integrative perspective. *The Chinese Journal of Communication and Society, 1*, 17–46.

Siegel, M., & Lotenberg, L. D. (2007). *Marketing public health: Strategies to promote social change* (2nd ed.). Sudbury, MA: Jones and Bartlett.

Sulzberger, A. G., & Meenan, M. (2010, April 25). Questions surround a delay in help for a dying man. *New York Times*. Retrieved from http://www.nytimes.com/2010/04/26/nyregion/26homeless.html?_r=0

Tuchman, G. (1972). Objectivity as strategic ritual: An examination of the newsmen's notion of objectivity. *The American Journal of Sociology, 77*(4), 660–679.

Van Dijk, T. A. (2013). *News as discourse*. New York: Routledge.

Wines, M. (2011, October 18). Bystanders' neglect of injured toddler sets off soul-searching on web sites in China. *New York Times*. Retrieved from http://www.nytimes.com/2011/10/19/world/asia/toddlers-accident-sets-off-soul-searching-in-china.html?pagewanted=all

Woods, N. (2014). *Describing discourse: A practical guide to discourse analysis*. New York: Routledge.

Yip. M. (2011, October 23). Anger and debate over hit-and-run toddler Wang Yue. *BBC News*. Retrieved from http://www.bbc.co.uk/news/world-asia-pacific-15401055

Zeng, Q. (2005). *News narratology*. Beijing: China Radio and TV Press.

CHAPTER SEVEN

Strange AND Familiar

The Othering of Chinese Writer Mo Yan in U.S. News

JING XIN AND DONALD MATHESON

Western media coverage of China has broadened in both quantity and kind since the country emerged as a major global force in the 1990s. China is no longer near-invisible to Western publics. Yet this shift brings its own problems, for the terms on which China and the Chinese people are represented show particular versions of Chineseness. A newly visible, rising China can be a threatening object.

Studies regularly show that Western-based broadcasters and newspapers devote an increasing amount of news space to China (Seib & Powers, 2010; Wilke, Heimprecht, & Cohen, 2012). This trend holds true also for the United States. While coverage of international news has plummeted since the 1950s, the percentage of that shrinking amount devoted to news on China has increased in elite U.S. media (Jones, Van Aelst, & Vliegenthart, 2011). There is, moreover, a long-term growth in news about matters beyond its relationship to U.S. geopolitical concerns as appeared to be the case in the immediate post–Cold War years (Goodman, 1999) and beyond the traditional focus on disaster and crisis (Sreberny-Mohammadi, Nordenstreng, Stevenson, & Ugboajah, 1985). China is now of interest for human interest stories (Peng, 2004).

Quantitative measures, however, only tell part of the story. There remain scholarly concerns that China is often reported in the West in narrow terms. To take one example, while CNN International devoted 6% of its news in February 2010 to China—of which a third were stories about Chinese society—on closer inspection, those social stories were dominated by the return of two pandas from the United States to a Chinese zoo and on the

Chinese New Year (Seib & Powers, 2010). If international news in the West operates by a dynamic of "localizing the global," in which the international is presented within the frames of interpretation of local audiences (Clausen, 2004), then a key dynamic appears to be the persistence of a narrow range of topics and frames within which China can be understood. A combination of U.S. neocolonial interests, ideological structures, and a hyper-commercial news environment raises the risk of more coverage in the U.S. media equating to more stereotypes. Places and people that are already culturally distant become symbolically associated with a few ideas, so that the news reproduces a world more or less already known in all but the latest details. Thussu (2000) argues, "With scant space to cover news from developing countries, these are often stereotyped into shorthand media clichés—Thailand is known for child prostitution, Colombia for cocaine, Ethiopia for famine" (p. 329).

China emerges in this chapter as an increasingly familiar but still strange Other in U.S. public discourse. It is familiar to the extent that Chinese business, politics, and social life is firmly established in news repertoires. But it remains strange to the extent that the localization of news about China for U.S. audiences happens in terms that fail to engage Chinese perspectives or understandings and inscribe Western imaginaries onto global public spaces.

This chapter analyzes the U.S. news reports of awarding the Nobel Prize in Literature to the Chinese novelist Mo Yan on October 11, 2012. Mo was the first Chinese citizen to win the prestigious prize,[1] and the event received substantial media coverage globally, placing China—especially Chinese writers and Chinese literature—in the limelight for weeks. The award of the 2012 prize was a global event involving a Chinese figure and was also a moment when Chinese high culture came to the fore. It therefore provides an opportunity to study how the U.S. media represent China and the Chinese when the market orientation of the news, ideology, and U.S. political interests might be imagined to be less prominent as determinants of reporting. The event is offered as a case study of the shifts in news reporting about China. Yet, as discussed below, awarding the prize to Mo demonstrates the power of those factors to determine the news: Mo is constructed as part of a highly homogenized Chinese Other, in stark juxtaposition to a Westernized universal. It seems also that U.S. journalists have highly limited resources by which to understand that Other, reaching for a few limited frames and tropes that have little to do with Mo's writings or Chinese ways of life.

THEORETICAL ISSUES

Representation is always dialogic, involving the sharing of encoded meanings, so there can be no certainty that any particular meaning will remain fixed.

When a symbol is used in a new context and is read by diverse individuals, its meaning is capable of being both reinflected and of referencing multiple meanings at once. Yet, as Stuart Hall emphasizes, drawing on Voloshinov (1986), the space of shared meaning must also be understood as one of contestation. When a shared reality is constructed, "*power* intervenes in *discourse*" (Hall, 1997, p. 10; italics in original), so that a "system of representation" (p. 21) takes shape. Of particular interest to us here is the extent to which power manifests itself in the construction of structures of meaning around self-identity and other identities. A global public event enables the coming together of strangers but may lead into an unreflexive cosmopolitanism that passes off certain forms of self-identity as universals (Corpus Ong, 2009).

One way to understand how these identities take shape is to study practices of framing. To the extent that the public nature of news makes it "a window on the world" (Tuchman, 1978), allowing the public to get to know and understand the world (Lippmann, 1922), it frames that world. For media critics, news is not found; stories created or constructed within specific narrative frames select and arrange symbolic events in a wider context (Wolfsfeld, 1997). In his initial and widely cited definition, Goffman (1974) characterized frames as basic cognitive structures that guide the perception and representation of reality. For Gitlin (1980), frames are identified as "principles of selection, emphasis and presentation composed of little tacit theories about what exists, what happens, and what matters" (p. 6). Such tacit knowledge is, however, hard to establish in empirical research, and Entman's (1993) definition is useful: "[T]o frame is to select some aspects of a perceived reality and make them more salient in a communicating text, in such a way as to promote a particular problem definition, causal interpretation, moral evaluation, and/or treatment recommendation" (p. 52). Such a definition emphasizes the active dimension of framing rather than the speaker's implication within an ideological structure. Scholarly discussion often emphasizes the active selection process in news framing. Tankard (2001) indicates that journalists at times circulate frames to deceive their audiences. Reese (2001, p. 13) suggests that researchers "should ask how much 'framing' is going on." For our purposes, to frame someone as Other is an act of othering, whether deliberate or not, in which power is being produced and deployed. By studying discursive mechanisms, such as excising, sanitizing, equalizing, personalizing, demonizing, and contextualizing, various frames can be identified (Liebes, 1997). This study, therefore, aims to explore the framing mechanisms that construct others, as well as contextual factors and the contestation of power in discourse.

These frames operate often to fix the meaning of an idea or person, so that representations perform not just the ongoing role of constructing identities in any given culture but stereotype others into fixed roles against which "we" can define ourselves (e.g., Grossberg, Wartella, Whitney, & Wise, 1998;

Hall, 1997). Stereotyping usually reduces people or objects "to a few, simple, essential characteristics, which are represented as fixed by nature" (Hall, 1997, p. 257). In this sense, the process of stereotyping fixes differences and thus leads to a naturalization of differences. By deploying a strategy of "splitting," stereotyping becomes a practice of separating the "normal" from the "abnormal," setting up boundaries through symbols, and excluding anything that does not fit or is simply different (Hall, 1997). It tends to take place where there are apparent inequalities of power. Laclau (1996) notes that these attempts to fix who "they" are or the meaning of key words that define the difference to "us" become particularly important when such fixities no longer have the power of being self-evident. Stereotypes can be read, then, as akin to Laclau's "empty signifiers." The attempt to establish the authority of a way of being lies partly in filling these discursive objects with meanings as the power to define those objects becomes contested.

The media, in this reading, not only exercise a regime of stereotyping that provides verbal definitions and graphic images concerning various social identities and groups but construct others and people's perceptions of "us" and "them" in the process (Kellner, 1995). They operate to misunderstand the Other, producing nationality, for example, out of overstating "our" differences to others (Anderson, 1991) and leaving political background and sociocultural context neglected or under-explored (Avraham, 2003; First, 2001; Hall, 1997; Weimann, 2000).

The discourse analysis below explores these conceptual categories and issues with respect to a sample of U.S. news media. U.S. news media texts throughout October 2012 were gathered from the *Factiva* database using a keyword search for "Mo Yan." Mo was announced as the winner of the Nobel Prize in Literature on October 11, 2012, and the news media began to speculate on top candidates for the prize at the beginning of October and continued heatedly discussing this event until the end of October. Thus the news sample extends from October 1 to October 31. Although coverage continued into November, topics tended to drift into less relevant and softer terrain, such as the boost in sales experienced by Chinese vodka brand Mo Yan Zui and a theme park planned for Mo's hometown. As a result, we limited the study to October. Among the media outlets represented in the sample were newspapers, magazines, news agencies, radio and TV programs, and news websites. These included elite, national outlets such as the *New York Times* and Associated Press, as well as regional newspapers such as the *Buffalo News* and *Ventura County Star*. Journalistic genres included news, commentary, book reviews, and transcripts of interview programs. Patterns were identified in these texts on the basis of the theoretical framework discussed above, that is, dominant media frames, mechanisms of framing (inclusion or exclusion, context, the dominant voice heard, source of information, and so forth), stereotypes, and forms of discourse favoring the production of stereotypes. The analysis begins with patterns in the news leads, then the representation of Mo Yan in the body of the texts, his literary style, and his novels.

FINDINGS AND ANALYSIS

Dominance of Political Frames

The headlines to the texts we studied were for the most part descriptive, working simply to link the key elements of Mo Yan, China, and the Nobel Prize in Literature, particularly in the earlier announcement texts. Thus the CNN Wire story of October 12 was headlined: "Mo Yan of China wins Nobel Prize for literature"; an Associated Press story was headlined: "Chinese writer Mo Yan wins Nobel literature prize." These headlines communicated the novelty of the co-occurrence of China and the Nobel Prize, carrying perhaps some implication that this was unexpected or even controversial. However, the leads to these texts consistently performed much more discursive work. As van Dijk (1988) notes, these initial sentences to news texts convey the prioritized elements of the news story and usually reveal the "underlying semantic macrostructure" of the text, that is, the key ideas that organize or subsume lower-level ideas presented later in the text (p. 189). Here, the macrostructure was one in which Mo and the literary prize were aligned with the Chinese state and authoritarianism and in opposition to critical or dissident voices and the Nobel Peace Prize, which were aligned with the West and with human rights.

The news was structured, then, around a highly politicized framing of the awarding of the literary prize, in which the top-level gist of the story was of a writer from an authoritarian state. Indeed, Mo Yan, together with the literary world he inhabits and the Nobel Prize in Literature, were marginal to many of the news intros. Instead, two subjects, namely the 2010 Nobel Peace Prize winner, Chinese dissident Liu Xiaobo, and political controversies in China, often eclipsed Mo's award. For example, the *Wall Street Journal* began its story this way:

> Chinese writer Mo Yan won the Nobel Prize for literature on Thursday, a move that could help offset a blow to China's image abroad two years after the Nobel Peace Prize went to a Chinese human-rights activist. (Chin, Mozur, & Trachtenberg, 2012)

Mo's win is here read as achieving political work in countervailing an (assumed) negative image of China. Similarly, the Associated Press wrote that Mo's win suggested a thaw to a two-year-old tension with Norway prompted by the awarding of the Nobel Peace Prize in 2010. Moreover, under the headline,

"After Past Fury for Peace Prize, China Embraces Nobel Choice," the *New York Times* wrote:

> Two years ago, when the jailed Chinese dissident Liu Xiaobo won the Nobel Peace Prize, the government reacted with contempt and fury, scrubbing the announcement from the Internet, condemning the award as a "desecration" and calling it a Western propaganda tool intended to insult and destabilize the ruling Communist Party. (Jacobs & Lyall, 2012)

In this item, both the headline and the lead set Mo Yan and the Nobel Literature Prize entirely to the side, concentrating on the Peace Prize winner in 2010 and the government's reaction. Elsewhere the shift in attention from Mo to Liu was less dramatic but consistently placed emphasis on the Chinese dissident and away from the current news event. Mo Yan's win was neglected or excluded in news leads and, to borrow Hall's (1997) term, the ostensible news subject was sent into "symbolic exile." There is some irony that the critical approach taken toward China here drifts itself toward a totalitarian discourse, in which all culture, individuality, and social activity are imagined to align with the state, for this is what the discourse itself criticizes the Chinese state for doing.

The news was, furthermore, frequently angled on controversy and particularly on political controversy. For example, the Associated Press defined Mo as "the first Chinese winner of the literature prize who is not a critic of the authoritarian government." This definition overstated the association of the prize with criticism of China, given that there had only been one previous Chinese winner of the prize, Gao Xingjian in 2000. That line was also reproduced in the *Pittsburgh Post-Gazette*'s account (Olesen & Nordstrom, 2012a). The Associated Press further explained Mo's writing in terms of tactical politics: "Mo is known for challenging the status quo without offending those who uphold it" (Olesen & Nordstrom, 2012b). The *Christian Science Monitor* told readers that Mo "has drawn criticism for his cozy relations with the government" (Ford, 2012). For the *Charleston Gazette*, the award engendered pride, "but critics say novelist is complicit with nation's history of censorship" (Olesen & Nordstrom, 2012c). In one of its texts, the *New York Times* gave Mo an unusually long attributive clause that exemplifies the way Mo was not only discussed in terms of a political context but defined by that context: "Mo Yan, a wildly prolific and internationally renowned Chinese author who considers himself nonpolitical but whose embrace by the ruling Communist Party has drawn criticism from dissident writers, was awarded the 2012 Nobel Prize in literature Thursday" (Lyall & Jacobs, 2012). The *Wall Street Journal* reminded its audience that "there was [*sic*] wild celebrations in some quarters, but strong disappointment in others" (Sala, 2012a). The news leads cited here indicate a trend of translating a cultural prize into a political object. The primary news value of the Chinese writer was as a symbol of China, and that symbol was invested almost universally with meanings around authoritarianism and the curtailment of human rights.

Mo Yan as Extension of the State

Set up in this way, the news texts then went on to expend considerable symbolic work on associating Mo Yan with the state and with censorship. The portrayal of Mo mainly focused on his pen name, his experiences in the People's Liberation Army, the official position he holds, and his relations with the Chinese government. Mo Yan, to a large extent, was depicted as a Chinese figure fixed within the communist system rather than as a writer who had made contributions to an artistic world or as an individual. Of concern here is that the writer became shoehorned into a stereotypical representation to the extent that he and his Chinese context became misrepresented.

Most media noted that Mo Yan is a pen name, which can be translated as "don't speak" (his real name being Guan Moye). Journalists tended to connect this name closely with censorship and political troubles in China, informing the audience that such a pen name was Mo's "parents' admonition" (Siems & Yang, 2012) and a reminder to "hold his tongue and stay out of trouble" (Olesen & Nordstrom, 2012b). CNN produced the only text in the sample to give an alternative explanation and also the only text to cite Mo about his name: "Mo told local media in 2003 that his pen name is a word play on his original middle name, but also a reminder to himself that he should talk less and write more" (Sterling & Jiang, 2012).

Few media mentioned the historical background of the naming, that is, its origination in a particularly sensitive period of China in the 1950s and 1960s. Instead, news media took every chance to make "Mr. Don't Speak" a symbol of the position of art in today's China. For example, the *Washington Post* chose a small part of Mo's interview with CCTV to reinforce the image of "Mr. Don't Speak." Mo was reported as answering, "I don't know" to CCTV's question "Are you happy?" after he won the prize (Yu, 2012). Mo's words immediately following "I don't know," which explored his understanding of happiness and his feelings about the pressures of fame, were omitted. However, those words would have given readers insight into the Chinese cultural value of self-deprecation that was at work here. Through these acts of cutting and emphasis, Mo Yan was depicted as a man who dares not talk.

Moreover, Mo's reply on hearing the winning news, "overjoyed and terrified," was quoted by news media as evidence of the name matching reality. For example, the *New York Times* regarded Mo's answer as "one of the most poignant Nobel reactions in memory" and explained that "it isn't hard to imagine why a writer who chose 'Mo Yan' as his pen name would find fear at the heart of such a happy occasion" (Siems & Yang, 2012). Yet, on the other hand, other comments by Mo, which related to politics or human rights, were used extensively in the texts, without entertaining the possibility that they weakened the symbolic construction of him as reticent and fearful. Mo was widely quoted stating that the political dissident, Liu, should be able to enjoy his freedom, as well as that some kind of censorship promotes creativity. It is possible to see a disjuncture between these different representations of Mo's talk, yet the texts tended instead to construct Mo's comments as "controversial," thereby privileging his position as normally subservient to the state. It should also be noted that Mo is not a prominent source in the news samples, despite his supposedly central position in the news event, and he was quoted mostly when he touched on political issues. Again, a prevalent political media frame can be seen to be at work fixing Mo Yan in a particular symbolic structure.

This trend was pervasive. Aspects of Mo's biography and talk were quoted that reinforced the interpretation of him as close to, if not subsumed within, the state. Besides the focus on his pen name, there was considerable media interest also in Mo's army experience and the official role he occupies. A set of oppositions were built up within and across sentences so as to produce a conflict between an idea of what kind of literary figure Mo is and an implicit sense of what a Chinese writer "should be." Many news media informed readers that Mo was both an artist and a former soldier in the People's Liberation Army. The Associated Press, for example, wrote: "Mo, who started writing while in the army, has steered clear from criticizing the government in public" (Olesen & Nordstrom, 2012b). In pragmatic terms, the mention of his army career is made relevant to understanding the literary career of someone who has been avowedly critical of the state (Wilson & Sperber, 2004). In making this information relevant, a base position is implied that a Chinese writer would criticize the state, unless she or he was somehow prevented from doing so. The *Wall Street Journal* draws upon the same assumption in slightly different form, writing that Mo's "belonging to the PLA offered cover so that, paradoxically, he could write more freely than others" (Sala, 2012b). This paradox only works in a binary set of oppositions about China: on the one hand, living in China, being oppressed, propaganda, and institutions of the state such as the army; on the other, being a writer, being critical of the state, and being independent. The text goes on to state that Mo "remained under the army's protective wing until 10 years ago," without providing further evidence. Mo's army experience is enough to work as proof for the Western media of a close relationship with the government and a lack of independence.

In the same way, Mo's official position as vice-chair of the Chinese Writers' Association drew much criticism in news reports. Within the news texts, the Chinese Writers' Association was widely labeled as "official," "government-run," "state sanctioned," and "government-sponsored," which underscored the tie between the association and the government. By emphasizing Mo's official position, Mo emerges again as a writer who lacks independence, who embraces the establishment, decides not to take a stand against the government, and thus is the object of much criticism. This criticism is sometimes made explicit, although the logical links producing the idea are not. The *New York Times* wrote that Mo "does not consider himself political, and his decision not to take a stand against the government—as well as his position as vice chairman of the state-run Chinese Writers' association—has drawn criticism from Chinese dissident writers" (Jacobs & Lyall, 2012). In the NPR program *Morning Edition*, host Renee Montagne introduced Mo Yan this way: "He is the first Chinese Nobel winner who is not in exile, or in prison; and that offers a clue as to why the choice has sparked criticism" (Lim, 2012). Throughout the texts, a simple syllogism, as pointed out by Julia Lovell (2006), is at work: a Chinese figure is good if a dissident and bad if associated with the state. The *Wall Street Journal* makes this point of view more clear:

> When writers from countries without freedom of expression are awarded important prizes, we expect them to have artistic merits, and to be capable of standing up to repressive governments. Mo Yan certainly is a worthy writer, but disappoints some on the second count. He is, after all, vice president of the government-sponsored National Writers Association and a Communist Party member. (Sala, 2012b)

The dichotomy between writers in countries with freedom of expression and those without can also be read as a dichotomy—for which the Nobel Prize in Literature has been criticized in the past—between Western writers who have an aesthetic role and those elsewhere who have more of a developmental role (Lovell, 2006). Mo "disappoints," by which we may assume he is thought of as a lesser writer, for not fitting the expected role of dissident political conscience.

The lack of explicitness in these constructions of Mo is significant, for it allows these dichotomies to emerge as self-evident. This can be seen in two further ways in which controversies were created around Mo. One was Mo's withdrawal from a seminar at the Frankfurt Book Fair in 2009 after Chinese dissidents were allowed to participate. The other was Mo's participation in hand-copying Mao Zedong's 1937 talks on art and literature, which it claimed is the basis for Chinese propaganda policies. Anonymous voices were widely employed when discussing the two events, such as "some have criticized Mr. Mo's failure to take a political stand," "he was also criticized for attending," "fellow writers, especially outside the establishment, mistrust," and so on. Particularly given the political frame within which the Nobel Prize in Literature announcement was discussed, the anonymous or abstract form that the criticism takes encourages the reader to occupy the position of those criticizing Mo. The criticism is allowed to be immanent and therefore harder to contextualize or question. Mo stands as an object of criticism, distanced from readers as an Other associated with things that people criticize.

Almost entirely absent from these news texts is any detail that would allow the U.S. public to understand Mo's career or his art in his own terms. Mo's military service is discussed without any mention of the requirement to serve; the status and function of the Chinese Writers' Association is not explained; the difference of the management of culture after the Cultural Revolution is neglected. Most importantly, the news texts make almost no mention of the symbolic importance within China of the award of the Nobel Prize in Literature to Mo Yan. Shih (2004) notes that the award of the prize in 2000 to the exiled avant-garde writer Gao Xingjian enraged intellectual as well as official figures in China as a political act and an attempt to vilify China (p. 25). Gao had approached the "universal validity" that is the central criterion of the prize by being less Chinese, in this view, condemning the great writers of mainstream Chinese literature for being unable to attain such a status of universality. This Chinese anger at a Western prize claiming the space of a universal aesthetic, and its counterpoint, the joy at receiving recognition 12 years later, imbue Mo with a quite different politics, which Western reporting was unable to communicate.

Overall, the U.S. news media's representation of Mo Yan is highly constrained by the political frame put on the award for the Nobel Prize in Literature. He becomes a mystified figure, filled with the meanings associated with an authoritarian state. Mo Yan was widely labeled "Mr. Don't Speak," and that image was reinforced by choosing to present only part of Mo's speech. His experience in the army together with his current official position were emphasized by many news media, positioning him within a set of oppositions between freedom and oppression. Selective events took on significance within that dichotomy and were allowed to become generalized and universalized through the use of anonymous voices and the omission of other perspectives. By the reduction and subjugation of his personality, humanity, and individual complexity, the media's representation of Mo turned him into a stereotyped Other composed of political and mystifying features. "By any standard, Mr. Mo is an enigma wrapped in Chinese characteristics" (Yu, 2012), as the *Washington Times* summarized.

Reducing the Cultural to the Political

The work to construct Mo, and the Chinese context he emerges from, as Others to a Western imaginary is nowhere clearer than in the treatment of his literary achievement. Mo's writing style is interpreted in relatively narrow terms as the product of censorship or alternatively as an extension of Western literary forms. The writing becomes knowable, then, in terms that rarely extend beyond the political and cultural reference points of the U.S. public, and indeed work to reinforce those reference points.

The literary technique of Mo's works was described in the Royal Swedish Academy of Sciences' citation as "hallucinatory realism [that] merges folk tales, history and the contemporary." In the news texts, again as a result of the political frame that dominates the reporting, this tends to be interpreted as a means of avoiding censorship. CNN quoted a *Time* magazine interview in which the interviewer reflected that "the adroit subtlety of his magic-realist style" aids Mo Yan in avoiding "stirring up the animosity of the country's ever vigilant censors" (Sterling & Jiang, 2012). Similarly, citing Mo's interview with British literary magazine *Granta*, the *Washington Post*, the *New York Times*, the *Star-Tribune*, the *Charleston Gazette,* and the Associated Press reported that Mo considered censorship as a great spur to creativity. For the *Tampa Bay Times*, the employment of "satire and fantasy" gives Mo "a virtual cushion against the government's wrath" (Maxwell, 2012). The *New York Times* noted that humor is "one way to describe Mo Yan's sentences" and added that "a certain amused distance makes it easier to take in his mostly rural Chinese universe, its unfairness, its casual violence, its stench, its tragedies, its Kafkaesque frustrations" (Bernstein, 2012).

The texts certainly contain brutal stories, but the harshness of the imagined world become read rather simplistically as a cipher for the harsh realities of rural China, in a way that one would not expect in a review of dark Western literature. More directly, the Associated Press deployed the citation to call Mo "a man of humor who has used that wit to avoid possible persecution." The *Wall Street Journal* pointed out that horror in Mo's work is represented by the Japanese invasion and his writings "purposefully avoid all mention of historical facts." It notes that Mo's reason for doing this is to achieve a sense of timelessness but interprets the technique as allowing him "to steer clear of directly describing, and criticizing, the current regime" (Sala, 2012b). The reductionism of these accounts, reducing literature to politics and constructing as a backdrop a horror-filled caricature of contemporary China, makes it less likely that any intercultural understanding would arise from reading about the award. The reader can easily dismiss Mo's award, as some commentators did explicitly, as a matter of its being China's turn rather than for literary merit.

Attempts to understand the literary achievement being rewarded by the academicians tended, perhaps inevitably, to use reference points in Western literature. In the tight space of initial news stories, these references were not elaborated. When journalists wrote at greater length, these reference points were expanded further only in one instance, instead for the most part portraying the Chinese author as a secondary figure dependent on the Western canon. Thus, the style of hallucinatory realism was widely reported as reminiscent of Western literature techniques, with only a few media noticing the impact of the Chinese literary tradition. The *Wall Street Journal*, the Dow Jones News Service, NPR, and PBS informed their audiences that Mo's mythic and absurd stories were influenced by Western writers like William Faulkner and Gabriel García Márquez; *USA Today* and the Gannett News Service called Mo Yan "China's Faulkner"; *WashingtonPost.com* described Mo's works as Dickensian, quoting Mo Yan's American translator Howard Goldblatt's words; the Dow Jones Global Equities News compared Mo Yan to William Faulkner, Charles Dickens, and François Rabelais, drawing on a Swedish radio interview with Peter Englund, the Academy's permanent secretary. It should be noted that most coverage or commentary only halted at these generalized terms, such as "China's Faulkner" and "Dickensian," leaving the comparison between Mo and Western writers rather vague. Some media, such as the *International Herald Tribune*, the *New York Times*, *Hollywood Reporter*, the *Virginian-Pilot*, the *Pittsburgh Post-Gazette*, and the *Atlanta Journal*, noted that Mo Yan had created a world reminiscent in its complexity of those in the writings of Western writers, and also found "a departure point in old Chinese literature and in oral tradition." However, little further explanation was provided.

The *Washington Post* is the only media outlet in the sample to elaborate on the influence of classic Chinese tales on Mo's literary style. It published, on October 12, an analysis of Mo's work by literary critic Steven Moore. Moore discusses his debt to traditional Chinese literature, such as animal characters, reincarnation, and an infernal descent to Lord Yama from Wu Chengen's novel *The Journey to the West* (circa 1570), reincarnation as a device from Cao Xueqin's *Story of the Stone* (circa 1760), and the philandering protagonist from *The Plum in the Golden Vase* (circa 1600). They were seen as "mashed up" with avant-garde techniques in Mo Yan's novels. Moore acknowledged the long history of Chinese novels and expressed that "it's satisfying to see the Nobel Prize go to a citizen of a country that was producing great novels long before Western novelists got in the game" (Moore, 2012). The rarity of this text, which frames Mo's work primarily as a literary achievement and uses description of Chinese politics to inform rather than determine the account, provides a sharp contrast to the reporting overall.

The treatment of the novels is significant for us because it was here more than any aspect of the reporting of the prize that the news media had an opportunity to cross cultural boundaries. The U.S. public, it should be said, is not exposed to many foreign novels (3% of novels are translations, by one account; Parks, 2014), but Nobel Prize–winning authors are among foreign literature that can expect to sell well. This opportunity was not embraced in the dominant media response to the announcement that subsumed the literary story under more newsworthy and familiar stories about China. In doing so, the longstanding cultural apparatus of colonialism was reinforced, as the East was represented as learning from the West, and as the aesthetic universal was associated with what the West produces. Culture here becomes an extension of politics rather than a moment when stereotypes and other tools of othering are made a little less stable.

Reading China in Well-Worn Themes

A number of news media discussed the novels in the longer stories that announced the prize and in their arts sections. Even when these texts were written by news rather than arts reporters, the paragraphs on the novels occurred lower down where the initial political frame of the lead was no longer such a structuring force. They also drew on what were clearly preexisting stories from news archives. The journalistic task here was to give some background information to the news, an element of news text that conventionally comprises uncontroversial facts that can "speak for themselves" (Tuchman, 1972). For all these reasons, the othering of Mo and of Chinese culture and politics was thought likely to be less evident. Instead, we found different forms of othering arising alongside and in interrelation with the dominant political frame.

A key feature of the representations of the novels was a tendency to reduce the novels to their themes, drawing out longstanding interpretations of China. Mo's novel *Red Sorghum* was widely mentioned in the sample, thanks in part to director Zhang Yimou's acclaimed 1987 film adaptation, and largely written about in these terms. The *Pittsburgh Post-Gazette* said *Red Sorghum* was "an account of the hardships endured by generations of a family in the Chinese countryside, including the brutality of the Japanese invasion" (Lasseter, 2012). The *New York Times* wrote similarly that *Red Sorghum* "takes on issues like the Japanese occupation, bandit culture and the harsh lives of rural Chinese" (Lyall & Jacobs, 2012). These references tend to describe the novel in terms of "headline" items of Chinese history and society that readers might already be familiar with. Although there is a stereotypical dimension here, the news texts do not draw on any easy Orientalism in speaking of the novels. They eschew the pleasurable images of the exotic, mysterious, sensual, and sentimental, despite the tendency among Western publishers to promote Chinese novels in these terms (Lovell, 2006). The *Wall Street Journal* wrote that the novel combined "gritty realism with surreal imagery" (O'Kane, 2012). The words *peasant*, *rural*, or *farmer* often occur in nearby sentences, grounding the accounts in the real rather than Oriental fantasy. Indeed, almost every sentence describing the novel is within a few sentences of one describing the author's peasant roots, his early poverty, and his careful negotiation of political control during the Cultural Revolution and since.

Not all the novels were treated in this way. A more Orientalist mode is evident in the brief discussion of *Big Breasts and Wide Hips* in one news text, describing the novel in terms of a "spoiled illegitimate child," with a "breast-obsession" and "skewed moral compass" (Sala, 2012a). The news texts did, however, tend to reduce the novel to its themes, neglecting the human dimension of the stories. Only the *Wall Street Journal* drew attention to the vivid characters of the novel. It told readers that in *Red Sorghum*, "history happens to those whose lives are usually forgotten, like peasants, bandits, beggars, mercenaries and even noodle-stall owners" and "each character is doggedly busy in countless acts of daily heroism in order to stay alive" (Sala, 2010b). The romance, social drama, and historical background of the family saga at the heart of the novel were less relevant for most commentators. Part of the reason for this is the compressed space of some of these texts; but in the longer texts, too, we found the novel, much like Mo himself, used in metonymic terms to talk about much that would be already familiar to a U.S. audience. The novel was about peasant China more than about peasants in China.

Similarly, Mo's novel *The Garlic Ballads* was summed up by the Associated Press as about "a peasant uprising and official corruption." This thematic statement was widely reused by, for example, the *Commercial Appeal*, *St. Louis Post-Dispatch*, and the *Charleston Gazette*. As in other aspects of the texts, this thematization drifted toward reducing the cultural to the political. For the *New York Times*, *The Garlic Ballads* describes "a peasant insurrection against government malfeasance, telling it in a semi-mythical fashion that avoids criticizing specific government officials" (Jacobs & Lyall, 2012) and laid bare "the brutality, greed and corruption that has flourished under Communist rule" (Lovell, 2012). The Dow Jones *Global Equities News* read the novel for its relevance to the political controversy over the award to a writer not avowedly anti-Communist. It excerpted a quote attributed to Stalin in *The Garlic Ballads*:

> Novelists are forever trying to distance themselves from politics, but the novel itself closes in on politics. Novelists are so concerned with "man's fate" that they tend to lose sight of their own fate. Therein lies their tragedy.[2]

By highlighting this excerpt, the reporter suggested that the quotation "takes on new resonance in the light of recent criticisms of Mo" for not being more outspoken on behalf of politically active writers (Dow Jones, 2012). Again, literary dimensions were restricted and read in terms of politics.

This reading was most explicit in relation to the novel *Frog*, where the political frame was overwhelming, despite the novel's central theme of sexism being easy to translate into the U.S. context. The novel was widely reported as looking at "forced abortions and other coercive aspects of the government's policies restricting most families to one child" (Olesen & Nordstrom, 2012c). The *Tampa Bay Times* depicted Mo as "having grown up under the brutality of

Maoist extremism" and as rejecting "the government's unforgiving one-child family planning program" (Maxwell, 2012). As evidence, it pointed to *Frog*. The *Wall Street Journal* reminded readers that "most of the atrocities Mo Yan's heroes must endure and fight against are from a pre-Communist era," while *Frog* is an exception that "addresses the brutality of the one-child policy" (Sala, 2012b). CNN looked for contemporary relevance, discussing how the traditional Chinese preference for boys over girls, as explored in the novel *Frog*, has fed the practice of aborting female fetuses or abandoning infant girls in rural parts of China (Sterling & Jiang, 2012). This framing occurred despite the expert sources drawn on. In NPR's program *All Things Considered*, Mo's primary English translator Howard Goldblatt was invited to talk about Mo's literature. After introducing the novel to the audience, he read his translation of a section, which narrates the heroine's terror when surrounded by the croaks of toads and frogs at night. The relationship between the heroine and frogs, and the metaphor of the frog, were not pursued, however. Instead, the host shifted the topic abruptly to political issues: "It turns out Mo Yan is afraid of frogs. In a *Granta* podcast from the London Book Fair this year, he said censorship is a fact of his literary life" (Ulaby, 2012). Then archived audio was played in which Mo talked about censorship. Even in such a longer-form treatment led by an expert voice, Mo's work was brought back sharply within the political frame.

The one exception was a republished review of *Big Breasts and Wide Hips* from the *Washington Post* (Yardley, 2012). This review by literary critic Jonathan Yardley, first published in 2004, was reproduced no doubt partly because it described the novel as pitched to the Nobel Prize. He elaborated the book's literary merit (laudable ambition, self-evident humanity), its literary shortcomings (it only infrequently achieved literary grace or distinction), prominent conviction (feminism), the difficulties in reading Chinese novels (the unfamiliarity of the Chinese proper names), and the main characters. *Big Breasts and Wide Hips*, in this review, seems to be the center of discussion and to be presented with context and cultural background. Yardley used Salman Rushdie's *Midnight's Children* and Gabriel García Márquez's *One Hundred Years of Solitude* to make sense of the history of Mo's country or continent and employed Ang Lee's film *Crouching Tiger, Hidden Dragon* to make sense of the "almost uniformly terrific" female characters in the novel. By connecting Western readers' cultural reference points to Mo's novel, Yardley's review facilitates an understanding of literature across cultures. Moreover, Yardley notices the difficulty in translating literary works from Chinese to English and expresses his difficulty when reading a Chinese novel. The space between cultures is made evident rather than conflated in ways that privilege the Western. While the novel draws upon some of the thematic material that other accounts of the novels did (the Red Guard, breast-obsession, Chinese women who are exploited, undervalued, and despised by a patriarchal society), the review carefully offered context for these features. After describing the perception of the Chinese preference for boys over girls, Yardley historicizes these attitudes to the inter-war years in particular and notes rights and opportunities gained by women in China in more recent years.

The novels, then, can be discussed in terms that extend beyond what U.S. audiences already (think they) know about China. However, none of the contemporary texts do this, only Yardley's reprinted review. In the sporadic mentions of Mo's novels, they are used metonymically to describe China. In losing some of the specificity of their characters, time, and Mo's rearticulation of social issues, they become subsumed under the central framing of the articles. Mo's writings are not fully assimilated to the frame of an authoritarian China and are not an exotic Oriental product, but they are decontextualized, leaving audiences with "headline" information about Chinese politics, society, and history that is likely to do little to broaden their horizons. Above all, the idea of an Eastern Other organizes the way the novels are referred to.

CONCLUSION

This study reveals an evident binary discourse of self/other. The U.S. news samples depicted Mo as a stereotyped Other and gave their audiences few ways to understand Mo or his literary contribution outside of those stereotypes. Through various mechanisms, namely politicized and mystified figures and events, symbolic exile, generalization, differentiation, and decontextualization, a consistent and limited set of frames emerges. Chinese writer Mo Yan was reduced to a Communist figure as well as an enigma wrapped in Chinese characteristics; Mo's prize was overshadowed by Chinese dissidents' previous Nobel prizes; Chinese literature was discussed largely in terms of challenging repressive regimes and struggling for artistic freedom. All of these align with findings of previous studies on Western media representations of China (e.g., Dorogi, 2001; Naduvath, 2014; Spence, 1990; Wang, 2005), contending that Western perceptions of China have been distorted, with a legacy of narrow and reductive representation.

The Nobel Prize in Literature is a rare moment in global cultural exchange, when literature makes it to the top of the news agenda and when boundaries between "our" literature and others' are broken. It is one of the rare global cultural events and has considerable authority and symbolic power, despite the Swedish Academy's protestations that it claims no power to judge the year's "best" literary figure. It is sobering, then, that when the Swedish Academy reached beyond Western literatures to reward a Chinese novelist, the U.S. news media struggled to report the event in ways that might broaden their audiences' horizons. In concluding, we wish to point to some of the factors we see at work in this relatively rigid structure of meaning.

First, it is clear that a perceived political dichotomy between the United States and China is a powerful force organizing the coverage. Herman and Chomsky's (1988) argument that an anti-Communist ideology filters the news that the U.S. public receives has been criticized as out of date. The analysis above should give that critique pause. The wholesale demonization of left-wing ideology and of Communist countries is perhaps harder to discern, but a similar role is played in the coverage of Mo's prize by a set of oppositions between authoritarianism and human rights. The particulars of Mo's life and literary career are immediately and powerfully lined up in accordance with the notion of China as lacking in human rights. As a non-dissident writer and as a writer celebrated at home (notwithstanding the banning of one of his books for a time), he becomes associated with that lack of human rights. There appears little middle ground available in the reporting. It is hard to discern, in the U.S. reporting of this Chinese figure, the multilayered global publicity that Reese (2009) describes as emerging or the globalized discursive spaces that Volkmer (1999) argues for.

Second, we would suggest that the West continues to need the East, despite the breakdown of formerly dominant Orientalizing structures. Mo Yan's novels cannot be understood in terms of the extraordinary discourse of the mysterious Orient stretching from Morocco to Japan (Said, 1979). But considerable identity work was going on in reporting the announcement of the Nobel Prize in Literature. The East continues to be a binary opposite for the West, politically, sociologically, ideologically, and imaginatively, if in different terms to the past. China and Chinese individuals are managed by the West through this understanding. Human rights are part of this discourse, as already noted, but the analysis suggests to us something more thoroughgoing: Mo and his novels are squeezed, with considerable symbolic violence, into a representation of China and of a non-Western Other more generally. As Sander L. Gilman noted, stereotypes perform powerful work when the self is unstable or weak. "Stereotypes arise when self-integration is threatened. They are therefore part of our way of dealing with the instabilities of our perception of the world" (in Hall, 1997, p. 284). Mo perhaps became an empty signifier (Laclau, 1996) in which the cultural political work of the West was able to take place, allowing a rational, progressive, civil, and humanistic self to be sustained. It is perhaps too strong to say that, as China rises in significance on the world stage and as people see and hear more about it through Western coverage of its economic, political, and social activities, this discursive work performs a role of validating a threatened U.S. political self. But it is available to understand a partially known China and allows for a stable U.S. self-identity in a changing world.

Third, due to the cultural distance between the United States and China, journalists reporting on the award of a literary prize to a Chinese figure have limited knowledge resources to draw on. As shown in the analysis, most of the texts relied upon "headline" knowledge when talking about Mo and his works, much as they scrambled in 2000 when reporting on Gao's Nobel Prize (Lovell, 2006). Stereotypes arise in a context of limited knowledge. Hermeneutics proposes that all knowledge begins with the already known (Gadamer, 1975) but that understanding depends upon the testing of previous knowledge through an encounter with the Other and through further information about the Other. It is telling that of the news organizations that produced the texts analyzed here, it was the elite media such as the *New York Times* and the *Washington Post* that produced the rare text that extended beyond the already known, through providing more detail on Mo and his literary work. Most news organizations had no encounter with the other but reworked Associated Press copy to refresh and extend that knowledge. A retreat into a political discourse can be partially explained by the foreignness of the Chinese literature in which Mo is embedded and of the Chinese social and historical concerns with which his novels are concerned. This case study saw opportunities for a cosmopolitan encounter with the Other in the U.S. news media.

To sum up, ideological divergence, cultural distance, and enduring stereotypes manifest themselves in a biased understanding of Chinese realities, contributing to the othering discourse and warped media representations in U.S. media texts. The stereotyped othering trend is a serious problem in international news reporting, partly because of China's newfound prominence. Fortunately, representation is a dynamic process, leading to the dynamic reconstruction of meanings. Accordingly, stereotypes can be breached, remolded, and dispelled to a certain extent. How to weaken or dispel stereotypes is of great importance to cross-cultural communication. It might be easy to agree with Hall's (1997) proposition that stereotypes can be disrupted through contesting meaning, acknowledging and praising differences, but it is not easy to follow those tactics. In this study, at least we see some twinkles of hope for the construction of reciprocal understanding between cultures. For example, China launched an English literature magazine named *Pathlight* in November 2011, providing Western readers with a selection of China's distinctive literary voices. As the title indicates, the magazine aims to lighten the path of cross-cultural communication from a Chinese perspective. Journalists from Dow Jones *Global Equities News* and the *Wall Street Journal* turned to the magazine's contributing editors for opinion on Mo Yan's literary works as well as advice on Chinese books. Such an interaction between Chinese and American sides suggests their effort to fill the gap and create opportunities for dialogue.

NOTES

1. The only previous Chinese writer to receive the Nobel Prize in Literature was Gao Xing-jian, but he had moved to France and was a French citizen by the time he won in 2000.
2. This quotation, as explained in the Preface to the second edition of *The Garlic Ballads,* was made up by Mo Yan.

BIBLIOGRAPHY

Anderson, B. (1991). *Imagined communities: Reflections on the origin and spread of nationalism.* London: Verso.

Avraham, E. (2003). *Behind media marginality: Coverage of social groups and places in the Israeli media.* Lanham, MD: Lexington Books.

Bernstein, R. (2012, October 12). In China, a writer finds a deep well. *New York Times.*

Bodeen, C. (2012, October 13). Nobel Prize for Literature winner Mo hopes for freedom for dissident Peace Prize winner Liu. Associated Press.

Chin, J., Mozur, P., & Tractenberg, J. A. (2012, October 12). World news: Nobel places China in focus again. *Wall Street Journal.*

Clausen, L. (2004). Localizing the global: Domestication processes in international news production. *Media, Culture & Society, 26*(1), 25–44.

Corpus Ong, J. (2009). The cosmopolitan continuum: Locating cosmopolitanism in media and cultural studies. *Media, Culture & Society, 31*(3), 449–466.

Dorogi, T. L. (2001). *Tainted perceptions: Liberal democracy and American popular images of China.* Lanham, MD: University Press of America.

Dow Jones. (2012, October 15). China real time: Found in translation. Five Chinese books you should read. Dow Jones *Global Inequities News.*

Entman, R. (1993). Framing: Toward clarification of a fractured paradigm. *Journal of Communication, 43*(4), 51–58.

First, A. (2001). The good, the dad and the missing. *Panim, 17,* 86–94.

Ford, P. (2012, October 11). Chinese author Mo Yan wins Nobel Prize in Literature. *Christian Science Monitor.*

Gadamer, H.-G. (1975). *Truth and method.* Trans. W. Glen-Dopel. London: Sheed and Ward.

Gitlin, T. (1980). *The whole world is watching: Mass media in the making and unmaking of the new left.* Berkeley: University of California Press.

Goffman, E. (1974). *Frame analysis: An essay on the organization of experience.* Boston, MA: Northeastern University Press.

Goodman, R. S. (1999). Prestige press coverage of US-China policy during the Cold War's collapse and post–Cold War years. *Gazette, 61,* 391–410.

Grossberg, L., Wartella, E., Whitney, C. D., & Wise, J. M. (1998). *Media making: Mass media in popular culture.* London: Sage.

Hall, S. (Ed.). (1997). *Representation: Cultural representations and signifying practices.* Milton Keynes, UK: Open University Press.

Herman, E. S., & Chomsky, N. (1988). *Manufacturing consent. The political economy of the mass media.* New York: Pantheon.

Jacobs, A., & Lyall, S. (2012, October 12). After past fury for Peace Prize, China embraces Nobel choice. *New York Times.*

Jones, T. M., Van Aelst, P., & Vliegenthart, R. (2011). Foreign nation visibility in US news coverage: A longitudinal analysis (1950–2006). *Communication Research*. DOI:10.1177/009365 0211415845

Kellner, D. (1995). *Media culture*. London: Routledge.

Laclau, E. (1996). *Emancipation(s)*. London: Verso.

Lasseter, T. (2012, October 12). China hails Nobel won by novelist who toes the line politically. *Pittsburgh Post-Gazette*.

Liebes, T. (1997). *Reporting the Arab-Israeli conflict*. London: Routledge.

Lim, L. (2012, October 12). Nobel literature winner sparks some controversy. NPR, *Morning Edition*.

Lippmann, W. (1922). *Public opinion*. New York: Harcourt, Brace and Company.

Lovell, J. (2006). *The politics of cultural capital: China's quest for a Nobel Prize in Literature*. Hawaii: University of Hawaii Press.

Lovell, J. (2012, October 16). Mo Yan's Creative Space. *New York Times*.

Lyall, S., & Jacobs, A. (2012, October 12). China's Mo Yan wins Nobel Prize in Literature. *New York Times*.

Maxwell, B. (2012, October 21). Fantasies and harsh truths. *Tampa Bay Times*.

Moore, S. (2012, October 12). China's Mo Yan wins Nobel in Literature. *Washington Post*.

Naduvath, J. (2014). Examining representation of the non-local: China in the UK media in the run-up to the Beijing Olympics. *China Report, 50*, 109–129.

O'Kane, B. (2012, October 15). Found in translation: Five Chinese books you should read. *China Real Time, Wall Street Journal* [blog]. Retrieved from http://blogs.wsj.com/chinarealtime

Olesen, A., & Nordstrom, L. (2012a, October 11). Chinese writer wins Nobel Literature Prize. *Pittsburgh Post-Gazette*.

Olesen, A., & Nordstrom, L. (2012b, October 12). Chinese writer Mo Yan wins Nobel Literature Prize; known for bawdy, sprawling tales. Associated Press.

Olesen, A., & Nordstrom, L. (2012c, October 12). Chinese author wins Nobel Prize; award draws pride, but critics say novelist is complicit with nation's history of censorship. *Charleston Gazette*.

Parks, T. (2014, July 11). Can books cross borders? *Financial Times*, July 11. Retrieved from http://www.ft.com/cms/s/2/a68127ea-0765-11e4-b1b0-00144feab7de.html#axzz3B-vz8x2jr

Peng, Z. (2004). Picturing China: A longitudinal analysis of the photo coverage in the *New York Times* and *Los Angeles Times*. Paper presented at International Communication Association conference, New Orleans. Retrieved from http://citation.allacademic.com//meta/p_mla_apa_research_citation/1/1/3/0/0/pages113002/p113002-1.php

Reese, S. D. (2001). Prologue-framing public life: A bridging model for media research. In S. D. Reese, O. H. Gandy Jr., & A. E. Grant (Eds.), *Framing public life: Perspectives on media and our understanding of the social world* (pp. 7–32). Mahwah, NJ: Lawrence Erlbaum.

Reese, S. D. (2009). The global village and the networked society: Reflections on the "media globalization myth." Paper presented at International Communication Association conference, Chicago. Retrieved from http://www.colorado.edu/journalism/globalmedia/kai%20hafez%20critique.pdf

Said, E. W. (1979). *Orientalism*. New York: Vintage.

Sala, I. M. (2012a, October 16). Mo Yan and Nobel expectations; Mo Yan has dodged politics up till now, but the Nobel confers new responsibility. *Wall Street Journal*.

Sala, I. M. (2012b, October 16). The Nobel Prize: A complicated honor. *Wall Street Journal*.

Seib, P., & Powers, S. (2010). *China in the news: A comparative analysis of the China coverage of BBC World, CNN International, and Deutsche Welle.* U.S. Center on Public Diplomacy, July 1. Retrieved from http://uscpublicdiplomacy.org/sites/uscpublicdiplomacy.org/files/legacy/media/China_in_the_News_Report.pdf.

Shih, S.-M. (2004). Global literature and the technologies of recognition. *PMLA, 119*(1), 16–30.

Siems, L., & Yang, J. (2012, October 18). China's Nobels. *New York Times.*

Spence, J. (1990). Western perceptions of China from the late sixteenth century to the present. In P. S. Ropp (Ed.), *Heritage of China: Contemporary perspectives of Chinese civilization* (pp. 1–14). Los Angeles: University of California Press.

Sreberny-Mohammadi, A., Nordenstreng, K., Stevenson, R., & Ugboajah, F. (Eds.). (1985). *Foreign news in the media: International reporting in 29 countries.* No. 93, UNESCO Reports and Papers on Mass Communication. Paris: UNESCO.

Sterling, J., & Jiang, S. (2012, October 12). Prolific Nobel Winner's pen name? "Not Talking." CNN Wire.

Tankard, J. W. (2001). The empirical approach to the study of media framing. In S. D. Reese, O. H. Gandy, & A. E. Grant (Eds.), *Framing public life: Perspectives on media and our understanding of the social world* (pp. 95–106). Mahwah, NJ: Lawrence Erlbaum.

Thussu, D. K. (2000). Development news versus globalized infotainment. In A. Malek & A. P. Kavoori (Eds.), *The global dynamics of news: International news coverage and news agenda* (pp. 323–340). Stamford, CT: Ablex.

Tuchman, G. (1972). Objectivity as strategic ritual: An examination of newsmen's notions of objectivity. *American Journal of Sociology, 77*(4), 660–679.

Tuchman, G. (1978). *Making news: A study in the construction of reality.* New York: Free Press.

Ulaby, N. (2012, October 11). Nobel-winning Chinese writer inspired by Faulkner. NPR, *All Things Considered.*

van Dijk, T. A. (1988). *News as discourse.* Hillsdale, NJ: Lawrence Erlbaum.

Volkmer, I. (1999). *News in the global sphere: A study of CNN and its impact on global communication.* Luton, UK: University of Luton Press.

Voloshinov, V. N. (1986). *Marxism and the philosophy of language.* Cambridge, MA: Harvard University Press.

Wang, H. (2005). National image building and Chinese foreign policy. In Y. Deng & F. L. Wang (Eds.), *China rising: Power and motivation in Chinese foreign policy* (pp. 73–102). Lanham, MD: Rowman & Littlefield.

Weimann, G. (2000). *Communication unreality: Modern media and the reconstruction of reality.* Thousand Oaks, CA: Sage.

Wilke, J., Heimprecht, C., & Cohen, A. (2012). The geography of foreign news on television: A comparative study of 17 countries. *International Communication Gazette, 74*(4), 301–322.

Wilson, D., & Sperber, D. (2004). Relevance theory. In L. R. Horn & G. Ward (Eds.), *The handbook of pragmatics* (pp. 607–632). Oxford, UK: Blackwell.

Wolfsfeld, G. (1997). *Media and political conflict: News from the Middle East.* Cambridge, UK: Cambridge University Press.

Yardley, J. (2012, October 11). Mo Yan: "Big Breasts and Wide Hips"; Jonathan Yardley's review of the Nobel Prize-Winner's novel. WashingtonPost.com.

Yu, M. (2012, October 18). Inside China, Mr. "Don't Speak" speaks. *Washington Times.*

The Presence OF Group Language Prejudice IN News Coverage AND Organizations

CHAPTER EIGHT

Discourse Bias AND
Face-TO-Face Negotiation

Intercultural Analysis of Coverage of the Wenchuan Earthquake

BO SHAN AND XUE LIU

Earthquakes struck Wenchuan, Sichuan province, in 2008. This disaster challenged the newly published *Regulations on Open Government Information.* The Chinese government executed a movement to rescue victims and rebuild life in the disaster area while learning to open information to the public. How the Chinese government distributed information of the disaster and how the Chinese media reported the disaster were reported in the Western media. The coverage showed that the Chinese mainstream media were satisfied to find that Western news reports about the Chinese government and media's role in the earthquake were positive. The Chinese public's anger at the Western media was fading. The website *anti-CNN*, which was launched to reveal the bias of the Western media, posted only a few articles about the Western media's reporting of the earthquake. However, can we see these changes as a dramatic turn in the relationship between China and the West?

Experimental research about the news media and stereotypes proved that the stereotype of others has existed widely in Western mainstream media. Stereotype has been passed on in Western culture ingeniously and effectively (Devine & Elliot, 1995; Eid, 2014; Gorham, 2006). Our research found that there was less negative coverage about the Wenchuan earthquake in comparison to the coverage of the disturbance in Lhasa, Tibet, in the same year. And there were more balanced strategies being employed in the reporting. However, the overall discourse structurally embodied intergroup bias. It is obviously a kind of selective interpretation out of context that the Chinese mainstream media interpreted the coverage of Western media as positive reporting. The selective interpretation demonstrates another aspect of inter-group bias—people tend to choose the discourse of others consistent with their own in-group identity to maintain the face of the group. Here are the questions to be answered: How was the discourse bias of the Western media produced? And how can the face of the self-group be maintained through dialogue when there is bias?

METHODOLOGY: INTERGROUP DISCOURSE BIAS AND FACE-NEGOTIATION THEORY

G. W. Allport (1954) argued that language can delicately reflect people's thought structure. Through language, we can trace the intergroup stereotypes and preferences of in-group people. Anne Maass and colleagues proposed a theory of linguistic intergroup bias. It argued that in the context of intergroup interaction, language reflects stereotypes when the information is inconsistent with preexisting notions about in-group or out-group behaviors (Maass, Salvi, Arcuri, & Semin, 1989). People tend to use more abstract language to describe positive behaviors of in-group members and negative behaviors of out-group members. Meanwhile, people use more concrete language to describe the neg-ative behaviors of in-group members and the positive behaviors of out-group members.

The theory introduces a key concept—abstractness of the language. It suggests a four-level classification that distinguishes between verbs and adjectives: descriptive action verbs (DAVs), interpretive action verbs (IAVs), state-of-things verbs (SVs), and adjectives (ADJs). The descriptive action verbs are at the most concrete level and the adjectives are at the most abstract level. Abstract language describes features and status such as honesty, creativity, belief, and envy, which are abstracted from concrete observable behaviors. Concrete language describes concrete behaviors that can be observed and have beginnings and ends, such as kiss, visit, help, and threat.

The classification of the abstractness of the language can reveal the deep meaning of the intergroup verbal interaction. For example, there are four different ways with different levels of abstractness to describe the action that A shakes his fist at B: (1) *A beats B*. "Beat" is a descriptive action verb that describes a certain behavior objectively under a certain situation without positive or negative meaning. (2) *A hurts B*. Although the description still focuses on certain behaviors under certain situations, it adds explanation to the behavior that makes the description show negative meaning. (3) *A hates B*. "Hate" is a state verb without a beginning or ending of the behavior. It not only describes but also illuminates. (4) *A is offensive*. "Offensive" is a relatively stable personal characteristic. The characteristic can exist not only in the present situation but also can exist at other times and under any other situations. Thus, it has the quality of a stereotype. If A is an in-group member, people tend to describe the negative behavior with concrete language. However, if A is an out-group member, people tend to describe the negative behavior with abstract language. This language-using strategy is intergroup linguistic bias. It reveals a phenomenon that preexisting intergroup bias promotes the use of language with bias, and the language with bias in turn maintains the preexisting intergroup bias.

There are two causes of linguistic intergroup bias (Maass, Ceccarelli, & Rudin, 1996). The first one is the in-group protective motive, that is, people have a motivation to protect in-group members. Linguistic intergroup bias can strengthen or maintain group identity. Concrete language describes the behavior of persons but not the characteristics of the persons themselves. So concrete language may separate the behavior from the actor. However, abstract language describes durable and stable characteristics of a person unconsciously. Therefore, linguistic intergroup bias is a mechanism to praise in-group members and thereby maintain in-group identity.

The second cause is people's cognitive pattern, that is, people tend to use more abstract language to describe behaviors consistent with their expectations than behaviors inconsistent with their expectations. People feel that behaviors consistent with their expectations appear to be stable and representative. So relatively stable abstract language is suitable to describe behaviors consistent with one's expectation. As a matter of fact, people have different expectations for in-group or out-group members. People expect in-group members to have more positive behaviors. On the other hand, people expect out-group members to have more negative behaviors to confirm the imagination of out-group members' negative characteristics. But people think that out-group members' positive behaviors have nothing to do with their characteristics. To separate out-group members' positive behavior from their characteristics and maintain the stereotype, people will describe out-group positive behavior with concrete language.

Although people can perceive the positive behaviors of out-group members, they are convinced by stereotype that there are more possibilities of out-group members' negative behaviors. Therefore, people generally distinguish accidental positive behavior from common behaviors or individual behaviors from collective behaviors to maintain the preexisting stereotype. Behavior inconsistent with the stereotype is thought to be an accidental phenomenon. Positive behavior inconsistent with the stereotype must be interrelated with the special situation and will disappear soon. This kind of psychological pattern will become visible in the form of linguistic intergroup bias, that is, concrete language will be used to describe out-group positive behavior that is inconsistent with the stereotype.

But the theory of linguistic intergroup bias overlooks the phenomenon that people sometimes will use abstract language to describe out-group members' positive behaviors. Moreover, the positive meaning of the abstract language may be consistent with the out-group members' identity. If language is not analyzed as an integrated discourse, discourse bias that is hidden in the context, narrative structure, and meaning structure will be overlooked. Thus the communication will be false. In fact, positive or negative meaning of any language is not abstract or fixed. Meaning comes into being within a concrete context, within cultural values and ideologies. The classification of linguistic abstractness is insufficient to understand the meaning of language. On the other hand, people may magnify or give prominence to others' positive description of "our" behaviors and overlook or avoid others' negative description of "our" behaviors. Thus, discourse that maintains in-group identity has a competitive relationship with others' discourse. So, to classify abstract and concrete language, positive and negative language is insufficient to reveal existing bias in intergroup dialogue. We need to explore if people describe others within a certain group's frame and make the discourse biased. We need a more sophisticated method to analyze intergroup discourse bias. It presumes that people are used to describing out-group behaviors with their own discourse frame and that stereotypes dominate the understanding of positive and negative meaning.

Furthermore, intergroup communication is a kind of social interaction. Negative or positive meaning of intergroup discourse bias is not determined by language or discourse alone but generated through the process in which people maintain self-image and seek others' approval. That is to say, it exists in the intergroup's "face-negotiation." Stella Ting-Toomey (1988) argues that the face is the individual's self-image emerging in a certain relational context, and it is a need that individuals expect social approval from others. Face-as-identity means actors define each other by communicating in certain situations. Members of each cultural group will communicate and negotiate with out-group members for faces they wish to cherish.

There are two categories of face: negative and positive. Eastern cultural members of "high-context culture" advocate collective needs and goals. They value collective needs and goals above individual needs and goals. The culture driven by collective values pursues positive face: face-assertion and face-giving. Face-assertion indicates that face is highly valuable. People living in a group have the desire to be accepted, protected, and included. Face-giving encourages, supports, and satisfies people's desire to be accepted, protected, and included. Western cultural members of "low-context culture" value individual values, needs, and goals more than collective ones. This culture driven by individual values pursues negative face: face-restoration and face-saving. Face-restoration claims personal freedom, space, and independent autonomy without interference from others. Face-saving is to respect the freedom, space, and preferences of others. Face-restoration and face-saving are negative or passive because their main functions are to maintain basic self-dignity but not to control or dominate others.

So face—the public image of oneself—is a kind of fundamental symbolic resource for individuals to live in groups. Negative face as a symbolic resource is closely related to the individual soul-personality structure and sub-consciousness of safety and fear. Positive face as a symbol resource is closely related to the power relationship of dominance and to the etiquette relationship of exchange between people. We hypothesize from this theory that to define others according to self-face will produce discourse bias. We can only face-negotiate with others by placing ourselves under others' faces.

But the theory has an obvious defect. It overly simplifies Eastern and Western cultures by overlooking their complexity and variability. It pays too much attention to the binary opposition of two cultures—culture driven by collective values and culture driven by individual values. In addition, it overlooks the possible overlapping of two faces, as well as the possible common face and new face generated in the interacting. Although Ting-Toomey and Chung (2012) realized later that further research is needed to explain the function of emotion, the influence of circumstance, and how face changes, their theory still pays too much attention to stereotyped face and overlooks contextualized face-negotiation.

It will be difficult to dynamically and comprehensively understand diversified face-negotiation. We should keep in mind that face-negotiation develops in relationship. When different faces overlap and accept some factors from each other, self-identities will vary. In some fields, new faces or an inter-subject common face may come into being. For this reason, the theory of intergroup language bias should be rethought. When the media report news events in the in- or out-group context, the interaction between the media representing different groups will demonstrate intergroup discourse bias and face-negotiation, which is significant for our rethinking.

WESTERN MEDIA'S COVERAGE OF WENCHUAN EARTHQUAKE: POSITIVE AND NEGATIVE IMPLICATIONS

Contemporary constructivist cognitive psychology found that people perceive and explain the external world in the frame of past experience and under the influence of social culture (Berger & Luckmann, 1967; Goffman, 1974). Journalists produce news discourse in a certain frame. For example, they depend on framing to process large amounts of information (Gitlin, 1980). Framing as a core notion or clue adds meaning to facts described by the news. It is a significant path to comprehensively understand the discourse structure of the Western media's coverage of the Wenchuan earthquake. This chapter examines four British and American newspapers' coverage of the Wenchuan earthquake to examine their strategies of choosing, opinion expressing, and rhetoric. Furthermore, this chapter's purpose is to reveal the reporting frame by which meaning is produced in the Western media's coverage of the Wenchuan earthquake and then to uncover the real meaning of the Western media's coverage.

Four representative newspapers were chosen to be examined: the *New York Times* and the *Chicago Tribune* in America, the *Times* and the *Guardian* in Britain. All of them are influential in America or Britain. To a greater or lesser degree, they represent the left-to-right spectrum. News reports published in these four newspapers from May 13 to June 13 are analyzed. June 13 was relevant to the period because the dangers of significant geographic instability and barrier lakes were reduced around this date. Moreover, the Chinese government announced on June 13 that the earthquake relief work had achieved great victory. Within that period, the *New York Times* published 34 reports and 2 editorial articles; the *Chicago Tribune* published 40 reports and 1 editorial article; the *Times* published 38 reports without an editorial article; the *Guardian* published 34 reports and 9 editorial articles. In total, there were 146 reports and 12 editorials.

There are no big gaps in the quantity of reports between the four newspapers. They adopted almost the same frame in the coverage of the earthquake in China, although these four newspapers have different political stands on reporting domestic events. But the four newspapers did have notable differences in the strategy of publishing editorial articles. The *New York Times* and the *Chicago Tribune* published fewer editorial articles, and they focused on the openness of information and society and the trend of democracy in China. The *Guardian* published more editorial articles that had more diverse opinions. Six of the articles compared China's rescue operation after the earthquake with Myanmar's rescue operation after the cyclone that hit Myanmar just before the earthquake hit China. Furthermore, these articles discussed the way that the Western world delivered help (for example, Jenkins, 2008a). Some articles commented that the Western media excessively reported Chinese victims of the earthquake but ignored Myanmar's victims of the cyclone (Jenkins, 2008b). Some other articles reflected the West-centrism embedded in the news reports, and suggested that the West should accept the changing status of China in the world. However, all of the nine editorial articles published in the *Guardian* held Western democratic political notions as their standpoint. And the diversity presented in these editorial articles had no influence upon the frame of news coverage in the *Guardian*. The reporting frame of the four newspapers can be organized on five levels:

1. Strong Earthquake Ravages China and China Rushes to Rescue Victims

The day after the earthquake, May 13, the four newspapers published 12 reports, most of which focused on the information of the disaster itself and the relief work. Here are some typical headlines: "Powerful Quake Ravages China, Killing Thousands" (*New York Times*, May 13, 2008); "Quake ravages China: Thousands killed, children trapped as buildings tumble; ruin hampers rescues" (*Chicago Tribune*, May 13, 2008); "Thousands perish as quake strikes China" (*Times*, May 13, 2008); "Thousands die in China quake" (*Guardian*, May 13, 2008). The follow-up coverage reported facts about the dangers of aftershocks and barrier lakes, the painful experiences of survivors, and the living condition of victims. Here are some typical descriptions:

> "Rescuers struggled this morning to reach victims of the devastating earthquake." (Branigan & agencies, 2008)

> "Thousands of rescue workers slogged on foot through mud and landslides all night trying to reach the mountainous epicenter. All roads in had been destroyed or seriously damaged. Treaded tanks also were employed to navigate the difficult terrain. Helicopters were turned back because of bad weather." (Magnier & Demick, 2008)

> "Troops rushed to carve a trench to drain the water before it floods the valley.... Downstream, officials rushed to evacuate people in the path of potential flood waters.... At Tangjiashan lake, hundreds of troops were working around the clock to dig a channel that would divert the rising waters before they breach the top of the rubble wall." (Ang, 2008)

> "In some areas there is insufficient electricity to provide power to keep the bodies. There is no option but a swift burial, with as much dignity as possible, in a land plunged into grief." (MacArtney & Yu, 2008)

> "At the stadium, arrivals received food and blankets and basic medical care, but by midday Wednesday the crowds had grown so large that officials with bullhorns at the front gate had to restrain the flow of newcomers." (Osnos, 2008a)

At this level, the language (effort, try to, rush to, struggle to) embodying positive meaning is restrained by the concrete facts of the disaster (damage, devastated, trapped, knocking down, kill), which naturally makes a clear distinction between atypical positive behaviors and stereotypes about out-group people. This method does not weaken the consistency of stereotypes. Nor does it hamper the converting of positive behavior to negative meaning.

2. Comments Comparing the Cyclone Disaster in Myanmar

Western media reports frequently compared the earthquake with the cyclone disaster in Myanmar. The comparison brought positive conclusions. For example: "The relatively vigorous flow of information and the fast response from top officials and rescue workers stood in stark contrast to the way China handled the Tangshan earthquake, or the way the military junta that rules neighboring Myanmar has managed the aftermath of a giant cyclone" (Hooker & Yardley, 2008). "In contrast to criticism levelled at the regime in Rangoon for its intransigent response to its disaster, the Chinese government are to be commended for their quick and efficient response" (MacAskill, 2008). "In terms of an official response, it seems like the authorities have done a good job, unlike Burma. They have said that their primary aim is to rescue people and calls have been made for international aid" (Branigan, 2008a). Moreover, a report objectively describes the fact that the Chinese government refused foreign relief workers. It points out that the Chinese government's response "appears to be based not on defensive secrecy but on the realistic assessment that China now has the manpower and experience to cope" (*Times*, 2008a). Beginning with this level, positive meaning is restrained in a concrete context.

3. China Builds a Good Atmosphere for the Olympic Games

Here are some typical discourses: "China's leadership knows that, with the Beijing Olympics less than 90 days away, it cannot afford another blow to its international reputation or to its domestic standing" (Macartney, 2008a). "China sees disaster relief as a tactical tool to improve ties with neighbors and soften its international image ahead of the Olympic Games in Beijing in August" (French & Wong, 2008). "Pressure for a rapid response was particularly intense, with the government already grappling with widespread unrest among Tibetans in Western China while trying to prepare for the Beijing Olympics in August" (Magnier & Demick, 2008). At this level of discourse, positive meaning begins to be transformed into negative meaning.

4. Earthquake Is Described as an Image of the Failure of Socialism

The *Chicago Tribune* even ran this headline: "A jolt to China's bedrock" (Osnos, 2008b). The news report says: "In another era, Chinese citizens would have asked whether these epic trials, particularly an earthquake in which 50,000 people are feared dead, might signal that the Communist Party had lost what the ancient Chinese called 'the mandate of heaven'—the political blessing of a higher power." By describing the victims, the report also tries to show how the authorities had modelled their people:

"Wen Jiabao wept," Gao Wenkai said, with awe in his voice. The 61-year-old farmer was standing in a shop owned by his niece, whose daughter was among hundreds of children killed in a collapsed school in this town southeast of the epicenter. "We will depend on the government to rebuild," Gao said, his face quivering with grief. That expectation—we will turn to the government—is the widespread refrain here in the hardest-hit sections of Sichuan. It is not only the response of a desperate population with no other means of support. It is also the product of a half-century of political training to rely on the Communist Party above all else.

"The government is a big comfort for us. If the leaders didn't come here, then we could never settle back down. It brings us peace," said Wang Yongjing, a 60-year-old farmer and mother, whose home was partly flattened. She spoke a short distance from the school where 900 students were in class at the time of the quake. Only a few dozen have been rescued.

The *Guardian* describes the authorities' influence on people with indirect language: "The couple had little water and not much food, they said. They also had nothing but praise for the rescue effort" (Branigan, 2008b). The *Chicago Tribune* quotes specialists' saying: "China is still a largely government-driven and controlled society" (Lee, 2008). The *New York Times* discussed in a report that "if China manages to handle a big natural disaster better than the United States handled Hurricane Katrina, the achievement may underscore Beijing's contention that its largely non-ideological brand of authoritarianism can deliver good government as well as fast growth" (Jacobs, 2008a). Then why did China's government make efforts for relief and show openness? "The government might have come to the realization that openness and accountability could bolster its legitimacy and counter growing anger over corruption, rising inflation, and the disparity between the urban rich and the rural poor." The *New York Times* explained again in another report: "After the international backlash over China's crackdown on ethnic Tibetans, the leaders have used the earthquake in an effort to show that their authoritarian government can be responsive, even populist, at crucial moments" (Jacobs, 2008b). At this level, the language has become a highly abstract political discourse where there are no positive implications.

5. Querying if Openness and Accountability Mean a Change of Politics

The *Times* doubted whether the Chinese authorities' openness and accountability were a sign of fundamental change by asking this question: "Can the new, open China outlive the huge relief effort?" (Macartney, 2008b). The *New York Times* gave its answer in a news report: "A brief flirtation with openness and responsiveness does not mean that China is headed toward Western-style democracy" (Jacobs, 2008a). The *Times* also reported: "The Chinese

Government remains a dictatorship that is staunchly undemocratic" (*Times*, 2008b). These doubts and statements straightforwardly articulated the democratic narrative frame adopted by the Western media. The reason why the Western media affirmatively described and even praised China's positive changes is that the way the Chinese responded was approaching Western democracy. For example, when a news report describes how Premier Wen directed the rescue work on site and showed his love of the civilians, it concludes: "Mr. Wen behaved like a politician in any democracy" (Macartney, 2008b).

The Western media's democratic frame is represented by the reporting of two more topics: (1) a schoolhouse collapsed and resulted in many students' deaths, which then sparked protests of the students' parents; and (2) the development of civil society symbolized by volunteers' wide participation and common public donation. From the Chinese perspective, the schoolhouse's collapse and parents' protest are typically negative topics. In reporting the former topic, the Western media's discourse is this: Disaster is caused by people as well as by natural forces. The latter topic shows Chinese volunteers' participation and common Chinese people's generous donations. "The devastating earthquake in China has given birth to a phenomenon unseen before in the country, a volunteer army" (Yu, 2008). "Developing a robust civil society is considered a major step if China is to become more democratic, and some advocates are hoping the earthquake proves to be a defining moment that will inspire the public to push for more change in the future" (Yardley & Barboza, 2008). On the other hand, reports on the topic of civil participation try to prove that "There is a limit to the government's tolerance of a stronger civil society. While many major international aid organizations were initially allowed into the area, controls on their movements have been tightened" (Watts, 2008d).

The Chinese government's open attitude to news reporting at the beginning of the relief work surprised Western reporters. The *Times* reported: "The response of China's rulers highlights the lessons that they have learned from the mishandling of several crises in the past few years. This time there is little sign, at least so far, of an attempt at a cover-up as there was during the Sars outbreak in 2003, when secrecy triggered rumor and panic" (Macartney, 2008a). One of the *New York Times* reports reads: "Mothers wailing over the bodies of their children. Emergency workers scrambling across pancaked buildings. And a grim-faced political leader comforting the stricken and reassuring an anguished nation. While such scenes are a staple of catastrophes in much of the world, the rescue effort playing nonstop on Chinese television is remarkable for a country that has a history of concealing the scope of natural calamities and then bungling its response" (Jacobs, 2008a). The *Guardian* reported that China's authorities opened the disaster area to foreign reporters. "Western journalists have been waved through police checkpoints around the epicenter, another sharp contrast to the practice 10 years ago when thousands of Chinese villagers were killed by flooding of the Yangtze River" (Borger, 2008). The *Times* reported that "Tens of millions of Chinese sat gripped by moment-by-moment coverage of the unfolding disaster on state-run television. The stodgy evening news broadcast was replaced by 24-hour scenes of rescues, of paratroops jumping into inaccessible villages, of weeping relatives and of ragged shocked survivors. These scenes are unprecedented in China." "The welcome by the ruling Communist Party to international participation is a first. Its willingness to allow people access to a wealth of detail about events breaking in their country is also unusual" (Macartney, 2008b). Another *Times* report said that Premier Wen's attitude to Western media "has been full of surprises" (Macartney, 2008c).

However, Western media began to disbelieve China's information openness when the situation changed. As the *Times* questioned, "It has been relatively easy for China's rulers to allow exceptional openness about such an exceptional disaster. They could be confident that the reports would follow a single line. Now the question must be whether they will allow any contradictory reporting and real freedom of expression" (Macartney, 2008b). On the same day, the *Guardian* found that "The Chinese media continued with blanket coverage of the quake, despite tighter reporting restrictions" (Watts, 2008c).

Later, more Western media found that China's authorities really were tightening reporting restrictions. The *Chicago Tribune* reported on May 22: "China in image-control mode. Reins in reporting" (Foreman & Chang, 2008). The news report described details of the controlling: "In the last day of a three-day national mourning period, the Communist government was reverting to well-tested methods to impose its authority. A message of unity in the face of adversity was prominent in state media and on the streets of the hard-hit city of Shifang. Billboards in the city center's shopping district showed pictures of the quake's damage, including collapsed buildings and injured people. A huge slogan read 'Everyone come together with one heart.' In the mid-term and late-term of the relief work, Western journalists interviewing students' parents were taken away" (Guan, 2008). On May 21, the *New York Times* reported that "China's propaganda authorities seemed to reassert their control over the nation's news media on Tuesday" (French, 2008). Another report published on June 2 read, "(Chinese) propaganda officials issued an order prohibiting the domestic media from continuing to publish articles about the schools controversy" (Jacobs, 2008c). On June 10, the *Guardian* reported, "Media controls are also being tightened after a period of relative openness" (Watts, 2008d). On June 13, the *Guardian* reported further, "The clampdown in Dujiangyuan and Juyuan came amid a tightening of media controls, as domestic journalists were instructed to focus on upbeat stories about the relief effort and foreign reporters were denied entry to the area." "Both towns (Dujiangyan and

Juyuan) are now out of bounds for foreign reporters, at least seven of whom have been temporarily detained in the past week by police. Others have been stopped at checkpoints or removed from the towns." The report noted that, "The restrictions are a step back ... The tightening reflects political concerns that the destroyed schools could become a focus for anti-government sentiment" (Watts, 2008e).

DISCOURSE LOGIC TO DEPRECIATE CHINESE FACE (IMAGE)

The five levels of discourse frame has some basic meanings: Strong earthquake ravaged China, brought ruinous destruction; Chinese people used to depend on government, which is a result of longtime political training. At the same time, some Chinese people didn't wait for the government passively. They hoped for governmental help while making their way in life by their own efforts. Relief work was launched actively with great difficulties. Chinese authorities' swift reaction and relatively active distribution of information are not only quite different from what happened after the Tangshan earthquake, but also totally different from Myanmar's handling of the cyclone disaster. China's impressive huge relief work indicates that it is still a largely government driven and -controlled society. China's active relief work and the openness of information are temporary strategies to build a good atmosphere for the coming Olympic Games in Beijing and to soften China's international image. The earthquake is an image of the failure of Chinese socialism. Chinese rulers have clearly associated the relief effort with maintaining stability. They have realized that openness and accountability can reinforce their legitimacy as rulers, and also can put down the increasing anger aroused by corruption, inflation, and extreme disparity between the rich and the poor. Temporary openness and accountability do not mean that China is marching toward Western democracy, although premier Wen directed the relief work on site and showed his love of ordinary people, which made him look like a politician of a democratic state. The Chinese government's open attitude for news reporting at the beginning of relief work surprised everyone. But the openness did not last long. The control of the information was weak at the beginning but increasingly strengthened. On the last day of the three national days of mourning, China went back to the image-control mode. Only upbeat reports were allowed to be published.

Obviously, preexisting Western bias against China turned the discourse frame into negative meaning. This discourse frame in turn maintained the preexisting bias and depreciated the Chinese face (image). Some people may excuse the Western media's bias through journalism professionalism, asserting that producing Western news discourse merely follows the watchdog role. The watchdog role typically constructs news discourse by uncovering problems that cannot be seen as unfriendly to out-group people. Jonathan Watts, the *Guardian*'s chief reporter in Beijing, said that the most significant function of the news media is to be a watchdog of the government and society, although the media have multiple functions. The watchdog tries to find the problems of society and report them, hoping people will change them. Watts believes that he did not come to China to write travel notes or to say how beautiful China was.

Western journalists tend to emphasize problems when reporting. They always focus on Chinese social and environmental problems and many other problems that they believe should be changed (Watts, 2008a). It is true that, if uncovering problems were bias, then bias is at most a "news bias," which focuses on conflict, abnormality, and negative and passive topics. In inter-group communication, bias is not relevant to what kind of problem the news reports—positive or negative—but is relevant to what kind of discourse is used to describe the topic, that is, if it is stereotype-driven news discourse. For example, the fact that the Chinese government's openness cannot last is negative for China. But the bias of a news report cannot be identified by the negative nature of the fact being reported. If the whole discourse is stereotype driven, more sophisticated observation is needed to verify bias.

According to previous analysis, the Western media's discourse frame has an overall characteristic: Western media not only reported the earthquake's massive destruction and the social and political changes displayed by the relief work in the information-open context but also described them using a Western discourse system. Positive advancements were reported with a "domestication" method, while negative rigid aspects were commented with a "deviance" method. In this way, the discourse structure brought Western bias—a legacy of Western discourse about Orientalism.

The method of "domestication" (Clausen, 2004; Cohen, Levy, Roeh, & Gurevitch, 1996) means to convert uncognizable Chinese events into a carrier of meaning with a Western perceptive frame (Berger & Luckmann, 1967). The logic of the news discourse is to identify others (China) with the face (image) held by the West.

The method of "deviance" is a reporting strategy that takes China as an evil other of Western society and a deviant from liberal ideology. This strategy is different from professionalism, which means objectively balanced reporting. On the contrary, the deviance method reports subjectively and critically and also selectively reports aspects of an event that fit certain ideological needs (Hackett & Zhao, 2005, p. 117; Hallin, 1986, p. 117). This strategy even makes negative reporting of China "political correctness." A typical discourse is like this: The earthquake is an image of the failure of Chinese socialism. Chinese rulers clearly associated the relief effort with maintaining stability.

Therefore, news discourse is completely controlled by stereotype. It can only depreciate the others' face (image).

Western journalists typically use the "watchdog" role of journalism to justify possible bias. Jonathan Watts talked frankly and bluntly about his own bias as a Western journalist:

> I don't think journalists can be objective or neutral. We have our own emotions, background and prejudices. We must know these prejudices. We should try our best to be fair and give both sides the same chances to appear in a report. In fact, we are people who have feelings. When an event happens, we have personal feeling. This feeling will partly influence our report. Although feeling cannot alter a report completely, it IS a factor which will have influence. (Watts, 2008a)

In the intercultural context, bias frequently emerges when Western journalists make judgments about topics of another culture from the perspective of the Western ideology frame, although they do not have comprehensive and accurate information. Furthermore, the bias can distort one's understanding of the other's culture. Psychology classifies prejudice into two categories according to the distortion of cognition and the fairness of attitude: (1) cognitive or epistemic prejudice, that is, the cognition is inconsistent with social reality; (2) moral prejudice, that is, the cognition or attitude violates the equal or fair principle needed by intercultural or intergroup understanding and communication (Li, 2007, pp. 6–7). The Western media's earthquake coverage displays both kinds of prejudice to different degrees.

The cognitive prejudice of Western journalists mainly comes from cultural prejudice and value intolerance and a news values system that emphasizes conflict and confrontation. For example, Western journalists did not understand when an earthquake victim said, "We will depend on the government." So the journalists made a deduction subjectively and explained that it was "the product of a half-century of political training to rely on the Communist Party above all else." Because of the lack of information symmetry and opacity, Western media reports covered topics by guessing and emphasized conflict and confrontation. A *Guardian* report on May 16 guessed that there was a rift over the rescue operation, since Prime Minister Wen shouted at PLA generals in a telephone conversation (Watts, 2008b). The *New York Times* published a report on May 21 guessing that "China's propaganda authorities seemed to reassert their control over the nation's news media on Tuesday" (French, 2008). The clue to this guess is that all Chinese newspapers adopted solemn, color-free front pages and, in one commonly repeated headline, urged the nation to move forward with the exclamation "Go, China!"

According to contemporary psychology theory, when facing unclear information, people tend to react in a way consistent with prejudice, even if they consciously reject prejudice (Devine, 1989). Accordingly, when Western journalists face unclear information on China, especially when some information is in blackout, they will report the topic according to prejudice. Therefore, information blackout can only accelerate prejudice's growth and expansion. The more an event is covered by the government, the more likely the Western media will report it on hearsay evidence to reinforce their prejudice. It is difficult for anybody, including ourselves, to be free of the psychological mechanism driven by prejudice when lacking comprehensive and transparent information.

The cognitive prejudice of Western journalists is also displayed when reporting Chinese events through the lens of Western ideology. This always is a binary opposition: thinking that the West is free and democratic while China is closed and despotic. Following this thinking, external and internal groups will be distinctly separated. The diversity and complexity of the world will be oversimplified in perception.

This is more conspicuous in deduction and induction. According to Pettigrew's (1979) attribution theory, if a person believes that another person's behavior is negative, he or she will explain that another person's behavior is a result of will (internal cause) when the person is an out-group member. However, he or she will explain that another person's behavior is a result of a conditional context (external cause) when the person is an in-group member. In the same way, when persons are out-group members, their positive behavior will be attributed to a conditional context; when they are in-group members, their positive behavior will be attributed to their will. China is an out-group of the West. China's positive relief effort as a positive behavior was attributed to conditional factors by the Western media, that is, the Chinese government was not willing to help the victims but was forced to act positively by political conditions.

When Western journalists hold a cognitive prejudice driven by ideology, their perception of and attitude toward Chinese topics will violate the equality and fairness principle and become a moral prejudice. Moral prejudice prevents journalists from reporting objectively. On the contrary, it drives the journalist to report incomplete stories because of the goals of dominating others, ideological hegemony, or race discrimination. For example, Western journalists tended to be critical that the government did not respond efficiently when reporting domestic disasters. But when reporting an efficient Chinese rescue operation, Western journalists looked down from the height of politics and morality, commenting that China was still a government-driven society, and lacking democratic qualities, the Chinese can only depend on government. This kind of moral prejudice can develop into political hostility and form discourses rejecting others and promoting deviance, just like what was published in the *Chicago Tribune*: The Wenchuan earthquake is "a jolt to China's bedrock." The report continued by suggesting that "In another era, Chinese citizens would have asked whether these epic trials, particularly an earthquake in which 50,000 people are feared dead, might signal that the Communist Party had lost what the ancient Chinese called 'the mandate of heaven'—the political blessing of a higher power."

The key to prejudice is to make irrational judgment on other cultures but without comprehensive and accurate information. There are two reasons why journalists cannot obtain comprehensive and accurate information. The first one is that information is ambiguous or blocked. Sometimes, journalists cannot get close enough and perceive the information sources. The second one is that journalists are dominated by the notion of conflict in politics, the economy, and culture. Then they filter the information within a certain value system. The first reason proves that news blackouts can only reinforce the Western media's bias. The *Guardian*'s journalist Jonathan Watts said that the policy of blackout does have negative influence on the Western media's reporting on China. Blackout has made it difficult for journalists to interview two sides of an event. Moreover, blackout itself becomes news (Watts, 2008a). The second reason shows that the most terrible prejudice has nothing to do with the information itself or cognitive limitation. It lies in the weakness of humanity—journalists participate in the construction and maintenance of a particular power system that benefits a certain group, race, or state. Some Western journalists' moral prejudice shows that the West-dominated power relationship with China is more influential in reporting than perceiving facts comprehensively. If journalists have only cognitive prejudice and admit the existence of cognitive prejudice like Jonathan Watts, they may develop multiple ways to understand truth by information exchange and cultural dialogue. However, moral prejudice produces only hostility and outrage, which reduces the possibility of information exchange and cultural dialogue.

CHINESE MAINSTREAM MEDIA'S FACE-NEGOTIATION UNDER SELECTIVE DECODING

Information openness, multiple exchange, and equal dialogue are the best ways to respond to and reduce the Western media's bias. These ways not only may eliminate bias but also may help to know others and cultivate the self-group in the bias. Otherwise, we may lose ourselves in bias, especially when we insist that the Western media must obey the "upbeat principle" in their reporting. If they do not, we claim the "demonization" of China in that their coverage is bias driven.

Surprisingly, the Western media's coverage of the Wenchuan earthquake had an unusual "influence" on Chinese mainstream media. From May 13 to June 16, all the main Chinese newspapers positively relayed or commented on the Western media's coverage of the Wenchuan earthquake. *Sina news* (htt://news.sina.com.cn) was searched for Chinese newspapers' quotes and comments on the Western media's coverage of the earthquake. Here is the result: the *New York Times* coverage was mentioned 8 times, the *Times* 6 times, the *Guardian* 4 times, and the *Chicago Tribune* 2 times. Those relays give people an overall impression that the Chinese mainstream media were selectively interpreting others' discourse to maintain the self-group's face. This is face-negotiation between the West and China. However, what is the nature of the face-negotiation in the perspectives of discourse interpretation and face concern?

In headline writing, Chinese newspapers used abstract language with the positive implication of generalizing the discourse of the four Western newspapers, such as "move the world," "positive comment," "highly concerned," "respond quickly," "surprised the world," "openness unprecedented," "transparency unprecedented," "accountable," "launch a new life," "more and more successful," and "display China's image with confidence." All of the language is positive. The Western media's discourse is converted into a new discourse, which is a single-goal-driven reconstruction of discourse: to magnify or stress others' positive description of "our" behaviors and to blur or hide others' negative description of "our" behaviors. Discourse reconstruction brings a competitive, tense relationship between discourse maintaining in-group identity and discourse by others.

When quoting the Western media's discourse, Chinese mainstream media deliberately ignored concrete context, discourse structure, cultural value, and ideology. The out-of-context quoting and generalizing reconstructed Western media discourse into discourse driven by in-group values.

The *Chicago Tribune* reported that China tried her best to deal with the newly happened natural disaster. "We saw the workings of a society that has opened up significantly over the last two decades. We see the new face of a Chinese leadership that is engaged with the outside world." (*Xinhua Daily Telegraph*, 2008.6.2. Quoted report: Huang, 2008)

"The very (in the original, "relatively") vigorous flow of information and the fast response from top officials and rescue workers stood in stark contrast to the way China handled the Tangshan earthquake." *New York Times in America*. Comment on May 13. (*Xinhua Daily Telegraph*, 2008.5.14. Quoted report: Hooker & Yardley, 2008)

The *New York Times* described *Xinhua News Agency's* coverage as "blot out the sky and cover up the earth." The report said *Xinhua News Agency* published regular updates on the situation, including latest death tolls, on its Chinese and English Web sites. (*People's Daily*, 2008.6.2. Quoted report: Hooker & Yardley, 2008)

The Times in Britain published a report on May 14 that highly praised the Chinese government's relief effort and the openness policy of disaster information. The report said it believed China has the ability and experience to cope with the disaster. (*Xinhua News Agency*, 2008.5.15. Quoted report: *Times*, 2008a)

Obviously, the method of traditional foreign propaganda filtered these quotations, which fundamentally changed the meaning of Western coverage. This method is to decode messages coded by Western ideologies with the Chinese ideological code system. As a kind of aberrant decoding (Eco, 1980), it manufactured an illusion that the Western media were reporting upbeat stories of China. The decoding method mixes "the negotiated reading" and "the oppositional reading" discussed by Stuart Hall (1999, p. 508). When there are some positive elements in the Western media's text, their positive elements will be accepted. But the interpretation will be modified to fit the need of Chinese society. The interpretation may have a completely opposite meaning than the ideological code of Western media. Even some Western words and expressions may be translated into Chinese-style discourse. A paradox emerges here: although the purpose is to use others' discourse to construct strength of identity and concern self-face (image), the positive meaning presented by others' discourse is in fact a false meaning because it is out of context.

In intergroup discourse interaction, people usually try to use the discourse of others to construct self-identity. This is rational, because the construction of identity is always associated with the others' understanding and cognition. Without the others' understanding and cognition, self-identity will become soliloquy and lose its meaning. However, if the others' discourse is interpreted by completely aberrant decoding, identity will become an illusion. Then intercultural face-negotiation is absurd.

According to Ting-Toomey's (1988) theory of face-negotiation, positive face pursued by the Chinese consists of face-assertion and face-giving. Face-assertion indicates that people living in a group have a need to be accepted and protected. Face-giving encourages, supports, and satisfies the need of being accepted and protected. The group's strategy in a values-driven culture for dealing with conflict is to seek group inclusion, that is, to satisfy people's need of face-assertion with continuous face-giving. Thus, conflict will be resolved.

This face-negotiation strategy is effective in personal or intergroup communication within the Chinese cultural context. It will not be effective once the face-negotiation moves into the intercultural context. Because of the cultural differences, people who do not share the meaning of face cannot communicate on face issues. Face-assertion seeking others' inclusion is difficult for the West to understand, whether or not it occurred when the Chinese felt hurt by the Western media or when the Chinese selectively collect the Western media's positive discourse. Selective interpretation of Western media coverage has an embarrassing effect. It seemed that the Western media changed suddenly and understood Chinese face-negotiation strategy and the resolution of cultural conflict through face-assertion and face-giving.

In fact, to face-negotiate with others, people can only try to understand the others' face. That is to say, to construct its self-image in Western news discourse, China must first understand Western face-negotiation. Western people pursue negative face and individual autonomy, which includes two strategies of face-negotiation: face-restoration and face-saving. Face-restoration claims personal freedom and space, thus preventing the others' invasion of personal independence or autonomy. Face-saving is to respect others' freedom, their space, and even strange preferences. When facing conflict, the strategy of negative face-negotiation generally is integrated. It aims to resolve a problem or seeks independent authority by competition. Its logic is this: If both or all sides of a conflict need to save or restore face, what they can do is only make a contract, that is, all sides establish and follow a basic game rule. If they follow the rule, all sides have faces, no matter if they win or lose. Therefore, the most effective way to get face in Western news discourse is to interpret Western coverage of China in terms of Western competitive rules of fairness, justice and equality, and the media rules of journalism's professionalism. Chinese people should not seek face by tracing what the Western media praise or criticize. They should experience what was driving Western discourse, in what context, and discover contradictions and problems in its discourse. Chinese-style positive face can be obtained by achieving Western-style negative face.

To maintain self-group image and reinforce self-identity, the Chinese media used the strategy of selective decoding to ignore Western discourse that depreciates China. It proves to be a resistance identity, just like criticizing the Western media for distorting the Chinese image. It stresses or magnifies the Western media's positive descriptions of "our" behaviors as well as blurs or hides the Western media's negative descriptions of "our" behaviors. The Chinese media's selective decoding made a tense relationship between others' discourse and discourse maintaining in-group image. However, it has another meaning: it embodies an attitude that accepts information openness and an open society while it produces ideological identity. There is project identity—a transformation plan of political culture—in the back of quoted words such as "openness" and "transparency." This is a new face formed in intercultural communication. It is also a common face between the West and China. If the Chinese media accept the new face and common face, they should view the Western media's coverage with an open attitude and quote comprehensively from multi-aspects and multi-angles. They should take these reports as a mirror to examine themselves and clearly reveal stereotype-driven discourse. In this way, their face may be restored. And Western journalists who distort the reporting will lose face.

Comparatively, Chinese netizens responded more rationally to Western coverage than did the Chinese mainstream media. *Qiangguo Forum* is an influential public forum in China. It is famous for posting serious political topics, although it is operated by *People's Daily*. From May 13 to June 13, there were 49 posts about the Western media's coverage of Wenchuan earthquake in the *Forum*. Those posts displayed diversified opinions. They consist of several types of discourse:

Warning:	"Don't exaggerate and be intoxicated with the Western media's word of praise."
Doubting:	"Some odd pieces of praise made some of us feel very bright. I will never believe it can be so easy for the Western media to put down their colored glasses, unless they are not Western media."
Reflecting:	"Each time CCTV likes to quote the Western media's comments to approve our people's achievements. It indicates that CCT is unconfident and irresponsible."

However, this shows a lack of understanding of Western face. If people are concerned with their own face but do not concern themselves with the face of others, "my face" can only be a result of self-comfort or self-isolation. It will make people's cultural soul fragile and sensitive but cannot deconstruct the tense, dominant relationship of power between China and the West.

CONCLUSION: CONSTRUCT SELF-IMAGE IN OPEN CULTURAL CONTEXT

People tend to understand out-group behaviors with their own discourse frame when they describe out-group people. The understanding of positive and negative implications thus is driven by stereotype. Certainly, this is a barrier to intergroup communication. It is also a challenge with which an open society is confronted. Western people have advocated equality, liberty, and fraternity for hundreds of years. But still, they cannot be free of prejudice. They are troubled by prejudice such as racist and orientalist discourse. The reason is that power and benefit have shadowed Western people's soul, and modernity reinforced the power of the West, which then dominated the relationship of the West and the East. China is establishing institutions of information openness. She takes the West as a frame of reference. But the corresponding openness of soul has not been established. The Chinese media's selective interpretation of Western news repelled or avoided negative reports. Western news discourse was displaced by simplistic positive discourse and finally was thrown into a closed discourse system. In this way, the Chinese can neither know others nor reflect self. The communicative relationship is broken off. Each side returns to an isolated group-self.

Intergroup communication is a process of social interaction. Negative and positive implications indicated by intergroup discourse bias are not identified by language or discourse but produced in the process of maintaining self-image and seeking the approval of others. Negative and positive implications exist in intergroup face-negotiation. That is to say, face is always constructed in relationship. Only in relationship can self-image be maintained and others' approval be obtained. The right way is to perceive a concrete context, context structure, cultural values, and ideologies of others' discourse, which can deconstruct stereotype-driven discourse on one hand and understand the group-self and construct a self-image in a cultural open context on the other hand.

The government's information openness and the media's freedom to report are important preconditions for the Chinese to open the group-self and innovate self-identity. They can display a relatively clear and abundant information environment to Western media, thus reducing the possibility of bias. However, prejudice may accompany humankind throughout its history because of humanistic weakness and games of power. What the Chinese can and should do is go with difference, facing prejudice calmly, taking Western prejudice as encouragement to innovate its group-self and surpass it. The government and the media should distribute comprehensive and open information to increase the chances of contact and understanding between Western and Chinese people and to dispel prejudice. The human being's moral strength should be recovered in understanding and communication. Only in this way can China's face (image) be constructed in the process of interaction.

BIBLIOGRAPHY

Allport, G. W. (1954). *The nature of prejudice*. Cambridge, MA: Addison-Wesley.

Ang, A. (2008, May 28). Chinese flee threat of floods: Looming rainy season adds to risk in quake's wake, prompting evacuations. *Chicago Tribune*, p. 12.

Berger, P. L., & Luckmann, T. (1967). *The social construction of reality: A treatise in the sociology of knowledge*. London: Penguin.

Borger, L. (2008, May 17). Beijing open to foreign aid and scrutiny in wake of tragedy. *The Guardian*, p. 26.

Branigan, T. (2008a, May 13). Surrounded by death, survivors fear more shocks: Beijing mobilises 8,000 troops as rescue effort intensifies. *The Guardian*, p. 4.

Branigan, T. (2008b, May 14). Desperate rescue effort at bank that dissolved into ground like a slab of melting butter. *The Guardian*, p. 2.

Branigan, T., & agencies. (2008, May 13). Thousands die in China quake. *The Guardian*, p. 1.

Clausen, L. (2004). Localizing the global: "Domestication" processes in international news production. *Media, Culture and Society, 26*(1), 25–44.

Cohen, A. A., Levy, M. R., Roeh, I., & Gurevitch, M. (Eds.). (1996). *Global newsrooms, local audiences: A study of the Eurovision News Exchange*. London: J. Libbey.

Devine, P. G. (1989). Stereotypes and prejudice: Their automatic and controlled components. *Journal of Personality and Social Psychology, 56*(1), 5–18.

Devine, P. G., & Elliot, A. J. (1995). Are racial stereotypes *really* fading? The Princeton Trilogy revisited. *Personality and Social Psychology Bulletin, 21*, 1139–1150.

Eco, U. (1980). Towards a semiotic enquiry into the television message. In J. Corner & J. Hawthorn (Eds.), *Communication studies: An introductory reader* (pp. 131–150). London: Edward Arnold.

Eid, M. (2014). Perceptions about Muslims in Western societies. In Eid & Karim (Eds.), *Re-imagining the other: Culture, media, and Western-Muslim intersections* (pp. 99–120). New York: Palgrave Macmillan.

Foreman, W., & Chang, A. (2008, May 22). China in image-control mode: Reins in reporting, vows rebuilding funds. *Chicago Tribune*, p. 20.

French, H. W. (2008, May 21). Rescues continue in China, but focus is shifting to the 5 million left homeless. *New York Times*, p. A16.

French, H. W., & Wong, E. (2008, May 16). In departure, China invites outside help. *New York Times*, p. A1.

Gitlin, T. (1980). *The whole world is watching: Mass media in the making and unmaking of the New Left*. Berkeley: University of California Press.

Goffman, E. (1974). *Frame analysis: An essay on the organization of experience*. New York: Harper & Row.

Gorham, B. W. (2006). News media's relationship with stereotyping: The linguistic intergroup bias in response to crime news. *Journal of Communication, 56*, 289–308.

Guan, H. (2008, June 4). Chinese quake outcry silenced. *Chicago Tribune*, p. 15.

Hackett, R. A., & Zhao, Y. (2005). *Sustaining democracy?: Journalism and the politics of objective* [Weixi Minzhu?: Xifang Zhengzhi yu Xinwen Keguanxing]. Trans. H. Shen & Y. Zhou. Peking: Tsinghua University Press.

Hall, S. (1999). Encoding, decoding. In S. During (Ed.), *The cultural studies reader* (pp. 507–517). London: Routledge.

Hallin, D. C. (1986). *The "uncensored war": The media and Vietnam*. New York: Oxford University Press.

Hooker, J., & Yardley, J. (2008, May 13). Powerful quake ravages China, killing thousands. *New York Times*, p. A1.

Huang, W. G. (2008, May 18). A changing China confronts disaster. *Chicago Tribune*, p. 1.

Jacobs, A. (2008a, May 14). Quake toll rises: China struggles to reach victims. *New York Times*, p. A1.

Jacobs, A. (2008b, May 21). In quake, apotheosis of Premier "Grandpa." *New York Times*, p. A6.

Jacobs, A. (2008c, June 2). Parents of quake victims protest at ruined schools. *New York Times*, p. A 9.

Jenkins, S. (2008a, May 14). As Burma dies, our macho invaders sit on their hands. *The Guardian*, p. 29.

Jenkins, S. (2008b, May 21). The world and its media are playing the dictators' game: Heroic Chinese rescuers and quake survivors lead the news. *The Guardian*, p. 35.

Lee, D. (2008, May 24). China orders cities to give aid: Wealthier provinces to help quake victims. *Chicago Tribune*, p. 15.

Li, S. (2007). *Prejudice* [Pianjian]. Peking: Oriental Publishing Center.

Maass, A., Ceccarelli, R., & Rudin, S. (1996). Linguistic intergroup bias: Evidence for an in-group-protective motivation. *Journal of Personality and Social Psychology, 71*, 512–526.

Maass, A., Salvi, D., Arcuri, A., & Semin, G. (1989). Language use in intergroup contexts: The linguistic intergroup bias. *Journal of Personality and Social Psychology, 57*, 981–993.

Macartney, J. (2008a, May 13). Olympic pressure helps to foster a caring response. *The Times,* p. 7.

Macartney, J. (2008b, May 24). Can the new, open China outlive the huge relief effort? *The Times,* p. 46.

Macartney, J. (2008c, May 26). A seismic shift in China's relations with West. *The Times,* p. 2.

Macartney, J., & Yu, S. (2008, May 17). March of death leaves its scars as countryside becomes a giant grave. *The Times,* p. 41.

MacAskill, E. (2008, May 13). Bush offers to share spy satellite data as Europe stands by with aid. *The Guardian,* p. 4.

Magnier, M., & Demick, B. (2008, May 13). Quake ravages China: Thousands killed, children trapped as buildings tumble. *Chicago Tribune,* p. 1.

Osnos, E. (2008a, May 15). Scrambling for refuge amid ruins—Clothes, medicine, food go short as China strains to cope with a flood of earthquake survivors. *Chicago Tribune,* p. 1.

Osnos, E. (2008b, May 18). A jolt to China's bedrock. *Chicago Tribune,* p. 13.

Pettigrew, T. F. (1979). The ultimate attribution error: Extending Allport's cognitive analysis of prejudice. *Personality and Social Psychology Bulletin, 5*, 461–476.

Semin, G. R., & Fiedler, K. (1988). The cognitive functions of linguistic categories in describing persons: Social cognition and language. *Journal of Personality and Social Psychology, 54*, 558–568.

Times. (2008a, May 14). Seismic shift: China responds to disaster with compassion, Burma remains criminally negligent. *The Times,* p. 16.

Times. (2008b, May 17). The Sichuan earthquake may have wider political implications in China. *Times,* p. 18.

Ting-Toomey, S. (1988). Intercultural conflict styles: A face-negotiation theory. In Y. Y. Kim & W. Gudykunst (Eds.), *Theories in intercultural communication* (pp. 213–237). Newbury Park, CA: Sage.

Ting-Toomey, S., & Chung, L. C. (2012). *Understanding intercultural communication* (2nd ed.). New York: Oxford University Press.

Watts, J. (2008a, April 2). How a foreign journalist reports China. Lecture at Wuhan University, PRC.

Watts, J. (2008b, May 16). Government appeals for rescue equipment as time runs out to find China quake survivors. *The Guardian,* p. 21.

Watts, J. (2008c, May 24). Quake patients face transfer as hospitals struggle to cope. *The Guardian,* p. 22.

Watts, J. (2008d, June 10). Tragedy brings new mood of unity: Government wins praise for reaction as the young lead surge in patriotic sentiment. *The Guardian,* p. 15.

Watts, J. (2008e, June 13). Chinese media blocked as parents seek justice over collapsed schools. *The Guardian,* p. 26.

Yardley, J., & Barboza, D. (2008, May 20). Many hands, not held by China, aid in Quake. *New York Times,* p. A1.

Yu, S. (2008, May 19). In sleek cars and "I love China" t-shirts, a New People's Army pours out to help victims of the quake. *Times,* p. 33.

CHAPTER NINE

Crime News

Defining the Boundaries

ROMAYNE SMITH FULLERTON AND
MARGARET JONES PATTERSON

The face is meaning all by itself. It leads you beyond ... The face speaks. It speaks, it is in this that it renders possible and begins all discourse ... The first word of the face is the "Thou Shalt Not Kill." It is an order. There is a commandment in the appearance of the face, as if a master spoke to me.

—(LEVINAS, 1985, PP. 87–89)

For philosopher Emmanuel Levinas, ethics begins and ends with the human face. By looking into the face of the Other, each of us becomes aware of our personal responsibility to and for another person. A face-to-face encounter ought to affect us profoundly because in this moment, both the mortality and vulnerability of the Other is revealed; we ought to hear and answer the plea not to be "killed." This fundamental alterity of another person manifests itself in our daily lives, for we are constantly surrounded by both ethics and our webs of connection with others. For Levinas, this is a primordial relationship (cf. Broadbent, 2014). The encounter with the Other reveals the a priori and fundamental responsibility the self has for the Other. From Levinas's perspective, we must welcome and be kind to the Other because he or she is our contact with the transcendent, or the divine. While this relationship with the Other is asymmetrical—"I" am responsible for the Other without knowing whether the caring will be reciprocated—such reciprocity is not to be considered because "I" am obligated or subject to the Other regardless of outcome (Lindahl, 2002). It was in this relation that Levinas located what it means to be human and what justice itself demands: consideration of the needs, wants, and desires of another person—articulated or not—and moreover, these concerns must be met ahead of one's own. In this way, ethics is "first philosophy." His is an appeal to a "metaphysical desire, a desire for goodness—obligations, responsibilities, the call to justice ... to the radical otherness of the other person" (Levinas, 1999, p. xii).

Levinas was critical of societies that depersonalize human relations and undermine face-to-face contact. In today's contemporary world where the Internet and social media are rapidly replacing more traditional modes of communication, the likelihood of genuine face-to-face encounters among citizens—even at a local or community level—is dropping rapidly. As technology conflates geography and removes or redraws national and international boundaries, countries are losing the legal and moral ability to control and contain the definitions and conversations that once defined them. As a result, creating and establishing meaningful intercultural communication is one of the greatest challenges facing scholars, journalists, and newsrooms today.

A consideration of the impact technology has had on journalism is particularly relevant when considering crime stories because these texts define the edges of a society by exploring what behaviors fall outside a culture's pale and how deviants should be treated. It is our contention that journalistic crime reporting practices have, until quite recently, generally reflected the dominant culture's norms, that practices differed significantly from country to country even when they share much common history, and that the practices have been both geographically and temporally specific. Now, however, the ready access to any and all information via the World Wide Web threatens to dissolve difference and render a near "tell-all" American style of storytelling the norm; after all, why uphold particular practices that protect the name of an accused or a victim when the "true identity" of virtually anyone is but the click of a mouse away? Thus, a comparison of crime reporting practices across advanced industrialized capitalist societies serves as a good exemplar of how the Internet disrupts the cultural integrity of these practices, as well as why and how newsrooms, in the Age of the Internet, ought to operate in more sensitive intercultural realities.

The West's Enlightenment attitudes, largely embraced and unquestioned by North American and United Kingdom news people, are often rooted in particular paradigms and epistemologies that can confuse equality with sameness and thereby trample the humanity of the Other. Routine practices of crime reporting have varied widely even within and among the countries of Western Europe and North America, which share similar history, culture, and democratic institutions, but those variations may be about to change in an increasingly multicultural age. To consider what may be lost or gained and to define what is at stake, this chapter compares those practices, explores the cultural assumptions they reflect, and evaluates the Internet's insensitivity to cultural difference. Finally, we suggest the need for new multicultural ethical standards.

A CASE FOR CONTEXT

New York, May, 2011: the unshaven and unkempt-looking managing director of the International Monetary Fund, Dominique Strauss-Kahn (DSK), was paraded in front of television cameras and photographers for what has been termed the "perp walk." Charged with a number of offenses including sexual assault and forcible confinement in an alleged attack on a hotel maid, he appeared publicly, shamed and embarrassed. But Strauss-Kahn had not yet been tried or convicted in court; legally, he was presumed innocent. Still, the perp walk has become a staple in American crime coverage, and defenders of the practice note that it offers the American people the opportunity to see the beginnings of its justice system in action, that one of the cornerstones of that system is the openness and transparency of the process, and, moreover, that publicity can act as a deterrent. Some journalists we interviewed, as well as public critics of the DSK case, have argued that the perp walk is indicative of the United States' attitude about equality: all persons, regardless of stature, can be made to face the public. The fact that this was a man held in high regard in both his own country of France and around the world does not matter; he, too, can be seen to be held to account. His status did not protect him from the watchful eye of the press. The photographs and video of DSK in shackles, escorted by New York police, were widely circulated.

Some French television stations even ran the footage. But in France, the reaction from commentators and politicians was swift and furious. Former justice minister Elisabeth Guigou found the images of a handcuffed Strauss-Kahn led by several police officers "to be brutal, violent and cruel" (Tompkins, 2011). In 2000, when she was justice minister, she had overseen the implementation of a law that forbids the publication or circulation of images depicting handcuffed criminal suspects because the French believe these visuals can undermine the presumption of innocence. Some French news outlets clearly ignored their country's law. "France's media is [*sic*] struggling to reconcile strict privacy laws with the age of twitter and the internet," the French international radio station reported (Diffley, 2012). Celebrities there were safe from public intrusion, but after the arrest in New York, Strauss-Kahn and his wife, Anne Sinclair, "were regularly snapped around Paris and numerous stories about the state of their marriage were published," Angela Diffley at Radio France Internationale (RFI) later said (Diffley, 2012).

In some parts of northern and central Europe, news outlets might well have ignored the Strauss-Kahn arrest if it had happened on their own soil because the alleged crime was not directly related to his performance in public office. At the same time, seven of eight French newspapers chose to run the name of the alleged victim of the attack, something American news outlets would normally avoid. In this case, as the accuser's veracity began to be questioned, most American news media eventually revealed her name, Nafissatou Diallo. All charges against Strauss-Kahn were ultimately dropped because of inconsistencies in Diallo's story and a lack of physical evidence; however, the damage to Strauss-Kahn's reputation was permanent, and investigations into other allegations in France continued.

BOUNDARIES OF DEVIANCE

The coverage of Dominique Strauss-Kahn's arrest in New York City reflects clear differences in routine journalistic practices from one country to the next. Moreover, these variations in law and journalistic ethics hint at deeper, more closely held values. These values—and the stories that contain them—constitute the very face of a culture—the face, Levinas said, that pleads not to be killed.

Crime stories play a key role in how a nation's values are discussed, reaffirmed, and perhaps how they change. As American sociologist Jack Katz (1987) pointed out, they delineate the behavioral borders of society by exploring what conduct falls outside the realm of "acceptable," as well as showing how deviants who cross those boundaries are treated. These types of stories both reflect the constant redrawing of these socially constructed borders and influence the direction in which they shift over time. Sometimes they bring inside behaviors that were once considered deviant. Other times, they push out what previously had been judged to be acceptable. In "What Makes 'Crime' News?" Katz (1987) pinpointed what lies behind the public's never-flagging interest in stories that are, he argued, remarkably similar and largely formulaic: they constitute a society's "daily moral workout." While geography once contained this ongoing exercise within the limited reach of news distribution, the Internet has broken down geographic and linguistic limits.

The Dominique Straus-Kahn story demonstrated this collapse. The story broke big in the American news media with sex, politics, money, and a powerful world figure all at play. Yet the story would have played differently—if it played at all—had the incident happened in Paris instead of New York. The story's international reach demonstrates ways in which French journalists and French culture are losing their grip on French news values. Cultures—all cultures, not just the French—define their own behavioral boundaries. But the Internet shows no respect for boundaries. Instead, it tears down the borders that contain laws that define crime, as well as journalistic practices that draw the margins of privacy and dignity.

For the French, the circulation of the DSK story served as a social catalyst, a story injected into French culture and politics from the outside. DSK quickly stepped down as head of the IMF and bowed out of his projected candidacy for president of France. The famous French broadmindedness about sexual peccadilloes and out-of-wedlock affairs had notoriously tolerated President Francois Mitterand's wife and mistress sharing space at his funeral in 1996, but DSK's arrest shifted the public conversation.

"Three weeks after DSK's arrest, France is in culture-shock. The French are re-examining, painfully, two of their fondest beliefs about themselves," John Lichfield (2011) wrote in the British newspaper the *Independent*. One belief, he said, was that their news media had a kinder, gentler attitude toward the private lives of public officials. The other belief was that the French are more relaxed about sex "than the uptight Anglo-Saxons, the frigid Germans or the silly Italians. The 'affaire DSK' has left both fond beliefs in tatters," Lichfield contended (2011). But Lichfield may have conflated a French laissez-faire attitude about sex with two equal if not greater French values: a commitment to the presumption of innocence often absent in the Anglo and American press and a belief that conduct that does not directly impinge on a public official's performance of duty is not the public's business. Both values hold great sway in the journalistic ethics of northern and central European nations.

Nonetheless, once the DSK story was unleashed inside France, French women broke their silence. French news media exploded with stories—some speculative, some verified—of DSK's previous aggressive and predatory exploits with women. The sexual behavior of other government officials came under scrutiny as well. Support groups in France reported a 600% increase in calls from women who claimed to have been victims of sexual harassment or blackmail at work, according to Lichfield (2011). The women were angered, French media reported, by the attitude of male politicians who were dismissing DSK's alleged behavior as trivial.

At the same time, French and American women began battling across the Atlantic for the right to say definitively what the interpretation of these events really meant. "Almost as repellent as the sexual entitlement of French men, with their insistence on their seigneurial right to 'heavy flirting,' is the docility and feminine-mystique-ization of the French women who enable them," Katha Pollitt (2011) wrote in the *Nation*. She quoted Anne Sinclair, DSK's wife, as saying in 2006: "I am quite proud! For a political man, it is important to seduce," even though he was rumored to have attempted to rape one of his daughter's young friends (Pollitt, 2011). Some French women accused the American feminists of being too uptight about sex, while others seemed to be just discovering the notion of sexual harassment. Pollitt (2011) wrote:

> Ironically, the DSK affair has given the small and internally conflicted French feminist movement new visibility and a great organizing issue. Petitions are going round against sexual harassment and male privilege. There's rage and mockery at DSK's pals and their dominance in the media. On May 22, hundreds of women demonstrated in Paris under banners with slogans like *Men lose it—Women pay for it*.

French sociologist Irene Théry, writing twice in *Le Monde* (2011a, 2011b), defended French feminism against what she saw as American attacks. She also argued for an assumption of the New York city maid's truthfulness equal to DSK's presumed innocence. Cross-cultural stereotypes and presumptions of values were pinching like ill-fitting shoes on both sides of this transatlantic spat. Depending on one's perspective, the American tell-all style of crime coverage and its routine publication of "perp walk" photos either opened up a much-needed conversation about predatory sexual behavior in France, or it cost that nation the leadership of a valued economist and politician. What was clear to the French is that the Internet had broken through their dikes, disrupting French law and reporting custom.

COMMUNITIES AND CONVERSATIONS

News stories about crime provide the fundamental materials for the social construction of boundaries. While some tales may just reassure the public that such boundaries remain in place, others alert citizens that a situation is dire and requires their attention.

Julia Kristeva (1982), cultural critic and literary theorist, explored the ways in which individuals and societies define such boundaries. In *Powers of Horror*, she argued these edges were founded on a concept of what she termed the "abject." Whatever form the abject takes—metaphorical or physical states, persons or a set of circumstances—it is simultaneously attractive and repulsive, but its effects are inescapable. We use the abject to separate the human from the non-human, the fully from the partially formed subject. The abject "disturbs identity, system, order. [The abject] does not respect borders, positions, rules. [It's] the in-between, the ambiguous, the composite" (p. 4). It is "the place where meaning collapses" (p. 2) and is, therefore, subversive. It threatens life itself and must be "radically excluded" (p. 2) from the human body (like feces, or vomit, or blood) or the body politic (like law-breakers who do not conform) and deposited on the other side of an imaginary border that separates self from not self, social from antisocial. While societies must exclude the abject because it threatens to destroy life, they must also tolerate it because its existence continually defines and delineates borders and reaffirms that we are alive and that our community remains distinct.

Society's criminals are often constructed as abject. Every society must delineate limits and expel the antisocial because the abject threatens the unity of that society by calling into question the boundaries upon which it is built and maintained. But those expelled must also be tolerated because they remind us of where the margins are continually drawn and redrawn. Each society with its unique history and culture will define the abject differently, and the criminal code and its interpretation will be one of the chief vehicles for negotiation of the abject.

Martin Innes and Nigel Fielding (2002) saw one way in which societies conduct this process by propelling a particular crime, or type of crime, into prominence, then using that crime to identify dark forces at the gate. Innes and Fielding coined the term "signal crimes" to describe the kind of crime stories that trigger the social process Kristeva described. They used this term "to capture the social semiotic processes by which particular types of criminal and disorderly conduct have a disproportionate impact upon fear of crime." Such crime stories tell their audiences about "events that, in addition to affecting the immediate participants (i.e. victims, witnesses, offenders) and those known to them, impact in some way upon a wider audience" (Innes & Fielding, 2002). They thereby cause people "to reconfigure their behaviors or beliefs in some way" (Innes, 2003, p. 52). The extensive news coverage such stories receive, Innes argued, enlarges the crime's semiotic properties because each is accompanied by "widespread popular concern that it signals that something is wrong with … society and its criminal justice process, which requires some form of corrective response" (p. 51).

DSK's arrest in New York fit into a larger narrative Americans had been exploring for decades about powerful men taking advantage of their might with women. From Gary Hart to Bill Clinton, John Edwards, and Anthony Weiner, sexual scandals became as much about arrogance and character as they were about sexuality. For Americans, bringing down great men might be seen as an exercise to prove their fallibility. They represent America's post-Vietnam and Watergate loss of faith in its leaders and political processes. They function as "dramatic articulations of popular fears about the seeming encroachment of the forces of disorder, drawing upon diffuse and inchoate existential anxieties about the state of contemporary society" (Giddens, quoted in Innes, 2002, p. 52).

The alleged DSK crime described above reflected the qualities of a "signal crime." It received widespread coverage about and reaction to the alleged crime itself, as well as about the manner in which the story was reported. Violence against women, an issue once hidden behind a curtain of privacy and relegated not to the public but to the private sphere, had been propelled into a worldwide spotlight by a series of signal crimes, including the DSK case, two high-profile suicides of Canadian teenage girls in the wake of online bullying and sexual harassment, and in one case of rape and circulation of photos on the Internet, as well as a series of gang rapes in India, the shooting of Malala Yousafzai in Pakistan, the National Football League's suspension of Baltimore running back Ray Rice for beating his fiancée, and most recently, Canadian CBC radio host Jian Gomeshi's alleged choking and beating of women before, during, or after sexual encounters, and allegations of drugging and rape by numerous women against comedian Bill Cosby. The list grows almost daily.

In our increasingly intercultural world where immigration, tribalism, border and racial tensions, and shifts in gender and sexual norms disrupt long-standing and traditional social patterns, such fears about large communication and social changes are commonplace but not surprising. The press and social media can either fan the public's incipient fears or quell them. The conventional press as "gatekeeper" has traditionally exerted the greatest and in some instances complete control over the semiotic process Innes described. Today, legacy media frequently cede that function to Internet bloggers and social media, which push their own agendas and employ their own means of both taking and affecting the public's pulse. The Internet now carries virtually all news—no matter its source or its reliability—across international borders. The construction of myth and meaning is no longer contained within national boundaries and is, instead, contested between and among media outlets, journalists and citizens, and different countries and nationalities, as well as differing cultural and/or reporting practices.

While signal crimes play an important social role, they are also central to the production of news itself. "Conceptions of deviance and control not only define the central object and character of news stories, but are woven into the methodology of journalists, influencing their choices from assignment through the selection and use of sources, to the final composition of the story," according to Ericson, Baranek, and Chan in their book, *Representing Order: Crime, Law, and Justice in the News Media* (1991, p. 239).

Until recent years when almost all news began traveling on the Internet, this process was largely confined within one culture. A community—on the local, regional, or even national level—conducted a conversation within its own boundaries about its limits of tolerance. Despite the fact that the Internet has now propelled almost all news into a stratosphere of international and intercultural communication, reporters generally conduct themselves as they always have. They continue to frame stories to reflect their parochial understanding of community concerns. As Gaye Tuchman observed in 1978, they perform much of what they do out of habit or what she referred to as the "routinization" of news production. These routines are comparable in many advanced Western democracies, countries that share much common cultural heritage. But after interviewing nearly 100 reporters and press experts in five European countries (England, Ireland, Italy, the Netherlands, and Sweden), Canada, and the United States, we have also found significant differences in the way crime is covered, differences that reflect each country's attitude toward crime as well as journalism's role within these democratic processes. Through our interviews, it became clear that few reporters or editors are aware that their reporting norms and routines, and the stories that result from them, can be out of step with those in the far corners to which their news stories now travel. Moreover, few considered how or whether these differences might be understood, and with what effect, in other locales.

To illustrate the contrast, consider two signal crime stories that happened within weeks of each other in 2009, one in the Netherlands and one in the United States. During the April Queensday celebration in the Netherlands, Karst Tates drove a small car through police barriers and into a crowd. While national television cameras were rolling and footage was being broadcast live to the Dutch people, he killed seven spectators and seriously injured 10 others. His attempt to assassinate the royal family failed when his car hit a stone memorial, and he suffered a fatal head injury. The story made news around the world, yet despite the spectacular nature of this crime and Tates's confession to police before he died, the Dutch Press Agency ANP (Algemeen Nederland Persbureau) and many other Dutch media withheld Tates's name and identifying information. They acted, Dutch reporters and editors later told us, to protect the man's innocent family, as they routinely do in reporting on crime.

Dutch journalists rarely use more than first name and last initial or simply initials to identify those accused, and in some cases even convicted, of serious crime. "You should have the presumption of innocence," said Thomas Brunig, general secretary for the Dutch Union of Journalists (personal interview, June 10, 2010). "You should be very careful because to be accused is not the same as being convicted, but when you see this in the paper, it doesn't look like that." Daphne Koene, secretary to the Dutch Press Council, said, "A suspect should not be convicted in the media before he or she goes to court. We have this value that the court decides the punishment, and there shouldn't be extra punishment by publication" (personal interview, June 11, 2010). But even after conviction, criminals' identities may be protected because the Dutch believe that one should not have to live with the stigma of conviction and should instead be rehabilitated into a productive life in the community, Brunig noted. "You should always live up to the things you have done," Brunig added, "but it makes it difficult to start over again … In Holland, the idea is more that you can always start again and better your life" (personal interview, June 10, 2010).

Six weeks after the Queensday incident, in the Netherlands, an elderly man shot a security guard to death inside the U.S. Holocaust Memorial Museum in Washington, DC, before being shot himself by police officers.

American reporters immediately named 88-year-old James Wenneker von Brunn, a native of Maryland who was well known to both police and civil rights groups for his ties to white supremacists and other hate groups. U.S. mainstream news media noted his previous criminal record and quoted from his books and online writings. Reporters sought quotes from former neighbors; some tracked down and named his son and his son's former girlfriend. Contrary to their Dutch counterparts, American reporters believe their duty is to probe and expose all possible motives and causes of the criminal mind, to act as the public's eyes and ears on the criminal justice process, and to help reveal the nature of dark forces in society. To them, this cannot be done without naming those accused and even tangentially connected to the alleged perpetrators, as well as outlining in detail all the relevant information they can dig up and verify. In part, it also matters because newspapers continue to be the medium of public record. As Daniel Nasaw, U.S. news editor for the Washington bureau of the BBC, told us, "I would say history needs to know the name of this person and who is the news person to judge?" (personal interview, August 6, 2013).

Most reporters in the English-speaking countries where we did interviews (the United States, Canada, England, and Ireland) characterized themselves as watchdogs acting in the public interest. They saw telling all that was newsworthy about the criminal defendant as their professional duty. "In every case we want as much info as we can about everyone including criminal defendants," said Peter Herman of the *Washington Post*. It's important "to get as quick, but also the most complete profile, we can of the person accused" (personal interview, August 8, 2013). Although the critics and the public often view the relentless pursuit of personal details in crime stories as sensationalism motivated by commercial greed, Herman offers a different explanation: "It's not voyeuristic," he said, using the Boston marathon bombers as an example. "It's (a question of) how did he become this?" In building the narrative of the bombers' lives, American reporters explored how the brothers originally entered the United States, whether they were on a watch list, and whether U.S. security protections are sufficient (personal interview, August 8, 2013).

Holding back from such a full and robust exploration was seen as dereliction of journalistic duty. "I disagree with those Dutch reporters," said Michael O'Toole, crime reporter for the *Irish Daily Star* in Dublin, commenting on the Dutch practice of withholding criminals' names from their reports. "I think it's a disgrace. We don't own the information. The people own that information. [Dutch reporters] are acting as a prism for the information. We shouldn't do that. What gives them the right to decide that we're going to hold this back from the public?" (personal interview, March 1, 2012).

These sharply distinct attitudes and practices in countries with similar democratic and economic institutions illustrate the two primary theories of communication that James Carey identified in his book, *Communication as Culture* (1988). Each reflects a different set of cultural values. North Americans reflect their history as settlers, Carey said, by subscribing to a "transmission" view in which messages are distributed in space to control or manage distance and people (p. 15). North Americans have an individualistic culture, Carey noted, and believe that thought is an "essentially private act" (p. 28). In a similar manner, they also conceptualize crime as an individual act of wrongdoing rather than as the failure of a social system. From this ethical perspective, reporters feel obligated to identify accused and convicted criminals as a public service. They approach government systems—including the criminal justice system—with skepticism, more so than some European journalists. "We trust in government here more than you do in the United States … and with good reason," said Tim Overdiek, then deputy editor-in-chief for the Dutch NOS (Nederlandse Omroep Stichting or the Dutch Broadcasting Foundation), who has been a foreign correspondent in the United States and the United Kingdom (personal interview, June 14, 2010).

Under the transmission model, truth is seen as a process, an idea John Milton first articulated during the English civil conflict in 1644: "Let her and Falsehood grapple; who ever knew Truth put to the worse, in a free and open encounter?" (Milton, 1644). The American news media will continue to pursue and report truth, and in the end, to quote an oft-employed British aphorism, "justice must not only be done, but must be seen to be done."[1]

Thus, the job of the press is to deliver the news and allow citizens to take action. "Give light and the people will find their own way," as the Scripps-Howard motto states. Within this transmission framework, withholding information that is generally seen as newsworthy—such as the identity of suspected and convicted criminals—can be viewed as a violation of journalism's basic mission. And most English, Irish, Canadian, and U.S. journalists we interviewed viewed it as such.

Europeans, in contrast, see communication as a way to maintain society—its culture, values, beliefs—over time, Carey (1988) wrote. "In [this] ritual definition, communication is linked to terms such as 'sharing,' 'participation,' 'association,' 'fellowship,' and the 'possession of a common faith.' This definition exploits the ancient identity and common roots of the terms 'commonness,' 'communion,' 'community,' and 'communication'" (p. 18). For those subscribing to this view, reading a newspaper is a ritual act, one that conveys not simply information but also a dramatic portrayal of contending forces at play in the world. For the Swedish and the Dutch, then, to engage in news reporting is to engage in community thinking, dialogue, and discussion. Historically, this interaction has not just been about gaining new information for the purposes of control so much as it is about confirming and maintaining attitudes about identity and their community over time—drawing and redrawing the boundaries of who and what belongs. For Dutch and Swedish news professionals and academics, the names, personal details, and identifying characteristics of suspected or convicted criminals are not a necessary part of this communal conversation. The specific identities of the "actors" are irrelevant; what matters are the deeper and less personal motivations and machinations of institutions, processes, and situations.

Carey challenges the North American notion that thought is private. "Thought is public," he contended, "because it depends on a publicly available stock of symbols. It is public in a second and stronger sense. Thinking consists of building maps of environments" (1988, p. 28). The maps, for Swedish and Dutch journalists, point to communities that, in the face of increasing technological and economic change, as well as pressure to conform to the "tell-all" model, still construct criminals as "one of us."

As we have argued in "Murder in Our Midst," crime coverage in North America, even when it tries to conform to best practices, often encourages a kind of prurient interest in the personal details of alleged perpetrators and their families (Fullerton and Patterson, 2006). From our perspective, identifying and naming those accused of serious crimes legitimizes the news media's focus on individuals' histories, idiosyncrasies, and perhaps irrelevant details that distract audiences from the genuine community issues at stake, about which they might conduct a more constructive conversation.

CONCLUDING THOUGHTS

All approaches to crime reporting have their critics. In England, writers like Yvonne Jewkes and Chris Greer (2005) have lambasted the sensationalism of British crime news. Building on older studies like that of Stanley Cohen (2002) about the news media's creation of "moral panics" and the characterization of criminals as "folk devils," they accuse the press of overheating public fears and thereby inciting repressive criminal justice policies in Great Britain and North America. In the Netherlands, Peter Berger, a media studies and journalism professor at Leiden University, said he doubts that withholding names and identifying characteristics keeps audiences from pointing fingers. Berger denied that the Dutch practice of using first name and initial or even two initials diminished the news' condemnation of the criminal. "My take on this as a journalism scholar is it's a minor ritual, to borrow from Gaye Tuchman's paper," he said in a personal interview (June 16, 2010). "By withholding names, [Dutch journalists] claim their actions are ethical," he said, but they are still guilty of conducting "trial by media" and demonizing parties involved in crime (personal interview, June 16, 2010). In recent years, he added, a change from using two initials to using first name and last initial "allows the press in these countries to distinguish ethnic status—the Mohammed T. as opposed to M.T." he said.

In the Netherlands and Sweden, obedience to their national press councils' ethics policies about naming is widespread but far from uniform. Most news organizations withhold names if both the crime and the person are considered "private," and most use the full name if a public person is arrested for a "public" crime, that is, one that directly involves his or her performance in office. But cases that fall between public and private are open to dispute. At the same time, some media professionals and scholars simply disagree with the policy.

Arendo Joustra, editor of the newsweekly *Elsevier*, argued that it is hypocritical not to identify "ordinary" people when the media routinely identify politicians or those with preexisting public profiles. If the *New York Times*, which Joustra calls the "icon of journalism," prints names of killers, then the practice "is not wrong *journalistic* behavior" (personal interview, June 15, 2010). Similarly, media scholar Ester Pollack of Stockholm University believes that Swedish media's privacy policies are motivated more by fear of legislative controls than by ethics commitments. Legislatures, she pointed out, frequently threaten to clamp down on what they see as trial by news media (personal interview, June 18, 2010).

Martin Jonsson, deputy editor-in-chief at *Svenska Dagbladet*, believes the policy of withholding names helps to establish trust in the news by displaying media professionals' commitment to ethics. But his newspaper explores the implications of every case, and sometimes, he said, you cause more harm by not naming. "For instance if we have a soccer player accused of drunk driving, it is better to publish his name rather than defame the other ten on his team" (personal interview, June 22, 2010).

Embedded within this debate is the larger discussion of who should control journalism ethics. While some of those interviewed believe that control should belong to the individual news outlet and others placed their faith in national press councils, all expressed the fear that control will soon cede to the anarchic Internet. Increasing incidents like the international circulation of photographs and video footage of Dominique Strauss-Kahn's perp walk will simply wrest control over journalistic practices and mute local and national conversations about which ethical values should prevail. Perhaps worst of all for those concerned about journalism ethics is that this process is likely to be mindless and heedless of cultural difference, driven solely by technology, not discussion.

This comparison of crime reporting practices serves as a good exemplar of why and how Internet Age newsrooms must operate in the new intercultural realities. Routine practices of crime reporting vary widely even within and among the countries of Western Europe and North America, which share similar history, culture, and democratic institutions. Traditional journalism ethics has been rooted in the West's Enlightenment attitudes, which can confuse equality with sameness. Many journalists we talked to failed to recognize that their convictions were rooted in a particular paradigm and epistemology and that their reporting practices reflected these cultural biases.

Only about 20% of our interview subjects expressed any awareness that crime-reporting practices differed elsewhere (mostly those who had been foreign correspondents or were educated abroad), much less how these practices differed. The majority thought only about local or national audiences. To the limited extent they had thought about the international pathway their stories now take on the Internet, they assumed sameness. "How could you do that to someone?" one Dutch reporter gasped when she learned the extent of personal information routinely reported in American news stories. Most North American and even British reporters were puzzled and amazed to learn that their continental counterparts gave so much privilege to privacy.

These reporters' assumption of sameness even as their own stories crisscross continents risk trampling the humanity of the Other. It brings to mind a famous quote by Wade Davis, Canadian anthropologist and ethnobotanist: "The world in which you were born is just one model of reality. Other cultures are not failed attempts at being you; they are unique manifestations of the human spirit."

All ethics, Levinas argued, flow from a fundamental obligation to the Other. But that consideration seemed to be missing in the transmission of the Dominique Strauss-Kahn images into the subject's home country with little regard for that nation's culture, law, or ethical practices. To Levinas, "Ethics is always relative to a particular Other" and that Other's particular needs (Murray, 2002, p. 186). This thinking rewrites the Golden Rule: "[Do] unto others as they would have us do unto them" (Murray, 2006, p. 176). And the change in pronouns changes everything: the ethical obligation develops within the encounter and the need evoked therein.

Levinas argued that all human institutions that allow us to function day to day—mass media, law, government, and politics—should be grounded in the primal ethical obligation to tend to the Other's needs. If not, human beings risk going adrift from their ethical moorings. Journalism runs such a risk if it fails to come to terms with its penetration into cultures far beyond its traditional circulation area.

NOTE

1. This phrase originated from a 1926 British case, *Rex v. Sussex Justices; Ex parte McCarthy*, and is attributed to Britain's Chief Justice Lord Hewart, who encapsulated the principle

of open justice. In the judgment, the phrase read, "it is not merely of some importance but is of fundamental importance, that justice should not only be done but should manifestly and undoubtedly be seen to be done" (cf. Spigelman, 1999). This document also makes reference to the detailed history of the use of the phrase.

BIBLIOGRAPHY

Broadbent, R. (2010, December 2). A Levinasian theory of justice in capital punishment cases. *Eidos*. Retrieved from http://www.academia.edu

Carey, J. W. (1988). *Communication as culture: Essays on media and society*. Boston, MA: Unwin Hyman.

Cohen, S. (2002). *Folk devils and moral panics: The creation of the mods and the rockers* (3rd ed.). New York: Routledge. (Originally published 1972)

Diffley, A. (2012, January 19). French Huffington Post will run Strauss-Kahn stories, says editor Anne Sinclair. RFI English. Web.

Ericson, R., Baranek, P., & Chan, J. (1991). *Representing order: Crime, law and justice in the news media*. Toronto: University of Toronto Press.

Fullerton, R. S., & Patterson, M. J. (2006). Murder in our midst: Expanding coverage to include care and responsibility. *Journal of Mass Media Ethics, 21*(4), 304–321.

Innes, M. (2003). "Signal crimes": Detective work, mass media and constructing collective memory." In P. Mason (Ed.), *Criminal visions: Media representations of crime and justice* (pp. 51–69). Cullompton, Devon: Willan.

Innes, M., & Fielding, N. (2002). From community to communicative policing: "Signal crimes" and the problem of public reassurance. *Sociological Research Online, 7*(2). Retrieved from http://www.socresonline.org.uk/7/2/innes.html

Jewkes, Y., & Greer, C. (2005). Extremes of otherness: Media images of social exclusion. *Social Justice, 32*(1), 20–31.

Katz, J. (1987). What makes "crime" news? Retrieved from http://www.sscnet.ucla.edu/soc/faculty/katz/pubs/WhatMakesCrimeNews.pdf?origin=publication_detail

Kristeva, J. (1982). *Powers of horror: An essay on abjection*. Trans. L. Roudiez. New York: Columbia University Press.

Levinas, E. (1985). *Ethics and infinity*. Trans. R. Cohen. Pittsburgh: Duquesne University Press.

Levinas, E. (1999). *Otherwise than being or beyond essence*. Trans. A. Lingis. Pittsburgh: Duquesne University Press.

Lichfield, J. (2011, June 4). The French more relaxed about sex? It's a myth. *The Independent*.

Lindahl, E. (2002, Summer). Face to face. *Piestisten: A Herald of Awakening and Spiritual Edification, 17*(1). Retrieved from http://www.pietisten.org/summer02/facetoface.html

Milton, J. (1644). *Areopagitica*. Retrieved from http://www.gutenberg.com

Murray, J. (2002). The other ethics of Emmanuel Levinas: Communication beyond relativism. In S. Bracci & C. Christians (Eds.), *Moral engagement in public life* (pp. 171–195). New York: Peter Lang.

Patterson, M. J., & Hall, M. W. (1998). Abortion, moral maturity, and civic journalism. *Critical Studies in Mass Communication, 15*(2), 91–115.

Pollitt, K. (2011, May 25). Dear France: We're so over. *Nation*.

Spigelman, J. J. (1999). Seen to be done: The principle of open justice. Keynote Address to 31st Legal Convention, Canberra. Retrieved from http://www.opentrial.info/images/2/20/ SEEN_TO_BE_DONE_THE_PRINCIPLE_OF_OPEN_JUSTICE.pdf

Théry, I. (2011a, May 23). La femme de chambre et le financier. *Le Monde.*

Théry, I. (2011b, May 28). Un féminisme à la française. *Le Monde.*

Tompkins, A. (2011, May 17). Cynics might call the perp walk the crime reporter's red carpet: How we justify images of IMF chief in handcuffs. Retrieved from http://www.poynter.org/ news/mediawire/132692/is-it-ethical-to-use-perp-walk-images-of-dominique-strauss-kahn-imf-chief-accused-of-attempted-rape/

Tuchman, G. (1978). *Making news: A study in the construction of reality.* New York: Free Press.

CHAPTER TEN

Cultural Sojourners

A Study of Western Sub-cultural Musicians in China

XUEWEI LIU

"Interculturality," a concept that is more attractive than "multiculturalism," refers to the communicative competence to interact between cultures, the forging of reciprocal understanding between cultures, and the building of a more complete self-awareness (Shan, 2010). It is not a static concept, but rather a process of constructing dynamic intercultural relations. Interculturality makes us face the prejudice, tensions, and conflicts between cultural groups and inspires us with various solutions to the significant problems in intercultural communication.

The sojourner is defined by Siu (1952) as "a stranger who spends many years of his lifetime in a foreign country without being assimilated by it." Siu (1952) demonstrates that "sojourner" is a derivative of the sociological form, "the stranger" (Simmel, 1950). The "cultural sojourner," however, is specific to an international migrant group that travels all over the world with the purpose of communicating with different cultures and building intercultural relations with people who come from the host cultures. The Western sub-cultural musicians whom I meet in China are a typical type of "cultural sojourner." The purpose of their sojourns is not only to share a particular culture with the Chinese people (underground live music to be specific) but also to develop everyday life interaction and intercultural relations with the common Chinese people they meet during their sojourns.

The essential character of cultural sojourners is that they are free to go anywhere, and their manner of staying is uncertain. According to Simmel, Western sub-cultural musicians who tour the world are a typical type of his notion of "stranger." Strangers represent a specific form of interaction, as Simmel demonstrated, which is the unity of nearness and remoteness. They are fixed within a particular spatial group but have not belonged to it from the beginning. They produce patterns of coordination and interaction while keeping distance from the host community by their own identity. Cultural sojourners, however, attempt to bring and import their qualities and culture to the community in which they sojourn, simultaneously becoming deeply involved in local social and cultural life and trying to diminish the distance between hearts.

Cultural sojourners do not belong to the majority of any society. They are unwilling to assimilate with others, and others can barely assimilate to them. They embrace difference and produce difference; even if they are influenced by a certain culture, there is always the possibility of change. Cultural sojourners are independent individuals, but with their co-cultural tendencies, they are likely to identify with others by the cultural symbols they share and construct intercultural relations with others through these common things. They are looking for ways to decrease the communicative limits between people of different countries, nations, races, religions, languages, and cultures, and in the meantime explore the various possibilities of interacting with them. And that is the way to build interculturality on the basis of understanding and respect and the way to make intercultural communication possible.

ENCOUNTER WITH CULTURAL SOJOURNERS

My encounter with Western cultural sojourners was due to my participation in the sub-cultural scene. In 2002, my friends and I decided to make a fanzine about punk music and distribute it at a nominal cost to others who share the same interests. This fanzine, CHAOS, was the first nonofficial publication about rock music in China. Although it was printed in small quantities and mostly promoted locally, it received a large amount of attention from friend to friend, even in the outside world. With the help of Catherine, an American sojourner who was active in the Wuhan punk scene, we made a bilingual Chinese and English language website, *Wuhan Punk*. Everyone could download the free webzines, contact us freely, and get information on how we work as a team.

As soon as the first two issues were circulated, Western musicians and activists started to contact us, even in one-sentence emails such as "I can't believe there are punks in China." Some of them sent their records and zines to us in exchange for the zines we had made, and some even asked for a direct conversation with us through email or phone calls. Initially, we just wanted to share new ideas with an alternative group of young peers in China interested in punk music. But surprisingly, the gates were opened to the outside world and bridges of communication were established. Western readers, on the other side of bridge—some of them whom we have never met—provided us with different ways of thinking and interpreting the world. In exchange, they were inspired by what we were trying to do in the sprouting punk scene in China, one of the most mysterious Eastern countries from their perspective. At that time, they could hardly believe that young Chinese peers with progressive views could discuss and spread punk-related ideologies, politics, ethics, and promote individual freedom and youth rights through printed booklets. The fourth issue of CHAOS zine is a collection of the conversations we had with those Western musicians and activists. It is not only about music but various topics, such as anarchism, anti-capitalism, the Zapatista movement, anti-sexism and antiracism, vegetarianism and animal rights, and so forth. Five hundred copies could not satisfy the demands of the readers, and we started to realize what we had gained and built in the previous two years.

Meeting Vialka, the progressive micro-orchestra duo from France/Canada, was a milestone in our sub-cultural practices. They contacted us by email and showed a lot of interest in touring China. In 2003, the touring system of rock bands was not well established in China, and there were no Western bands coming to China for noncommercial underground tours on a large scale.[1] Neither of us had any experience or knew how to find contacts or venues beside Beijing, Shanghai, and Wuhan. It was full of challenges, but Vialka gave us a lot of encouragement and courage through the hundreds of emails we sent to each other. Eric and Marylise, the young couple based in the European punk scene and who have specific interests in art, told us of the countries they had traveled, about their nomadic way of living, and their improvised ideas about communication in the international music scene. The most important aspect of their artistic role, according to them, is the personal touch they develop through their art to develop trust, friendship, a community of common open thoughts, and the place and the responsibility of art. From this perspective, they see the artist's role as working on a language of honest feelings that build true impressions and real thoughts and new experiences.

The Do It Yourself ethic, which is tied to the punk aesthetic and ideology, was not a fresh thing for us, but there is a long way to go from talking to taking action. We decided to accumulate contacts and organize their tour, and 15 cities and towns were eventually booked. The moment Vialka landed in China with their instruments, curiosity, and openness toward different cultures, they showed us a strong determination to build relationships and interact with Chinese people using a specific means of musical communication that is beyond art. They became one of the typical cultural sojourners whom I met in the past 10 years.

Features of Participants

The researched Western cultural sojourners are from 13 countries in Europe and America, who sojourned in China multiple times ranging from a few weeks to several years, comprising 12 French, 11 Swedish, 6 Swiss, 11 German, 9 Italians, 7 Americans, 2 Canadians, 1 Pole, 4 British, 3 Spanish, 4 Norwegians, 5 Uruguayans, and 3 Australians. There are five major differences between the cultural sojourners and the majority of Western sojourners in China. First, the researched cultural sojourners at both the amateur and professional levels are/were doing activities related to intercultural practices and interactions in China. Second, the desire for communication and interaction with the Chinese people makes them act more freely and with more initiative on various levels than the majority of Western sojourners. Third, most of the places of their sojourn are not Chinese international metropolises such as Beijing, Shanghai, and Guangzhou but many small cities, towns, and villages, which brings them to a closer observation and experience of Chinese society and Chinese daily life. Fourth, they are not from the vast majority of any society but cultural citizens who interact with others from a cosmopolitan point of view. And last, with the multiple cultural identities they carry, cultural sojourners can construct intercultural relations with others in multiple ways.

Questions in Four Stages

Distance. I did not have personal contact with any foreigner before I joined the editorial team of CHAOS zine in 2003. As contact with the Western world developed, it became increasingly necessary and important to respond to our Western readers and communicate with them. It made me feel excited and curious. After organizing Vialka's first tour in China, we helped five other bands from the U.K., Germany, Sweden, and Austria tour China over the next two years. Although relations were established and they were standing right in front of us, I felt a distance between our minds and hearts. They were strangers in my eyes, close at hand, yet far away. What is life like in their countries? What do they believe in and value most? What interested and motivated them to come to China?

Trust. In 2006, some of the participants of the CHAOS editorial team graduated from colleges and started careers in other cities. The zine ceased publication, and the bridge of communication that we built over several years gradually fell apart. With the courage to take action, one of the virtues I had learned from cultural sojourners, I started to independently help Western bands who were interested in touring in China. Before coming, I was the only contact they had in China; when in China, I was the person whom they trusted most. I booked their shows and organized their tours, traveling together with them, taking night trains (sometimes without reserved seats and places to sit), carrying heavy gear and being refused by taxi drivers, sharing rooms in cheap hostels, arguing in restaurants and trying to make the waiters understand what vegetarian food is. Touring was always difficult. We were facing difficulties and conquering them together, and the pleasures of intercultural practices replaced the feelings of anxiety. What did they think about China and what did they pay attention to? What interested, surprised, and disappointed them? Did their prejudices change during their sojourn in China? Where did the courage come from, and what empowered them to make these unprecedented intercultural communications and interactions happen with the Chinese people?

Equality. Invited by a French grindcore band, I went to Europe in the summer of 2008 for a four-wheel driving tour of France, Germany, Poland, Czech Republic, Switzerland, and Italy. Most of the venues they played at were punk/political squats and nonprofit youth centers. "We would like to do something for you in return"—in an intercultural way, nothing can be better than this. It was a stage of equality, in which we could truly call each other friends. We could open ourselves to each other, joke with each other, debate with each other, and express our emotions freely. At this stage, my view of the Western world and its cultures, ethical values, social norms, and political systems was changed. So what about theirs? How did their sojourn affect them? Did their perspectives on China change? Did their experiences in China influence their lives and value systems? And what do they think about these changes?

Veil. Until 2013, I've helped 24 Western D.I.Y. bands and have organized 32 tours for them. I met these cultural sojourners in China and engaged in social practices and intercultural interactions with them in their respective fields. Music is still an important part of their way of life and communication, but the things they shared and how they interacted with Chinese people became diversified. My ability to communicate, negotiate, and effectively work with people from other cultures developed, but the confidence I had led to new problems, and I realized that achieving perfection in intercultural communication is by no means an easy task. Sometimes self-doubt held me back when conflicts showed up between my Western friends and me. It seems that the barrier between us had been torn down, but we could see a looming veil interfering with our communication and interaction. Is there any possibility to pierce the veil and uncover the mystery of people from different cultures?

RESEARCH

Questions

This study investigates how cultural sojourners construct relations in the cognitive, affective, and behavioral dimensions with the host Chinese people in the context of globalization (cf. Park & Burgess, 2014). Three sets of questions are raised based on this research. First, how do cultural sojourners observe and develop differences between different cultures? Second, what values and attitudes do they have in the process of intercultural communication as cultural sojourners? Third, how do they behave and how do they take action with the host Chinese people for building connections and constructing relations together?

RQ1: How did they build their precognition of China before coming? What were their initial motivations and purposes? During their sojourn, what were the most positive and negative images of China in their view? Are they different from what they expected? What most interested them, surprised them, and disappointed them? Did they have any conflicts and misunderstandings with Chinese people?

RQ2: How did cultural sojourners experience emotional development in certain situations? Facing cultural shock and conflicts with Chinese people, how did they react and behave based on emotions? How did cultural sojourners experience and work through their positive, neutral, and negative feelings? What skills did they use to deal with their emotions?

RQ3: What were cultural sojourners trying to do to break the language barrier? What is the role of nonverbal communication in the interaction between cultural sojourners and the host Chinese? What were the strategies cultural sojourners commonly used to decrease cultural differences? What directed their behaviors during their sojourn? How did they monitor, control, and regulate their behaviors?

Methods

Communication ethnography, as a particular research method, is primarily used in this qualitative research. The researcher observes and analyzes how researched participants interact with, socialize, and influence the host Chinese people in their ways of communication through accumulations of data.

I have tagged along with Western cultural sojourners during 12 tours and journeys to conduct field studies. As their tour organizer and manager, I eventually became one of the in-group members, having the advantage of being an insider to record their life experiences and events, without having to make extra efforts to immerse myself in their lives. However, to avoid the trap of being too much on the inside, I often left problems to the participants themselves when conflicts showed up between cultures. The various roles in which I engaged myself were manageable, and generally it was quite understandable for the participants. It was often a pleasure for them to face the challenges of the language barrier and cultural differences, finding explanations and solving the problems by themselves. Meanwhile, to keep minimal intervention in the observation, I would try to behave as naturally as possible when I conducted in-depth interviews and discussed the findings with them.

I acquired various genres of ethnographic data and materials during this study, such as field diaries, recorded interviews and conversations, and photos and videos that I took on tour. Various documents provided by the participants have an important role in this study, such as tour diaries, written articles and interviews published in newspapers and magazines, music and art works, biographies and autobiographies, and photos and videos they took on tour.

A total of 167 materials were selected for analysis and classified. See Figure 10.1 for the distribution of the classified data and materials.

	Classified Data and Materials	Total Number
Observations of Researcher	Journals by Researcher	14
	Photos by Researcher	12
	Videos by Researcher	4
	Interviews by Researcher	59
Materials Provided by Participants	Journals by Participants	9
	Written Texts by Participants	3
	Written Texts and Interviews published in newspapers and magazines	4
	Photos by Participants	38
	Art Works by Participants	18
	Videos by Participants	6

Figure 10.1. Number of Classified Data and Materials.

COGNITIVE PERSPECTIVE OF CULTURAL SOJOURNERS

Cultural cognition of the sojourners is the process though which symbols get stored and cumulated, corrected, supplemented, and extended in their sojourn and communication process. Cultural cognition is examined by the researcher on the following three levels. First, how they built their cognition system before coming to China is discussed; then I examine how the stereotype weakened to some degree during their sojourns; and on the last level, I discuss the cultural distance and psychological barrier between Western sojourners and the Chinese.

Precognition

There are several major sources that the participants typically use to learn about China before coming. Internet, media, travel guidebooks, literature, and movies are the first and most important in forming their precognition of China and its culture. "Before my first visit, I only got to know about China from Hong Kong movies," said Fred, who is a fan of the Shaw Brothers; "but without stepping on its soil, I could never brag about what I know about this country." The tour organizer becomes the one who provides them with most of their information, and some of the participants also get impressions of China from their Chinese friends and friends who have been to China. Yidao, a Chinese graduate student who studied in France for four years, became an activist in the local punk scene and moved into a political squat: "I'm not the only Asian face in the local scene, but the only Chinese. Everyone wants to know more about China from me, especially the development of the D.I.Y. scene, and I always suggest that they go to China and find out for themselves." The Chinese communities abroad and their way of living help form a precognition of the local residents, but it is not a significant factor for participants who live in small towns where there are not many Chinese people.

Stereotype

Stereotypes are commonly held and shared by the participants and can be used to create images of relevant outgroups and explain their observations on certain social and cultural events. I conducted a survey of 30 participants randomly chosen from the researched subjects about their preconceptions about China before coming and how they were corrected during their sojourns. Among the first preconceived ideas on their lists, there are 11 answers about ideologies and social forms, 11 answers about government control and security supervision, and 8 answers about cultural social life in China. The results showed that most of them were corrected to different degrees during their first sojourn in China based on what they saw, heard, and experienced, and that due to face-to-face communication with the host Chinese people, their attention was often drawn to something other than what they had expected. However, similar stereotypes are hardly to be changed for foreigners who never have been to China (see Figure 10.2).

Participant Information	Year of First Visit	Impression Before Visit	Change of Impression
Dennis, Swedish	1999	We put on Mao-style cos-tumes for coming to China, and we think Chinese people will like it.	Two of our concerts were canceled because our lyrics are too political. Apparently the censorship bureau would not be more tolerant because of our belief in socialism.
Julien, Swiss	2006	Communist propaganda is everywhere on the street, and you can see a lot of statues of Chairman Mao.	I only saw two statues of Mao inside the university campus. And there are a lot more commercial advertisements than government propaganda on the streets.
Thierry, French	2011	China is a country of bicycles, and you can see thousands of them during rush hour. The view must be amazing.	The road is packed with all kinds of vehicles, buses, cars, scooters, and motor-bikes; everything except bicycles.
Andre, Swedish	2002	Kungfu masters with long white beards practice under the trees at Shaolin Temple.	The monks are too busy selling products, they have no time to practice Kungfu.

Figure 10.2. Examples of Impressions Before and After the Visit.

Cultural Distance and Psychological Barrier

1. Mr. L told me that the best way to get to know about a Chinese city is by talking with taxi drivers, and the best way to get to know about the whole of Chinese society is by taking trains and observing the people on them. The Long-distance Train, as the widely used transportation tool of a touring band in China, is one of the most important public spaces in which the cultural sojourners meet and communicate with ordinary Chinese people from various backgrounds. It shows that in certain circumstances, the desire to communicate could bridge the gaps between different nations, cultures, languages, and ethnics. Julien explained the differences between train traveling in Europe and in China.

In Europe, people are usually reading, surfing the Internet, or listening to music on the train. But on the trains in China, you can get to know a stranger and start conversation very easily. It is a public space that makes me feel most communist, and people know the ethics of sharing. If someone watches a movie on their laptop, they are very likely to share it with the seven or eight people around them. One would not listen to music on earphones, but play it loud for everyone to hear. They share snacks too: sunflower seeds, chicken feet, and spicy tofu, which they usually eat while chatting. It made me feel bad to eat my own food without sharing it with others.

2. There is a significant cognitive gap between Western sojourners and the Chinese people in some culture-related phenomena, which can be only realized through daily life activities in China. Vegetarianism and veganism, for instance, is a typical ethic-related lifestyle that can prove hard to achieve mutual-understandings with Chinese people. Among the 78 participants in this study, there were 36 vegetarians and 18 vegans, and almost everyone felt that it is difficult to be a strict vegetarian in China. Jonas, a member of a straight-edge band from Sweden, has been a vegan for 26 years. During his seven sojourns in China, the most difficult thing in his opinion is to get the right food in restaurants.

> I told the waiter that I don't eat meat, she asked, "do you eat chicken?" I said, "no, I don't eat chicken or any other meat." Then she asked, "do you eat fish?" Every single time I go to the restaurant I have to waste so much time and energy explaining that I don't eat all kinds of meat including pork, chicken, beef, fish, eggs, dairy, etc., but I can still end up finding small pieces of mince meat or sausage in the dish or soup, and sometimes the food is cooked in oil made from animals or spiced with lots of meat taste. Before coming to China, I thought China would be heaven for vegetarians because they have thousands of food products made with tofu. But I was wrong, most of the delicious tofu is cooked with mince or meat-flavor spices.

Viklund, having similar experiences and feelings as Jonas, also explained his confusions:

> We still have a lot of trouble ordering food in restaurants even with the help of our Chinese organizer. It is not a problem of language, but cultural differences. Most of the Chinese don't understand that vegetarianism is based on the moral concerns about the industrialization of animal slaughter and the consumption of animals in general. They simply consider that we just don't want to spend money on food or we don't trust that they can cook it well, and adding small pieces of meat is not a problem because it's just a little and will make it taste good, and they think it's a generous deed.

3. The media environment and the limits of free expression are indeed a communication barrier. Almost all the participants experienced frustration when finding out that many of the networks they commonly use, such as Facebook, Twitter, YouTube, Google, and Gmail, did not work in China. But for some of the participants who sojourn long term in China, they discovered various ways to make communication happen.

> Learning how to get information and communicate with people through Chinese networks is very necessary; such as WeChat, Weibo (Chinese "Twitter"), Douban

(Chinese "Facebook") and Youku (Chinese "YouTube"), and it is not as difficult as we thought. I was used to reading news about China on Western news websites, until I found out "ChinaSMACK."[2] It's not only about news, I can also read about Chinese netizens' reactions, and join the discussions and debates between Chinese and Westerners.

"For our tour in China, we have to promote our band and communicate with the Chinese people in their way. Of course, it would be better if Facebook worked in China, but to only communicate with Chinese people who can speak English is not enough. There are many more people getting to know us on our Douban band page," Susi said.

4. An interesting finding of this study is the significant changes in the stereotypes of communist ideologies, government control, and social security supervision, and the "Chinese" experiences that bring new confusions to the participants. Although stereotypes can be corrected on a certain level, Western sojourners are still outsiders. "Before my first visit, I thought there would be many Red Guards patrolling the streets," Gabriel said, "but they no longer have Red Guards in China, and actually there aren't even many police officers on the street. Instead, I see people in different uniforms everywhere, and they are very friendly and smile at us. I've been told that they are security guards, but it makes me feel strange that they don't look strong enough to protect others, many of them are in pretty old age. But anyway, I feel very safe in China, more so than in France."

Cultural censorship does exist in China, but during my 10 years of experience in organizing tours for Western bands, there have been only two bands that ran into trouble because of censorship. Vialka, for example, were deported from China in the middle of their first tour in 2003 after being reported to police because of a poster portraying a political idea:[3]

> We stayed at the Police Station for two days, and were asked many personal questions. We were not treated badly, they were quite polite to us and fed us. I believe that they didn't want to create problems for us, but they had to obey their superior officers. I don't think such things happen in China very often. We toured China eight times, and that was the only problem we had with the police.

AFFECTIVE PERSPECTIVE OF CULTURAL SOJOURNERS

The storage of knowledge is the basis of intercultural communication; however, a more crucial element is the attitude of the cultural sojourners and their abilities to adjust it. The second part of this chapter explores the affective perspective of cultural sojourners, identifying which attitudes are helpful for constructing these intercultural relations and which sentiments may be negative. Furthermore, the ability of Western sojourners for cultural empathy is discussed as a crucial component.

Elastic Limit of Cultural Sojourners

The emotions of cultural sojourners swell and subside during their sojourns, and as all materials that have limits to a degree of distortion, they have their elastic limits as well. Most of the time, the participants in this study were able to endure all kinds of situations and conflicts. However, in some circumstances, the cultural conflict went far beyond their limits. Cultural differences in dining manners and different ethical views of meat consumption, as Desiree explains in the following text, is a typical example.

> Offering food or buying dinner for guests is one of the most important ways of showing hospitality in China. We have been treated to dinner by the local promoter or venue owner very often. Apparently, we don't have many choices of what we eat, but I think it's very kind of them to introduce the local specialties to us. I'm not a vegetarian, but some of the people in the band are. Most of the dishes are with meat, and the vegetarians would not even touch them. I feel that it's not very polite, so I always force myself to eat as much as I can and persuade myself to try everything, even chicken feet, fish head and hundred-year egg. But once in Zhuhai, we were treated to a dog pot (a specialty in southern China), and that was the main dish on the table. I have two dogs at home, they are my friends and my family. I will never forget how much I suffered that night, I vomited most of my dinner afterwards. Since that day, I am afraid when we get invited to dinner. We ask our manager to announce that we're all vegetarians in order to not have to eat some strange food. I'm not proud of acting that way, but I just don't want to challenge the limits in my mind.

Don Vito, a German D.I.Y. noise band that are always on tour, and of which the three members are open-minded about different cultures, played 22 gigs in 18 cities and towns in a four-week China tour in 2009. "I think we'd prepared ourselves for all the kinds of difficulties that we could possibly meet in China, but sometimes it was still too hard to endure the situation."

> We ran to the train station in Changsha at 3:00 a.m., right after the gig, and we were informed that the train was canceled because of a snowstorm in the north. We didn't want to miss our concert in Shenzhen that night, so we decided to wait on the platform to see what was going to happen. After waiting for eight hours, the staff of the train station tried to arrange for us to get onto a passing train, but that train was packed with standing passengers like us. We tried to tell them that it was not possible for us since we were carrying so much equipment, but it seemed that there was no other choice. Susi, our bass player and the only woman in the band, was quite rudely pushed into the wagon following the so-called "Ladies First" principle. When all of us got into the train, we didn't even know where she was. We finally found her crying and trembling in the middle of the wagon with some people pointing fingers at her,

mocking, laughing and smoking; that was so rude and it absolutely scared her. We had known each other for more than 10 years, and it was the first time I saw her crying on tour. At the beginning of the China tour, we pretended that "nothing is going to be a problem for us," even though everyone knew that the tour was going to be very hard. The communication among us was not enough to face the various difficulties, and it was too late when we realized that Susi had lost control of her emotions.

Empathy

Cultural empathy, as one of the most important competencies in intercultural communication and interactions, could not be investigated in a short-term observation. Mr. A, a musician and architect, was the most popular person in his band when they toured in China in 2006. He was a very active communicator, always smiley, polite, and had a good sense of humor. But five years later, when he returned to China to visit a remote village in Yunnan province,[4] many cultural conflicts with the local residents came to light. For example, Mr. A liked showing off a tattoo that impressed and interested many young Chinese people on his first tour, but most of the farmers in this underprivileged village are Christians[5] and didn't have any appreciation of a punk tattoo with skull heads. "I think he looks scary, and I'm a little afraid of him," one villager told me; "I don't think the tattoo looks good." However, Mr. A didn't hide his tattoo even though he knew that it scared the villagers, "This is what I am, and I don't really care about how they look at me."

There's no doubt that Mr. A is a person who is open-minded about different cultures, and his passions and interest in China made him return to this country and visit one of its most original and underprivileged places. He was doing quite well on interpersonal communication during his first sojourn, but he failed under certain circumstances when he was trying to discover more about China. However, this is an individual case. In this study, many cultural sojourners have a high level of ability to feel and share emotions of others cognitively and affectively. A rich intercultural background and sojourn experiences help cultural sojourners form diverse sociocultural values and discard self-cultural centralism and ethnocentrism. They learn the social values and culture norms of the host country and interpret and broadcast them in a very Chinese way. Campbell, an activist in the Beijing underground scene, interprets Chinese rock & roll as "yaogun" in his book Red Rock. Cezard, a French musician and photographer who currently lives in Wuhan, refers to Westerners who work in China as "Yangminggong"[6] in his photographic work China 2050. "The situation of Chinese Nongmingong is very different from how we illustrate migrant workers in a Western country," Cezard said. "The Westerners who work in China, who are certainly in a different situation, can be better illustrated as part of mingong popularity, and that is how I feel as though I am one of them."

Furthermore, the participants who have a high level of empathy tend to be more concerned with the "face" of others. Although the face, as one of the top concerns of people from collectivist cultures, is not well understood by people from individualistic cultures, cultural sojourners learn how important it is in daily-life interactions with Chinese people.

> We often meet Chinese people who want to offer us alcohol at concerts. It is very kind, but they force us to Ganbei[7] with them all the time. Chinese people have an absolutely different drinking culture, I think it's quite common to insist on drinking until the body collapses, and they can be very proud of it. They offer us alcohol and drink toasts, and it can be associated with their dignity. But if we don't Ganbei in response to them, we'll make them lose face. I don't want any conflict to happen because they have their face threatened because of me. So very often, I have to Ganbei to make them happy even though I don't enjoy it at all.

BEHAVIORAL PERSPECTIVE OF CULTURAL SOJOURNERS

Effective and efficient intercultural communication is based on the cognition system cultural sojourners build, and their behaviors are led by a positive attitude toward cultural differences. At the same time, we also need to seek out techniques to master the "toolbox of culture." In this part, I investigate the strategies and ethics of Western cultural sojourners in communicating and building relationships with the Chinese, how they use language and nonverbal language to communicate, and how they adjust their behaviors in the face of problems and difficulties.

Language and Intercultural Communication

Compared to other forms of communication, human language is unique in expressing feelings, emotions, and facts of daily life and as a social tool for constructing relations between cultural groups. However, the understanding of language could be different between users from different cultures. "Every time I said I'm an open-minded person (开放的) in Chinese, people understand that I'm very sexually open," Gaia said. "I've been studying Chinese language and cultures for such a long time, but I still don't know how to express 'open-minded' without such an embarrassing ambiguity."

As friend and tour manager of the Swedish band INVSN, I encountered a typical intercultural conflict by misunderstanding an expression from a different cultural background. The Swedish said "thanks for the food" to me after every single meal, with eye contact and a very smiley face. After a few responses such as "You're welcome" or "My pleasure," I started to feel confused and upset about such polite expression. In Chinese culture, "thanks" cannot be overused among close friends, as an old saying goes: "it is not necessary to say thanks between friends." As ordering food for the band is one of my duties and all the meals were paid for with the band's money, their courtesy produced a distance between us to a large extent. At the end of the tour I told them how I felt, and it did surprise them. "I'm very sorry about that," Sara said; "in our culture, 'thanks for the food' is commonly used as one of the basic courtesy expressions to show our appreciation to friends. We're saying it to you just because we treat you as a good friend." "Thanks for the food," a simple sentence that I understand literally, implies much more culturally in the Swedish context, and that caused cultural misunderstandings.

Nonverbal Communication and Interactions

Western musicians in this study always planned additional performances for the end of concerts. However, the bands who toured in China in earlier years rarely received an "encore," even though it had always been expected. Sometimes there was someone screaming "Zailai Yige![8]" or "One more!", and the bands would directly return to the stage to play the extra songs and express their appreciation to the audience. With the rapid development of the underground scene in China, Chinese young people are quite familiar with this procedure nowadays. "Encore" can be currently heard in every single concert of foreign and domestic bands as a universal argot.

Likewise, the Chinese audience is gradually mastering the gestures and sign language to communicate with the musicians on the stage. The corna, for example, by stretching the index and little fingers while holding the middle and ring fingers down with the thumb, is commonly seen at rock concerts. Some audience members mix it up with the sign for "I love you" by extending the thumb, and get mocked by others. Raising the fist and the gesture of stretching the index finger are commonly used in punk gigs, as well as pogo, slam, and other forms of character dance. "I'm so glad to see those changes in the underground scene in China," Vincent said; "our communication with Chinese people mostly relies on the language, but it becomes different when we're on stage. We use music as language, and they respond to us in multiple ways, from which we know that they enjoy our shows and they know exactly how to express their feelings. That is very interesting and emotional."

The Closer, the Better

The closer, the better—a principle of most of the cultural sojourners in this study—is reflected in the daily communication situation. Many participants expressed interest in eating with the Chinese around a big table with the dishes placed in the middle, especially at late-night outdoor barbecues.

> The table will soon be piled with chicken bones, barbecue skewers, empty beer bottles and cigarette butts. Everyone talks and laughs loud, the same as people at other tables. We don't need to mind our dining manners and there's no distance or privacy. It feels so good to be natural and open up to the Chinese people who we might meet only once in our life. I don't really care what we eat; you know, the food is not important here, but I do enjoy this unique atmosphere and feeling.

With regard to accommodations, many participants wish to stay with local Chinese in their home.

> The hostels in China are extremely cheap compared with those in Western countries, but we much prefer to stay with local Chinese in their homes, and we really don't mind sleeping on the couch or on the floor. I bring my sleeping bag and a travel mattress every time I tour China. I don't know if we'll have any luck to get invited but I don't want to miss any opportunities. This is an experience that money cannot buy. I feel so glad and honored to get such invitations for homestays. It reflects their trust in us and provides us with an opportunity to know more about their lives.

Regarding transportation, most of the participants prefer taking the train, not only with economic concerns in mind but also for a better communicative environment. "When our band toured China in 1999 and 2004, we had arranged for a van trip as we usually do in Europe. When the distance was too far between two cities, flight became the option," Dennis said, "until the tour in 2011, I got the chance to travel by train in China, and I love it. I never got bored of seeing what the Chinese people around me were doing, eating, talking, and sharing things. And they're often interested in us, you know, and they start to ask many questions."

> At the beginning when I knew that there would be a lot of train traveling by sitting, or even without a seat for more than 10 hours, I was a little panicked. But after taking long-distance trains a few times, I found that it was not bad at all. We're not isolated in this society, and our white faces haven't increased the sense of distance between us. We've been asked so many questions, and sometimes they're too strange and private, but it's not a big deal. Once there was a middle-aged Chinese woman who came close up and touching the piercings on my nose and lips, she seriously asked if it hurts. It's very funny and it would never happen in Europe.

Cultural Identities

I was once doing an in-depth interview with Mr. R, who is a musician and social activist from Germany, in a small pub in Wuhan. Another German friend of mine came inside and I spontaneously introduced him to Mr. R as "this is Chris also from Germany." The atmosphere suddenly became very weird, and at that moment they didn't even know how to react to each other. After a while, they greeted each other and started to talk in the universal English language. "Every time I travel abroad, I try to forget my identity as a German," Mr. R told me, "or you can say that the German identity and the German way of thinking are not important anymore when I'm abroad. It helps me to get rid of the stereotypes in my head, and reduces the differences between me and others."

"The most awkward feeling on tour in China is meeting white guys at concerts, especially the French," Thomas said. "They come to our concerts because we're a band from France, but it's so strange for us to play for French people after having traveled thousands of miles."

> Honestly I don't really like to play concerts in the international metropolises such as Beijing or Shanghai, you can see that half of the audience are white. I know that Westerners contribute a lot to the underground music scene in China, and they influence Chinese people just as we do. But still, I hope that there are more Chinese people that come to our gigs and who are interested in our music, as that is our reason and purpose for touring in China.

Other than music, the multiple sociocultural identities of the participants help them enter the interactive circle of Chinese people (cf. Gordon, 2005). The French hardcore band Amer Beton coincidentally met Mr. R for the second time at Autonomous8 (Social Movement Resource Centre) in Hong Kong. The first encounter was at a squat in Lausanne, Switzerland. Mr. R was visiting a sociologist at Hong Kong Baptist University, and Amer Beton were applying for their Chinese visas. All of them—as Western cultural sojourners in China—got permission to stay at Autonomous8, and they all appreciated and cherished the opportunities to share experiences and communicate with the Chinese activist group who devotes itself to social, political, and economic change.

> We stayed there for two weeks, sharing the electricity, water and food, cooking for ourselves every day. It's so similar to the punk/political squat scene in Europe, we definitely didn't expect to see it in China. The important thing is, the Autonomous8 is not the only place like this. There's a scene and a network, and we had visited several places like this in Mainland China. It is so impressive.

CONCLUSIONS

Intercultural relations built in the sub-cultural scene through the efforts made by Western musicians sojourning in China are represented by the following three facts:

The relation with China: The sojourn experience itself, such as concerts, art performance, workshops, and discussions, is the relation Western musicians build with China. They form their perceptions of China-related facts and develop their cognition during their sojourns, producing a significant impact on the people around them who have never been to China.

The relation with the Chinese and its maintenance: Generally, Western cultural sojourners make a lot of effort to interact with the Chinese people as much as they can—tour organizer, local promoters, venues and festivals, activities, audience, and ordinary people they meet and talk with in their sojourns in China. The relations with some of them do not end after the tour finishes. The maintenance of relations produces a desire for further communication and motivates them to return to China again and again.

The contributions to the Chinese sub-cultural music scene: In the past two decades, Western musicians and bands inspired a whole generation of Chinese young people, and this influence is still expanding. China is no longer a desert on the international sub-culture map, but an essential part of it. Nowadays, some Chinese musicians and bands start to go abroad to show their music and attitudes to the outside world, which is primarily influenced by the Western sojourners with whom they built relationships.

How Do Western Cultural Sojourners Construct Intercultural Relations with the Chinese in a Global Context?

1. *Cognitive Dimension*. New opportunities and possibilities are provided by modern information and communication technologies, which offer rapid access to a large amount of information and the resources to enable people to know the outside world and its people and cultures. Based on the discussion in the cognitive perspective, the following conclusions could be derived:

First, the cultural sojourners in this study do not simply use Western or non-Western discourses to interpret the world. The information from the Internet or other media could not satisfy their desires to learn about China and its culture. Going on site, stepping on the soil, viewing the pictures, and talking with people is the first and most important thing they do to acquire a specific knowledge of China and to get true images and a representation of what China looks like.

Second, although stereotyping is unavoidable, it can quickly be corrected to varying degrees, but new stereotypes are most likely formed at the same time. Cultural learning is a developmental, dynamic, and ongoing process. The general and specific knowledge of a certain culture is enriched and varied through real-life experiences and the communication practices of cultural sojourners.

And last, interactive cognition, as the base of equal communication, plays a key role in the process of constructing relations between people from different cultures. To achieve the ultimate goal of intercultural communication and understanding, cultural sojourners go inside the world of others and explore their thoughts and behavior. In this way, they can better examine themselves and make themselves better understood.

2. *Affective Dimension.* Intercultural communication is a process of emotional development. The attitudes cultural sojourners carry with them and their ability to control and adjust their feelings play an important role in the interaction process with people from different cultures. Based on the discussion in the affective perspective, the following conclusions can be derived.

First, the process of constructing relations between different cultures accompanies the desire for communication and its production, in relation to the real-life experience of cultural sojourners. The rich sojourn experiences and the various people they meet in the host country are helpful in constructing relations with different cultures and increasing curiosity in the process of communication and interaction, providing incentives to keep it active and persistent. New desires appear, while old ones disappear. The desire to communicate, which is hardly limited to what they learned from the domestic culture or killed by the conflicts between cultures, flows and extends in an unlimited expansion of interactive networks. As long as these desires last, the pursuit of effective intercultural communication will not stop.

Second, cultural sojourners with high self-esteem and self-confidence usually have a positive attitude toward cultural differences, which helps to develop their abilities to deal with frustration and alienation. Persons with cultural tolerance and open-minded curiosity are willing to listen to others and stay open to different opinions. Instead of labeling others according to their subjective judgment, they pay more attention to self-examination and self-improvement. These individual virtues have been widely found in the researched cultural sojourners in this study, allowing for the construction of relations with people from different cultures and producing pro-social effects.

And finally, in any situation or circumstance in which we encounter conflicts, cultural empathy is always one of the most important competencies in intercultural communication. Cultivation of cultural empathy and empathy-induced altruism is a long-term process. Even those who often share emotions with others may fail in certain circumstances once having lost the capacity to feel empathy. But generally, cultural sojourners who have a high level of cognitive and affective empathy are not only able to reduce psychic distance in short-term interactions but also correct stereotypes that have formed in their mind in the process of building long-term relations with other cultures. They are willing to learn the social values and cultural norms of the host country and interpret and broadcast them in a way that can be mutually beneficial.

3. *Behavioral Dimension.* Communication between different cultures is not a process in which everyone speaks his or her own words and opinions. The ultimate goal of intercultural communication is to reach a consensus on the way of thinking and acting. Based on the discussion of the strategies and ethics of the cultural sojourners, the following conclusions can be derived.

First, the nomadic sojourning experiences of the Western cultural sojourners in this study represent an alternative intercultural innovation in the global context. They practice a rhizomatic (Deleuze & Guattari, 2004) way of thinking and acting in the world-culture map as they establish connections and relations with other cultures. They are not creating a new model but drawing a map of various connections and possibilities. Although every single relation has the possibility to be cut off, new relations and connections are developed prolifically.

Second, what these cultural sojourners are trying to do is bridge the gaps with multiple entries and exits. We need dialogue, not only through language but also through new means of communication and interaction that are creative and imaginative.

Third, the cultural sojourners in this study are independent individuals but can be united by the cultural identities and symbols they shared and created. Furthermore, their ultimate goal is to cooperate and act together to fight all kinds of cultural inequalities.

China's Role in a Global Society for Better East and West Cultural Understanding

In the 21st century, a period of accelerated global change, culture is developed and driven by various international factors. The conflicts and misunderstandings between different cultures cannot be solved by violence but through dialogue, communication, cooperation, and interaction.

In the cognitive perspective, obtaining knowledge and understanding an outside world divided by countries, regions, and ethnics is not enough. China should take on a broader view of humanity as a whole. We live on the same earth and look up at the same sky. There are always facts, ethics, and topics that are beyond cultures and boundaries, particularly the ultimate concerns of human existence: the environment, human and animal rights, poverty, social inequality, and so forth. The ultimate goal of communication and interaction beyond cultural boundaries is to work together to make the world a better place, and China still has a long way to go as a responsible major country.

In the affective perspective, China should be more tolerant and open-minded toward others, especially in the face of criticism from the international community. Intercultural communication and relationships will not help China achieve perfection. We must learn skills to deal with our emotions and attitudes and understand and affect the emotional states of others to be able to mediate the relationships in a changing international social environment.

Last, the Chinese people should use imaginative and creative means of communication to break through the barriers of language and spark the motivation, courage, and spirit necessary to act together with people from the outside world, dealing with problems through cooperation and negotiation rather than with menace and threat.

NOTES

1. The Swedish punk rock band The (International) Noise Conspiracy had a tour in China in 1999, but all of their 15 shows were in Beijing, Shanghai, and Hongkong. In the same year, the American/Czech duo Sabot arrived in China as the terminal of their Silk Road Tour, but they hardly managed to find any venues or opportunities to play.
2. ChinaSMACK (http://www.chinasmack.com/) provides non-Chinese language readers with a glimpse into modern China and Chinese society by translating into English popular and trending Chinese Internet content and netizen discussions from China's largest and most influential websites, discussion forums, and social networks.
3. The poster of Vialka's tour in 2003 was against the war in Iraq.
4. Bingzhongluo (丙中洛), the village Mr. A visited, is located in the northernmost part of Nujiang Prefecture in Yunnan Province, which shares a national boundary with Myanmar and provincial boundary with Tibet.
5. Christianity has become the largest religion in this area.
6. Yangminggong (洋民工) refers to foreign workers in China. This item comes from the Chinese word "nongmingong" (农民工), which refers to the vast amount of migrant workers from the Chinese countryside doing labor jobs in cities.
7. Ganbei (干杯) means "bottoms up" in Chinese.
8. Zailai Yige (再来一个) means "one more" in Chinese.

BIBLIOGRAPHY

Campbell, J. (2011). *Red rock: The long, strange march of Chinese rock & roll*. Hong Kong: Earnshaw Books.

Deleuze, G., & Guattari, F. (2004). *A thousand plateaus: Capitalism and schizophrenia* (5th ed.). London: Continuum International.

Gordon, M. M. (2005). The concept of sub-culture and its application. In K. Gelder & S. Thornton (Eds.), *The subcultures reader* (2nd ed.). London: Routledge.

Park, R. E. (1928). Human migration and the marginal man. *The American Journal of Sociology*, *33*(6), 881–893.

Park, R. E., & Burgess, E. W. (2014). *Introduction to the science of sociology*. Charleston, NC: CreateSpace.

Shan, Bo. (2010). *The problems and possibilities of intercultural communication*. Wuhan: Wuhan University Press.

Simmel, G. (1950). The stranger. In K. Wolff (Trans), *The sociology of Georg Simmel* (pp. 402–408). London: Free Press.

Siu, P. C. P. (1952). The sojourner. *American Journal of Sociology*, *58*(1), 34–44.

Siu, P. C. P. (1988). *The Chinese laundryman: A study of social isolation*. New York: New York University Press.

CHAPTER ELEVEN

The Self-Salvation Path
OF Communication

BO SHAN

As sociology is a discipline to answer how society is possible, communication is a discipline to answer how communication is possible. It provides the mechanisms of cognition and repair for human communication. Therefore, it also provides the hope of better communication.

However, reality mocks communication studies again and again. Look at the Xiao Yueyue incident, the continuing suicides of Foxconn employees, and the lonely victims of Wenchuan earthquake.[1] Such repeatedly occurring communication dilemmas inquire of scholars: Have you really found the true problem of human communication? Can you find a pathway out of communication dilemmas?

In the end, the understanding of "how communication is possible" is still weak. And this weakness makes communication studies seem unnecessary, because they cannot provide the possibility of improving communication. They haven't taken any action to improve real-life communicating. Furthermore, they can't provide any hope of good communication. What communication studies has done is merely copy the cold reality by looking on someone's trouble indifferently and objectively or dodging the dilemma of communication by moral criticism.

In this revolutionary communication era, human communication is more and more unstable and in danger. Communication scholars tend to analyze the political and technological aspect of the communication revolution, such as the rise of neo-liberalism that leads to the centralization of the media and the collapse of democracy. The revolution in communication technology brings out media convergence and makes new challenges to the existing media institutions and communication modes, and so on.

Actually, the most profound aspect of the communication revolution is pushing humans into the mediated society. Mediated society is now making us live in the condition of fast-growing interpersonal relationships. On the one hand, this narrows the time-and-space distance between people—both might be extinguished at last. And we have more communications with "the other." People have more freedom in choosing their audience and the character of their interaction. We can build an almost infinite number of bridges.

On the other hand, the symbolized reality created by the media—and the saturation of information, knowledge, and symbols led by the explosion of communication methods—isolates humans from objective reality, real history, and culture. This makes people keen on one kind of communication but distant from another, and thus leads people to have bias toward one kind of cognition but isolated from holistic cognition. People linger around the mutual construction of images between intercultural interactions created by the media and are alienated from real intercultural contact (Bolden, 2014). They are used to face-to-face communication constructed by the media but lose real interpersonal face-to-face interaction and shape an omnipresent gap (Shan, 2010, p. 20).

The double cultural roles that the media play as both "bridge" and "gap" are two sides of the same coin—media control. As an infinite "bridge," the media control the path, method, and modes of communication. As an omnipresent gap, the media extend cognitive bias and cultural bias.

This two-sided phenomenon can also be expressed as "mediation" (Zengotita, 2009). It can be understood as people facing reality through the media, and also as manifesting the emotional experience communicated by the media that is created by all the arts and human power. At the same time, "bridge" and "gap" include especially those influences that the media have on us toward everyone's experience of personal life and of this world. Because of such a change, "how communication is possible" becomes a most fundamental question.

The possibility of communication is rooted in the dilemma of reality. It concerns the legitimacy of communication studies. It is not difficult to understand this if we observe the development of sociology that is close to communication studies.

Sociologists construct a holistic view based on the relationship between people and society: People do not have the concept of society anymore. Public man[2] (Sennett, 2008) is falling, the same as social capital.[3] Specifically, people do not participate in and understand the public sphere by actual social contact. They are now used to not communicating with others, using the excuse of "freedom from interference." They are unwilling to spend their free time chatting with neighbors or participating in group activities. Hence, sociologists advocate the use of Foucault's words: *Il faut défendre la société!*[4] [Then society must be defended!]

Discovering society in its founding period to defending society today seems to construct a circle from the birth to the rebirth of sociology. In the middle of the 19th century, the breaking of traditional society discredited the orthodox view at that time that had believed that human behavior was determined either by God or by physiology. Émile Durkheim's study on suicide discovered the significance of social integration to persons, which means social power influences individual action. The higher the social integration of a group, the lower the rate of suicide will be (Durkheim, 1996). Durkheim's study presents an important fact: Society is an external entity for individuals and obtains real power equal to the physical world. Sociological studies later on discovered that societies are processes of continual social criticism and reconstruction. Fromm's "sane society" means reconstructing society after criticizing it. "Sane society" is described as letting "people take activities in the scale [they] can control and perceive, make people become active and responsible participators in social life and become the Lord of [their] life" (Fromm, 2007, p. 279).

Real society can scarcely be the "sane society." It hardly lets people feel comfortable or happy. On the contrary, real society typically brings people into suppression or even suffocation. However, if there were no society, there would be no significant existence for human beings. If we take no step to construct and protect "the sane society" in our heart, we cannot escape the death of self-reclusiveness or the infringement of power (including nation power). At the same time, at the important moment when a citizen society slips into a market society or greedy society, the decomposition of "society" means the decomposition of the legitimacy of sociology. Therefore, defending society is the opportunity for sociology's rebirth.

In fact, the moment that people discovered society is the moment when people rediscovered human communication. According to Karl Marx, the ideas of common material communication and consciousness communication happened after the industrial revolution. The common interaction between people makes it possible for social organizations crossing clan, kinship, and territory to come into being as well as diverse groups, communities, culture, structure, and identity, and for the breaking down and reorganization of society.

The discovery of society means to discover models of relationships and social networks in structural perspective; the relationship constructed between people and the outside world in cultural perspective (physical culture, cognitive culture, and prescriptive culture); and the exchange of cultural resources inside our structural status in interactionist perspective. Every perspective of society is activated and maintained by communication. Society operates in communication. Meanwhile, all intrapersonal communication, interpersonal communication, organizational communication, and mass communication happen in society.

According to Wilbur Schramm (1994), it is not coincidental that the two words "community" and "communication" have the same linguistic root. People cannot be isolated from society. Some kinds of communication will take place as long as people get together to make a living (p. 55). Simultaneously, human beings desire to communicate, but they also hurt each other. Plato described a story of human communication:

> It is because humans had a share of the divine dispensation that they alone among animals worshipped the gods, with whom they had a kind of kinship, and erected altars and sacred images. It wasn't long before they were articulating speech and words and had invented houses, clothes, shoes, and blankets, and were nourished by food from the earth. Thus equipped, human beings at first lived in scattered isolation; there were no cities. They were being destroyed by wild beasts because they were weaker in every way, and although their technology was adequate to obtain food, it was deficient when it came to fighting wild animals. This was because they did not yet possess the art of politics, of which the art of war is a part. They did indeed try to band together and survive by founding cities. The outcome when they did so was that they wronged each other, because they did not possess the art of politics, and so they would scatter and again be destroyed. (in Cooper, 1997, pp. 322–323)

We can feel from Plato's description that "how communication is possible" has been a long-standing and in-depth question. Modern communication studies detail this problem into all kinds of problems. Sometimes communication studies face the problem of how to construct a community by communication, such as the relationship between communication and democracy. Sometimes communication studies face problems like human attitudes and behavior, such as interpersonal communication or cognitive effects in the communication process. Communication studies also refer to the power relationship in communication, such as the ownership of media, the construction of the public sphere, ethnicity in communication, communication and the differentiation of social structures, production and consumption, and so forth.

Though these problems come from different perspectives across the field of media and society, deviation toward the technicalization of the question "How is communication possible?" has led to a continuous narrowing of the problems and has caused a crisis in the communication discipline. As Wolfgang Donsbach (2006), the former chair of International Communication Association, has put it: "With more personnel striving for professional distinction, the research questions become smaller and more remote all the time" (p.447).

As summarized by John Durham Peters (2003), there are two dominant discourses in communication studies after World War II: technical and therapeutic discourses (p. 18). The former turns common information in daily life into a kind of technology and thus shapes an information concept of communication that combines natural science (DNA is the great password), the humanities (language is communication), and social science (communication is a basic social process) together. The therapeutic trajectory puts the emphasis on the failure and dilemma of human communication, exploring the salvation path of human communication through multiple dimensions such as psychological therapy, social criticism, cultural studies, political economy of communication, and media ecology.

The innovation logic of technology is that every time when media technology, communication technology, and information technology are out of control, technical rationality always leads people to pursue a more powerful controlling technology. This is an innovation of technical rationality, that is to say, people should not only program for media development following the logic of technical rationality and form the media environment and spectacle according to their own needs but also influence others by the media through building more elaborate controlling mechanisms.

Therapeutic discourse tends to presume that good communication has a function to treat the alienation, rootlessness, drifting, and indifference of human beings. Or it can counter people's loss of value and significance. From this perspective, we have to clarify the value of communication and find an antidote to unfair power-dominating relationships in the process of communication.

Unfortunately, technical and therapeutic discourses have neither liberated people's communication nor freed their thoughts of communication. While deconstructing the restrictions of communication, technical discourse is also constructing the rational control of communication. It seems that rational control is an inevitable rule of modern social order, as Harold D. Lasswell (2009) observes: "If the public wants to break the iron chains, they must accept silver chains" (p.177). In fact, rational control is even stricter than the old social control relying on brute power. Therapeutic discourse is keen to examine the restrictions from communication and the power-dominant relationships in communication. But, in the meantime, it divides the moral boundary and value boundary between us and others, which results in an inability of communication studies to lead to daily conversation.

Let's go back to China in 1978 when ideological emancipation brought Western communication studies. At that time, common people were liberated from mental control and transformed the uniformity and monotony of daily life. They put themselves out of mental control and went back to warm interactive personal lives from numb and cold group living. Once the common

Chinese went back to personal life, restored the choice and judgment of their lives, the desire of communication became uncontainable. Therefore, the introduction of Western communication studies was pretty natural for China, which in the absence of modern communication concepts was eager to come out of its closed circle of culture.

However, that emancipation has not occurred. The old ideological shackles weren't eliminated, while the new mental control came into reality. People stepped into the ivory tower of Western communication studies and lived in the shadow of several "gods" of communication. The Chinese obeyed the direction of thinking designated by the West, persisted or obsessed in what they had learned from the West, and could not make independent innovation on Chinese communication problems. Therefore, intellectual custom blocked or obstructed the wisdom of communication studies.

By 1992 when second thought liberation started in China,[5] people broke the binary opposition of socialism and capitalism and tended to a socialist market economy.[6] As a result, Chinese scholars turned their attention to communication studies once again. They grasped the change in media structure through the competition of the multimedia and observed diverse media functions in the communication process. They focused on audience studies and communication effects to seek control of the media market and the innovation of the mode of business operations (Li & Li, 1998). At the same time, the Chinese widened their vision from freedom of the press to communication rights and freedom of information; from media competition to media convergence through the new technology; from one-dimensional communication to multidimensional and interactive communication.

Furthermore, the third ideological emancipation starting in 1997 got rid of the worship of ownership.[7] While some people criticized the social inequality of China's market economy and blamed it on the invasion of international firms and the global capitalist system, the Chinese had already begun pushing themselves into the tide of globalization. When people examined media globalization and made globalization a concept, consciousness, and thinking method, their thoughts were opened to the Western world unprecedentedly.

First, Chinese academics tried, in approaching the Western news media, to understand the media's tendency toward fragmentation, massification, integration, and gigantism, as well as the concept of global management. Chinese scholars got to know the idea of media operations and the concept of news reports from dialogue with the West (Gu, 2004; Su, 2005). Second, Chinese scholars analyzed the structure of the Western news media's ownership system and operation mode, the dilemma of journalistic professionalism in the market mode, the path to make the media bigger and stronger, the relationship of the media and democratic politics, and the problems of the media and the public sphere. They also grasped the concept system of Western media comprehensively. Third, they explored the relationship between the Chinese media and Western media in the context of globalization. They rethought the conflict between social instruments and profit maximization, the conflict between market choice and government regularity, the impact of foreign media on Chinese media markets, the difference between Chinese and foreign media operations, and they looked for ways to transform Chinese media (Zhou, 2002).

Emancipation from ideology brought Chinese society closer to communication from one time to the next. Chinese communication studies also become more professional in the process of learning from the West. However, the defects of Western communication studies have also been brought to China: it did not contribute to either the liberation of human communication or the emancipation of communication ideas, or to daily communication practice. Besides, it also has left a Chinese style problem: Westernization and de-Westernization (Waisbord & Mellado, 2014). Westernization makes Chinese communication studies lose themselves; following the theory and concepts from the West makes the Chinese unable to face their own communication problems. Hence it hasn't brought people innovative thoughts and imaginative theory. De-Westernization tends to reject Western thoughts and theory instead of sharing ideas with the West or providing comprehensive creations. Therefore, it results in the closing of thoughts and the danger of the Chinese speaking to themselves.

The mediated transformation of society has tremendously changed the relationship between humans, the media, and society. The media have become a way for people to deal with reality. The media infinitely extend people's communication space and alleviate loneliness. But the media have also reduced face-to-face interaction and thus made people's leisure time more and more private, passive, and thus fastened to the decline of society and "public man." There are increasingly more people who are "bowling alone," in Putnam's terms (2000). People prefer to stay at home alone, watch TV, surf the Internet, and live a kind of virtual public life online rather than spend their spare time in communicating, chatting, and participating in public lives. In the 1920s, Walter Lippmann observed that the dilemma of communication was the impossibility to look, listen, contact, or understand the world where we live because it was too large, too complex, and too fast. We could only take action based on reports from other people (Lippmann, 2006). The situation now is that the world where we live is mediated. We are used to dealing with reality through the media and are willing to create mediated reality ourselves.

When facing the interpersonal communication problem, the imagination of communication study has been greatly decreased. In the perspective of interpersonal communication, Robinson Crusoe's world does not exist in the real society or in the inner world. Persons cannot speak only to themselves or build an isolated island in their minds, for language is social. There is no private language. However, we still imagine realizing the conversation between the Freudian ego of reason and the id of desire, the superego of morality. This communication would undoubtedly be the most stable. But a danger exists in this kind of stability. No matter how stable the ego, id, and superego's communications are, paranoia of the self will be inevitable. In a group, we extend from the pursuit for stability of self to the group. This makes the danger of group paranoia hide behind successful communication. Think of fascism, fundamentalism, and so forth. In daily life, we seek persons who are similar to us in mind and in emotion, as the poem says: "birds singing for friends" (*The Book of Songs*). The saying "dissidence of opinions makes it useless to talk" also means we can only have conversation with those who have the same discourse as us. That is also a kind of self-paranoia in appealing for stability. That means to communicate from self. The goal of communication is "You equal me, I equal you." If not, stable interaction will be hard to seek. In that case, we can't help sighing over the failure of communication, screaming that "hell is other people" and "the human heart is incomprehensible." We can see that people's personal imagination of communication is limited.

In real life, the dilemma of communication is that people have lost the freedom of communication. The relationship of "people, media, and society" is in serious imbalance. People and society have disappeared in mediated society. In this kind of crisis, communication studies should face up to the dilemma of communication, help people restore the imagination to communication, rebuild a relationship of unity between the media and human beings. For one thing, communication creates the mediated world by communication practice, and for another, we should understand communication bias in terms of the mediated extension of the human body. Communication studies should direct the relationship between media and society by practical wisdom, that is, to focus on the authenticity of mediated social interaction and on constructing the common rule of mediated society. In this way, communication studies could offer us a cognitive and repair system of human communication in our daily lives. In this sense, communication studies can realize the freedom of communication and construct a harmonious relationship among people, media, and society to liberate communication from technical discourse and therapeutic discourse and liberate people's communication ideas.

NOTES

1. Xiao Yueyue: a 2-year-old girl named Wang Yue who died after being run over and then lay unaided on the street while 18 pedestrians passed by. The continuing suicides of Foxconn employees: 18 Foxconn employees attempted suicide with 14 deaths between January and

November 2010. Both of the cases illustrate the absence of the Chinese people's ability to trust each other, as well as a lack of mutual communication. They lost the spiritual space to communicate freely with others.

2. Sennett's concept of "Public Man" is not a permanent or eternal word. In the 18th century, when public life was in its fullest flowering, being "public" meant to behave with strangers in an emotionally satisfying way while remaining aloof from them. Being public was thus man-made, whereas one's private self was natural. The post-Augustine Roman pursued his private life outside the public world. In the 19th century, "public man" refers to those who were earnest about political issues and cultivated a public characteristic based on individuality; the latter also became a social category. After carefully reviewing the history of public life, Sennett concludes that in modern times, we are suffering from impersonality, with emptiness in private life, as well as public life becoming distorted. This impedes our personalities from fully developing (see Sennett, 2008).

3. For Robert D. Putnam, "social capital" refers to "features of social organization such as networks, norms, and social trust that facilitate coordination and cooperation for mutual benefit. For a variety of reasons, life is easier in a community blessed with a substantial stock of social capital." However, from the1960s, the voting booth, organizational membership, religious affiliation, workers' affiliation with labor unions, trust in American government, membership in civic and fraternal organizations, and volunteers for mainline civic organizations, etc. have all increasingly declined or have been deserted by Americans. Putnam thus concludes that "more Americans are bowling today than ever before, but bowling in organized leagues has plummeted in the last decade or so" (Putnam, 1995).

4. Michel Foucault thinks that we should abandon the traditional way of analyzing power only in its legal form, or through Marxist "economism" theory. He proposed a new way of analyzing power through sets of relations. Foucault presents his historical investigations with the common critique of "liberal" economism and "Marxist" political power. Meanwhile, Foucault says we must defy the economic functionality that "Marxism" attributed to power and revise the notions of "war," "tension," "power," and "history" by analyzing their mutual relations. (See Jacques Luzi, 1998.)

5. China launched the great debate on "practice is the sole criterion for testing truth" in 1978. In retrospect of old ideological ossification and thought slavery, the Chinese people confirmed the priority of practice. This procedure is regarded as China's first ideological emancipation and thought liberation. In 1992, Deng Xiaoping put forward the idea of getting rid of the dualism between socialism and capitalism after his inspection of southern China. This inspection speech led to a big discussion about China's socialist market economy and the choice of the path of market, thus giving China its second thought liberation.

6. The shift from a central planning system to a socialist market economy in China can briefly be understood as giving more power to the liberal market and less power to the central government, but the latter still plays an important role in the social economy.

7. The so-called worship of ownership refers to the traditional concept of seeing the state-owned system as equivalent to socialism. It believed that the development of the non-public economy would make the public ownership economy lose its dominant position. Since 1997, China started another great discussion that contributed to a thorough understanding of Marx's concept of social ownership. As people gradually realized the important role various economic sectors play in the real development of socialism, they have begun to seek coordination and healthy development of economic elements and thus pursued innovation for the socialist system. This is regarded as China's third ideological emancipation.

BIBLIOGRAPHY

Bolden, G. B. (2014). Negotiating understanding in "intercultural moments" in immigrant family interactions. *Communication Monographs, 81*(2), 208–238.

Cooper, J. M. (Ed.). (1997). *Plato complete works.* Indianapolis, IN: Hackett.

Donsbach, W. (2006). The identity of communication research. *Journal of Communication, 56*(3), 437–448.

Durkheim, É. (1996). *Le suicide.* Trans. Y. Feng. Beijing: Commercial Press.

Fromm, E. (2007). *The sane society.* Trans. D. Wang et al. Beijing: International Culture Press.

Gu, X. (2004). *Meeting U.S. newspapers.* Guangzhou: Nanfang Daily Press.

Lasswell, H. D. (2009). *Propaganda technique in World War.* Trans. J. Zhang & Q. Tian. Beijing: Renmin University of China Press.

Li, L. (2003). *Contemporary Western news media.* Shanghai: Fudan University Press.

Li, L., & Li, X. (1998, Fall). Journalism needs to turn to mass communication. *Journalism Bimonthly, 57*, 17–20.

Lippmann, W. (2006). *Public opinion.* Trans. K. Yan & J. Hong. Shanghai: Shanghai Century Publishing Group.

Luzi, J. (1998). Il faut défendre la société, par Michel Foucault, *Neutralité & engagement du savoir, Agone 18 et 19*, 237–247.

Marx, K., & Engels, F. (1961, 1965, 1972). *Complete works of Marx and Engels* (vol. 9, 22, 24). Beijing: People's Publishing House.

Peters, J. D. (2003). *Speaking into the air: A history of the idea of communication.* Trans. D. He. Beijing: Huaxia Press.

Putnam, R. D. (1995). Bowling alone: America's declining social capital. *Journal of Democracy, 6*(1), 65–78.

Putnam, R. D. (2000). *Bowling alone: The collapse and revival of American community.* New York: Simon & Schuster.

Schramm, W. (1994). *The story of human communication.* Trans. Z. Yu & Y. Wu. Taiwan: Yuan-Liou Publishing.

Sennett, R. (2008). *The fall of public man.* Trans. J. Li. Shanghai: Shanghai Translation Publishing House.

Shan, B. (2008, Summer). How to unfold the wisdom of Chinese communication studies. *Journalism Bimonthly, 96*, 49–51.

Shan, B. (2010). *The problems and possibilities of intercultural mediated communication.* Wuhan: Wuhan University Press.

Su, R. (2005). *A probe into media conglomerates in the U.S.* Guangzhou: Nanfang Daily Press.

Waisbord, S., & Mellado, C. (2014). De-Westernizing communication studies: A reassessment. *Communication Theory, 24*(4), 361–372.

Zengotita, T. D. (2009). *Mediated: How the media shape your world and the way you live in it.* Trans. S. Wang. Shanghai: Shanghai Translation Publishing House.

Zhou, W. (Ed.). (2002). *Cutting-edge media report: The prospect and direction in transformation of an industry.* Beijing: Guangming Daily Press.

Intercultural Competence OF Journalists: Surveys AND Reflection

Intercultural News Reports AND Intercultural Competence OF Western Journalists IN China

DAN YANG

Research on foreign correspondents, such as a wide survey of American international reporting and foreign correspondents (Hess, 1996), an anthropological study of foreign correspondents (Hannerz, 2004), field work on war correspondents based in Salvador (Pedelty, 1995), and recent research on foreign correspondents in China (Qian, 2012; Zhang & Ye, 2009) suggest that foreign correspondents in modern media institutions form a professional community, sharing the same professional values. "Is it fair? Is it true? Is it accurate?" One of the respondents in this research has repeated these questions to emphasize they are what come first when evaluating his and his colleagues' work.

This research explains why foreign correspondents, whether "parachutists" or stationed journalists, are able to make news stories on the first day they arrive at a place, finish their daily tasks, and even make well-known and highly praised news reports without knowing the local language, understanding the local culture, or communicating deeply with local people. They are defined as foreign correspondents by working with a set of operational codes, routines, and ethics, in which cultural sensitivity is not necessarily ignored but is marginalized.

Research on journalistic gate keeping finds that individual influence on news production is insignificant. Instead, media institutions embedded in larger political and economic structures decide what should be reported and how the story goes, following their sophisticated routines of news production. But the reality may call for a renewed perception of special issues in foreign correspondence. (1) Only a few media institutions send a small number of journalists to cover a foreign country. According to Chinese official data, until 2012, 58 countries had sent more than 700 foreign correspondents representing more than 421 media organizations to work in China.[1] (2) Foreign correspondents are more independent compared to newsrooms in their home countries. They are situated in a more complicated working environment, which potentially empowers them with more autonomy to make decisions. (3) New media technologies provide opportunities for journalists to have more individual influence on news coverage than before. (4) Audiences of certain media outlets become unprecedentedly global and diverse. Showing on the news websites and journalists' blogs, a story may receive feedback more instantly and directly, not only from regular consumers of the media but also from people who are referred to in the story and anyone who feels connected with the story. The status quo raises questions: Is it enough to merely report accurate facts in foreign correspondence? Should news reports be culturally sensitive to the Other?

The inner limitation of news production is that it is a construction of the outside world. The professional ethics of journalism sets the "reporting of facts" as a target, but reporters do not remind their audience anywhere in their stories that the facts they present are chosen and restructured. Instead, the news media always claim they are presenting truth to their constituency.

Journalistic representations of the Other have been criticized for decades in terms of both national and international news. But how can a breakthrough be made in both journalistic theory and practice? Some researchers have been working on theorizing a new approach to journalism and seeking solutions. Since the 1990s, ethical theorists have discussed possibilities to establish a globally acknowledged cultural ethics that enables different cultural groups to communicate and get along with each other. This trend has also thrown a shadow on the study of journalism, presumably a mediated way of communication between different cultures.

Some researchers have advised journalistic education to provide courses and training for students to enhance their intercultural awareness and competence. After examining the role of culture in the work of foreign correspondents and conducting in-depth interviews with six correspondents, Starck and Villanueva (1992) have raised such questions as, "Is there such a practice as 'intercultural' reporting? If so, how does this differ from traditional journalism?" They have suggested that journalists striving for a clear understanding of events in another culture should use methods that are sensitive to local conditions and, to some extent, that attempt to portray other cultures on their own terms rather than merely through the cultural filters of the journalist.

There also has been a trend of approaching intercultural journalism through an anthropological perspective. Fürsich (2002) has transferred the concept of "representations of the Other" to current global media practice and explored new strategies to overcome the epistemological dilemma journalists face when covering others. She has pointed out that only self-reflective and critical approaches toward traditional ritualistic reporting and production strategies can help to disentangle problematic media representations.

Some journalists have appealed to reforming news genres and reporting methods. For example, Luyendijk (2010), a former foreign correspondent based in the Middle East, has contended that the criticism of journalism should go beyond prejudice and ideology to see the dilemmas in news production, which requires a fundamental rethinking of what news is on the part of both journalists and audiences.

In recent years, researchers have made efforts to establish a global journalism ethics, calling for "development of a richer theoretical basis for journalism ethics and a more adequate set of practical newsroom-based norms for a multiplatform journalism with global reach, which leads to a more cosmopolitan journalism ethics in theory and practice" (Ward, 2009). After reviewing the development of global journalism ethics, Ji and Huang (2014) concluded that most researchers on establishing a global journalism ethics, despite their different approaches and theoretical frames, recognize the importance of cultural diversity and the possibility of finding a widely acknowledged base of global journalism ethics. As a result, the notion of global journalism ethics might not be a utopian imagination but become a consensus of journalists all over the world.

Researchers such as Downing and Husband (2005) and Garyantes (2010) have discussed the concept of intercultural competence as a new approach to journalism. Both researchers have tried to transcend the existing structure of journalistic professionalism and find a new approach to the study of journalism. To sum up, they suggest that there are three core elements for being an interculturally competent journalist: (1) reflection on the inner limitations of news production and their own cultural bias; (2) knowledge of the Other; and (3) skills in making culturally sensitive news stories.

However, the research of Downing and Husband and of Garyantes is focused on journalistic practice within a nation or multicultural community. The question for this chapter is whether intercultural competence is a valid approach for perceiving international news reporting. According to the above three core elements of journalistic intercultural competence, this study raises the following four research questions.

RQ1:   Are foreign correspondents aware of the inner limitations of news production and their own cultural bias?

RQ2:   How do the foreign correspondents value the knowledge of the Other's culture?

RQ3:   Will foreign correspondents apply skills to make their news coverage more culturally sensitive?

RQ4:   What factors influence foreign correspondents' awareness, knowledge, and skills to report the Other in a culturally sensitive way?

METHOD

To answer the above research questions, eight foreign correspondents in China were interviewed in this study. All of them have worked with mainstream Western media institutions including AP, Thomson Reuters, AFP, Agencia EFE, the *Guardian*, PRI (Public Radio International), CNN, and the *New York Times*. There are seven reporters and one editor. They have been foreign correspondents from 4 years to 30 years.

All respondents can use English to accomplish their daily tasks. Two respondents can speak and write in Chinese, with educational backgrounds in the Chinese language or related areas. Three respondents can read and speak in Chinese; three respondents can only speak some words in Chinese.

There were two stages of interviews. In the first stage, researchers sent the eight respondents outlines of a semi-structured interview, which included three aspects: (1) respondents' professional experiences, such as their understanding of journalistic values, ideas, and principles; (2) the respondents' cultural experiences, such as their cultural backgrounds, personal education, and the cultural differences they encounter while working in China; and (3) the respondents' understanding of cultural bias in their work. These questions are designed to explore the respondents' awareness and understanding of news production and cultural differences.

After this first stage, each respondent was asked to provide one or two pieces of their news stories that they thought were their masterpieces in reporting in China (the editor respondent is not included). At the second stage of the interview, respondents and the researcher discussed their chosen news stories to explore how they have produced the stories. This part of the interview is meant to examine two aspects: (1) to what extent the respondents' ideas and awareness are reflected in their news coverage on China; and (2) what kind of skills the respondents have assumed to use or actually did use to make their stories more culturally sensitive.

All eight respondents participated in the first-stage interviews, on average for more than one hour. Three respondents participated separately in the second-stage interviews, talking about their best stories in detail.

AWARENESS OF INNER LIMITATIONS OF NEWS PRODUCTION AND CULTURAL BIAS

Whose Bias?

Most respondents have recognized that their cultural backgrounds might influence their work. There is a tendency to criticize bias and prejudice in the

Western media's coverage of China as a whole while accepting the fact that cultural baggage and upbringing are unavoidable for individual journalists. However, they are more aware of the problem than editors and audiences back home, who often make mistakes due to technical or other more complicated reasons.

Some respondents have criticized the bias in the Western news media and their audiences as a whole, which include (1) stereotypes, such as Chinese people still wear Mao tunics, or dress like blue ants; (2) deviation in news choices, such as a preference for negative events; (3) black-and-white stances, such as the government is bad, or the Chinese people are brainwashed; and (4) cliché rhetoric, such as "authoritarian government."

Some respondents attribute bias in news to the following factors: (1) ignorance of China's practical situation by editors, some journalists, and audience, because they cannot read in Chinese, or they do not bother to verify what they read about; (2) people's lack of reflection on old concepts and ideological bias; and (3) economic pressures on media institutions.

Most respondents claim that they take precautions to avoid bias and have tried their best to fight with them, but as individuals, they cannot avoid mistakes at work. They attributed these mistakes to the following factors: (1) technical problems; (2) complicated situations in collecting information due to government control; (3) the journalist's lack of experience, training, or knowledge; and (4) editors' inappropriate modification of the journalist's original story.

Some respondents tend to recognize bias and stereotypes as a general characteristic in the Western media's reports of China, which are caused by ignorance and disregard by media institutions, audiences, and journalists. But for individual foreign correspondents, they are more careful of their cultural baggage and make efforts to fight bias. One of the respondents who speaks fluent Chinese frequently uses the phrase "we Western media" when he refers to clichés in news stories, which actually gives a sense of what he is talking about, such as "We Western media often write about human rights issues, Internet policies, or other problems, but always in the same way. In fact, there are very complicated things behind the event, from which you can see a changing China. I can only utter a sigh at this."

Separating institutional or group "bias" from the individual journalist's "mistakes" may indicate the potential limitation of producing interculturally competent news content. Journalists are commonly aware that bias is problematic in foreign correspondence, while they tend to believe that in specific situations, individual mistakes in news work are unavoidable, just as the same in any other occupational situations. As a result, mistakes can be noticed and revised, while nobody needs to take responsibility for bias in the news as a whole.

All respondents show a high cultural sensitivity when talking about cultural bias in news. They are prepared to fight stereotypes and clichés and try their best to avoid and fix mistakes. This is not only an ethical demand on themselves but also a way of maintaining their autonomy at work. In fact, some veteran correspondents say that they have been far away from their motherlands for so many years that they know better what happens in their host country than in their home country.

Some respondents, especially those working for news agencies, experience more institutional control. For example, the editors based in Singapore modified one respondent's story about the Olympic torch arriving at the top of Mt. Qomolangma by adding a paragraph about the political symbolic meaning of the event at the beginning of the story. The respondent was not happy with this kind of editorship because his name is shown in the byline.

In other situations, more autonomy at work may enable the journalist to make more interculturally competent news stories. One respondent working with PRI who enjoys high autonomy and freedom at work uses an ethnographic style in making her stories. When she has done a series such as a story about young people in China, she has prepared for months by reading, talking to people, interviewing, thinking, and feeling. Only 5% to 10% of the materials are used in the final stories.

Most respondents agree that the most effective methods to make anti-bias news coverage are (1) inviting editors back home to go to China to get firsthand experience and (2) telling the story in as much detail as possible.

Professionalism of Foreign Correspondents

Recognizing bias in news does not mean that foreign correspondents think communicating between cultures is what they should do at work. Instead, all respondents deny that journalists should play a role as cultural communicators. Helping people from different cultures to understand each other is only a possible objective result of their work.

In terms of the role a foreign correspondent plays, all respondents agree that there is no essential difference between a domestic journalist and a foreign correspondent. Either with a journalistic educational background or not, all respondents primarily identify themselves as fact reporters. Furthermore, in terms of function of journalism, all respondents show approval of the watchdog function, journalistic values, and universal values such as speaking for the suffering and the powerless.

When the researcher raises the question that foreign correspondents may potentially have a bigger influence on how people in their home country see China than they have imagined, some respondents admit it may be true. But for them it does not mean that journalists should be responsible for this; this is the job of a diplomat or a public relations expert.

One respondent goes deeper to explain that if a journalist's work can promote people's understanding of another culture, it is because he or she always keeps a high professional standard in seeking truth, to find more facts, and to dig out more behind the phenomenon. People's better understanding is not because the journalist tries to make people have a good impression of another culture. In this sense, news can either build a bridge or destroy a bridge between cultures, but neither is a journalist's mission.

Some respondents realize that prejudice is unavoidable in news production. When someone knows nothing about a place, he or she has to find an entry point. Since journalists have their own upbringing and cultural baggage, they understand what to cover from a more or less prejudiced perspective.

Some respondents agree that objectivity is only an ideal in news practice. Journalists should try their best to pursue objectivity, but it is hard to be purely objective in news. One respondent admits, for example, that making news means making a series of choices of facts. As soon as you choose some facts to report over other facts, you are leading opinions in one direction away from another one.

All respondents, in spite of their cultural backgrounds or viewpoints, agree that there are common values in quality news stories, both in national and international journalism, that is, authenticity (truth) and fairness. But it is interesting that they have different judgments whether these values are also implemented in Chinese news culture. Some respondents feel that Chinese media institutions are controlled by the government, so they do not have a modern journalistic culture. Other respondents understand that even though there is journalistic censorship in China, these common values can be seen in the work of many Chinese journalists.

Most respondents do not agree that cultural differences can override universal values such as human rights, freedom, and speaking for the suffering. On one hand, pursuing these values may promote cultural sensitivity in news reporting, because journalists will try their best to get closer to common people, especially lower-class and subcultural groups, listen to them, and learn how they live. On the other hand, preconceived notions of suffering people may lead to a savior complex, which has happened to a few senior foreign correspondents in China in recent years.[2]

Insider/Outsider Status

Although there is consistency in all respondents' identification of their role as journalists reporting facts instead of cultural communication, there are also big differences in their attitudes and behaviors toward covering specific events.

Respondents show different levels of intimacy with Chinese culture due to differences in their language skills, length of stay, and integration into the society. This study describes this as a characteristic of insider/outsider status. It should be noticed that respondents should not be divided into two groups as outsiders or insiders. Instead, all respondents have both tendencies, that is, reporting facts as professional journalists while maintaining cultural sensitivity in their news stories.

One respondent has been a journalist in China for a long time. He also has a life here. He has more contacts and sources than any newcomer from his media institution, so he can help to push a story through various barriers. However, this is also the reason why he is not recognized as a "frontline" correspondent. In most stories, his name does not appear in the bylines but on the contributors' list. He says that he only provides "dry facts," which will be restructured and modified in the final story by a "frontline" journalist. He is more an insider than his colleagues. He thinks that many newly distributed journalists have no concept of many events in China. They do their jobs only to finish tasks they are assigned.

Some respondents have been reporting on China for a long time, with rich experiences and knowledge about the country. They have enjoyed a high reputation in the community of foreign correspondents in China. They are referred to as an "expert on China issues," which means not only that they are professional journalists but also that they own political, cultural, and image capital in the professional community. One such respondent emphasized keeping balance between insider and outsider perspectives. In his words, "When in Rome, do as the Romans do; this has both positive and negative effects on foreign correspondence. Now and then, I will go outside China to see different people and different cultures in order to maintain sensitivity. One foot inside, another foot outside."

However, for most regular journalists, the media institution's mobility rule doesn't allow them to remain an insider. Just before the interview, two respondents were informed that they would soon be sent to another country, after four years working in China. The insider/outsider status leads to different attitudes toward the mobility policy. One of the two respondents, who loves Chinese traditional culture and can read and speak in Chinese, says that he wants to stay longer and be able to write more in-depth stories. But the respondent who wrote the Olympic torch story says that he has stayed enough. The former respondent understands that the news agency he works with has the mobility rule because the media institution does not want the journalist to stay in a country too long to maintain a fresh insight of the country. But he thinks five years would be just a start if you want to write good stories on China. But the sport journalist argues that if journalists have stayed in China for 20 years, they will become localized insiders who might lose the wood for the trees. Another factor for his preference to have an outsider perspective is that he is not satisfied with the working environment in China, which has brought many obstacles for him in finishing his job.

To sum up, the respondents are more or less aware of the inner limitations of news and cultural bias. The factors that may influence their reflections are:

1. Autonomy at work. Most respondents consider themselves to be able to see China in a more fair and integrated way than their editors and media institutions back home. Adequate autonomy at work potentially allows foreign correspondents to approach a story in a more culturally sensitive manner. On the other hand, lacking autonomy at work may hinder journalists from getting an in-depth investigation of what they cover.
2. Professional role identity. All respondents identify themselves as professional reporters, not cultural communicators. Cultural communication is only a natural result of professional behavior, not a target of journalism.
3. Insider/outsider status. Insider status allows journalists to understand and report on China in a more empathic way.

KNOWLEDGE OF THE OTHER'S CULTURE

Multifaceted Understandings of Culture

Most respondents said that culture is too big a word and should be examined on different levels. For example, a British respondent referred to class culture as a factor that may lead to different angles of news stories on the same event. The *Guardian* and *Daily Telegraph* may have distinct stories on the Hainan government's project of developing golf courses in local rainforests, because the two newspapers' audiences belong to different classes.

He also refers to the fact that he feels closer to the Chinese people of his own age, who have experienced wars and revolutions, than much younger people in his own country whose worldviews are basically constructed by the Internet.

Some respondents suggest that a journalist's interest in Chinese culture may influence his or her attitude in reporting on China. One respondent is interested in the Chinese language. He thinks that many people say that Chinese traditional culture is lost in many aspects, and he doesn't agree, because culture lives in language and the daily use of language.

One respondent says that the political and diplomatic face of China may look largely different from the civil society face of China. There are more similarities in civil societies between different nations.

The respondents' multifaceted understanding of culture resonates with the researchers' discussion of what culture is when we talk about intercultural competence. The concept of culture includes "'macro' aspects involving cultural practices that conform to common codes and norms, shared language and common historical, political, social and economic development, as well as 'micro' aspects, including internal contradictions and inconsistencies, continual change due to internal and external influences, and the multiple identities of individuals within the culture" (Garyantes, 2010, pp. 87–88).

Respondents in this study all agree that culture should not be understood as an essentialized concept. One respondent reminds us that it is dangerous to assume Chinese culture is this way and Western culture is that way. Knowing more about China can be the knowledge of language, history, politics, economics, and society, as well as knowledge about what people think, behavior, and change. Respondents address both "macro" aspects and "micro" aspects of knowledge about China, with a different focus by different individuals. However, all respondents agree that reporting in China means catching up with the rapid changes of the country that happen every day, making the country a rich mine of original news stories.

Language Skills

Most respondents say that language competence enables them to go deeper into the complicated issues, know the society better, communicate with people, and write stories without a translator. One respondent says that it is particularly important to know the Chinese language if you want to understand the real environment of speech in China; otherwise you may easily get wrong conclusions. For example, an influential French journalist who doesn't read or speak in Chinese once wrote in his blog that the Chinese media still have a problem in facing the Cultural Revolution, because they haven't reported the death of Liu Shaoqi's wife. But this respondent had just read a story about her death in the *Beijing News*. He was astonished that this reporter made his comment only quoting a newspaper in English. He also mentioned that if journalists do not know the language in interviews, they are not able to feel what the people involved in the story feel. This is a barrier for the journalist's understanding of what the interviewee is really talking about.

One respondent says that another reason that language is so important is that if you interview common people in China with a translator behind you, they will become nervous and uneasy, and maybe they won't tell you what they really think and feel.

Knowledge of History, Customs, Economy, Politics, and Society

Nearly all respondents consider this type of knowledge to be necessary. One respondent has a degree in history, so she pays close attention to Chinese history, which enables her to have her own style of reporting on China, observing the events she covers by putting them in their historical context. For example, in the beginning of a story about creativity in China, which is one of her best stories, she traced the problem of creativity in China back to the Ming Dynasty.

Another respondent has taken courses on Chinese art at the Central Academy of Fine Arts. She has been making efforts to expand her journalistic work on Chinese art and artists. She insists that knowledge of Chinese history could help journalists get rid of a self-centered perspective such as the "Marco Polo complex." By this she means that some journalists think they come to discover a new China with an ambition to become a superpower, neglecting the fact that China has always been a superpower, only to have a crisis in the recent 100–200 years.

A veteran correspondent who has reported on China for 30 years says that his knowledge of recent Chinese history and society helps him observe news events within appropriate contexts with less misreading caused by comparing China with other countries. It helps him to see small changes and reflect them in his stories, as well as helping his colleagues to be more informed.

Another respondent has claimed that the knowledge of Chinese politics, economy, and society helps journalists to realize that they shouldn't simplify what happens in this complicated country. For example, it is important to bear in mind that there are huge gaps between urban and rural areas. Two respondents who work with news agencies have argued that a rich knowledge of China is important also if a journalist wants to make more original news stories that allow journalists to become experts in reporting on China.

There are three sources that all respondents agree are necessary for getting knowledge.

Reading. Reading books, newspapers, and news reports by ex-reporters is endorsed by many respondents. One respondent says that reading different materials provides all kinds of perspectives on approaching an issue. These perspectives work not by disabusing all prejudice but by providing the audience with as many angles as possible to balance the old ones.

But there are two problems in reading. One is the depth of reading may influence the depth of understanding. Some journalists have enough time and vigor to do comprehensive reading for one issue; others may only have a little time to do some homework just before they have to produce the news story.

It depends on the quantity and quality of tasks that the media institution distributes to them.

Another problem is that some respondents can only read in their mother languages and in English, but those materials may include some prejudices in the first place. Sometimes it seems that some books or articles provide a fresh point of view, but it is hard to tell whether it is only another biased viewpoint.

Asking experts. Expert databases are important sources for foreign correspondents. There are three types of experts: (a) experts on China outside China; (b) local experts on particular issues; and (c) native-speaking colleagues.

Most respondents say that local experts can provide the most authoritative opinions on many local issues, but in China it is relatively difficult to interview local experts. This makes their work more difficult, so they have to turn to experts outside China, who surely do not see many issues as thoroughly and inclusively as their Chinese counterparts.

Taking courses. Four respondents have taken relevant courses before and after they came to China as foreign correspondents, including art courses, courses on Chinese history, and Chinese literature courses. Other respondents have taken short-term training in the Chinese language, but none of them feels it has helped them cope with the difficulties of living or working here.

Knowing About the Reality on the Ground

If the "macro" aspects of culture ask journalists to read, require, and learn information about static facts regarding the Other, then the "micro" aspects of culture ask journalists to observe and interpret what happens every day in specific places and how people make sense of their lives. Static knowledge about the Other is structured, conformed, and logical, while the reality on the ground is often complicated, contradictory, and difficult to be conveyed properly through a well-structured logical narration. However, all respondents attach great importance to this kind of knowledge. Most respondents, especially those who enjoy more autonomy at work and are able to make more original stories, approve this kind of knowledge as important.

Two respondents say that reporting in China is more challenging yet more interesting than reporting a war. It is relatively easy to write an original story in China. One respondent who was based in Japan before he came to China says that he has achieved much more in China than in Japan. He is more proud of his China stories than his Japan stories. He says, "I've had more opportunities here. I think it's a stronger story, more powerful things. Opportunities for journalists here are huge. In Japan it's a very mature media market with very few domestic media constraints. It's not such a big country so most of the news in the Japanese media probably has already been done … It is very difficult to actually find a story that nobody has done."

A clear emphasis in the narratives of most respondents is that China is under constant change, with considerable complexities and contradictions in every issue they cover. But there are two restraints in digging out all the details, let alone demonstrating them all in their stories. One is the control of foreign correspondents by the Chinese government. The other constraint is the limitations of news production including time, space, editorial policy, and audience interest.

Respondents find that once they come to China, they see more similarities than differences in the micro aspects of culture. One respondent comes from Spain. She has found both in China and Spain that there has been a period of cultural opening, and the young people have been crazy. The other respondent says that when he comes to China, he finds similarities between the Chinese and French or British societies, especially when he talks to people. British people might be as proud of their country as the Chinese people are proud of theirs.

All respondents believe that culture influences people's behavior, so it's the best way to understand China through reporting what people do and how people think. This is also considered the best way to write original stories, using more direct impressions and firsthand materials.

Skills for Interculturally Competent Journalism

All respondents agree that it is necessary for a foreign correspondent to apply skills to avoid cultural misreading and bias.

Talk to people. It is commonly believed that going out to investigate by oneself and talking to people is the best way to avoid bias and stereotypes. One respondent says that when he goes to dinner with his Chinese friends and has discussions on many topics, he always finds how open and interesting they are. One respondent says that when she has an opinion on an issue, she will talk to local people to examine whether this is a prejudice, which helps her to reflect on herself all the time.

Another respondent has made a comparison between "shiny shoes journalism" and "muddy boots journalism" by saying, "Shiny shoes is that you have to dress and wear shiny shoes and talk to people who are business leaders and political leaders, working in the high buildings in big cities. The other journalism is muddy boots. You travel into the countryside and you walk with individuals and see the dirty side of life. I think good journalism should be both."

Add as much context as possible into the stories. All respondents mention context as the most important tool in avoiding cultural prejudice and misreading. One respondent says that one of his tasks is to explain to his audience what happens here in China, and adding contexts can explain a lot of things.

But some respondents remind us that if a context has been used to explain most of the related events, such as Mao's time and the Cultural Revolution, it may also lead to stereotypes. One respondent has noticed that for foreign correspondence to be more competitive, the less journalists will use this kind of context; otherwise their stories can be seen as out of date, not original pieces of work.

Be careful with prejudiced rhetoric in news stories. Three respondents with a high level of Chinese language ability are sensitive to linguistic bias in journalism. One respondent who has stayed in China for 30 years made the analysis that common usage of prejudiced expressions in China news coverage can be ascribed to both ignorance of Chinese culture and the ethnocentrism of the journalist. He always fights with such expressions as red China, communist China, blue ants (a phrase referring to Chinese people in the 1960s because most of them wore blue clothes), and so forth. He understands that journalists might use these expressions unconsciously, but he thinks they should avoid using them.

Demonstrate the complexity of problems and events without black-and-white narration. The respondent who studied Chinese classic literature has a clear understanding of "representation." He does not believe that news can show a real China, but there is a difference between good representation and bad representation. Good representation is showing, not telling, which means to describe how things have happened in detail instead of using abstract words. But more details need more space in the media, which is not available most of the time.

Use alternative news frames and narrative models to demonstrate perspectives from multiple angles. One respondent has been using "alternative framing strategy" to make different news stories. For example, in his story on Zhang Yimou's film *Founding Ceremony*, he chose to present how people feel about this film. People are not represented as ideologically brainwashed. Instead, they are common people who are proud of their motherland and are fond of Hollywood-style movies as well. The journalist believes that this story is still a critical report, but it has been criticized from a different angle that is more real.

CONCLUSION

This study is based on interviewing eight foreign correspondents working with Western mainstream media, examining their work from a cultural competence approach using the three dimensions of awareness, knowledge, and skills. Although these journalists all approve of and adhere closely to professional journalistic ethics, they show great differences in their attitudes and practice in reporting on China. These differences can be investigated and analyzed by the concept of cultural competence.

To answer RQ1 regarding the aspect of awareness, all respondents are aware of cultural bias in news and prepared to fight against whatever they consider bias. But their criticism of bias is more at the institutional and group level. Individual journalists tend to admit that personal prejudice and objective mistakes are unavoidable. All respondents refuse to identify themselves as cultural communicators, acknowledging their work to be only a natural result of reporting facts. The result is that individual mistakes are unavoidable, while nobody takes responsibility for the bias as a whole. This may indicate that to make more interculturally competent news content, intercultural competence should also be conducted not only by individual journalists but also by editors and other news workers who may influence news production.

The desire for autonomy at work may be a factor that can influence a journalist's enthusiasm to do more culturally competent work. Although it cannot be concluded that being free from institutional control will surely lead to more cultural sensitivity, it can be seen that lacking autonomy at work leaves no room for foreign correspondents to make more culturally competent stories.

To answer RQ2 regarding the aspect of cultural knowledge of the Other in both macro and micro aspects, most respondents agree that the macro aspect of cultural knowledge such as language, history, and political, economic, and social knowledge is important. They learn this kind of cultural knowledge by reading, taking courses, and asking experts. However, all eight respondents have endorsed the idea that reporting what happens in a constantly changing China is important, such as going out to see the real society, acknowledging the complexity of the issues they cover, and understanding events through people's behavior.

This study finds that a possible predictor of differences in knowledge among foreign correspondents might be the desire for originality at work. More knowledge about Chinese history, political and social structure, traditional culture, and literature empowers journalists to make an in-depth analysis of an event. On the other hand, knowledge of the micro aspect—such as the details of how people live and think—might enable journalists to find fresh angles and topics that never have been reported in the past. The ability of recording and writing about China undergoing great change is challenging but rewarding for those journalists who are committed to make firsthand stories about this country.

To answer RQ3 regarding the aspect of skills, it is commonly believed that talking to Chinese people is the best way to overcome bias and stereotypes. Adding contexts as much as possible is also highly approved, but it is severely limited by media space and editorship. It is also a problem to treat contexts and stereotypes discriminately. Avoiding linguistic bias and black-and-white narration is also addressed. A few respondents also try to use alternative frames and angles in their stories.

To answer RQ4, this study finds that both institutional and individual factors might influence the above three aspects:

1. Institutional power and news production routines, such as intrusive editorship, limits of space and time, the bureaucratic structure of foreign correspondence, overly detailed division of tasks, and mobility rules as well. These institutional elements essentially weaken journalists' autonomy at work and, as a result, might keep them away from self-reflection on the inner limitations of news production and their cultural bias.

2. The individual journalist's desire for autonomy and originality at work. When foreign correspondents want to have more control over their own work—such as what kind of events to cover, how to make decisions, and how to frame a story—they tend to give a second thought to the limits of media institutions, the ideological framing of the story, and the cultural bias of their editors and audience back home. What is more, when foreign correspondents want to make their stories original and unique, they might make an effort to understand the whole situation, get a deeper understanding of a particular issue, and try more actively to apply skills that make the story more culturally competent.

EPILOGUE

This is tentative research on an intercultural approach to foreign correspondence, which focuses on the foreign correspondents and their news production in three aspects of the operational definition of intercultural competence: awareness of the inner limitation of journalism and cultural bias, knowledge of the Other's culture, and skills to practice interculturally competent journalism. By interviewing eight foreign correspondents working with Western mainstream media in China, this study verifies that an intercultural competence approach to journalism may explain differences among individual journalists in reporting on China. Nevertheless, these differences are still confined within an ideology of professionalism and of media institutional control. Institutional limits and the individuals' desire for autonomy and originality at work might be factors that predict the levels of intercultural competence in news production.

NOTES

1. This is the number of officially registered foreign correspondents who are stationed in China for a long period, not including parachuting journalists, freelancers, and local assistants.
2. In recent years, a few foreign correspondents have made well-known in-depth investigative reports on China, with a focus on Chinese society and common people. Some of them have expressed opinions on how to remove a Western-centered attitude toward China. Such reporters as Evan Osnos, Leslie Chiang, and Peter Hessler have addressed similar opinions on this issue.

BIBLIOGRAPHY

Downing, J., & Husband, C. (2005). *Representing race: Racisms, ethnicities and media*. London: Sage.

Fürsich, E. (2002). How can global journalists represent the "Other"? A critical assessment of the cultural studies concept for media practice. *Journalism, 3*(1), 57–84.

Garyantes, D. M. (2010). *Toward a new norm of understanding: A culturally competent approach to journalism*. Doctoral dissertation, Temple University.

Hannerz, U. (2004). *Foreign news: Exploring the world of foreign correspondents*. Chicago: University of Chicago Press.

Hess, S. (1996). *International news and foreign correspondents*. Washington, DC: Brookings Institution.

Ji, L., & Huang, Y. (2014). Establishing global journalism ethics in international communication. *Journalism Bimonthly, 127*, 1–7.

Luyendijk, J. (2010). Beyond Orientalism. *International Communication Gazette, 72*(1), 9–20.

Pedelty, M. (1995). *War stories: The culture of foreign correspondents*. New York: Routledge.

Qian, J. (2012). *A study of foreign correspondents in China as a mobilized occupational community*. Doctoral dissertation, Fudan University.

Starck, K., & Villanueva, E. (1992, August 5–8). *Cultural framing: Foreign correspondents and their work*. Paper presented at the Annual Meeting of the Association for Education in Journalism and Mass Communication. Montreal, Canada.

Ward, S. (2009). Global journalism ethics: Widening the conceptual base. *Global Media Journal (Canadian Edition), 1*(1), 137–149.

Zhang, Z., & Ye, L. (2009). *What about China: How do foreign correspondents tell stories on China*. Guang Zhou: Nanfang Daily Press.

CHAPTER THIRTEEN

Original Voices AND New Paradigms

Indigenous Media and Social Transformation in Canada[1]

VALERIE ALIA

Native people are doing for themselves what cannot be accomplished by the mainstream media. They are sharing their communities' concerns in their own voices, uninterrupted by cultural interpreters and reporters who lack the background to understand the complex issues of contemporary Native life.
—PEGGY BERRYHILL, NATIVE AMERICAN BROADCAST PRODUCER (ALIA, 2010, P. XI)

Some of the world's least powerful people have become world leaders in creative and ethical media citizenship. Indigenous peoples are using radio, television, print, and a range of digital media to amplify their voices, extend the range of reception, and expand their collective power. Many of the major developments originated in Canada or were nurtured by Canadian Inuit, First Nations, and Métis journalists. I have extended Ien Ang's (1996) idea of the "progressive transnationalization of media audiencehood" to the *inter*nationalization of media audiencehood and production, which I call the New Media Nation. It is a global movement that includes Indigenous media in North America, Europe, Africa, Australia, New Zealand, and Latin America.[2] No real "nation" in the political science sense, it originates in a shared colonial inheritance and an international political and social movement of Indigenous peoples that foster important social, political, and technological innovations. Its creators and users engage in transcultural and transnational lobbying and access information that is sometimes inaccessible within state borders. To promote and sustain itself, the New Media Nation uses what the interdisciplinary, postcolonial scholar of ethics, human rights, and globalization Gayatri

Chakravorty Spivak (1990, 1995) has called "strategic essentialism," in which particularities and differences are set aside to maximize collective power by forefronting common experiences, issues, and goals. Thus, the New Media Nation operates under an essentialized pan-indigeneity while also serving and incorporating an array of culturally specific communities and media.

This discussion focuses on Canada's pivotal experiences as a case study in New Media Nation building. We begin with an example of the impact of low-tech, small-scale media on larger-scale political events.

> The phone lines are down to the Yukon's most remote community. The people of Old Crow won't have any way of letting the Chief Returning Officer know who won in their riding, short of renting a plane and flying the results in. Those results could be crucial. (CBC Radio, Whitehorse, Alia, 2010, p. 79)

The results were indeed crucial, and they arrived in an unusual way. A "ham" radio operator picked up the information from a message radioed from an airplane that was flying over the small Gwich'in First Nation community of Old Crow in northern Yukon Territory, and relayed the information to Whitehorse, Yukon's capital city. That convoluted but effective mode of transporting information may seem unnecessary and peculiar to those in urban centers. In remote and northern regions, such occurrences are part of daily life. The New Media Nation includes people and news organizations in large urban centers, such as Toronto, Helsinki, Melbourne, Osaka, and New York, along with small communities such as Rovaniemi (Finland), Sisimiut (Greenland), Pangnirtung (Nunavut, Canada), Hotevilla (Arizona), and Old Crow. In the Indigenous media universe, polls, profits, and audience ratings count for little; no place is too big or too small to be considered important. The power of those accumulated voices is widely recognized, though not always celebrated. In Guatemala, government attempts to suppress Indigenous radio caused decades of political, social, and cultural loss and loss of lives. Indigenous-language broadcasting and, to a lesser extent, publication is an important New Media Nation contribution to cultural and sometimes physical survival.

Indigenous people are used to improvising. In remote regions, communication and transportation are inseparable, and interdependence is not a theory but a daily reality. In Arctic winter, a breakdown in transportation can be a matter of life or death. Breakdowns in transportation are not the only crises. A communications breakdown can also mean life or death in a land where radio or telephone lines link people with survival as well as with each other.

Although "access" is often used to mean availability of technology, it is really about hierarchies of power. In Arctic Canada, as in other remote regions, people are informationally disadvantaged. Knowing this, they often make extensive use of communication technologies to improve their access to information. In 1995, *YukonNet* joined the information universe. Yukoners could now access the World Wide Web, and the twice-weekly *Yukon News* was online before it hit the local newsstands.

> I find it ironic that even though I live in a small community in a remote corner of the planet, somebody in New Zealand can read my local newspaper on the World Wide Web before I can get it from across the street. For information to flow like this in major urban centres may be commonplace; but here in Whitehorse, where people still talk to each other on the street ... the delivery of our community broadsheet via cyberspace seems absolutely Orwellian. ... Perhaps the most salient benefit from the Internet's arrival here is not that we can access [the Web] but that the Web can access US. (Alia, 2010, p. 80)

JOURNALISM AND POLITICS: A TANGLED HISTORY

Early English-language "news books" emerged in London (England) in the 1620s (Steffens, 1998). The first newspaper in North America, *Publick Occurrences Both Foreign and Domestick*, began publishing in Boston in 1690 (Alia, 2010, p. 82). Newspapers arrived relatively late in Canada, starting in Nova Scotia with the *Halifax Gazette* in 1752. They were usually founded by printers and often began as newsletters, a pattern still seen in Indigenous communities, where newsletters often evolve into newspapers. Because they relied on government funding, their coverage of "news" was controlled by government priorities and blatantly biased. The early years of journalism were full of violence. Newspaper editors and publishers were jailed for their behavior in what are sometimes mildly called "disputes." Mobs smashed equipment, burned newspapers, and destroyed print shops. The violence coexisted with an at least superficially more benign pattern of symbiotic intimacy between journalism and government. At least five of the "fathers" of the Canadian Confederation were journalists. In the 1860s, editors of newspapers in Toronto, Brantford (Ontario), and Montreal held cabinet posts. Although today's news media tend to separate themselves more sharply from the political arena, the tradition continues, especially in northern and Indigenous media.

The invention of the telegraph in 1844 transformed the distribution of news and information and started the revolution in information technologies that would lead to broadcast and digital media. It was not until 1917 that Canada had its own wire service—not because technological capability was lacking but because the Canadian railway's monopoly over dissemination of the news, and ill-considered business decisions, resulted in an absurdly convoluted system. Canada did use the wires, but in a different way from the direct transmission that was now possible. The Great North Western Telegraph system, an affiliate of the Grand Trunk Railway, sent information by wire from station to station. When the news arrived at a station, it was translated from

Morse code to English, transferred to paper, and carried by runner to each separate newspaper office. In 1858 came the first transatlantic cable and a communication revolution. It started in Newfoundland, then an independent British colony, which would become part of Canada a century later.

In the New Media Nation, the connection between journalism and politics is tied less to government and corporate empire building than to leadership skills building. In all of the countries I have observed, there is a tendency for Indigenous leaders to spend part of their careers in journalism. This is especially true in Canada, where a number of the most prominent leaders started in broadcasting. Among them are Jose Kusugak, who was heard on BBC and IBC before moving to Inuit politics, and Mary Simon, Rosemarie Kuptana, Nellie Cournoyea, and John Amagoalik, whose careers are sketched below.

The appointment in 1994 of Mary Simon as Canada's first Ambassador for Circumpolar Affairs marked the first time an Inuk would hold an ambassadorial position in Canada. Like many Indigenous leaders, Simon began in journalism, broadcasting on the CBC Northern Service and writing for *Inuit Today*. She moved to politics in 1973, and from 1986 to 1992, she served as the first president of the Inuit Circumpolar Council (ICC), where she developed close ties to Greenland, sought "a significantly expanded role for Inuit at the international level," and supported ICC's push for international cooperation and designation of the Canadian Arctic as a nuclear-free zone. This latter is a position Inuit continue to promote despite challenges from U.S., Canadian, and other government and corporate interests. Her opposition to President Reagan's Star Wars Strategic Defense Initiative was timely. Simon attributes her early awareness of Inuit internationality to hearing Greenlandic music on her family's short-wave radio as they traveled among hunting and fishing camps in northern Québec and to her grandmother's dream that Inuit from different countries would someday work together. As Ambassador for Circumpolar Affairs, her main responsibility was to help develop the Arctic Council. At its First Ministerial Meeting in 1998, the council issued the "Iqaluit Declaration: An Agenda for 2000." It called for circumpolar cooperation, an initiative on children and youth, and a northern foreign policy for Canada.

Nellie Cournoyea is best known for her leadership of the Northwest Territories government. She was an announcer and manager for CBC radio and, with Agnes Semmler, co-founded the Inuvialuit political and advocacy organization COPE, the Committee for Original People's Entitlement. In 1991, after several years serving in the Northwest Territories legislature, she became government leader and the first Indigenous woman to lead a provincial or territorial government in Canada.

Rosemarie Kuptana is an internationally prominent Inuvialuit broadcaster, political leader, environmental and political activist, negotiator, and consultant. She was the first woman to serve as president of the Inuit Broadcasting Corporation, from 1983 to 1988. Her traumatic childhood experience in a government residential school inspired a lifelong determination to resist assimilationist programs and policies. From the mid-1970s, she participated in early land-claims discussions between Inuit and the Canadian government. In 1979, she joined the CBC Northern Service as host of CBC Inuvik's radio public affairs magazines. She moved on to the Inuit Broadcasting Corporation (IBC), and as president of the corporation she bolstered IBC's commitment to develop programming to promote Inuit traditional life and languages, broadcasting in Inuktitut and Inuvialuktun. She was a key member of the group of Indigenous leaders who envisioned, designed, and developed Television Northern Canada (TVNC).

In 1982, she made a landmark presentation to the Canadian Radio-Television and Telecommunications Commission (CRTC) on behalf of Inuit Broadcasting Corporation (IBC) and its northern Quebec companion broadcaster, Taqramiut Nipingat Incorporated (TNI). The following excerpt includes one of the most widely quoted passages in the history of Canadian broadcasting, which became known as the "neutron bomb speech."

> IBC is a non-profit public television service dedicated to serving the needs of 25,000 Inuit in the Canadian Arctic. [It] is presently broadcasting five hours per week with production centres in Frobisher Bay, Baker Lake, Eskimo Point and Igloolik. TNI is an independent communications society based in Salluit, Northern Quebec [which] provides programming for the IBC network.
>
> ... The subjects of this hearing represent but a further phase in the accelerating introduction in Canada of the Information society. We fear, not that we will be left behind, but that we will be run over. ... The great southern organizations ... [are] preparing for a feast of tiers of television and channels within tiers ... as we have visions of being subjected to multiples of Southern programming, irrelevant to our culture and lifestyle. ... We want ... our own facility for distributing our own programming to our own people.
>
> We might liken the onslaught of Southern television, and the absence of Native television, to the Neutron bomb. This is the bomb that kills the people but leaves the buildings standing. Neutron-bomb television is the kind of television that destroys the soul of a people but leaves the shell of a people walking around. This is television in which the traditions, the skills, the culture, the language, count for nothing. The pressure, especially on our children, to join the invading culture and language and leave behind the language and culture that count for nothing is explosively powerful.
>
> ... This does not mean that we find Southern culture lethal. Nor does it mean we want to deprive non-Native peoples living and working in the North of access to their own culture on television, in the way we are being deprived. We want, first, a basic, coherent, comprehensive television programming service for the Native people of the North.
>
> ... The time has come for us to benefit from the advances in communications technology. ... We ask that ... a portion of the first tier of service of a universal pay-TV system be reserved for Northern Native broadcasting.

Kuptana left broadcasting to become Canadian vice president of the Inuit Circumpolar Conference (ICC) from 1986 to 1989, and from 1991 to 1996 president of the Inuit Tapirisat of Canada (ITC), now Inuit Tapiriit Kanatami (ITK). She was principal negotiator for Inuit in the attempt to win constitutional recognition of Indigenous people's inherent right to self-government. Despite strong lobbying and work at the negotiating table, that effort failed and remains a sore point for those who consider the Nunavut Agreement inadequate. Kuptana had greater success negotiating an amendment to an international treaty, gaining recognition and constitutional protection of Inuit hunting rights.

Her predecessor as ITC president was the broadcaster and political leader John Amagoalik, who is often called the "father of Nunavut." He was a prime mover in the creation of Nunavut Territory and development of TVNC and APTN and was always a master at seeing the big picture. Declaring there is more to literacy than reading and more to "reading" than the printed page or computer screen, he eloquently clarified the cultural core of literacy while unraveling the layers of colonial thinking:

> If we are to survive as a race, we must have the understanding and patience of the dominant cultures of this country. We do not need the pity, the welfare, the paternalism and the colonialism which has been heaped upon us over the years. We must teach our children their mother tongue. We must teach them what they are and where they came from. We must teach them the values which have guided our society over the thousands of years … our philosophies which go back beyond the memory of man. We must keep the embers burning from the fires which used to burn in our villages so that we may gather around them again. It is this spirit we must keep alive so that it may guide us again in a new life in a changed world. (Alia, 2010, p. 97)

BROADCASTING, CULTURAL SURVIVAL, AND CONFLICT RESOLUTION

Broadcast and digital projects have received the most consistent government funding and tend to be more durable than print. The first northern broadcast services originated elsewhere and were sent *to* the North. Today, northerners produce their own programming. Like northern politics, northern broadcasting is a wild mix of global, local, and everything in between. Listeners and viewers can access an array of radio and television ranging from high-budget regional, national, and international to low-budget local programming.

Canada's national broadcaster, the Canadian Broadcasting Corporation (CBC), launched its Northern Service in 1958. More than 20 years later, a report commissioned by the national regulatory body, Canadian Radio and Telecommunications Commission (CRTC), said communications had a key role in preserving Indigenous languages and cultures (Alia, 2010, p. 84). It set the stage for a new era in Indigenous broadcasting, not only in Canada but also worldwide. Canadian programs and policies continue to set precedents and inspire Indigenous projects in many regions and countries. In 1983, Canada launched its Northern Broadcasting Policy and Northern Native Broadcast Access Program (NNBAP) and funded 13 northern Aboriginal Communications Societies. Some were already in place and were incorporated into the new framework. Their mandate was to serve Aboriginal communities across Canada, with a focus on remote and under-serviced areas. Under the umbrella of the National Aboriginal Communications Society (NACS), they became regional centers for production and distribution of radio, television, and print media.

Radio has been called the most grassroots of media. It is well adapted to oral cultures and to, nomadic, and remote-community life. Where languages are threatened, Indigenous-language programming is the main attraction, with talk radio providing a forum for social and political dialogue. Despite increasing globalization, radio remains a medium of linguistic and cultural continuity and sometimes of survival. Indigenous stations regularly broadcast in the local language.

Conway Jocks, the Mohawk broadcaster, historian, writer, and cartoonist, often spoke of the (inter)connectedness and intimacy that radio brings to people living in small and/or remote communities. "Phone-in shows are lively extended family affairs," and while most North American talk radio is AM, in Indigenous communities, the less costly and more easily established FM and trail radio dominate. In Indigenous communities, "FM, easier and cheaper to build, is king, followed by trail radio, sometimes called 'moccasin telegraph;'" talk-back radio "forges the communication links in ethnic neighborhoods, small towns and Aboriginal communities from the farthest Arctic coasts to the outskirts of major Canadian cities, sending hundreds of languages through the air" (Jocks, 1996). CKRK, the station he founded in 1978, began as "the communication voice of the Kanienkehaka Raotitiohkwa Cultural Center," a local institution dedicated to the promotion and reinforcement of Mohawk culture and language. It provided support for students in the Mohawk immersion schools. Its "secondary objective was to inform non-Mohawk people, whom Jocks called 'our drop-in listeners, of who we are and what we believe in'" (Roth in Alia, 2010, p. 88).

Along with linguistic and cultural survival, radio can also mean physical survival, as it did during the 1990 "Oka Crisis." Townspeople sought to extend a golf course onto a sacred Mohawk burial ground. Mohawk resistance, police, and military intervention led to a blockade of the community of Kanehsatake. To assure continuing news coverage, Mohawk broadcasters Marie David and Bev Nelson camped out in the Kanehsatake radio station CKHQ until the crisis ended four months later. Throughout the history of

Indigenous broadcasting, some of the most effective communications strategies were low tech. When David and Nelson found themselves trapped inside their radio station, living on rationed food supplies and sleeping in the station, the Internet was not yet an option. Yet they managed to create a network that reached across their own community to other First Peoples and, ultimately, to an international audience.

In a sense, the telephone "made it possible … to be in two places at the same time" through "party lines" on which conversations could take place simultaneously in many homes. In "the early systems, bells rang along the entire line and everyone who was interested could listen in" (Roth in Alia, 2010, p. 89). Using the radio station's single telephone and fax line, Nelson and David were able to link their relatively isolated community to individual and group supporters and others, bringing their eyewitness account to the ears of the world. From the local Mohawk community and immediate region, the listening audience rapidly expanded, as other radio stations within and outside Canada picked up their broadcasts. They were interviewed almost daily by Canadian and international radio and television services. Excerpts from CKHQ reached other stations by telephone and occasionally were "sneaked out by a supportive Montreal journalist for rebroadcast" on stations in Montreal, across Canada, and internationally.

Nearby, the larger community of Kahnawake provided important support. Unlike Kanehsatake, it was not occupied by Canadian authorities and thus had more freedom to operate. Led by station manager Conway Jocks, Radio Kahnawake CKRK "became the loudest First Nations broadcast voice in southern Québec," reaching more than 300,000 listeners during peak listening periods and playing "a pivotal role in providing alternative forms of information [by building] a public opinion support base for the Mohawk position and acting as a conflict mediator." At the center of the service was CKRK's phone-in show, *The Party Line* (Roth in Alia, 2010, p. 90).

During the confrontation, CKRK's policy was to act as "normal" as possible, though music playlists "tended to have high message value, e.g., *Give Peace a Chance* by John Lennon or *The Freedom Song* by Frosty, a well-known resident of Kahnawake" (Roth in Alia, 2010, p. 90). The programming featured surveillance information; tips on surviving with limited resources; public service announcements of military and police maneuvers; "the comings and goings of residents"; updates on political negotiations; appeals from members of the Band council to maintain calm and sobriety; suggested ways to answer public questions; conversations with witnesses and participants from the front lines; advertisements and political statements. The station became one of the most important vehicles for keeping the town informed and keeping the channels to outside communities open. Talk-back radio was the most effective way to encourage and promote communication with outsiders—a "potent medium for producing public debate" that opened up a safe mediaspace where audiences can join the discussion while remaining anonymous. The discussion was limited only by the judgment of CKRK's directors and broadcasters and constraints imposed by Canada's 1991 Broadcasting Act (Taylor, 2013) and Radio Regulations 1986 that proscribe transmitting racist comment.

Conway Jocks believed that rumor is the most dangerous incendiary device. He insisted on confirming the facts and would not broadcast anything that could not be confirmed—a departure from the usual style of talk-back radio. CKRK could not afford to join the Bureau of Broadcast Measurement (BBM) to obtain official ratings, but their "mole at one of Montreal's major radio stations told us that we were pulling in almost half a million listeners during our phone-in segment. If true, that is the biggest story of all—and the best kept secret." The first phone-in broadcasts got such large audiences and were so important to helping to defuse conflict, Jocks decided to extend *Party Line*'s broadcast hours and bring in a former announcer, Nathalie Foote. "The program soon turned into a barricade jumper, the only direct link with the outside world for us inside who were rapidly taking on a fortress mentality" (Jocks quoted in Roth, 1993).

In the non-Indigenous world, talk-back radio is known for its provocative and confrontational style. In Mohawk country, it took a diametrically opposite direction. During the summer of 1990, each *Party Line* broadcast opened with a prayer:

> Great Spirit, whose voice I hear in the winds and whose breath gives life to all the world, hear me. I come before you—one of your many children. I am small and weak. I need your strength and wisdom. Let me walk in beauty and make my eyes ever behold the red and purple sunset. Make my hands respect the things you have made, my ears sharp to hear your voice. Make me wise so that I may know the things you have taught my people, the lesson you have hidden in every leaf and drop. I seek strength not to be superior to my brothers, but to be able to fight my greatest enemy—myself. Make me ever ready to come to you with clean hands and straight eyes so when life fades as a fading sunset, my spirit may come to you—without shame.

The prayer was followed by the rules of conduct prohibiting foul language, use of last names, and naming of anyone entering or leaving Kahnawake. Nathalie handled crisis radio by using a soft voice and a friendly and "chatty" manner. Coping with more than 100 calls an hour some of the time, she invited callers to share their feelings and helped to defuse some of the verbal violence. She even encouraged expressions of racism, deflecting calls for violent action to (angry and offensive) speech. She helped divert angry outsiders and Mohawk "effigy-burners and rock-throwers" by encouraging them to call in and explain their actions—redirecting violence to talk. She was influenced by Martin Luther King Jr.'s Gandhian view that "if violence is the language of the inarticulate," the opportunity to speak can provide an outlet for anger and frustration and diminish physical violence. When callers made hostile comments, Nathalie quietly thanked them and hung up. She rarely "blew her cool" and managed to maintain diplomacy "through some very tense periods. Nat developed new ways of using radio to diffuse hostile energy." Using radio "for catharsis and conflict mediation ... she developed a technique for diffusing tension—psychotherapeutic radio" (Roth, 1993).

AS TECHNOLOGY EVOLVES, THE NEW MEDIA NATION THRIVES

Each technological development has provided new opportunities to report and spread the news. Keith Battarbee's research points to the potential for mobile phones and digital radio to maintain Indigenous languages. He finds that telephony is "essentially language-neutral," and its accessibility and ability to cover distances is a significant support for minority languages. He notes the "rapid growth of other-language websites and, alongside these positive developments, a computer technology that remains biased towards written language and dominated by English" (Alia, 2010, p. 92). In 2006, Canada funded a Broadband for Rural and Northern Development Pilot Program, partnered with the Kittiwake Economic Development Corporation to expand broadband and high-capacity Internet to new communities.

Television Northern Canada (TVNC)

> At exactly 8:30 p.m., an Inuktitut voice signals the start of the world's largest aboriginal television network. Elder Akeeshoo Joamie of Iqaluit asks Jesus to guide TVNC to success. An English translation rolls slowly across the screen. ... The vision of TVNC became a reality with a montage of Inuit, Dene, Metis, Gwich'in, Kaska, Tuchone, Tlingit and non-aboriginal faces beamed to 22,000 households from Northern Labrador to the Yukon-Alaska border. ... TVNC is a non-profit consortium which aims to use television for social change. (Thomas in Alia, 2010, p. 97)

Indigenous television programming developed in response to the invasion of foreign television signals into Arctic airwaves. In the late 1970s and early 1980s, Canada's Department of Communications responded to Indigenous pressure by developing the Anik B (satellite) trial-access program. In 1976, the satellite carried an experimental interactive audio project, Naalakvik I, across northern Quebec, linking eight radio stations and run by the Aboriginal Communications Society Taqramiut Nipingat Incorporated (TNI) (Roth & Valaskakis, 1989, p. 225). Two years later, Anik B carried the launch of programs from Project Inukshuk, a media project named for the human-form stone sculptures Inuit use to mark important features on the land. The federally funded Inukshuk project heralded the start of Inuit-produced television broadcasts and was sponsored and organized by Inuit Tapirisat of Canada (ITC, now ITK), with video production facilities in Frobisher Bay (now Iqaluit) and Baker Lake. The purpose was to train Inuit film and video producers, establish Inuit production centers, and conduct interactive audio/video experiments linking six Arctic communities via satellite. When Inukshuk first went to air in 1980, it sent 16.5 hours a week of television programming and teleconferencing.

In 1980, the CRTC struck a committee to consider proposals for satellite television services to remote communities. The nine-member committee, headed by Réal Thérrien, included John Amagoalik, who would become the first Indigenous person to help set national communications policy in Canada. The committee emphasized the role of broadcasting in preserving and maintaining Indigenous languages and cultures and foresaw "A New Broadcasting Universe":

> Our first unanimous conclusion is that immediate action must be taken to meet the needs of the many Canadians who believe that, as regards broadcasting, they are being treated as second-class citizens. ... We cannot stress too strongly the immediacy of the problem: alternative television programming must be provided from Canadian satellites with no further delay. (Thérrien, 1980, p. 1)

The authors of the Thérrien Report wrote that the new satellite-delivered television posed both "the most damaging threat to native objectives and the most potentially feasible means of achieving them." Ken Kane of Northern Native Broadcasting Yukon, TVNC's first chairperson, said:

> When I first heard about this new technology coming to the North, I realized that along with it would come a lot of change and a lot of impact for my people. That is why we got involved. To make sure that this time we got in on the ground floor: not to oppose it or go against it, but to grow with it. To learn and develop with it. (Alia, 2010, pp. 98–99)

TVNC served 100,000 viewers north of 55 degrees latitude, covering one third of Canada. Its mandate was to broadcast "cultural, social, political and educational programming" in English, French, and several indigenous languages to Canada's northern Indigenous people, via satellite to an audience of approximately a hundred thousand. Its leaders represented the 13 Aboriginal communications societies and a handful of associate member organizations. TVNC was a precedent-setting experiment that succeeded beyond its founders' expectations, using Canada's pioneering Anik communications satellites to transmit its programming to an increasingly widening audience.

In 1998, TVNC produced a position paper that included the following statement from a section titled "Facing the New Era":

> Aboriginal peoples in the North are again at a crossroads. Digital video compression (DVC), universal addressability, direct-to-home satellite services (DTH) and the expansion of the information highway have [changed] and will dramatically change business, information and cultural environment. The paradox identified in the Therrien Report is still true today ... Aboriginal participation in the design, ownership and operation of communications services ... will strengthen the foundation of the northern communications infrastructure and ensure that the new services support the practice of self-government. (Alia, 2010, pp. 98–99)

The Aboriginal People's Television Network (APTN)

TVNC's founders saw the media and communications projects as inherently and importantly linked to the emergence of Indigenous self-government, on- and off-line education, and cultural and political survival. Their position paper reminded the government that the "inherent right to self-government places aboriginal people in control of all aspects of community life. Programs which were historically administered by the Department of Indian Affairs are being devolved to aboriginal governments." They considered access to information essential to effective self-governance and economic development, which would enable Indigenous communities to become self-sufficient. After several years of successful broadcasts, they were granted permission to become a national television service—the Aboriginal People's Television Network (APTN). Launched in 1991, it broadcasts nationwide, and its programming reaches far beyond Canada's borders, the world's largest Indigenous television network.

One of the most popular programs on TVNC was "Super Shamou," an amalgam of Inuit and *Qallunaat* (non-Inuit) characters and traditions with distinctively Inuit qualities and values. "Super Shamou" echoed the familiar Superman legend, offering both a send-up of Superman and a uniquely Inuit character. It gave birth to another popular TVNC children's program, "The Takuginai Family." *Takuginai* means *look here* in Inuktitut. The program taught respect for elders and Inuit culture and language. These characters and programs carried over, and evolved on APTN. APTN is run and produced by Aboriginal people for a nationwide, multicultural audience who receive it as part of their basic cable television package. It is the first national Aboriginal television network in the world with programming by and about Aboriginal Peoples and is available to some 10 million Canadian households and commercial establishments.

About one third of APTN's programs are in Aboriginal languages; about 15% are in French, with the remainder in English. The range of languages is extended by subtitles. The network shuns government funding, surviving on subscriber fees, advertising sales, and strategic partnerships. The broadcast day comprises mainly independently produced programming, along with three national news shows, produced in house and broadcast from APTN headquarters in Winnipeg. Newscasts are supported by interviews and reports from 11 news bureaus across Canada. Following the long tradition of community participation and engagement in Indigenous radio, there is also a live call-in show, "Contact."

Indigenous call-in shows bear little resemblance to those seen and heard on mainstream networks. The difference in production values was brought home to me in the early 1990s during a stay in Whitehorse, Yukon. I was in the studios of NNBY, observing a live broadcast of the radio phone-in show, during the "Oka Crisis" based at the Kanehsatake (Mohawk) community in Quebec. Callers were sharing important and emotionally charged information. The show was scheduled for a one-hour time slot, but as the hour ended, the phones were still ringing, with no sign of letup. In the space of a few minutes, a decision was made to continue the show, immediately following the planned, remote/spot coverage of a healing circle and demonstration in solidarity with the Mohawks at Kanehsatake. Following the demonstration, the camera crew returned to the studio and resumed broadcasting the phone-in show, which continued until all of the callers had an opportunity to speak.

Community programming continues to have that kind of flexibility. As a national broadcaster, APTN maintains a less flexible, fixed schedule while providing alternative perspectives and ways of interviewing, editing, and presenting. In celebration of the launch of the new network, the October/November 1999 issue of *Aboriginal Voices* magazine ran a cover photo of APTN's first chair, the journalist Abraham Tagalik (a veteran of both the Inuit Broadcasting Corporation, IBC, and TVNC) headlined: "Please Adjust the Color On Your Set" (*Aboriginal Voices,* 1999, cover). In Whitehorse, Yukon, on September 10, 2000, just after APTN's first anniversary, I tuned in midway through an Inuit current affairs magazine featuring mini-documentaries on northern Nunavut Day celebrations and a skidoo race captured with energetic and creative camera work. Its leaders see APTN as a "digital gathering place" that can inform Indigenous people and the wider public. That public is increasingly global.

Indigenous media in Canada continue to develop. APTN's broadcast week includes outstanding music programs, such as "Rez Blues." In 2008, APTN expanded its commitment to Indigenous musicians by cosponsoring a new national distribution program aimed at bringing Indigenous music to the mainstream market.

On June 11, 2008, my husband, Pete Steffens, and I wept as we watched the coverage of Canada's official apology to Indigenous people for the sexual, physical, and psychological abuse that occurred in residential schools. We watched the day's events unfold on CBC, Canada's public broadcaster, and on APTN, the Aboriginal People's Television Network. The live broadcast and commentary on APTN was itself a testament to the survival of First Peoples. APTN provided full, live coverage and streaming video available 24/7 on its website. Throughout the proceedings, APTN kept reporting the availability of the AFN's 24-hour phone line for survivors and others needing support.

Canadian Prime Minister Stephen Harper reluctantly and belatedly followed the lead of Australian Prime Minister Kevin Rudd and apologized for the abuse and efforts to obliterate Indigenous languages and cultures. After the politicians had spoken, five Indigenous leaders, seated in a circle with six former residential school students, were given an opportunity to speak.

The U.S. media are notoriously inattentive to Canadian news. This occasion was an exception. The *Washington Post* reported:

> Canadian Prime Minister Stephen Harper delivered a long-anticipated apology yesterday to tens of thousands of indigenous people who as children were ripped from their families and sent to boarding schools … part of official government policy to "kill the Indian in the child" … thousands of Indian, Inuit and Métis children suffered mental, physical and sexual abuse in 132 boarding schools, most of them run by churches [from the late 1800s to 1996]. "The treatment of children in Indian residential schools is a sad chapter in our history," said Harper, facing indigenous leaders who sat in a circle in the House chamber [and] listened silently or wept for what their people suffered and are still suffering. (Alia, 2010, p. 105)

ITK President Mary Simon told the House: "Let us not be lulled into believing that when the sun rises tomorrow, the pain and scars will be gone. They won't. But a new day has dawned." Some years ago, when Mary Simon was the international ICC president, I was commissioned to write an article about her for a major magazine. When the piece was cut to an insulting single paragraph, I consulted Simon and, on her advice, withdrew it. As is so often the case with mainstream media, the magazine had missed an opportunity. This time, the media paid attention. In the years of the residential schools, those media were silent.

"The memory of residential schools cuts like merciless knives at our souls," said Phil Fontaine, national chief of the Assembly of First Nations [AFN], which represents 633 indigenous communities across Canada. "I was one of the people who suffered physical abuse as well as sexual abuse. Sadly, I am not unique." Duncan Campbell Scott, deputy superintendent of Indian Affairs from 1913 to 1932, set the tone for decades of abuse in his contribution to a government document, expressing his policy objectives: "I want to get rid of the Indian problem … Our objective is to continue until there is not a single Indian in Canada that has not been absorbed into the body politic" (Alia, 2010, pp. 105–107).

The U.S. media were not just reporting on Canada. They were pointing inky fingers at their own national policy. In February 2008, the U.S. Senate passed a resolution apologizing for "atrocities committed against Native Americans as part of the assimilationist policies, appropriation of Indigenous lands, and forcible removal of children from their families to distant boarding schools" (Brown in Alia, 2010, p. 106). The resolution urged President George W. Bush to acknowledge and apologize for the mistakes. President Obama quietly signed the resolution in 2009 without making a public statement.

Some reports got it partly wrong. "Canada tells its Indians: We're sorry," headlined a story published in the *Chicago Tribune* and, under a more accurate headline referring to "Canada's Native People," in the *Los Angeles Times* (Alia, 2010). By contrast, a Canwest News Service story published in several Canadian papers referred to "First Nations, Inuit and Métis peoples," but its unequivocally celebratory tone suggests that the journalists may have listened selectively, and rather narrowly, to Indigenous people. Others were less celebratory:

> The apology was billed by the government as a chance to redress a dark chapter in Canadian history and to move forward in reconciliation. But the hours before the landmark statement were marked by wrangling over whether native leaders were adequately consulted … and anger that they would not be allowed to respond in the House of Commons. Just before Harper's speech, opposition leaders led a successful motion to allow aboriginal representatives to reply in the chamber. Some survivors … said the apology came only grudgingly under intense pressure from native groups, and must be matched by action. (Guly & Farley in Alia, 2010, p. 107)

Where Australian Prime Minister Kevin Rudd had *campaigned* on his promise to apologize to Indigenous people and issued an apology soon after his election, Canadian Prime Minister Stephen Harper was *pressured* and shamed into his apology, first refusing and then stalling before finally delivering it. More than a year earlier, Liberal MP Tina Keeper posted the following comments on her website: "The Minister of Indian Affairs must honor the federal government's pledge to Canada's First Nation, Métis and Inuit peoples and issue a formal apology to residential schools survivors" (Alia, 2010, p. 107).

Before being elected MP for Churchill Manitoba, Tina Keeper was a well-known actor. She starred as an Indigenous RCMP officer in the television series *North of Sixty*, and one particularly moving episode recounted her character's personal struggle with the effects of her residential school experience. As a politician, Keeper played a major role for several years in efforts to pressure the Harper government to apologize to First Peoples. Yet her considerable influence and leadership were written out of much of the political history-making and mainstream media coverage.

Harper expressed remorse but made no promises to improve social conditions and continues to cling to that unfortunate policy. In 2013, in "a rare show of solidarity, Canada's premiers and territorial leaders [agreed] that there needs to be an inquiry into the hundreds of Aboriginal women and girls who go and have gone missing in Canada. But the Harper government is still resisting the idea" (APTN National News, 2013). Again in 2014, after the alleged murder of a 15-year-old Aboriginal girl in Manitoba, Harper again refused to consider a formal inquiry into Canada's more than 1,200 missing and murdered Indigenous girls and women, insisting, "these particular things … [are] not all one phenomenon. We should not view this as a sociological phenomenon. We should view it as crime" (*CBC News Manitoba*, online 2014). APTN and other Indigenous media continue to press for an inquiry and to cover the underlying issues and conditions.

Straightening the Record: The Wider Significance of the New Media Nation

The New Media Nation does not just serve Indigenous people. It provides a wider range of knowledge and perspectives and, often, greater accuracy. Few would question the importance of accuracy in journalism, and journalists who cover unfamiliar places and people are expected to check correct usage. Many writers, broadcasters, and editors have learned that the people they used to call "Eskimo" usually prefer to be called "Inuit." Yet even seasoned professionals keep getting it wrong. In 2014, a writer for Canada's *National Post* described a boy from Igloolik "who speaks no Inuk" (Atkinson, 2014, p. B3). Had she checked a reputable source, she'd have learned that nobody speaks "Inuk"; there is no such language. "Inuk" is an Inuit individual. The language is *Inuktitut*. I am willing to bet that if the text described a boy "who speaks no Frenchman (or Frenchwoman)," the editor would have corrected the error and questioned the writer's qualifications. There are persistent double standards, and however unintentional, such carelessness borders on racism.

Along with correcting errors, Indigenous media provide information that is often missed in mainstream media. *Windspeaker* is a Canada-wide newspaper based in Edmonton, Alberta. Each issue includes an array of news from individual Indigenous communities; items of wider interest (e.g., its *Health Watch* section; jobs and scholarship listings); and issues that are un- or under-reported elsewhere—for example, a story from a remote Haida community on a heart attack death that might have been prevented by better ambulance and paramedic services. The story includes proactive measures the community is taking to update its ambulance service; details about the man and his family; and broader concerns about medical care in British Columbia (McKenna, 2014, p. 18). In the same issue are articles on the missing and murdered girls and women; a U.S.-Canadian cross-border, intertribal treaty aimed at protecting the Salish Sea from oil tankers and other environmental threats; a feature on Mohawk artist Greg Staats; and "The Urbane Indian," a monthly column by Ojibway playwright, humorist, and journalist Drew Hayden Taylor. Taylor often looks at cultural change and (sometimes inadvertent) racism in fresh ways, making serious points with humor. This time, he recalls a non-Indigenous critic's response to a performance of the internationally celebrated Cree playwright Tomson Highway's play *The Rez Sisters*. The reviewer applauded the production but added that "Western dramatic theatre was not an art form known to Aboriginal people." Taylor responded by noting that the flush toilet was not an instrument previously known to Aboriginal people, "but we seemed to have mastered its intricacies" (Taylor, 2014, p. 6).

While the New Media Nation is mainly a constellation of smaller organizations and outlets, it is fostering a range of larger organizations that, in turn, support its members. The international Inuit Circumpolar Council (ICC) established a committee in 1982, which expanded to become the Circumpolar Communications Commission. Things became increasingly global and cross-cultural, and in 2008, the World Indigenous Television Broadcasters Network was born. Its founding members include Maori Television in Aotearoa/New Zealand, NRK Sámi Radio in Norway, Indigenous broadcasters in Taiwan, Ireland, Australia, and Scotland, and APTN in Canada.

Digital technology continues to improve and is enhancing networking in remote regions, particularly the Arctic. In 2014, several companies began fiber-optic projects aimed at using the Arctic Ocean and Northwest Passage to connect Alaska, Greenland, England, and Japan. Ironically, this is made possible by climate change—the global warming that also threatens the Arctic ecosystem (Arctic Fibre.com, 2014; CBC online, 2014; *The Globe and Mail* online, 2014).

Despite the new technologies, some of the simplest media and distribution methods remain the most effective. Remote communities in Canada and other countries access radio and television transmitters and programming by CD, DVD, or flash drive via snowmobile, dogsled, or all-terrain vehicle (ATV). Radio remains the dominant medium. Television and an array of visual media are delivered in various ways to an expanding audience, and the Internet is becoming the main cross-border forum for discussion and debate, a tool for global and regional constituency building and cross-border organizing.

The Sámi poet and scholar Harald Gaski speaks of living on the cultural borderlines, "where all the fun takes place." I think we will see an increasingly complex array of multilayered experiences and experiments. Political and profit motives will continue to challenge and threaten Indigenous media priorities and principles. But the foundations are in place, the technologies make it increasingly difficult to contain or sabotage communications, and the networking is in constant motion, ready to welcome new voices.

NOTES

1. *Media Nation: Indigenous Peoples and Global Communication*, New York and Oxford, UK: Berghahn Books; and "Gender and 'The New Media Nation,'" presentation to *Conference on Gender Equality in the Arctic: Current Realities and Future Challenges*, Akureyri, Iceland, October 30–31, 2014, Government of Iceland, Ministry of Foreign Affairs.
2. A note about terminology: "Indigenous" is the term most widely used and accepted internationally. I have capitalized it to clarify the difference between Indigenous, or First Peoples, and other uses of "indigenous." Preferred terms differ among countries and cultures. In Canada, it is used interchangeably with "Native," "Aboriginal," and "First Nations" (usually capitalized). "First Peoples" is equivalent to "Indigenous." "First Nations" are the peoples referred to as Native Americans in the United States, where Alaskan Inuit sometimes call themselves Eskimos (a term discarded in Canada). A single Inuit person is an *Inuk* and the main language is *Inuktitut*. Inuvialuit are Inuit of the western Canadian Arctic. Their language is *Inuvialuktun*.

BIBLIOGRAPHY

Aboriginal Voices. (1999, October/November). Cover photograph and caption.

Alia, V. (2010). *The New Media Nation: Indigenous peoples and global communication.* New York and Oxford, UK: Berghahn Books.

Alia, V. (2014). Gender and the New Media Nation. Presentation to the *Conference on Gender Equality in the Arctic: Current Realities and Future Challenges*, Akureyri, Iceland, October 30–31. Government of Iceland, Ministry of Foreign Affairs.

Ang, I. (1996). *Living room wars: Rethinking media audiences for a postmodern world.* London: Routledge.

APTN National News Online. (2013, July 26). Harper government says no to inquiry into missing and murdered Aboriginal women. Retrieved from http://aptn.ca/news/2013/07/26/harper-government-says-no-to-inquiry-into-missing-and-murdered-aboriginal-women/

Arctic Fibre.com. (2014). Retrieved from http://arcticfibre.com/arctic-fibre-extends-network-to-northwest-alaskan-communities/

Atkinson, N. (2014, June 20). The north remembers, even if you're just a kid who's never been there before. *National Post*, B3.

Barents Press Website. (2014). Retrieved from http://www.barentspress.org/

CBC News Manitoba Online. (2014, August 21). Harper rebuffs renewed calls for murdered, missing women inquiry. Retrieved from http://www.cbc.ca/player/News/Canada/Manitoba/ID/2494404330/

CBC News Online. (2013, August 20). Company surveys Arctic fiber optic cable route. Retrieved from http://www.cbc.ca/news/canada/north/company-surveys-arctic-fibre-optic-cable-route-1.1389176

The Globe and Mail Online. (2014). Retrieved from http://www.theglobeandmail.com/report-on-business/shrinking-arctic-ice-and-a-golden-fibre-optic-opportunity/article4714817/

Jocks, C. (1996). "Talk of the Town": Talk radio. In V. Alia, B. Brennan, & B. Hoffmaster (Eds.), *Deadlines and diversity: Journalism ethics in a changing world* (pp. 151–172). Halifax: Fernwood.

Keeper, T. (2007a, March 27). Conservative government must issue apology to residential school victims. Website of Tina Keeper, Member of Parliament for Churchill, Manitoba.

Keeper, T. (2007b, August 30). Harper government fails Canada with UN vote. Website of Tina Keeper, Member of Parliament for Churchill, Manitoba.Kuptana, R. (1982). Inuit Broadcasting Corporation presentation to the CRTC on cable tiering and universal pay TV. Speech, Inuit Broadcasting Corporation.

McKenna, C. (2014, November). Councillor's death jolts health services into action. *Windspeaker*, p. 18.

Radio Regulations. (1986). Justice laws website. Retrieved from http://laws,justice.gc-ca/eng/regualtions/SOR-86-982

Roth, L. (1993). Mohawk airwaves and cultural challenges: Some reflections on the politics of recognition and cultural appropriation after the summer of 1990. *Canadian Journal of Communication, 18*(3), 315–331.

Roth, L. (2006). *Something new in the air: The story of First Peoples television broadcasting in Canada*. Montreal: McGill-Queen's University Press.

Roth, L., & Valaskakis, G. G. (1989). Aboriginal broadcasting in Canada: A case study in democratization. In M. Raboy & P. A. Bruck (Eds.), *Communication for and against democracy* (pp. 221–234). Montreal: Black Rose.

Taylor, D. H. (2014, November). Aboriginal evolution and yesterday's social movement: The urbane Indian. *Windspeaker*, 6.

Taylor, G. (2013). The 1991 Broadcasting Act, communication law, historical Canada online. Retrieved from http://www.thecanadiancyclopedia.ca

Spivak, G. C. (1990). *The post-Colonial critic: Interviews, strategies, dialogues*. New York: Routledge.

Spivak, G. C. (1995). Subaltern studies: Deconstructing historiography. In D. Landry & M. MacLean (Eds.), *The Spivak reader: Selected works of Gayatri Spivak*. NewYork: Routledge.

Steffens, P. (1998). Excerpt from notes for a book on journalism history (unpublished).

Thérrien, R. (1980). *The 1980s: A decade of diversity-broadcasting, satellites, and pay-TV. Report from the Committee on Extension of Service to Northern and Remote Communities (The Therrien Report)*. Ottawa: Minister of Supply and Services Canada (CRTC), Catalogue No. BC 92-24/1980E.

CHAPTER FOURTEEN

Moral Motivation Within Media Cultures

PATRICK LEE PLAISANCE

The power of communitarianism as a normative framework for intercultural media ethics theorizing is undeniable. The criticism of Clifford Christians that our media theorizing has been overwhelmingly monocultural to date is an important one. Compelling calls have proliferated in recent years for the field of media ethics to better reflect the global nature of mediated communication itself, to find purchase in a forceful moral realism and thus gain legitimacy for efforts to construct normative claims that overcome cultural relativism. With landmark works such as *Ethics for Public Communication* (Christians, Fackler, & Ferré, 2012), Christians and colleagues clear a way forward to an exciting realm of global theorizing that rests on a cornerstone of communitarianism. This approach draws on the work of Michael Sandel, Charles Taylor, and others and "is a way of thinking about the moral life that fixes our attention away from the rights and obligations of the self, and centers instead on the social matrix in which we gather all we know about the true, the good, and the beautiful. In communitarianism, we understand that we are social beings who are constituted through others" (Christians et al., 2012, p. x).

Communitarianism recasts the arc of history to highlight how the relatively novel idea of the autonomous individual is borne out of Enlightenment thinking. As the North Atlantic's ideology, vigorous individualism is assumed to be the natural and desirable state of affairs, the "enlightened" perspective on moral agency. Yet Christians and colleagues argue that this individualism is a relatively new and historically disruptive phenomenon: "autonomy is a concept that arose after the development of movable type in the fifteenth century" (p. x) and flowered with the claims of John Locke that "the innermost self" was what lay at the heart of humanity and that autonomous agency must be protected from outside forces. Theorists such as Taylor, Sandel, and Michael Walzer have argued compellingly that individual identity is constituted through a social process that locates the good. They show how Enlightenment thinkers such as Locke and John Stuart Mill isolated the individual from their history and culture. "We flatter ourselves with the illusion of being autonomous," Christians and colleagues wrote. "Rather than individual rights as the integrating norm, our obligations to sustain one another define our existence" (p. xi). Similarly, Alasdair MacIntyre has argued that Enlightenment thinking warped our understanding of autonomous agency by urging us "to think atomistically about human action and to analyze complex actions and transactions in terms of simple components" (2007, p. 204). Drawing on this perspective in their *Ethics for Public Communication* book, Christians and colleagues showcase a collection of valuable instances of media practices—they can be called moral media tales—that represent manifestations of communitarian theory.

This chapter embraces the power of communitarianism as illustrated in these tales, and it aligns itself with the broader claim that this approach provides a useful normative framework that transcends cultural value distinctions. Yet Christians continues by dismissing the formalist framework of virtue ethics, as it traditionally has been harnessed to promote the same individualistic Enlightenment ethic that communitarianism seeks to counter. While it is true that Aristotle's virtue-based ethical system "promoted self-realization" (Christians et al., 2012, p. xiv), a considerable portion of his writings also is concerned with the notion of societal "fitness" and another key function of virtue contemplation: ensuring that individuals develop into effective participants in the polis. "The point or rationale of the virtues is meeting appropriately 'the demands of the world,'" virtue theorist Christine Swanton writes. "This includes self-realization, but is not exhausted by self-realization" (2003, p. 14). Virtue ethics in general arguably provides an inherently pro-social agenda; even Aristotle's framing of moral education is implicitly focused on its broader community value. Its goal, as Meyer (2011) frames it, is "to produce a fully autonomous individual who *merits* praise or blame" (p. 3; author's emphasis). Similarly, Swanton's (2003) pluralistic theory of virtue ethics implicitly rests on an assumption of social exchange or communion, an assumption that virtuous behavior does not manifest itself in a vacuum but instead in gestures responding to the social contexts and encounters in which we live. Her "profile" of virtue denotes "that constellation of modes of moral responsiveness or acknowledgement which comprise the virtuous disposition" (p. 3). As a branch of the formalist approaches that have dominated ethics theory, virtue ethics is limited in its usefulness because of its focus on self-development, Christians and colleagues argued. Its compatibility with a communitarian approach, they write, is deeply in question. "[M]orality is a community product: Moral values unfold through human interaction," they write. "Only in community are there ethical formation, action, and accountability" (p. xv).

This chapter challenges that skepticism. As have all formalist approaches, virtue ethics has evolved as contemporary theorists have compellingly refined initial precepts from ancient Greece and arguably transcends such narrow readings. David Solomon (1997) and others have effectively disposed of the common objection to virtue ethics as being individualist-centered. A fuller accounting of the framework of virtue ethics provides a vision of how, by understanding key features of mature moral motivation, virtue ethics theory in fact reinforces key communitarian claims. Recent moral psychology research, focused on notions of moral motivation and development of self, may appear at odds with the communitarian paradigm, but a close analysis reveals some key, enduring links. Selected "exemplars" from various professions, including media, show how virtues and moral concerns—including those tied to community flourishing and promotion of the common good—are internalized in such ways as to leave little daylight between perceptions of virtue and actual behavior. Rather than reinforce Enlightenment abstractions about the centrality of the self, moral psychology efforts can help media ethics researchers demonstrate how a communitarian ethic is embedded in the morally motivated self. This self-orientation, subsequently, can and should have a significant influence on intercultural media theorizing and on the evolving cultures of digital newsrooms and citizen-journalism community initiatives.

The link between communitarianism and the morally motivated self is further strengthened by the *ethical naturalism* detailed in the works of neo-Aristotelian theorists such as Rosalind Hursthouse, Alasdair MacIntyre, and Philippa Foot. In his articulation of how the neo-Aristotelian approach is usefully brought to bear on questions of media practice, Nick Couldry (2013) implicitly links virtue theory with key elements of communitarianism:

> The basic question for media ethics flows quite readily: How should we act in relation to media, so that we contribute to lives that, both individually and together, we would value on all scales, up to and including the global? ... Far from claiming to start out from some accepted and already authoritative norm by which contemporary journalists can be judged, media ethics in the neo-Aristotelian tradition asks what, in today's factual conditions, can we expect that media as a practice *might* contribute to our possibilities of living well together. (pp. 25–26; author's emphasis)

THE VALUE OF MORAL PSYCHOLOGY

Recent research in moral psychology identifies features of cognition, environment, and behavior and traces their links with moral virtues. As a discipline, moral psychology concerns itself with the intersection of human sciences and moral deliberation. It is a central focus of researchers in philosophy, psychology, neuroscience, and even anthropology and economics. As such, the field touches on both the profound and the prosaic. More broadly, moral psychology research represents a valuable effort to provide a strong empirical foundation for normative ethics theorizing by suggesting connections between the theories and methodologies of psychology and the values and principles of moral philosophy. The link between virtue theory and moral psychology in fact was made as early as 1958, when Anscombe sought to shift the focus of the philosophy of ethics away from systems analysis to the concept of virtue. Virtuous action, as more applied ethics research is suggesting, is not contingent on character *or* context but on the complex interchange between character *and* context. As Solomon (2005), a contemporary philosopher, noted, "circumstances and character cannot be pried apart and should not be used competitively as alternative explanations of virtuous or vicious behavior" (p. 654). Moral psychology is less concerned with justifying the rightness of specific *actions*, as is the case with Kantianism, utilitarianism, and other frameworks, and aligns itself instead with virtue ethics and the concern of what constitutes notable *character*. With a range of empirical and more qualitative instruments that have been refined over decades, researchers have been able to "operationalize" or quantify important philosophical and ethical concepts such as moral development, empathy, and people's relative emphasis placed on concerns about pursuing justice and avoiding harm. Moral psychology "investigates human functioning in moral contexts, and asks how these results may impact debate in ethical theory," according to Doris and Stich (2006, p. 1). Rather than provide merely a descriptive ethics, moral psychology provides a basis to develop an interpretive analysis of our roles, obligations, connections, and relationships.

A recent study of selected "exemplars" in the U.S. media system—prize-winning journalists and public relations executives known for their ethical leadership—identified a shared profile of morally motivated self-identity that extended far beyond mere "self-realization." These exemplars manifested a pattern of marrying their conception of the self with external moral principles and thus transforming "objective" virtue into a key part of how they are motivated to perform their work and live their lives (Plaisance, 2014). This moral orientation, or successful integration of issues of morality into the self, echoes the theories of moral identity developed by Maslow (1971), Blasi (1984), Lapsley (2008), and others. It also echoes the conclusions of Anne Colby and William Damon in their 1992 landmark study of moral exemplars, *Some Do Care*. Media exemplars' moral identity profile can be linked directly to descriptions of the virtuous agent by neo-Aristotelian theorists: "Built into the theory is the claim that part of the virtuous person's practical wisdom is her knowledge, her correct appreciation, of what is truly good, and, indeed, of what is truly pleasant, truly advantageous, truly worthwhile, truly important, truly serious (and, correspondingly, of what is truly bad, unpleasant, or painful, disadvantageous, worthless, unimportant, and trivial)" (Hursthouse, 2012, p. 73). In earlier work, Hursthouse (1999) elaborates on the nature of moral motivation:

> [B]eing "morally motivated" is not solely a matter of acting, on a particular occasion, for a special kind of reason, let alone one that is vitally different from other kinds of reasons … but, primarily, acting *from virtue*—from a settled state of good character. … "[B]ecause she thought she was right" (from "a sense of duty," etc.) is an ascription that goes far beyond the moment of action. It is not merely, as grammatically it might appear to be, a claim about how things are with the agent and her reasons at the moment. It is also a substantial claim about the future (with respect to reliability) and, most importantly, a claim about what sort of person the agent is—a claim that goes "all the way down." … [W]e are not insisting that she have explicit thoughts about right action, duty or principle. … Such explicit thoughts are not a necessary condition for being morally motivated. (pp. 123, 140; author's emphasis)

This moral motivation manifests itself on the individual level, but an equal part of its value lies in the translation of virtue into notions of community connectedness and social health. Nussbaum (1995), too, reinforced the basis for the connection between the morally motivated self and the wider world in her rejection of claims that human nature—and by extension our understanding of morality—is "internal" rather than "external": that personal identity and notions of the self provide an objective foundation for moral thought that need not require independent validation beyond morality itself. "Human nature cannot, and need not, be validated from the outside, because human nature just *is* an inside perspective, not a *thing* at all, but rather the most fundamental and broadly shared experiences of human beings living and reasoning together" (p. 121; author's emphasis). Correspondingly, the model of the "morally motivated self" that emerges from the media exemplar study appears to be largely shaped by features of (a) their moral development, (b) their ethical ideology, (c) their personality traits, and (d) their professional environment, or moral ecology (Figure 14.1). The suggested model arguably reflects a communitarian approach through the constellation of principles that the media exemplars explicitly prioritized in their personal and professional lives—principles including social justice, concern for the welfare of others, and moral courage.

The idea of the morally motivated self also suggests links to what Kevin DeLapp (2013) refers to as "motivational externalism," which acknowledges that moral judgments often require additional (nonmoral) motivating factors to move people to act, even though this does not undermine the existence of the moral values in question. This is an important part of a *moral realism* that states that "moral values exist in a way that is causally and evidentially (though not conceptually) independent from the beliefs of anyone and everyone (including idealized agents) such that evidence and beliefs do not determine or constitute those values, though they may adequately and reliably measure or reflect them" (p. 17). The relevance of moral psychology approaches becomes clearer when communitarian claims are understood as expressions of a moral realism—a way of thinking about the moral life, as Christians and colleagues (2012) argue, "that fixes our attention away from the rights and obligations of the self, and centers instead on the social matrix in which we gather all we know about the true, the good, and the beautiful" (p. x).

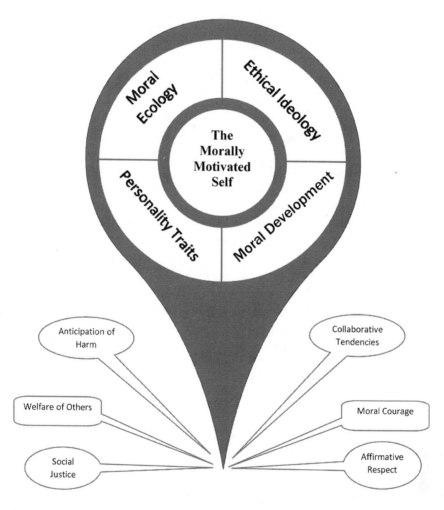

Figure 14.1. Model of the Morally Motivated Self (Plaisance, 2014, p. 204).

INTERCULTURAL IMPLICATIONS

Moral psychology approaches also offer significant promise for global media theorizing. As we will see, some key lines of empirical inquiry, including examinations of moral development and value systems, have established a robust validity that holds across cultural distinctions. Indeed, systematically rejecting the notion of cultural relativism served as a primary aim of the research agenda of Lawrence Kohlberg (1971; Kohlberg, Levine, & Hewer, 1983), whose theory of moral development has provided a dominant approach for several decades. That said, claims of moral universals, or the specifics of an "objective moral charter," continue to be subject to ongoing debate. Cultural psychologist Richard Shweder and others (Shweder, 2003; Shweder & Power, 2013) have argued that the moral domain is broader than liberal values as commonly understood in the West and should not be restricted to the study of autonomous agency, nor should they focus exclusively on "liberal" moral concepts such as harm, individual rights, and justice.

At the very least, moral psychology approaches hold enormous potential for deepening our understanding of cultural differences in the context of value systems found in most all societies. Shweder and Power (2013) point to this function for cultural psychology as well, and the suggested link to questions of cultural value sharing and media is worth noting:

> We live in a world that is globalizing, boundaries are coming down and we are faced with cultural collisions of one type or another as people move into common territorial spaces. Cultural psychologists have a very important role to play in promoting human understanding of cultural differences which, at least in principle, might support a more tolerant live-and-let-live attitude, especially if you can get over your initial reactions of indignation or disgust at what other people are doing when we encounter unfamiliar practices. That responsibility arises in part because of the technologies associated with media. These days you can stick a camera in someone else's valley and show a very provocative or even incendiary image which gets people to want to react very quickly, even before they necessarily understand what they are seeing. I can see how cultural psychology might have a part to play in the world of journalism, for example. (pp. 679–680)

Shweder and others have expressed skepticism toward any attempt to standardize measures of moral growth across cultures. And the words above focus on ethical implications of media framing and audience effects; the value of applications of moral psychology approaches in media ethics research while focused on media production—the other side of the media equation—is analogous.

Moral Development

Lawrence Kohlberg's theory of moral development stages has been dominant for decades. And while Kohlberg's research was monocultural, he was
unequivocal about the validity of its intercultural application:

> Almost all individuals in all cultures have the same ... basic moral categories, con-
> cepts, principles [and values], and ... all individuals in all cultures go through the
> same order or sequence of gross stages of development, though they vary in rate and
> terminal point of development ... [given different] opportunities for role-taking.
> (1971, pp. 176, 183)

Theorists such as John Snarey (1985) offer an anthropological critique of
Kohlberg's approach that simultaneously sympathizes with his anti-relativist
project yet insists on taking cultural difference on questions of moral agency
seriously. Kohlberg's system is based on assumptions of rationality, so that
what follows is the claim that people in all cultures should move through his
stages as their moral reasoning matures. Consequently, we should see more or
less consistent development through the early stages across cultures. Research
has suggested this is indeed the case: In studies across more than three dozen
countries, progression from stages 1 to 2 occurred in most cultures by late
childhood; stage 3 thinking predominates in late adolescence, and most young
adults attain stage 4. But, Snarey and colleagues suggest, moral development
into the higher stages also should correlate with factors indicating "affordance
and accumulation of diverse social experiences and perspective-taking opportunities through social participation" (Gibbs, Basinger, Grime, & Snarey,
2007, p. 446). Here, universality claims appear to greatly weaken. Indeed,
Kohlberg (1981) himself later acknowledged that his descriptions of the highest post-conventional stages of development did not appear to be applicable
across all cultures.

The concern of Gibbs, Snarey, and other critics is that Kohlberg's stage-
based system of moral development glosses over the complexity and different manifestations of more highly developmental modes of moral agency in
non-Western cultures. Perhaps, they say, Kohlberg's emphasis on conscious
rationality disallows recognition of other routes for moral growth. The work of
Carol Gilligan (1982) is among the more prominent lines of inquiry that has
challenged the unidimensional focus of Kohlberg's theory. Yet a more ambitious analysis of 75 cross-cultural studies and applications of revised models
of moral maturity indicated a "convergence" for "common moral values, basic
moral judgment stage development, and related social perspective-taking
across cultural groups" (Gibbs et al., 2007, p. 444). Specifically, the "qualitative
shift from instrumental (Stage 2) to mutualistic (Stage 3) moral judgment was
robust enough to manifest across different methods of assessment and diverse

cultures" (p. 489). "Although the question of the universality of values continues to need research attention," the researchers conclude, "persons around the world do seem to understand and appreciate values such as life, affiliation, contract or truth, and property or law ... [M]oral development is not entirely relative to particular cultures and socialization practices" (pp. 488, 491).

And there are others who continue to hold the possibility of discovering more broadly universal elements of moral reasoning that link Kohlberg's higher stages of development with other "elaborations" on conventional morality, as Gibbs and colleagues suggest (2007, p. 489). Other theorists such as Darcia Narvaez (2002) are "neo-Kohlbergian" in their efforts to modify his approach to encompass the possibility of multiple manifestations of moral reasoning, some of which may be implicit, and they draw on schema theory (Roskos-Ewoldsen, Roskos-Ewoldsen, & Carpenter, 2009) from cognitive psychology to do so.

Value Systems

Begun soon after the turn of the century, research on human value systems culminated in sophisticated instruments that point to a robust theoretical cross-cultural framework. Earlier empirical work by Milton Rokeach (1968) suggested a widely shared group of variously ranked values—defined as "single belief[s] that transcendentally guide actions and judgments across specific objects and situations, and beyond immediate goals to more ultimate end-states of existence" (p. 160). More ambitious intercultural testing and refining of value notions by Shalom Schwartz and colleagues has culminated in a high-reliability structure theory of human values that illuminate broad similarities and differences that are culturally based. In research conducted in more than 70 countries (e.g., Schwartz, 1992; Schwartz & Bilsky, 1990; Schwartz & Boehnke, 2004), their results have suggested that there are strong patterns in how value sets are distinguished within and among cultures. Not only have they identified common values embraced in cultures, but they have found these values are commonly clustered in two dimensions on a value circumplex: "self-enhancement/self-transcendence" and "conservation/openness to change" (Figure 14.2). Schwartz and colleagues identify how individual values tend to be related to others across cultures and how different cultures emphasize differences among values. Support for one value in the circumplex tends to correlate with support for adjacent ones and less support for those on the opposite pole.

While there are clearly differences in how values are embraced among cultures, there are also patterns to those differences, as Schwartz's values circumplex indicates. Other lines of research echo these patterns. The work of Hofstede (2001) and Inglehart and Welzel (2005) regarding value structures across the globe all point to patterns in the ways that cultures agree and disagree on moral issues. Other theorists have explored more complex explanations of the "moral ecologies," as Huff, Barnard, and Frey (2008) use the term, that constitute the interplay of individual and cultural influences shaping moral claims and moral identity. Markus and Kitayama (2010), for instance, suggest what they call a model of the "cycle of mutual constitution" of cultures and selves. Walker and colleagues (Walker, Frimer, & Dunlop, 2010) have also found that selected moral exemplars emphasize "communal" characteristics.

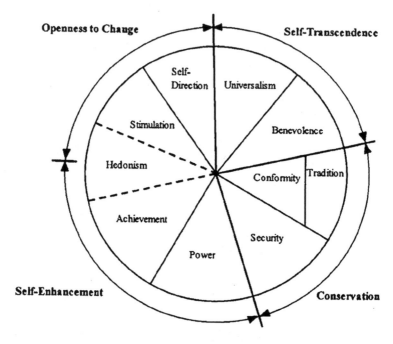

Figure 14.2. Circumplex Structure of Values (Schwartz & Boehnke, 2004).

For all the empirical research that points to robust patterns of values and moral perspectives around the globe, the field of moral psychology also offers cautionary notes about the limits of its postpositivist approach. When considering the complexity of patterns in intercultural agreement, the words of Shweder are worth noting:

> [There are] universal questions that have to be faced for the sake of personal identity and social existence—they are unavoidable. But it's not as though science or logic is going to provide a definitive answer binding all; and different historical traditions have developed different kinds of answers and built different types of institutions around those answers. There is not a single way to trace group inclusion or kinship affiliation. There is not a single universally binding conception for gender relations,

one that all rational and morally sensitive human beings must abide by. Morally sensible and reasonable people can disagree without being involved in error, ignorance or confusion. Or if there is error or ignorance that may be a concomitant of the ultimate limits of human reason. There are some questions that can't be decided solely using rational procedures and some truths that are just unknowable. (Shweder & Power, 2013, p. 680)

VIRTUE ETHICS AND COMMUNITARIANISM

Moral psychology reveals the enduring links between the broad, pro-social concerns emerging from the morally motivated self and key communitarian precepts. The fact that these realms are not mutually exclusive should not be surprising. Aristotle arguably focused as much on virtues' pro-social ends as much as he did on the nature of the virtues themselves. More contemporary virtue ethics theorists have done the same. For Philippa Foot, the virtues (e.g., courage, wisdom, justice, temperance) all share three key features: they are dispositions of the will; they serve as correctives for some bad general tendency among humans; and of most relevance here, they are beneficial to either its possessor or to others, or both. Referring to the more complex virtue of justice, Foot (2002b) noted, "communities where justice and charity are lacking are apt to be wretched places to live, as Russia was under the Stalinists, or Sicily under the Mafia" (p. 3). Just as Taylor argues that communitarianism more properly accounts for the sociology of identity and daily life, Foot (2002a) argues that the nature of the virtues extends beyond individual dispositions and are connected with human goodness broadly understood. Her work also allows for the assertion of virtues across cultural lines. There is room, she says, for individual societies to specify a "moral system" or "system of virtue."

Foot, according to one analysis of her work, "forwards a critical social vision that is shared with other moral and social philosophers such as Jürgen Habermas, John Rawls, and Tim Scanlon. At the center of this critical vision is the idea of the individual persons as more than just 'cells in a collective whole,' as Warren Quinn puts it" (Hacker-Wright, 2013, p. 151). While Christine Swanton distinguishes herself from Foot and other neo-Aristotelians with her "pluralistic" virtue theory, she also nonetheless emphasizes how virtue ethics speaks to the socially situated self. Here she draws from Karen Horney in making her point about the role of culture in defining virtuous behavior:

[W]e are not simply a "self" but a self existing "within a matrix of concentric fields extending from the intra-psychic through the interpersonal to the larger culture in which we are all immersed." As a result, distinctions such as that between "vicious" and "neurotic" ambition and a healthy ambition or pursuit of success rely on a sensitivity to, and informed critique of, cultures in which ambition or relative lack of ambition are salient. (2003, pp. 10–11)

The *ethical naturalism* of neo-Aristotelian thinkers also comports well with the communitarian framework. Ethical naturalism, Hursthouse (1999) wrote, helps us examine "whether my beliefs about which character traits are the virtues can survive my reflective scrutiny and be given some rational justification" (p. 194). Such a naturalist agenda, she suggested, does not assert a singular—and thus suspicious—notion of the right, but encourages us "to think about what empirical assumptions we make about ourselves as a kind of animal with a contingent nature when we talk about ethics" (2012, p. 179).

Foot, in her landmark book *Natural Goodness*, made a compelling case that we do indeed have objective reasons for acting in ways we call virtuous, quite apart from any claim that, as Kant argued, we are morally obligated to do something when we properly understand what is "right." Rather than focusing on abstract concepts such as sacredness of life, goodness, and duty, Foot argued we must concentrate on traditional virtues and vices, and by doing so, we can see the concrete connections between the conditions of human life and the objective reasons for acting morally. She rejected the longstanding distinction insisted upon by philosophers between the nature of a fact and the nature of a value. The "negative value" of vice, she argued, is a defect in humans the same way that poor roots are a defect in an oak tree or poor vision a defect in an owl: the two assessments have clear normative implications, yet are also entirely factual.

The model of the morally motivated self challenges conventional, one-dimensional perceptions of ethical behavior that emphasize either deontological reasoning or simplistic claims of personal integrity and grounds its approach in a more complex—and more useful—neo-Aristotelian framework of contextualized virtues. Claims about conscientiousness, about commitment, about care all can easily be inferred from moral psychology findings. These claims suggest why the virtue ethics of neo-Aristotelian philosophers of Philippa Foot, Rosalind Hursthouse, Martha Nussbaum, Alasdair MacIntyre, and others provides a compelling philosophical framework that has clear areas of overlap with communitarian priorities. The constellation of personality dispositions, experiences, moral ecologies, and moral schemas all fit better with virtue ethics theory, which in turn has evolved into a neo-Aristotelian framework that covers far more than mere self-development. This framework firmly situates the self within community and underscores the same concerns of justice, engagement, and social conscience found in communitarianism. While the empirical, individual-based variables mentioned above may on their surface suggest a narrow focus on individual self-realization, they in fact direct our focus on what is essential for human flourishing and competent engagement in the polis. These broader community goals necessarily emphasize the process of interpreting and selecting inputs, the internalization of values, and development of perceptions of virtuous motivations.

BIBLIOGRAPHY

Blasi, A. (1984). Moral identity: Its role in moral functioning. In W. M. Kurtines & J. L. Gewirtz (Eds.), *Morality, moral behavior, and moral development* (pp. 129–139). New York: John Wiley.

Christians, C. G., Fackler, P. M., & Ferré, J. P. (2012). *Ethics for public communication: Defining moments in media history*. New York: Oxford University Press.

Colby, A., & Damon, W. (1992). *Some do care: Contemporary lives of moral commitment*. New York: Free Press.

Couldry, N. (2013). Why media ethics still matters. In S. J. A. Ward (Ed.), *Global media ethics: Problems and perspectives* (pp. 13–29). Malden, MA: Wiley-Blackwell.

DeLapp, K. (2013). *Moral realism*. London: Bloomsbury.

Doris, J., & Stich, S. (2006). Moral psychology: Empirical approaches. *Stanford encyclopedia of philosophy*. Retrieved from http://plato.stanford.edu/entries/moral-psych-emp/

Foot, P. (2001). *Natural goodness*. Oxford, UK: Oxford University Press.

Foot, P. (2002a). *Moral dilemmas and other topics in moral philosophy*. Oxford, UK: Oxford University Press.

Foot, P. (2002b). *Virtues and vices and other essays in moral philosophy* (2nd ed.). Oxford, UK: Oxford University Press.

Gibbs, J. C., Basinger, K. S., Grime, R. L., & Snarey, J. R. (2007). Moral judgment development across cultures: Revisiting Kohlberg's universality claims. *Developmental Review, 27*, 443–500.

Gilligan, C. (1982). *In a different voice: Psychological theory and women's development*. Cambridge, UK: Cambridge University Press.

Hacker-Wright, J. (2013). *Philippa Foot's moral thought*. London: Bloomsbury.

Hofstede, G. (2001). *Culture's consequences: Comparing values, behaviors, institutions and organizations across nations*. Los Angeles, CA: Sage.

Huff, C. W., Barnard, L., & Frey, W. (2008). Good computing: A pedagogically focused model of virtue in the practice of computing (part 2). *Journal of Information, Communication and Ethics in Society, 6*(4), 284–316.

Hursthouse, R. (1999). *On virtue ethics*. Oxford, UK: Oxford University Press.

Hursthouse, R. (2012). Human nature and Aristotelian virtue ethics. *Royal Institute of Philosophy Supplement, 70*, 169–188.

Inglehart, R., & Welzel, C. (2005). *Modernization, cultural change, and democracy: The human development sequence*. Cambridge, UK: Cambridge University Press.

Kohlberg, L. (1971). From is to ought: How to commit the naturalistic fallacy and get away with it in the study of moral development. In T. Mischel (Ed.), *Cognitive development and epistemology* (pp. 151–235). New York: Academic Press.

Kohlberg, L. (1981). *The philosophy of moral development: Vol. 1. Moral stages and the idea of justice: Essays on moral development*. San Francisco: Harper & Row.

Kohlberg, L., Levine, C., & Hewer, A. (1983). *Moral stages: A current formulation and a response to critics*. Basel, Switzerland: Karger.

Lapsley, D. K. (2008). Moral self-identity as the aim of education. In L. P. Nucci & D. Narvaez (Eds.), *Handbook of moral and character education* (pp. 30–52). New York: Routledge.

MacIntyre, A. (2007). *After virtue* (3rd Ed.). Notre Dame, IN: University of Notre Dame Press.

Markus, H. R., & Kitayama, S. (2010). Cultures and selves: A cycle of mutual constitution. *Perspectives on Psychological Science, 5*(4), 420–430.

Maslow, A. (1971). *The farther reaches of human nature*. New York: Viking Press.

Meyer, S. S. (2011). *Aristotle on moral responsibility: Character and cause*. New York: Oxford University Press.

Narvaez, D. (2002). Integrative ethical education. In M. Killen & J. Smetana (Eds.), *Handbook of moral development* (pp. 703–732). Mahwah, NJ: Lawrence Erlbaum Associates.

Nussbaum, M. C. (1995). Aristotle on human nature and the foundations of ethics. In J. E. J. Altham & R. Harrison (Eds.), *World, mind and ethics: Essays on the ethical philosophy of Bernard Williams* (pp. 86–131). Cambridge, UK: Cambridge University Press.

Plaisance, P. L. (2014). *Virtue in media: The moral psychology of excellence in news and public relations*. New York: Routledge.

Rokeach, M. (1968). *Beliefs, attitudes and values: A theory of organization and change*. San Francisco: Jossey-Bass.

Roskos-Ewoldsen, D. R., Roskos-Ewoldsen, B., & Carpenter, F. D. (2009). Media priming: An updated synthesis. In J. Bryant & M. B. Oliver (Eds.), *Media effects: Advances in theory and research* (pp. 74–93). New York: Routledge.

Schwartz, S. H. (1992). Universals in the content and structure of values: Theoretical advances and empirical tests in 20 countries. *Advances in Experimental Psychology, 25*, 1–65.

Schwartz, S. H., & Bilsky, W. (1990). Toward a theory of the universal content and structure of values: Extensions and cross-cultural replications. *Journal of Personality and Social Psychology, 58*(5), 878–891.

Schwartz, S. H., & Boehnke, K. (2004). Evaluating the structure of human values with confirmatory factor analysis. *Journal of Research in Personality, 38*, 230–255.

Shweder, R. A. (2003). *Why do men barbecue? Recipes for cultural psychology*. Cambridge, MA: Harvard University Press.

Shweder, R. A., & Power, S. A. (2013). Robust cultural pluralism: An interview with Professor Richard A. Schweder. *Europe's Journal of Psychology, 9*(4), 671–686.

Snarey, J. R. (1985). The cross-cultural universality of social-moral development: A critical review of Kohlbergian research. *Psychological Bulletin, 97*, 202–232.

Solomon, D. (1997). Internal objections to virtue ethics. In D. Statman (Ed.), *Virtue ethics: A critical reader* (pp. 165–179). Edinburgh, Scotland: Edinburgh University Press.

Solomon, R. C. (2005, November). What's character got to do with it? *Philosophy and Phenomenological Research, 71*(3), 648–655.

Swanton, C. (2003). *Virtue ethics: A pluralistic view*. New York: Oxford University Press.

Walker, L. J., Frimer, J. A., & Dunlop, W. L. (2010). Varieties of moral personality: Beyond the banality of heroism. *Journal of Personality, 78*(3), 907–942.

CHAPTER FIFTEEN

Casuistry's Strengths FOR Intercultural Journalism Ethics

A Case in Point

SANDRA L. BORDEN AND DAVID E. BOEYINK

Ursula Rakova, a resident of the Carteret Islands near Papua New Guinea, is a rare example of a Pacific Islander whose voice has been featured prominently in Western news stories about the rising water levels that are pushing people like her out of their homes. She, like others who are migrating from their homeland because of the effects of climate change, worries about losing her language and her culture: "Our culture is about connectedness to the island. It makes us who we are" (Potter, 2009). For those familiar with the conventions of sourcing in Western journalism, the reason for Rakova's exceptionalism will not be surprising. She left the Carteret Islands to go to college, worked for OXFAM, and has become adept at accessing the levers of power that control the international resources her people need. She has learned to "play the game." But she also retains her distinct perspective and uses her position to turn the dominant climate-change narrative on its head. She is helping to create a detailed migration plan, upsetting the stereotype of "climate refugees," and she is pointing fingers: "In Canada, climate change probably will mean making a choice about lifestyle," she told a *Toronto Star* reporter. "For those of us on the islands, it is a choice of life and death."

Rakova's plight is illustrative of recent developments that have hastened the need for what the editors of this volume call a "new media ethics of interculturalism." The rapid expansion of electronic communication technologies has created new spaces for intercultural encounters. Global media corporations have enabled diverse voices to be disseminated well beyond their places of origin at the same time that these corporations have promoted homogenization in accord with market incentives. And, as structural economic changes and other global stressors make their impact felt, journalists find themselves struggling ethically to mediate the resulting cross-cultural upheavals. The tension between the universal and the particular is central to intercultural media ethics. As editors Shan and Christians noted in their introductory dialogue to this book:

> The new technologies are international—ICT's, data clouds, communication satellites, the cyber world of search engines—but we live in communities and practice our professions within them. Ethics needs to work effectively on the ground as research and lived experience indicate. We need a media ethics that is actionable and pluralistic. (p. 10)

Climate change illustrates how areas of media content increasingly cross cultures and raise ethical problems precisely at the boundaries of cultures. An ethical challenge for journalists is to frame their climate coverage in ways that avoid both hegemony and relativism. If journalists use frames that are hegemonic, they tell stories that are actionable but not pluralistic. If they use frames that are relativistic, they tell stories that are pluralistic but not actionable. The purpose of this chapter is to demonstrate the usefulness of an ethical decision-making method known as casuistry for navigating this challenge.

Borden (2014) has suggested that casuistry has the following advantages in intercultural media ethics: (1) the method does not require convergence at the level of principle; (2) it avoids dilution of difference for the sake of resolution; and (3) its modest epistemology is appropriate to the perplexing nature of intercultural ethics.[1] After explaining these methodological advantages, we test Borden's argument by applying casuistry to news coverage of the effects of climate change in Oceania. Using a casuistical strategy, we explore ways in which Western media frame the problem of rising ocean levels for Pacific Islanders. We conclude with a discussion of casuistry's strengths and limitations for tackling such cases in the future.

CASUISTRY: RECENT HISTORY AND THEORY

Practical Resolution, Not Theoretical Consensus

Reflecting on their experience developing federal recommendations for research with vulnerable subjects, Jonsen and Toulmin (1988) noticed that the members of the National Commission for the Protection of Human Subjects of Biomedical and Behavioral Research were able to formulate joint recommendations despite deep religious and philosophical differences. The secret was case-based reasoning, which allowed the commissioners to work *with* difference rather than ignoring or diluting it. Their focus was practical: coming up with workable recommendations that captured their key moral concerns. They did this by working inductively with the details of cases rather than deductively from first principles.

Indeed, casuistry has not depended historically on any particular version of the good life or on a common set of principles to deliberate about difficult ethical choices. As Jonsen and Toulmin (1988) noted, "It was a simple practical exercise directed at attempting a satisfactory resolution of practical problems" (p. 242). By approaching moral problems in this way rather than as a competition between adversarial theories, casuistry can help us make progress on difficult intercultural problems without leaving behind our philosophical, religious, or social commitments. "The result is not a regrettable compromise, but a new creation—perhaps even a new 'language'—that would have been impossible without such an encounter" (Borden, 2014, p. 17).

Casuistry, to be clear, is not the same thing as a casual, unsystematic "situation ethics." It is a well-established, rigorous method that provides logical grounds for justifying and criticizing particular moral judgments. Casuistical deliberation begins by classifying the case that must be decided and then identifying a clear-cut case of the same kind—a paradigm—to guide an inductive ethical analysis. This analysis proceeds by comparing the case in question to the paradigm and to other analogical cases on the basis of the cases' morally relevant characteristics. Facts are deemed morally relevant on the basis of moral concepts, such as truth telling and nonviolence, which have *prima facie* validity within certain limits. These limits are determined by particular understandings of which resolutions will be most cogent in the circumstances, as well as resolutions that will be ruled out altogether (Wallace, 2009). In other words, casuistry's moral categories are situated, not abstract. For example, truth telling in journalism could entail reproducing a quotation exactly "as is" but may also allow for slight "cleaning up" to eliminate a distracting stutter. What it will not allow, no matter how much more clearly stated the speaker's ideas might be, is "putting words in people's mouths."

The "thick ethical concepts" in play "are notions that reasonable people know" and can use well given sufficient experience (Kuczewski, 1997, p. 5). They may be traced to a variety of ethical theories and may be clarified through philosophical reflection. However, they cannot be simply reduced to principles nor are they derived from principles. And, perhaps most important, they are not absolute, timeless, and speculative (the top-down approach of applied ethics that interprets cases as instances of theories). Rather, they are grounded in experience and subject to qualification and revision. "Casuists are committed to the principle that no principle is absolute but that each is applicable within certain limits" (p. 75). Casuistical presuppositions are similar to precedents in case law; they have presumptive force, but it is the details of the case at hand that determine whether and how these "precedents" ultimately hold sway. Justification is secondary to cases.

Although casuistry does not depend on any one theoretical orientation, it nevertheless has not been a free-standing method historically. Casuistry's moral presumptions could be traced, in different places and different times, to a wide variety of moral and religious traditions, ranging from Roman juris-prudence to rabbinical Judaism. Whatever you call them—"maxims" (Jonsen & Toulmin, 1988), "presuppositions" (Miller, 1996), or "middle principles" (Kuczewski, 1997)—the moral categories in question are domain specific; they require a "background of customary practice" to understand their scope and meaning (Wallace, 2009, p. 41). In other words, casuistical norms have always been "thick" ones, flowing from specific ways of being in the world, embodied in concrete practices and activities in actually existing communities.

Resisting Abstraction and Overgeneralization

As Boeyink and Borden (2010) noted, casuistry offers a way to give con-crete meaning to general moral notions by directing our attention to specific cultural contexts. For journalists, their understanding of autonomy and truth telling, for example, will invoke the entire system of interrelated commitments and activities that constitute "being a journalist"—not as a general proposition but within a given life narrative in a given tradition in a given community.

Ethical deliberation may start out on the basis of a norm's manifest con-tent, or minimal morality (Walzer, 1994), but the process of working through cases helps decision makers dig down to the latent content, or maximal moral-ity. It is at this level of maximal morality that decision makers rely on a sub-stantial amount of moral expertise with the social roles, relationships, and histories at stake in a particular case. Casuists do not water down morality to achieve consensus. Indeed, paradigm cases have moral resonance because they encapsulate worldviews with their sociocultural biases and limitations. When it is necessary to work with more than one culture, casuists must identify par-adigms that are preloaded with moral categories traceable to more than one tradition, one history, one language. One of the limits on the practical reso-lution of such cases will be the resolution's compatibility with the different cultures in play. Instructional examples are the joint activities of those involved in contemporary hospice care despite their varying attitudes toward religion and euthanasia (Bretherton, 2006) and those who advocate for immigrants despite being variously motivated by the claims of civil liberties, religion, human rights, or ethnic identity.

The casuist's task is not to subsume or transcend the various contexts involved in intercultural media ethics cases but to work with them and through them. Our common humanity is not based on sameness; it is based on the fact that "we participate, all of us, in thick cultures that are our own" (Walzer, 1994, p. 83). This is not to say that our differences are absolute, however. "Since social actors inhabit a common world, their language games are permeable and communication between them possible ... The *incommensurability* is not universal but always local, temporal, and partial, just as commensurability is" (Volf, 1996, p. 109, emphasis in original). Provisional commensurability is enough for the casuist to move forward.

By staying close to the ground, casuistry avoids the overgeneralizations and abstractions of "cosmopolitan" approaches to intercultural ethics.[2] Instead, casuistry acknowledges what international relations theorist Scott Thomas (2000) calls the "deeper pluralism" of the world's various cultures. Nevertheless, the casuist values consistency and does not resort to a crude relativism to settle matters. We will take a closer look at casuistry's methodology next.

A Modest Epistemology

Epistemological modesty is inherent to the casuistical method and, we argue, an appropriate orientation to vexing intercultural problems. Casuistry is flexible, incremental, and tentative in how it defines moral concepts, classifies cases, generalizes moral judgments, and estimates the level of confidence such judgments should engender.

For starters, the moral concepts used in casuistry are always provisional. Although they operate as presumptions at the outset of a case analysis, the ways in which these "maxims" are applied get worked out in the process of analyzing the details of cases. As a matter of fact, the moral concepts themselves may undergo specification as a result of casuistical deliberation. We will see how this works when we analyze our test case. Another assumption is that paradigms themselves may be revised or replaced if warranted by new circumstances or advances in moral understanding. Casuists may have to refine or abandon paradigms if they no longer "fit" the problem as previously conceived. Or they may find their paradigms challenged by others. A poster depicting a political leader as a Nazi may count as "free speech" in the United States but be seen as "incitement" in the volatile context of Israeli society (Cohen-Almagor, 2000).

Casuistry is similar to case law in that casuists strive to generalize moral judgments only to cases that are sufficiently similar to the original ones. As Jonsen and Toulmin (1988) put it, we are talking only about what is "permissible in certain special circumstances" (p. 346). For example, publishing the college marijuana habits of a political candidate who now campaigns on a law-and-order platform does not justify the same for every person in the news—or even every politician. Casuistry's agenda, then, is not to come up with a core list of principles for media ethics across cultures, which often are experienced as "extrinsic" Western-centric principles "imposed from without" (Miller,

1996, p. 15). Rather, the goal is to make incremental progress in developing provisional guidelines grounded in the experience of working through cases.

Finally, casuistical judgments sometimes include an assessment of their "probability," that is, an estimate of how much confidence one should have in the judgments. Extrinsic probability refers to the casuist's reputation; intrinsic probability refers to the merits of the casuist's argument. In Richard Miller's (1996) words, "We approach practical deliberation as local, topical, and persuasive, seeking to provide sound judgments about substantive issues of the day rather than airtight demonstrations about what abstract, theoretical principles entail for human action" (p. 16). Now we will test our argument on an actual case.

OCEANIA AND THE CASE OF "CLIMATE REFUGEES"

With roughly 70% of the earth's surface covered by water, the impact of melting glaciers and polar ice caps on sea levels is a worldwide problem. Sea levels have risen about 1.5 mm a year since 1870. Current sea levels are rising at double that rate (Lindsey, 2013). Predictions vary on the future rate of sea-level increases—between 6 and 23 inches by the end of the 21st century, according to one source (Intergovernmental Panel on Climate Change, 1997).

Most coastal areas, including U.S. cities such as Miami and New York, will be at risk with a rise of 20 inches in ocean levels. Today, most cities are not prepared for the flooding and incursion of sea water that would result (Howard, 2014). Little wonder that this issue made the news in U.S. media more than 550 times in 2014. Many of those stories reported on local impacts of rising seas, such as stories about the loss of beach property and homes or the super storms that threaten New York's infrastructure. But what happens when Western news reports shift the focus to the populations most threatened by the rise in sea levels, such as the islands of Oceania? More important, how ought Western journalists cover the threat to persons in other cultures?

Oceania comprises a large area of the tropical Pacific Ocean. Large and small islands and atolls, often separated by vast expanses of water, dot this massive area. All of these islands have experienced a rise in sea levels. But the smallest, lowest islands—such as Rakova's Carteret Islands—are the most threatened. With rising sea levels, "king tides" flood low areas and compromise crops on these territories, which also include Tuvalu, Kiribati, Vanuatu, and the Maldives.

So, if you are a consumer of Western media sources, what do you know about this problem? According to two media critiques, not much. Or more accurately, only what you can see through the lens many media stories adopt. A systemic problem of media coverage is the framing of the story as one about "refugees." Carol Farbotko (2012) argued that terms such as "climate refugee" and "environmental refugee" have framed much of the news coverage since the 1980s as convenient labels for those threatened by rising sea levels (pp. 119, 121–125). Ethical implications for journalism ethics are profound.

The Refugee as Powerless

The problem with this framing of the story is that the term *refugee* portrays people like Rakova at the mercy of climate change. The Pacific Islanders have no power to alter rising sea levels. Their islands and their fresh-water supplies are shrinking; sea water is invading formerly arable land; houses must be moved to higher ground. If they are not refugees now, they are likely to be among a predicted 200 million "global warming refugees" expected by the middle of the century (Agence France-Presse, 2007). Indeed, Farbotko (2012) argued, reporting on the climate refugee "serves the function to create an apparently visible embodiment of the effects of climate change" (p. 123).

Over the decades, numerous stories have been written that outline the impending tragedy facing the "climate refugees." These stories often convey alarm, as illustrated in an early story from Australia that frames its lead around the "wave of environmental refugees" that may be coming (Quiddington, 1988). Even more sympathetic stories, such as a report in UK's *Guardian*, use the threat of the refugee crisis to push for action on global warming without any sense of a role for Pacific Islanders. The stories do not provide any agency for those most vulnerable to rising sea levels (Vidal, 2009). It is as if the idea of a refugee almost precludes it.

The Refugee as One Dimensional

An analysis by Trudy Rebert (2006) concluded that "environmental refugee" is misleading in another way:

> In the end, "environmental refugee" is not a useful term. It overshadows the complex factors leading to migration … The literature lumps refugees (forced migration across international boundaries), internally displaced peoples (forced migration within national boundaries), and migrants responding to a variety of different environmental, ecological, and societal factors, into one category. (p. 28)

One can see an example of this in a *Toronto Star* story, "Fleeing Fiji's Floods" (Aulakh, 2014). Despite the fact that the classic definition of "refugee" is someone who has crossed international borders, the story labeled the Fiji villagers of Vunidogolo, who merely moved inland to escape coastal flooding, as refugees of climate change.

The refugee frame also allows news stories to oversimplify a story's theme in another way. By definition, the term *refugee* means someone on the move, if not in the past or present, then in the future. The results are stories that look only at the impact on host countries. For example, the only dimension of the "refugee" explored by stories in the *Daily Mirror* (McTague, 2014) and the *Independent* (Razzouk, 2014) is the effect of mass migration on host countries. The *Independent* (London) noted the xenophobia of the current immigration climate in the UK. But the story then used the fear of massive immigration by "climate refugees" as a reason to consider changes in environmental policies. Ironically, despite citing the UN's recent publication of the Intergovernmental Panel on Climate Change (March 31, 2014), the story ignored the report's extensive calls for mitigation and adaptation (alternatives that imply the power to make changes that would allow islanders to stay home), focusing instead on a prediction of up to one billion "climate refugees."

The Refugee as Cipher

As the previous example suggests, the use of *refugee* can shift the focus from the effects of migration on the people who are at risk from rising sea levels to the effects of large-scale migrations on the countries to which they might go. However, a more subtle—and more significant—shift is from human beings at risk to the faceless category of "refugees." Although exceptions like Rakova can be found, many news stories do not allow their audiences to meet real persons who live in Oceania. Not only are their faces missing, their voices are silent. In short, they are a problem, dehumanized through statistics. Stories like this are not necessarily mean spirited. An Agence France-Press story focuses on the harsh reality that the poorest people in the world are also most vulnerable to disasters brought on by climate change (Tandon, 2014). Yet the story contains not a single one of these voices. Environmental studies and experts stand in for the perspective of the poor. Refugees as a class become a cipher for the person standing on the disappearing sand.

To this point, our exploration of Oceania and rising sea levels presents an unflattering case for media coverage. However, both Farbotko (2012) and Rebert (2006) were able to build such bipolar accounts (news media gets it wrong; Pacific Islanders get it right) because they keyed almost exclusively on some variant of the "refugee" language. They make a critical point: The "refugee" framing of the media's narrative about Pacific Islanders connotes an image of persons helpless against the rise in sea level and dependent on the kindness of strangers to provide the necessities of life, including a spot of dry land on which to relocate. The contrast between the displaced islanders and their settled hosts stokes fears of needy, primitive foreigners "flooding" or "knocking on the doors" of well-off countries.

In that context, alternative narratives are ignored or submerged. For example, Farbotko (2012) documented possible counter-narratives from the Islanders' perspective: the *vaka* discourse, celebrating the seafaring prowess of the Islanders' ancestors who originally settled the islands, and a "drifting" discourse, reflecting the ocean survival knowledge necessary to cope with the always-present danger of getting lost at sea. These discourses, acknowledging the unpredictability of life and the Islanders' ability to adjust to unwanted and unexpected developments, more closely reflect the way the Carteret Islanders, for example, have explained their views. Rakova is heading an indigenous organization with a phased migration to land donated on the nearby island of Bougainville that began in 2009 with plans to grow cocoa as a cash crop (Rakova, Patron, & Williams, 2009).

To be sure, the potentially misleading use of the language *climate refugee* is significant. However, what emerges from this narrow focus is an analysis that is itself misleading. As we will see, casuistry can build a more nuanced critique of media accounts by building its analysis from the bottom up, looking at *all* the relevant facets of each story. In doing so, one is able to see a more varied scorecard of media coverage. Not all stories buy into the "refugee" narrative simply because the stories use that word. Using a paradigm case as a guide, more dimensions of the story emerge, and more nuanced judgments can be made that sketch a richer picture of media performance—both bad and good. A paradigm case is a clear-cut example of great reporting, a case (nearly) everyone would agree exemplifies the highest ideals of journalism. When it comes to reporting on displaced persons, that paradigm is "Feeding on the Hungry" (Cramer & Wohlmuth, 1981).

MADE-TO-ORDER "REFUGEES" IN SOMALIA

In the late 1970s, a war and a drought delivered a one-two punch on the nomadic people of the Ogaden, the contested bushland bordering Ethiopia and Somalia. Lacking food, water, and security, they crossed into Somalia and headed to central food distribution sites, where they built their traditional huts in crowded conditions that taxed natural resources and fostered disease. It was an oft-repeated crisis from Africa. Journalists had written about displaced persons before; they had filmed dying children with bloated stomachs; they detailed the work of relief agencies to save lives. But the *Philadelphia Inquirer* told a different story in a series based on intensive reporting on the ground in Somalia. Richard Cramer laid out the drama of the situation:

- Relief agencies had sent more than enough food. However, children still died because half of the food was stolen before it reached the distribution sites, strategically dubbed "refugee camps" by the government for political purposes and to "fatten its own economy."

- The government of Somalia claimed 1.5 million "refugees," twice the actual number.
- All the parties knew this, but no one wanted to upset the gravy train. Said one representative of Save the Children, "It's a competitive world. And you're basically going after the same refugee dollar" (p. 22).
- The Ogadenis are a people whose life in the best of times is a search for food and water. So when the war and drought ended, the refugees stayed where they could get that food and water. "In their fathers' time, this was called a migration: When the rains came and greened the plain, when the war died down on their pastureland, the nomads would wander back. Now it was labeled a refugee crisis" (p. 7). A culture was being destroyed.

Even though the immediate cause of the Ogadenis' displacement was not climate change, we have reason to think that this story belongs to the same "type" as climate-related displacement in Oceania. This classification step is important for proceeding with relevant moral presumptions as we evaluate the Oceania coverage in light of the *Inquirer* paradigm. Just as "disappearing islands" and "climate refugees" are dominant ways for Western news media to frame the mass movement of peoples from low-lying Pacific Island nations, the news media constructed the situation in Somalia as a "refugee crisis" fueled by "war and drought." These designations reflect the priorities of international organizations, advocacy groups, governments, researchers, and relief organizations that want to set policy agendas and attract resources. They also reflect ideological narratives that construct non-Western traditional societies as vulnerable and dependent (rather than efficacious and self-determining) because of their lack of infrastructure, widespread corruption, intransigent tribalism, and so forth. These narratives construe mass movements in these societies as episodes of flight (rather than adaptation) proceeding in a disorderly (rather than orderly) fashion within the context of acute crisis (rather than normal scarcity and journeying) (Farbotko, 2012).

So far, so good, but we will have to dig deeper into the details of the *Inquirer* case to see why it is a compelling paradigm for Oceania coverage. What about the *Inquirer* series is morally relevant for our purposes? Here are our suggestions:

- The key players in the stories and the photos were those persons who were displaced, moving from desert to dependency. Their voices echoed through the stories. In the "Feeding on the Hungry" series, we listen in on the refugees huddled in a tent debating why more children are dying in the camps when there is more food than in the desert where food was scarce. Here, the migrant voices rarely heard in other news accounts tell their own story. Cramer and photographer Sharon J. Wohlmuth put the Ogadenis first.

- However, the story also featured the black marketeers and their customers, the warehouse workers handling food donations at the Mogadishu port, thieves and the food monitors trying to catch them, relief workers and the government agents complicit in inflating the number of "refugees." Cramer and Wohlmuth allowed these players to give their take in their own voice, but we also heard them describe each other *as well as* the implied audience of the *Inquirer* series: the people in the United States and elsewhere who were still sending donations to Somalia. In a startling example of "reversal of perspective" (Seymour, 2003), Cramer's readers back home hear themselves described not as saviors but as unwitting accomplices in a cycle of misery. The handling of these multiple perspectives went well beyond standard "he said–she said" reporting, which was appropriate to the complexity of the situation on the ground.

- The story presented the Ogadenis' situation in all its messiness and ambiguity. By giving a comprehensive account, the series was more accurate.

- However, the story did not leave readers scratching their heads about what it all meant. The reporting team wove the various aspects of the "refugee crisis" into a coherent whole, giving readers a realistic sense of what had gone wrong and what alternatives there were for improving the situation.

- The story used thick description that conveyed the situation in all its particularity, including cultural, political, religious, and historical context often missing from intercultural news stories. For example, one story in the series detailed a nighttime bush medicine ritual in which the parents of a sick boy attempted to exorcise his "spirits of starvation." This example vividly illustrated the cultural gap between the Ogadenis and the relief workers trying to help them and hinted at the distinct blend of folk beliefs and Islam that defined the Ogadenis' way of life.

- Cramer also was unusually self-reflexive about the role of the media in contributing to the dependency of the Ogadenis. He noted how the media had cooperated in framing the story as a "refugee crisis." By making the constructedness of the "crisis" transparent, Cramer also was able to attend to the hidden costs and benefits of framing the story in this way.

Having settled on a paradigm and articulated its relevant characteristics, we now need to reflect on the ethical norms that emerge from the "Feeding on the Hungry" series:

- **Truth telling** has multiple dimensions, and a number of them are evident in these stories. *Accuracy* is always a relevant norm for the journalist, but it is crucial when describing the concrete details of the life of displaced persons. *Completeness* means providing context, telling a story from all relevant perspectives. Finally, *holistic scope* means giving attention to the whole problem. It means looking at the *causes* of the migrants' condition, not simply spotlighting the migrants' precarious position.

- **Dignity** is also a marker of the paradigm case. It respects the actors in the story. In this series, these refugees are the protagonists at the core of the story. To capture their story, journalists must have *empathy*, the ability to see the world through the eyes of these persons, but also to see themselves in those persons. Dignity means the journalist gives the refugee *autonomy* through the voice that controls how she and her people are represented.

- **Justice** is at the core of the paradigm case. This is another norm with a number of possible dimensions. At a minimum, this means *avoiding stereotyping*, if only by minimizing the language of "refugee." By definition, this is a story of persons who are vulnerable to environmental, social, and political forces beyond their control. Journalists should attend especially to the perspective of those most affected by the threat or reality of displacement. Elevating the voices of those whose futures are at stake may be the single most important quality missing from many news stories. *The voice of the dispossessed has primacy.* Moreover, part of this entails calling attention to those who benefit from injustice (for example, the volunteer agencies using the Somalia "refugee crisis" to compete with each other for prestige and resources). Stories must *address any misuse of power* to be excellent journalism.

- Put another way, the best journalism explores **accountability**. Are institutions, professions, governments, and aid agencies *living up to stated (or mandated) responsibilities*? These parties include journalism itself, which is in a unique position to shed light on possible courses of action that people can jointly undertake to address common goals and problems. *Journalists must also be accountable for the part they play* in getting others to see the world in ways that, not infrequently, can be traced to "prejudices and unspoken interests" (Miller, 1996, p. 153). By doing so, they can emancipate themselves and their audiences from unquestioned assumptions such as "refugee" that hide alternative ways of telling stories. This is especially crucial in stories where "cultural blinders" color the very way in which journalists discern relevance and coherence.

Now that we have spelled out some of the relevant norms, we can determine how well they "fit" the circumstances. As we noted in Boeyink and Borden (2010):

> In casuistry … cases provide occasions for exploring the meaning of those ethical norms and even for *revising* them; it is the norms themselves that are being judged based on whether they are consistent with our moral judgments about cases. It is the rules that must bend to the cases, not the other way around. (p. 70)

If we do a good job with this step, we will be in a position to appreciate the morally relevant characteristics of *any* news story we would consider paradigmatic of excellent coverage of displaced persons, as well as discern when any given story is different enough from the paradigm to warrant alternative treatment. A closer look at the *Inquirer* series suggests, in fact, that our provisional norms need some specification. For example, Cramer acknowledged that "Muslim values" may provide an alternative lens through which to understand the Ogadenis' "fatalism"; he did not go into any detail. He alluded to the political complications caused by tribal rivalries without really giving readers any real sense of what belonging to a tribe really means. These gaps, unfortunately, reinforce some stereotypes and cultural blind spots in Western journalism.

Truth telling as an ethical norm can be traced to a number of Western sources: the ethics code of the Society of Professional Journalists ("Seek the Truth and Report It"), the Aristotelian notion of human activities being ordered to a specific good based on their function, the humanity formulation of Kant's Categorical Imperative. However, the challenges of truth telling in a case like this have more to do with conveying meaning. Alan Durant's (2010) book, *Meaning in the Media*, talked about the "meaning-related disputes" in the media and how these can lead to the disruption of communication. Durant said we need to focus on these moments in discourse when understanding breaks down. The Somalia series—and intercultural stories generally—present journalists with just such moments. The actors in news stories should recognize journalists' representations of them as plausible. This means that journalists have to dig deeper than colorful anecdotes and strive to become "cultural bilinguals" (Ricoeur, 1996).

In respect to the norm of dignity, likewise, many Western journalists would ground dignity as an ethical norm in Enlightenment notions of individual rights (owing much to Kant). However, dignity as a norm also can be traced to traditions that are less individualistic and more focused on commitments, such as Ubuntuism. Alternative traditions might ground dignity instead in community membership, meaningful work, one's place in the natural order, and so on. Given that the dignity of Ogadenis, as they themselves understand it, seems to encompass such considerations, this norm also needs to be further specified for a good "fit" with the case. Empathy and autonomy do not become irrelevant in such a move. However, we see how enacting dignity also means that journalists should attend to the importance of actors' relationships to family, tribe, religion, practices, professions, communities, and even the environment, depending on the case. To make these commitments intelligible to their audiences, journalists should research the particular histories of these commitments and how they are lived out.

Now that we have detailed the facts and norms that are morally relevant to our paradigm case (moving back and forth between general and particular), we will see how the paradigm fares as a template for evaluating news stories about "climate refugees" in Oceania. We begin with a *Mother Jones* story that Farbotko (2012) cast in a negative frame with other "refugee" stories that have a narrative dominated by "foreign journalists, researchers, environmentalists, and documentary-makers rather than island inhabitants" (p. 124). In fact, a look at the story of the nation of Tuvalu will find it closer to our paradigm case than to the stories Farbotko uniformly criticized. We will then examine several analogous cases. Based on their ability to meet the standards of the paradigm case, these will be found at different places on a continuum from the best case to worst case in media coverage, offering a more nuanced picture of media performance than we see in Farbotko's analysis.

MOTHER JONES: A TEST CASE

The *Mother Jones* story had an unpromising headline: "What happens when your country drowns? Meet the people of Tuvalu, the world's first climate refugees." Yet the text itself contained many of the markers we identified as ethically desirable for a news story on displaced persons. The story began inside a community of people who have migrated from Tuvalu to New Zealand. After setting the stage with physical descriptions of the community and outlining the basic facts of the threat of sea-level rises to Tuvalu, the author let us hear the voices of those who have resettled in New Zealand. Their resettlement had been planned and orderly, the migrants maintaining a level of control (autonomy) over their lives. Even as they made plans for more migrants, they were clear about the cultural risks. "The next generation gets caught by two cultures," said one Tuvalu man. "Before Tuvalu sinks physically, our identity might sink in a foreign country" (Morris, 2009).

The story even challenged aspects of the climate-change narrative, pointing out that predictions of 200 million "environmental refugees" by 2050 are crude extrapolations, a worst-case scenario. Some people will have options, argued Alex de Sherbinin of Columbia University's Earth Institute. Many residents of Tuvalu and other nations could stay in place, he said, if only people paid attention to the available science. The text also implied that the world's powerful institutions have a responsibility to provide information and tools for planning so that people have "power to make sensible decisions." Said Thomas Fingar, formerly of the National Intelligence Council, "Shouldn't we start thinking about coping strategies? Stop ringing the damn alarm bell and go buy some buckets" (Morris, 2009). Moses Saitala, one of the Tuvalu residents now living in New Zealand, did not have a plan to keep Tuvaluans in their island homes. But neither was he without ideas. "Tuvalu has a lot of resources—$100 million in reserve," he said. That money could buy uninhabited islands for 10,000 people.

One could criticize the *Mother Jones* story because it does not do enough. It could use more context and depth; it could focus more clearly on the responsibility of countries whose pollution is raising world temperatures and sea levels. Yet this story has many of the qualities we identified as excellent journalism:

- Accuracy and completeness in its reporting on the lives of Tuvalu migrants and in its presentation of the larger "climate-change" crisis. Multiple perspectives—experts, refugees, politicians, community leaders—were woven through the story.

- That strategy allowed seeing the problem through the eyes of the displaced themselves, and it conferred a level of dignity and respect by letting their voices shape the narrative while also affirming their national and cultural commitments. ·

- Although the language of "refugee" was used, those who have migrated to New Zealand were clearly autonomous in this narrative. The church in New Zealand wanted future migrants to be prepared, so it was taking "matters into its own hands." One Tuvaluan wanted people to know what to expect rather than simply reacting. "What is the plan?" she asked. "What is the plan?" Another had a plan: to buy uninhabited islands. This seems to be precisely the kind of alternative narrative Farbotko found in her interviews with Pacific Islanders.

- Concerns for justice and accountability were more muted here than in our paradigm case. One could argue that a larger focus on the causes of global warming (fueled by the industrial world) would push the story more clearly into financial responsibility for mitigating its effects in places like Tuvalu. Yet the voice of the dispossessed clearly had a leading role in the story. We learn about the economic and social costs migration has inflicted on the displaced. Moreover, through its careful investigation of extreme predictions for numbers of "environmental refugees," it developed a factual challenge to climate orthodoxy, much like the *Philadelphia Inquirer*'s challenge to the accuracy of refugee numbers in Somalia. It also took up the crucial question of what is needed from the international community to empower Pacific Islanders: scientific information on which to plan for the future. Again, we see a "reversal of perspective," where Western audiences are confronted with how they appear to others.

In short, the standards developed in our paradigm case served us well in the analysis of the *Mother Jones* story, both in seeing its strengths and pointing to areas that might have been developed further. Case-based reasoning can also be refined through the use of analogous cases. We can look at other stories that may not be as ethical as the case from *Mother Jones*, testing how close they come to the paradigm—and whether the missing elements are morally fatal. For example:

- We already noted that one of the weaknesses of a 2005 Agence France-Presse story was its failure to include any voices of persons in vulnerable environmental conditions. Yet that story did contain an important focus on a report from the Norwegian Refugee Council that advocated helping vulnerable people to be more "resilient." Its model was the 2004 Indian Ocean tsunami for which $13 billion was spent "not only for reconstruction, but for resilience to future disaster."

- A 2014 story from *Africa News* began with a rich portrait of the effects of climate change in a hot, dry region of Africa. Despite its harshness, Amina Aliyu refused to leave, arguing that she could not leave her family. "This is my only home," she said (UN Integrated Regional Information Networks, 2014, "Difficult to leave"). The story then segued into a longer discussion of initiatives seeking to reduce the pressure on fragile environments and allow vulnerable persons to avoid migration. The story never returned to Aliyu. Nor did it show how these initiatives would apply to her life. How should we evaluate this case? Is this a story that should be credited for having the perspective of the vulnerable? Or was she just a prop to allow the reporter to talk about the Nansen Initiative centered in Europe?

- Using the language of "climate migrant," a 2014 *Toronto Star* story focused sharply on justice. Using a study from the Canadian Centre for Policy Alternatives, the story explored the link between Canada's greenhouse gas emissions and its "climate debt" to nations bearing the impact. "This is not a matter of charity or generosity but one of justice and reparation," argued the study's authors (Keung). How should we evaluate this single-source story? It contained few of the markers of our paradigm case, yet it offered the best inquiry into the place of justice of any story we have seen.

The number of analogous cases used can continue as long as they help to sharpen the analysis of the issue at hand. Hypothetical cases can also be used. The key will be the point when one feels ready to accept the provisional guidelines we have established. As we add more cases of reporting on displaced persons from different cultures to our taxonomy, we should be able to draw finer moral distinctions among cases, recognize circumstances that warrant exceptions to the standards we have developed, and further specify the scope and meaning of relevant ethical norms. Throughout this process, our judgments will be qualified and extend only to sufficiently similar cases.

DISCUSSION

We have argued that the casuistical method is well suited to a media ethics that is intercultural and comparative because of its analogical process, its use of situated ethical concepts in all their particularity, and its modest aspirations for justification. As seen in our discussion of the Somalia paradigm case, norms such as dignity and truth telling can be grounded in more than one theory or tradition without having to settle on a singular rationale. In this sense, casuistry is itself "multivocal." It makes room for difference without trying to come up with a knock-down proof or "super-principle" to transcend or subsume it. This clears the way for agreement on provisional reporting guidelines for even the most complex intercultural stories. If, instead, we were to approach moral disagreement about intercultural stories as a competition between master narratives or rival theories, we could quickly reach an impasse. Not only would this approach prove to be unhelpful in providing moral guidance, but it also would prevent precisely the kinds of insights we can obtain from stretching our moral imaginations beyond our cultural comfort zones.

Despite casuistry's merits for intercultural media ethics, a few caveats and limitations are in order. First, we should note that casuistry has always been intended for limited use with "hard cases." These are cases that, by definition, do not lend themselves to a "top-down" theoretical approach using moral rules because the applicability of the rules is doubtful or because the rules conflict in a way that defies easy resolution (Boeyink & Borden, 2010). "Garden-variety" ethical problems in the media do not require a casuistical approach. However, it is our position that intercultural cases lend themselves to the casuistical method precisely because they defy easy resolution by appeal to general principles.

A more serious objection concerns the method's potential hegemonic tendencies, given the importance of shared histories and moral commitments in ascertaining relevance and limits in casuistical decision making. A lack of critical distance could reproduce oppression in some intercultural cases. Miller (1996) cautioned casuists to always question whether the moral coherence of a casuistical analysis is the product of unspoken ideology (he illustrated this by using feminist techniques to critique the casuistry of the papal encyclical declaring that artificial contraception is wrong). For this reason, we agree with Miller that casuists should practice what he calls a "hermeneutics of suspicion" (p. 16) that makes use of the tools developed for ideological and cultural criticism. Fittingly, these tools are a staple of scholarly work in media studies. Thus a modern area of study developed in the context of media can enrich an ancient method for ethical decision making when applied to the media.

We attempted to do this in our discussion of our paradigm case. Arguably, our first pass at explicating the relevant ethical norms had a Western philosophical stamp on it. Proceeding without more specification might simply have reproduced this bias in our analysis of the Oceania cases (illustrating how important it is to get the paradigm case right). We had to take a second look at the norms we used with a more critical eye. Even so, we could have benefited from the input of others with experience covering displaced persons and with cultural knowledge of Somalia and Oceania that we do not possess. Thus, we do not claim the highest probability for our analysis. More work will need to be done. Fortunately, casuistry provides a useful way forward.

NOTES

1. Borden (2014) suggested that virtue ethics is a natural theoretical fit with casuistry's methodological assumptions. However, our argument about casuistry's advantages for intercultural media ethics does not depend on its complementarity with virtue ethics.
2. See Ong (2009) for a discussion of cosmopolitanism in the media literature.

BIBLIOGRAPHY

Agence France-Presse. (2007, June 19). Greenpeace warns of 200 mln global warming refugees by 2040. *Space Daily*. Retrieved from http://www.spacedaily.com/2006/0706190936. w811co8z.html

Aulakh, R. (2014, February 8). Fleeing Fiji's floods. *Toronto Star*. Retrieved from http://www. thestar.com/

Boeyink, D. E, & Borden, S. L. (2010). *Making hard choices in journalism ethics: Cases and practice*. New York: Routledge.

Borden, S. L. (2014, August 9). *Aristotle, casuistry, and global media ethics*. Paper presented to the Association for Education in Journalism and Mass Communication, Montreal, Canada.

Bretherton, L. (2006). *Hospitality as holiness: Christian witness amid moral diversity*. Surrey, England: Ashgate.

Cohen-Almagor, R. (2000). Boundaries of freedom of expression before and after Prime Minister Rabin's assassination. In R. Cohen-Almagor (Ed.), *Liberal democracy and the limits of tolerance: Essays in honor and memory of Yitzhak Rabin*. Ann Arbor: University of Michigan Press.

Cramer, R. B., & Wohlmuth, S. J. (1981). Feeding on the hungry: How a relief program based on a government's fraud and mankind's greed lures nomadic tribesmen to a life of dependency in Somali refugee camps. *Philadelphia Inquirer*. (Reprinted from a series published September 27–30, 1981.)

Durant, A. (2010). *Meaning in the media: Discourse, controversy and debate*. Cambridge, UK: Cambridge University Press.

Farbotko, C. (2012). Skillful seafarers, Oceanic drifters or climate refugees? Pacific people, news value and the climate refugee crisis. In K. Moore, B. Gross, & R. Threadgold (Eds.), *Migrations and the media* (pp. 119–142). New York: Peter Lang.

Howard, B. C. (2014, July 13). West Antarctica glaciers collapsing, adding to sea-level rise. *National Geographic*. Retrieved from www.nationalgeographic.com

Intergovernmental Panel on Climate Change. (1997). *The regional impacts of climate change: An assessment of vulnerability*. Retrieved from https://www.ipcc.ch/pdf/special-reports/spm/region-en.pdf

Jonsen, A., & Toulmin, S. (1988). *The abuse of casuistry: A history of moral reasoning*. Berkeley: University of California Press.

Keung, N. (2014, November 5). Ottawa urged to open doors to "climate migrants. *Toronto Star*. Retrieved from http://www.thestar.com/

Kuczewski, M. G. (1997). *Fragmentation and consensus: Communitarian and casuist bioethics*. Washington, DC: Georgetown University Press.

Lindsey, R. (2013). *2012 State of the Climate: Global sea level*. National Oceanic and Atmospheric Administration. Retrieved from http://www.climate.gov/news-features/understanding-climate/2012-state-climate-global-sea-level

McTague, T. (2014, April 1). GLOBAL WARNING; extreme weather threat to all, says UN; West faces climate change refugee surge; higher food prices & heatwaves to come. *Daily Mirror*. Retrieved from http://www.mirror.co.uk/

Miller, R. B. (1996). *Casuistry and modern ethics: A poetics of practical reasoning*. Chicago: University of Chicago Press.

Morris, R. (2009, November 30). What happens when your country drowns? Meet the people of Tuvalu, the world's first climate refugees. *Mother Jones*. Retrieved from http://www.motherjones.com/

Ong, J. C. (2009). The cosmopolitan continuum: Locating cosmopolitanism in media and cultural studies. *Media, Culture & Society, 31*(3), 449–466. doi:10.1177/0163443709102716

Potter, M. (2009, September 23). Rising seas create first climate refugees: When sharks started showing up in the garden, Ursula Rakova knew her home and native islands were doomed. *Toronto Star*. Retrieved from http://www.thestar.com/

Quiddington, P. (1988, August 23). Scientists warn of islands' peril. *Sydney Morning Herald*, p. 7.

Rakova, U., Patron, L., & Williams, C. (2009, June 16). How-to guide for environmental refugees. *Our World*. Retrieved from http://ourworld.unu.edu/en/contributors/ursula-rakova

Razzouk, A. W. (2014, November 3). If you're worried about immigration, then you should be terrified about climate change; our politicians appear content to jump on the xenophobic band-wagon driven by the likes of Ukip, yet no one is talking about climate refugees. *The Independent*. Retrieved from www.independent.co.uk

Rebert, T. S. (2006). The rising flood? Environmental refugees in a political ecology perspective. Retrieved from http://www.macalester.edu/academics/geography/courses/coursepages/rebert.pdf

Ricoeur, P. (1996). Reflections on a new ethos for Europe. In R. Kearney (Ed.), *Paul Ricoeur: The hermeneutics of action* (pp. 10–21). London: Sage.

Seymour, R. (2003). Story stances. (Unpublished copy given to authors)

Tandon, S. (2014, September 21). Wiping out the vulnerable. *The Nation* (Thailand). Retrieved from LexisNexis Academic database.

Thomas, S. M. (2000). Taking religious and cultural pluralism seriously: The global resurgence of religion and the transformation of international society. *Millennium: Journal of International Studies, 29*(3), 815–841.

UN Integrated Regional Information Networks (Nairobi). (2014, June 12). A fresh start for climate change refugees. *Africa News*. Retrieved from http://www.irinnews.org/report/100206/a-fresh-start-for-climate-change-refugees

Vidal, J. (2009, November 2). Global warming could create 150 million climate refugees by 2050. *The Guardian*. Retrieved from www.theguardian.com/

Volf, M. (1996). *Exclusion and embrace: A theological exploration of identity, otherness, and reconciliation*. Nashville, TN: Abingdon Press.

Wallace, J. D. (2009). *Norms and practices*. Ithaca, NY: Cornell University Press.

Walzer, M. (1994). *Thick and thin: Moral argument at home and abroad*. Notre Dame, IN: University of Notre Dame Press.

CHAPTER SIXTEEN

A Media Ethics Code FOR ALL Time Zones? The Global Use and Implications OF THE Society OF Professional Journalists' Code

CHRIS ROBERTS[1]

Kevin Z. Smith traveled the world during his 24 years as head of the ethics committee for the Society of Professional Journalists, spreading the news of the society's code of ethics. As an ambassador for America's most-cited journalism ethics code created by members of America's largest journalism organization, he has talked about the code to journalists from nations whose governments are described in all four original theories of the press (Siebert, Peterson, & Schramm, 1956) and to journalists working in nations with other press-political approaches that include Asian (Yin, 2008) and post-colonial (Rao & Wasserman, 2007).

His travels taught him that many journalists across the globe see the First Amendment to the United States Constitution, and the SPJ code it inspired, as influential or at least aspirational for the reporting and commentary they wish to produce. Reporters and editors worldwide "take their cues from American media," said Smith, deputy director of the Kiplinger program in public affairs journalism at The Ohio State University (personal communication, September 5, 2014). The Society understands the code's influence, translating its 1996 version into more than a dozen languages as an exemplar of the minimum expectations and maximum aspirations for socially responsible journalists. Joe Skeel, the Society's executive director, said journalists worldwide use the code as a way to seek "credibility in the profession" and differentiate themselves "from those who aren't on the up-and-up" (personal communication, October 28, 2014).

But the SPJ code is not always an easy sell outside of the United States, and Smith has heard journalists of many nations tell horror stories of how they have been hurt for following the code's principles that conflict with powers opposed to independent, oppositional truth-tellers. A journalist from a southern Asian nation told him of being beaten multiple times by thugs hired by a businessman angry at news stories "that were accurate but didn't rise to the level of taking on government," a reminder that "you don't have to take on political power to end up in pain." At a 2007 conference in North Korea, Smith met a journalist from another southern Asian nation who told him, "If we tried to abide by the ethics that you do, we would end up being killed" (K. Smith, personal communication, September 5, 2014).

Those sorts of stories reveal the ultimate dilemma for advocates of a universal media ethic—the practicality of delineating agreed-upon values and standards of journalism, and ensuring that ethical forms of journalism are respected across nations and cultures. Some advocate a global media ethic based on protonorms such as sacredness of life (Cooper, 2010), while others criticize such approaches (Steiner, 2010). Some argue for a global ethic using anthropological realism (Christians & Ward, 2012). Others argue that pursuing universal standards is futile for reasons ranging from the inability to move beyond mere professionalism and human primordialism to systemic failures of the United Nations and of international political systems (Alleyne, 2009).

Nearly all of the debate, however, has been academic. The reality is that media practitioners are subject to harm when their truth-seeking mission and practices are not protected by their nations' law or, even when protected by law, are not tolerated by the actions of their nations' political apparatus and other powers. This reality threatens journalists who dare question their community's powerful or create work that offends other religions or cultures. It also threatens correspondents from one nation using their culture's standards when reporting in nations with different standards. Ward (2005) defined a professional journalist as someone who "is obligated to speak to the public in a manner that is different from partisan public communicators such as the social advocate, the government official, the lobbyist, the public relations person promoting a product, or the lawyer representing a client" (p. 9). In nearly every nation, however, jails and graves are filled with journalists who did just that, following their own consciences and expressing truth or opinion that opposed the powerful. The Committee to Protect Journalists (2015) reported more than 1,100 journalists were killed between 1992 and mid-2015, including 61 killed and 221 imprisoned during 2014. And in nearly every nation, newsrooms are filled with journalists contemplating the consequences of following their conscience, journalists speaking truth to power while waiting for consequences, journalists seeking ways to be subversive without directly challenging the powerful, or journalists living in quiet desperation after being cowed into submission. They face laws and practices that expressly prohibit the truth telling they wish to perform or inscrutable rules that are fuzzy enough to chill journalists who cannot know precisely what could lead to punishment.

This chapter considers the practicality of a universal code of media ethics through the prism of the Society of Professional Journalists' code (2014), a Western document that likely has had more global impact than most of the world's many media ethics codes. It describes the code's concepts in terms of moral philosophies, providing examples of both the code's inner conflicts and its conflicts with non-Western media-state relations. It ultimately argues that while the code includes journalistic virtues that deserve consideration in constructing a global media ethic, the practical reality is that some of its most aspirational tenets would require journalists in some nations and cultures to make personal sacrifices that go beyond the duties expected of journalists working in societies where the personal risk is much less.

MEDIA ETHICS CODES AND THE SPJ CODE

Codes of media ethics codes are nearly a century old, and debates about their usefulness and global transferability are almost as old. A seminal moment in the debate over a global media ethic was the 1980 report by UNESCO's International Commission for the Study of Communication Problems, better known as the MacBride report for chair Sean MacBride. The report acknowledged the utility of national and regional codes "prepared and adopted by the profession itself" (UNESCO, 1980, p. 243) but could not seem to make up its mind about international codes. The report described a need for journalism to be more "professional," yet it worried whether allowing governments to define what "professional" means would let governments control journalists through licensing and other means. It concluded by saying that the plurality of nations and media systems makes a universal code all but impossible to create at present:

> While it is true that it is at present difficult to formulate a code …, there are no reasons to consider it unattainable or that its pursuit should be abandoned for reasons of principle. All the more so if it is acknowledged that our universe is becoming ever smaller and ever more interdependent, and that it is important to take account not only of the rights of those disseminating the messages but also of the concerns, interests and needs of those to whom they are addressed. (UNESCO, 1980, p. 244)

It suggested that any international code should echo UNESCO's 1978 declaration on the mass media, which appealed for global free speech rights to stem war, strengthen peace, educate citizens worldwide, curb racism, protect journalists, and limit cultural imperialism by balancing the flow of information from more powerful nations. This UNESCO declaration and the Mac-Bride report were perceived by some as an attack on press freedom, which is among the reasons the United States withdrew from UNESCO (Mansell & Nordenstreng, 2006).

In footnotes to the MacBride report's discussion of media ethics codes, the commission stated that "it is for the professional themselves and not for government to ensure" that ethical standards are created and respected. Others were less sure of the panel's findings. Member Elie Abel, a Canadian-born journalist and American journalism educator, said government-issue codes "must necessarily be rejected by journalists" who see their roles as watchdogs of the powerful (UNESCO, 1980, p. 244).

It is no surprise, then, that Abel often spoke at events sponsored by the Society of Professional Journalists (Associated Press, 1971), which printed his obituary in its *Quill* magazine ("Deaths," 2004). The SPJ claims its nearly 10,000 members, mostly in the United States, make it "the nation's most broad-based journalism organization" (Society of Professional Journalists, n.d.-a). Membership is voluntary, and it is doubtful that any news organization requires employees to join. A large number of members are freelancers, students, and journalists not working in traditional newsrooms, who hope that membership will give them an imprimatur of professionalism that often comes from affiliation with larger news organizations.

The society began in 1909 as Sigma Delta Chi, a fraternity for journalism students at DePauw University in Greencastle, Indiana, as one of the many ways that journalists began to seek professionalism early in the 20th century. It added off-campus professional chapters by 1916, and in 1926, its members adopted a code of ethics taken heavily from the American Society of Newspaper Editors' 1922 "Canons of Journalism" (Society of Professional Journalists, n.d.-b). Sigma Delta Chi's code remained untouched until 1973, when members approved a revision while changing the group's name to the Society of Professional Journalists, Sigma Delta Chi. (It later dropped the Greek letters from its name.) Convention delegates approved updated codes in 1984, 1987, and 1996 (Brown, 2011) and most recently in September 2014 (Society of Professional Journalists, 2014). The newest version retains the same general format of the 1996 code. Three of the four key principles—"Seek Truth and Report It," "Minimize Harm," and "Act Independently"—went unchanged. The fourth added two words: "and Transparent" after "Be Accountable." Underneath those four principles are 35 bullet points describing the minimum standards and highest aspirations of Western journalism.[2]

Ward said that a global journalism ethic should be derived through contractualism, which he defined as "the attempt to identify and justify principles that govern actions in general and actions within professions and fields of endeavor" (2005, p. 6). The creation of the latest version of the SPJ code was an exercise in contractualism among members and non-members (for example, see Buttry, 2014). Debates and discussions online and in person included everything from key principles to punctuation placement. SPJ delegates approved the updated code after a year-long process that included a survey of members, Twitter chats, three rounds of drafts published online to give anyone opportunity to comment on each draft, and changes suggested at the convention before and during the final business meeting. The conversations sparked some fierce debate in its focus to bring the code into the Internet era. Delegates, for example, rejected a line that would have warned journalists to take special care when reporting on suicide. But they accepted the committee's deliberate decision to not specifically mention online media, to remind its readers that journalistic principles should remain consistent across communication channels. If contractualism can be defined as a political process, then the SPJ code is a product of contracturalism—meaning that, like most work crafted by committee, subject to suggestions from thousands and approved by vote, no one is completely satisfied with the final product.

Despite the code's flaws, it remains widely cited as part of journalism's appeal to be perceived as having professional status, or at least as having practitioners who work as professionals. The code is often used as justification by practitioners when defending decisions and as evidence by those who accuse journalists of real or imagined ethical breaches. It has become "probably the most recognized" (Berkowitz, Limor, & Singer, 2004, p. 162) journalistic code in the United States.

VALUES WITHOUT FRAMEWORK

SPJ's code is firmly set in Western and American values, calling the public enlightenment that journalism provides the "foundation of democracy" and citing the First Amendment to the U.S. Constitution's declaration that "Congress shall make no law ... abridging the freedom of speech, or of the press" in its post-script as a reminder that the code is not legally enforceable by or against anyone who uses it. The code pushes journalists toward social responsibility, yet offers relief for the libertarian who would not feel bound by this or any other code when exercising free speech and press.

The code also reflects Article 19 of the United Nations' Universal Declaration of Human Rights: "Everyone has the right to freedom of opinion and expression; this right includes freedom to hold opinions without interference and to seek, receive and impart information and ideas through any media and regardless of frontiers" (United Nations, 1948). For this and other reasons, the

Society sees its code as a model for other cultures. The 1996 code has been translated from English into Arabic, Chinese, Croatian, French, German, Greek, Hungarian, Macedonian, Persian, Portuguese, Slovenian, and Spanish. Work to translate the 2014 code is already underway.

The code has evolved as journalism's technology and epistemology evolve. As an example of changing technology, the 1973 version replaced "newspaper" references with "mass media," and the newest edition's inclusion of the words "broadcast" and "publish" recognizes television and radio broadcasting and print and online publishing. As an example of journalistic epistemology, the 1973 and 1987 versions of the code call objectivity a goal for journalists, while the 1996 and 2014 versions do not include the word. Instead, the newest version describes ethical journalism as "accurate," "fair," "transparent," based on "original sources," and designed to "provide context." As part of its goal to be a broad-based code, the 2014 version makes no mention of new online technologies that deliver news faster and allow nearly anyone with a Web connection to communicate news and opinion, but many of its additions (such as "[p]rovide access to source material when it is relevant and appropriate" and "[c]onsider the long-term implications of the extended reach and permanence of publication") were written with an eye toward online publishing.

The code's epilogue describes the code as "a statement of abiding principles" and "not a set of rules." With one exception—"Never plagiarize. Always attribute"—the code is an aspirational statement in identifying values that describe ethical journalists and are acted upon by ethical journalists. Its value types, as defined by Schwartz (1992), fall exclusively in categories of universalism and benevolence (Roberts, 2012), both of which are social-context outcomes that connote self-transcendence (Rohan, 2000) and speak of journalism's ultimate obligation to serve others. That is partly because of the nature of all ethics codes (what ethics code trumpets Machiavelli?), but also because, by nearly every definition, ethical journalism is perceived as being a public service. Yet the aspirational nature of the SPJ code and its voluntary nature as a code adopted by a voluntary organization make it difficult to apply and impossible to enforce. This has led to considerable criticism of it and other codes as little more than a heads-up to neophytes and/or a tool to serve the organization's public relations needs (Black & Barney, 1985).

Moreover, the SPJ code has no single philosophical framework, and its use can cut across multiple moral philosophies:

- Utilitarianism, which is "prevalent in the media professions, and in quasi-form is the mind-set of most students preparing for careers, such as journalism" (Christians, 2007, p. 113), has plenty of weights and counter-weights in the SPJ code from which to measure potential goods and harms. The four principles often conflict, leaving the user the task of maximizing journalistic happiness while understanding and balancing the conflicts—to seek and report truth while minimizing harm, and to work independently while showing accountability.

- Deontological approaches also are possible in the code, especially for those with a Russian bent (Meyers, 2011), as the code's competing claims can be understood as prima facie duties that ultimately become the actual duties that journalists should perform. Furthermore, the code can be seen as a pledge to the right and good duties that members take upon themselves when choosing to be a Society member.

- Virtue has a place in the code, too, as through balancing its four principles, users can find an Aristotelian mean for individual decisions, and as its many bullet points describe the actions that become the habits of virtuous journalists. The code also describes the values and actions that a virtue-focused person would seek to find in a role model.

The code also hints at other philosophical approaches. "Justice" is the code's 16th word, a nod to Rawls (1971, 1999), along with a reminder to show compassion for the weak and those who deserve special consideration, such as juveniles and sex-crime victims. Even communitarianism can be found in the code, with reminders to engage in civil exchanges of views with news consumers and to support such exchanges among users. In all, the SPJ code is a philosophical chameleon, able to match most shades of ethical approaches taken by its users. Depending upon perspective, this philosophic-agnostic approach can be seen as either a positive or a negative for the code's practical use or some of both. It could be argued that the code's omission of philosophical approaches is good, because the code provides insight to journalists who use differing philosophies (or none, or whether aware of those theories or not) when making decisions. On the other hand, it could be argued that the code could be stronger and more helpful if it addressed differing philosophies or suggested (for example) when duties may be more important than utilitarian concerns.

THE SPJ CODE'S CALL TO DUTIES THROUGH RIGHTS

Like many media codes, the SPJ code was conceived as a statement of both rights and duties. The code's bullet points describe the perceived duties of an ethical journalist, as perceived through traditional Western social responsibility and/or libertarian systems of government. The First Amendment gives journalists both the freedom and the legal rights to assume the duties associated with socially responsible journalism—although libertarians might say the First Amendment also gives practitioners the right to ignore these duties and communicate as they wish. The SPJ code is most compatible with the "detached watchdog" approach to journalism and most at odds with the "opportunist facilitator" approach, which Hanitzsch (2011) described as giving journalists the least individual freedom in a journalism designed to promote governmental policies and support the powerful.

Although it goes unstated in the SPJ code, it assumes the rights granted by the First Amendment are a requirement for practitioners who choose to adopt the code's duties. Moghaddam, Slocum, Finkel, Mor, and Harré (2000) define rights as "domains in which individuals tend to try to exercise control over others," noting that the exercising of a right "implicitly repudiates the demands of others" (p. 276). Their example, appropriate for this chapter, is the right of free speech, which when exercised "curtails the actions of censors, those who would deny it" (p. 276). The First Amendment, then, gives U.S. journalists and others the right to repudiate censorship.

A glance through the 2014 edition of the code reveals multiple instances of duties that are more likely to be more easily exercised in societies with more granted individual liberties. Many of the instances reside beneath the code's "Seek Truth and Report It" section, which includes this bullet point: "Recognize a special obligation to serve as watchdogs over public affairs and government. Seek to ensure that the public's business is conducted in the open, and that public records are open to all." This duty, defined in the code as an "obligation," suggests that journalists should bring to light the actions of governments, businesses, and other powers who would secretly influence the public or benefit themselves. Elsewhere in the "Seek Truth" section, the code tells journalists to "[b]e vigilant and courageous about holding those with power accountable" and to "[s]upport the open and civil exchange of views," all duties more easily exercised in nations that provide the right to free speech.

The code's "Act Independently" section states that the "highest and primary obligation of ethical journalism is to serve the public," which the bullet points underneath identify as avoiding conflicts of interest, refusing material goods and avoiding activities that could compromise impartiality, and denying favoritism to advertisers or others. New to the 2014 code is a call for journalists to "resist internal and external pressure to influence coverage," added as a way to boost journalists who would seek to act against those who would seek to limit journalistic independence required to serve the public. The call implies an injunction against the sorts of media owners whom Lee (2000) said seek press freedom "to advance their personal and class interests" (as quoted in Christians, Glasser, McQuail, Nordenstreng, & White, 2009, p. 203), a concern of critics of Western and overly commercial journalistic enterprises.

The call for independence puts the code in conflict with other media-government approaches—in authoritarian systems where the press serves the political agenda of those in power, in communist systems where the state-owned press serves its needs (Siebert et al., 1956), in developmental approaches where journalists work with politicians and others to help build society (Musa & Domatob, 2007), and in Eastern approaches where media often promote group harmony over individualism in approaches that balance freedom and responsibility (Yin, 2008). While Altschull (1995), Nordenstreng (1997), and others criticized simple press models defined by levels of government control, a focus on government is important for this discussion because governments have the power to provide and limit the rights of journalists who would accept the duties of the SPJ code, and external power plays a factor in the ability of individuals to accept duty.

DUTIES, RIGHTS, AND THE ROLE OF THE SPJ ETHICS CODE

If it can be agreed that the SPJ code provides a useful definition of the values and practices of ethical journalism, at least as defined in a Western context and seen as aspirational by many others worldwide, then two questions emerge. The first is for Western journalism: "Do those who call themselves journalists have a moral obligation to follow the SPJ code of ethics?"

The easiest answer is "no," because of the code's voluntary nature, and because the First Amendment neither defines what is ethical nor requires ethical practice. While the meaning of "freedom" in the First Amendment remains subject to debate (Mendelson, 1962), the contrarian and partisan press already in existence when the amendment passed in 1791 was far from ethical standards of social responsibility defined in 20th-century codes.

Yet the answer is a tentative "yes." The code's four overarching principles—to seek truth, to minimize harm, to act independently, and to be accountable and transparent—are intuitively accepted not just as journalistic virtues but as general virtues by nearly all moral objectivists and as principles lived by virtuous people across nearly all cultures. The pantheon of thinkers espousing the moral philosophies mentioned in this chapter likely would accept this list as a general guide for behaving ethically. Drilling into the particulars of the code, however, makes this answer tentative. The code describes journalistic virtues and provides general guidance about general and specific ethical questions a journalist might face; it was never designed to provide mere answers to thorny dilemmas beyond the sin of plagiarism. Nevertheless, while journalists can argue about the code's particulars—such as anonymous sources or naming juvenile suspects—the code's four key principles should be moral obligations for journalists and non-journalists alike.

The second question takes the code beyond its Western context and seeks to apply it to all journalists everywhere: "If the SPJ code is indeed ethical, then do journalists worldwide have a moral obligation to follow it?"

The answer is "no"—unless an existential journalist willingly decides otherwise. This answer is predicated on the original definition of "realpolitik," defined as "how to achieve liberal-enlightened goals in a world that does not follow liberal-enlightened rules" (Bew, 2014), as well as on the "ought-implies-can" relationship to moral obligation.

The SPJ's decision to translate its code into so many languages is an effort to promote the normative theory of social responsibility to journalists worldwide. The U.S. government, which says it works to "support the development of open and responsible media abroad and to assist in building the infrastructure needed for a free press to operate" (U.S. Department of State, 2003), has both promoted the SPJ code as a model for responsible journalism and sponsored SPJ leaders' travels to other nations to discuss media ethics (see, for example, U.S. Department of State, 2006). This is a useful enterprise and should be replicated by purveyors of journalism codes and rules everywhere in the attempt to provide more cross-cultural understanding. Without considering the actual merits of the ethical standards being promoted, however, promoting the code also can be seen as an example of realpolitik of the U.S. government's efforts to bring Western-style democracy to other nations, for which the United States has long been criticized by some for cultural imperialism of both media content and systems of government. Some who see Western media's commercialism, support of status quo, lack of harmony, and continuous examples of ethical failings may not perceive Western journalism's guidelines as better than their current media system.

As the SPJ code espouses many of the standards agreed upon by moral philosophies and expounds upon UNESCO's definition of journalistic rights to access sources, to transmit information, and to interpretation and fair comment, the MacBride report's findings are as true now as then: "Despite the high-sounding principles enshrined in laws and constitutions, journalists in many countries are not free to tell the truth" (UNESCO, 1980, pp. 240–241). This statement brings into sharp focus the Aristotelian and Kantian principle of "ought implies can," which states that "a person is morally obliged to do something only if it is in his power to do it or not to do it" (Kekes, 1984, p. 459).

Journalists (or, for that matter, anyone) might well be relieved from moral obligation under the "ought implies can" principle if they live under authorities who harshly punish those who dare serve as independent speakers of truth to power or otherwise stray from the party line. While rejecting Aristotle's belief in natural slavery—instead accepting contemporary understanding and United Nations declarations that all humanity deserves freedom—Aristotle's discussion of "slavery by law" (*Politics*, 1255a5) informs the previous sentence. Journalists harmed by authorities for their speech or chilled into silence by being threatened with harm may well be defined as being under "slavery by law," stripped of their natural rights and subject to duties assigned to them, unable to easily perform self-assigned duties assumed by Kantian-described pure reason. As Aristotle wrote, those who are slaves by law are less likely to be friends with or share common interests with their masters (*Politics*, 1255b13-15).

If this is the case, then, it can be argued that journalists in repressive states may not have the obligation to risk death or debilitating harm to speak freely. When discussing the question of anyone's moral obligation to take violent military action against regimes caught violating rights, Buchanan argued that we have a "presumptive duty to help ensure that all persons can live in conditions in which their basic rights are respected, *at least if we can do so without excessive costs to ourselves*" (1999, p. 85, italics added). Much less, then, would be our duty when we have no personal defense and comrades to protect us from death or physical harm.

Having said that, many living under "slavery by law" yet feeling the obligations described of ethical journalism may well have the "can" ability to speak—if only for a while, and with the possibility of punishment. Such actions would be considered supererogatory, beyond the call of duty as morally best but not morally obligated (Horgan & Timmons, 2010) for the reasons of freedom and repercussion stated earlier. They may be able to find a place along the doctrine of the mean, a middle way, or another path that allows them to best serve society and themselves. Or they may choose a path more fraught with peril. This is an existential decision. It can lead to personal disaster—or the societal change that is the nature of some journalism—and sometimes both.

CONCLUSION: AN EXISTENTIAL DECISION

The decision to take up individual freedom is, indeed, an existential decision for all journalists operating under any system, as the late John C. Merrill argued in *Existential Journalism* (1977/1996), his argument against corporate journalism. He was contemptuous of the SPJ's 1973 code, filling three pages of the book with examples of its contradictions, fuzziness, and "guidelines for the organization-persons." He may have better appreciated the Online News Association's (ONA's) current "build your own ethics code" (2014), which lets individual journalists and nontraditional organizations with newsgathering functions design their own approach. Even the ONA approach, however, includes the SPJ code as a touchstone, further cementing it in the discussion of media ethics definitions.

Merrill wrote that an ethics code "hanging on the wall is meaningless; a code of ethics internalized within the journalist and guiding his actions is what is meaningful" (1977/1996, p. 45). Those who wrote the SPJ code could not agree more. As SPJ Executive Director Skeel said (personal communication, October 28, 2014), journalists in other nations who see the code "know not everything can be applied directly to their scenario." This is equally true for Western journalists.

The point of the Society of Professional Journalists code has always been to provide a starting point for those who would internalize their own ethics code. It can do no more, and it expects nothing less of those who seek to use journalism to improve their own societies.

NOTES

1. The author was a member of the SPJ Ethics Committee that wrote the new version of SPJ's ethics code approved by delegates at the association's annual convention in September 2014.

2. From the SPJ Code, available at https://www.spj.org/ethicscode.asp: "The SPJ Code of Ethics is a statement of abiding principles supported by additional explanations and position papers (at spj.org) that address changing journalistic practices. It is not a set of rules, rather a guide that encourages all who engage in journalism to take responsibility for the information they provide, regardless of medium. The code should be read as a whole; individual principles should not be taken out of context. It is not, nor can it be under the First Amendment, legally enforceable. Sigma Delta Chi's first Code of Ethics was borrowed from the American Society of Newspaper Editors in 1926. In 1973, Sigma Delta Chi wrote its own code, which was revised in 1984, 1987, 1996 and 2014."

BIBLIOGRAPHY

Alleyne, M. C. (2009). Global media ecology: Why there is no global media ethics standard. In L. Wilkins & C. Christians (Eds.), *The handbook of mass media ethics* (pp. 382–393). New York: Routledge.

Altschull, J. H. (1995). *Agents of power: The media and public policy* (2nd ed.). White Plains, NY: Longman.

Associated Press. (1971, April 4). Objectivity in reporting discussed by journalists. *The Toledo Blade.*

Berkowitz, D., Limor, Y., & Singer, J. (2004). A cross-cultural look at serving the public interest: American and Israeli journalists consider ethical scenarios. *Journalism, 5*(2), 159–181. doi:10.1177/146488490452001

Bew, J. (2014). Real realpolitik: A history. Retrieved from http://www.loc.gov/today/cyberlc/transcripts/2014/140410klu1600.txt

Black, J., & Barney, R. D. (1985). The case against mass media codes of ethics. *Journal of Mass Media Ethics, 1*(1), 27–36.

Brown, F. (2011). *Journalism ethics: A casebook of professional conduct for news media* (4th ed.). Portland, OR: Marion Street.

Buchanan, A. (1999). The internal legitimacy of humanitarian intervention. *Journal of Political Philosophy, 7*(1), 71–87.

Buttry, S. (2014). New SPJ code of ethics: An improvement but a disappointment. Retrieved from http://stevebuttry.wordpress.com/2014/09/08/new-spj-code-of-ethics-an-improvement-but-a-disappointment/

Christians, C. (2007). Utilitarianism in media ethics and its discontents. *Journal of Mass Media Ethics, 22*(2–3), 113–131.

Christians, C., Glasser, T. L., McQuail, D., Nordenstreng, K., & White, R. A. (2009). *Normative theories of the media: Journalism in Democratic societies.* Urbana: University of Illinois Press.

Christians, C., & Ward, S. J. A. (2012). Anthropological realism for global media ethics. In N. Couldry, M. Madianou, & A. Pinchevski (Eds.), *Ethics of media* (pp. 72–88). London: Palgrave Macmillan.

Committee to Protect Journalists. (2015). 1129 journalists killed since 1992. Retrieved from https://www.cpj.org/killed/

Cooper, T. W. (2010). The quintessential Christians: Judging his books by their covers and leitmotifs. *Journal of Mass Media Ethics, 25*(2), 99–109. doi:10.1080/08900521003640652

Deaths. (2004, September). *Quill, 92,* 37–38.

Hanitzsch, T. (2011). Populist disseminators, detached watchdogs, critical change agents and opportunist facilitators professional milieus, the journalistic field and autonomy in 18 countries. *International Communication Gazette, 73*(6), 477–494.

Horgan, T., & Timmons, M. (2010). Untying a knot from the inside out: Reflections on the "paradox" of supererogation. In E. F. Paul, F. D. Miller Jr., & J. Paul (Eds.), *Moral obligation* (pp. 29–63). New York: Cambridge University Press.

Kekes, J. (1984). "Ought implies can" and two kinds of morality. *The Philosophical Quarterly,* 459–467.

Lee, K. Y. (2000). From Third World to First: The Singapore story from 1965–2000. *Memoirs of Lee Kuan Yew* (pp. 212–225). Singapore: Times Publishing and Singapore Press Holdings.

Mansell, R., & Nordenstreng, K. (2006). Great media and communication debates: WSIS and the MacBride Report. *Information Technologies & International Development, 3*(4), 15–36.

Mendelson, W. (1962). On the meaning of the First Amendment: Absolutes in the balance. *California Law Review, 50,* 828.

Merrill, J. C. (1977/1996). *Existential journalism.* Ames: Iowa State University Press.

Meyers, C. (2011). Re-appreciating WD Ross: Naturalizing *Prima Facie* duties and a proposed method. *Journal of Mass Media Ethics, 26*(4), 316–331.

Moghaddam, F. M., Slocum, N. R., Finkel, N., Mor, T., & Harré, R. (2000). Toward a cultural theory of duties. *Culture & Psychology, 6*(3), 275–302. doi:10.1177/1354067x0063001

Musa, B. A., & Domatob, J. K. (2007). Who is a development journalist? Perspectives on media ethics and professionalism in post-colonial societies. *Journal of Mass Media Ethics, 22*(4), 315–331.

Nordenstreng, K. (1997). Beyond the four theories of the press. *Media and politics in transition* (pp. 97–109). Leuven: Acco.

Online News Association. (2014). Build your own ethics code. Retrieved from http://journalists.org/resources/build-your-own-ethics-code/

Rao, S., & Wasserman, H. (2007). Global media ethics revisited: A postcolonial critique. *Global Media and Communication, 3*(1), 29–50. doi:10.1177/1742766507074358

Rawls, J. (1971, 1999). *A theory of justice* (Rev. ed.). Cambridge, MA: Harvard University Press.

Roberts, C. (2012). Identifying and defining values in media codes of ethics. *Journal of Mass Media Ethics, 27*(2), 115–129.

Rohan, M. (2000). A rose by any name? The values construct. *Personality and Social Psychology Review, 4*(3), 255.

Schwartz, S. H. (1992). Universals in the content and structure of values: Theoretical advances and empirical tests in 20 countries. *Advances in Experimental Social Psychology, 25*(1), 1–65.

Siebert, F. S., Peterson, T., & Schramm, W. (1956). *Four theories of the press: The authoritarian, libertarian, social responsibility, and Soviet communist concepts of what the press should be and do.* Urbana: University of Illinois Press.

Society of Professional Journalists. (2014). SPJ code of ethics. Retrieved from http://www.spj.org/ethicscode.asp

Society of Professional Journalists. (n.d.-a). About the Society. Retrieved from http://www.spj.org/spjinfo.asp

Society of Professional Journalists. (n.d.-b). About the Society: History of the Society. Retrieved from http://www.spj.org/spjhistory.asp

Steiner, L. (2010). The value of (universal) values in the work of Clifford Christians. *Journal of Mass Media Ethics, 25*(2), 110–120.

U.S. Department of State. (2003). *Global issues: Seeking free and responsible media,* vol. 8. Retrieved from http://photos.state.gov/libraries/amgov/30145/publications-english/EJ-free-media-0203.pdf

U.S. Department of State. (2006). Supporting human rights and democracy: The U.S. record 2005–2006. Retrieved from http://www.state.gov/j/drl/rls/shrd/2005/63949.htm

UNESCO. (1980). *Many voices one world: Report by the International Commission for the Study of Communication Problems.* New York: Unipub.

United Nations. (1948). Universal Declaration of Human Rights. Retrieved from http://www.un.org/en/documents/udhr/

Ward, S. J. A. (2005). Philosophical foundations for global journalism ethics. *Journal of Mass Media Ethics, 20*(1), 3–21. doi:10.1207/s15327728jmme2001_2

Yin, J. (2008). Beyond the four theories of the press: A new model for the Asian & the world press. *Journalism & Communication Monographs, 10*(1), 3–62.

Constructing AN Intercultural Public Sphere

CHAPTER SEVENTEEN

The Global Imaginary IN Mumford AND McLuhan

JACK LULE

This chapter looks at one of the crucial but sometimes overlooked intercultural dimensions of news media: They have been essential to globalization.[1] The chapter starts from an understanding that globalization is made possible by the work of the *imagination*. That is, people have needed to be able to truly imagine the world—and imagine themselves acting in the world—for globalization to proceed. And the media—which bring stories, pictures, sights, and sounds from other peoples and places, even outer space—often have been the means by which the imagination of the world has been made possible.

People today perhaps take "the world" for granted. We all know that with enough money, we can hop on a plane and go anywhere, or make a transcontinental phone call, or use Google or Wikipedia to find photographs and information on even the most remote places. That imagination, however, was a long time coming for humankind. For centuries, many parts of the world were unknown to other parts of the world. People told fantastic stories of these other places. They told stories of primitive villages and fearful savages. They told stories of unfathomable wealth and streets made of gold. They could not imagine what life was like elsewhere.

As Arjun Appadurai (1996) has argued, the imagination is not a trifling fantasy but a "social fact." The imagination is a "staging ground for action" (p. 22). The Irish people, starving from a potato famine in the 1800s, *imagined* a better life in America, and millions emigrated. The Egyptian people, suffering under a dictatorship, *imagined* a better life for themselves in 2011.

They filled Tahrir Square in Cairo and overthrew the dictator, "imagining a new nation" (Kadry, 2014). The imagination—in the context of news media and globalization—can be an especially fertile concept for study.

We will start our study with *the imaginary*, a term that scholars often use, and one that has enriched research in numerous fields, including journalism and communication. We will look at the ways theorists have employed the imaginary in studying how individuals, nations, and societies imagine themselves and the world.[2] Then we will look at the role of news media. In this perspective, the media have not only physically linked the globe with cables, broadband, and wireless networks but have also linked the globe with stories, images, myths, and metaphors. The media are helping to bring about a fundamentally new imaginary, what scholar Manfred Steger (2008) has called a rising *global imaginary*—the globe itself as imagined community. In the past, only a few, privileged people thought of themselves as "cosmopolitan"—citizens of the world. Cosmopolitanism, I argue, is now a feature of modern life. People imagine themselves as part of the world (Durante, 2015).

What are the implications of this global imaginary? Here we will turn to media scholar Marshall McLuhan (1962, 1964). The global imaginary surely seems like a modern notion. But in the 1960s, McLuhan anticipated this phenomenon with his conception of the global village. The global village, McLuhan felt, would bring about a utopia. Drawn closely together by media, people would be like neighbors. From its introduction, though, the global village has been a source of controversy. We will look at the global village debate, with particular attention to a critique offered by the historian of technology and science Lewis Mumford (1951, 1970). Years before McLuhan, with strikingly similar language, Mumford too found utopian hope in media technology. He too hoped for a village-like world of community and grace. However, Mumford watched with dismay as media technology was used instead for capitalism, militarism, profit, and power. His dreams became nightmares. Mumford's later work savaged the possibility of the global village and railed against its implications. Mumford became one of McLuhan's most ferocious critics.

Ultimately, however, this chapter will argue that the news media and globalization are producing a macabre marriage of the visions of Mumford and McLuhan. The dawning global imaginary is the realization of McLuhan's global village. As McLuhan predicted, media and globalization have connected the world and its people from end to end so that we can indeed imagine the world as a village. However, the connection, closeness, and interdependence of the global village have brought no collective harmony or peace. Instead, we will conclude, globalization and media are combining to create the dark, dystopian world that Mumford dreaded. We will thus arrive at a construct we need to understand the world today: the global village of Babel.

The ethics of interculturalism developed in this book have never been more necessary and complicated.

STUDY OF THE IMAGINARY

People have long used *imaginary* as an adjective to describe imagined beings or objects, such as imaginary friends or imaginary selves. It makes sense that a psychiatrist would be intrigued by the imaginary. The French psychoanalyst and social theorist Jacques Lacan (1968, 1977) took special interest in this process. His psychoanalytic system is rich, intricate, and difficult to distill. Yet much of his work has had great influence in philosophy, critical studies, literary theory, and other arenas. Unlike many Freudian analysts, Lacan does not place his primary focus on the unconscious. Instead, Lacan, who was heavily influenced by Marx, emphasizes the impact of society and culture on people and their psyches.

Lacan (1968) argues that people perceive the world in three ways, or orders—the imaginary, the symbolic, and the real (pp. 29–87). For Lacan, the imaginary is perception shaped by images, imagination, illusion, and, in particular, fantasy. For example, Lacan discusses the fantasies a person builds around a perceived, imagined self and says that the person "ends up by recognizing that this being has never been anything more than his construct in the imaginary and that this construct disappoints all his certainties" (1977, p. 42). For Lacan, then, the imaginary largely is, in Marx's terms, illusion and, in Freud's terms, fantasy. The imaginary is a way in which individuals deceive and are deceived, in which they alienate and are alienated.

Cornelius Castoriadis, a Greek philosopher and economist, shared much intellectual kinship with Lacan. Also a social theorist and psychoanalyst, influenced too by Marx and Freud, as well as by Lacan, Castoriadis nevertheless argues for a much different understanding of the imaginary. In *The Imaginary Institution of Society*, Castoriadis (1987) extends the imaginary from the individual to society.

He believes that groups of people share imaginings—a social imaginary—that capture essential values and beliefs of the people. The ancient Jews' understandings of the Old Testament God are a social imaginary, Castoriadis (1987) says. The Jews believed in that God, who could be stern and unforgiving as well as munificent and kind. That shared belief is a social imaginary. Another example would be the political and philosophical structure established and accepted by the ancient Greeks (pp. 128–129). Ultimately, societies need social imaginaries for unity and cohesion. Castoriadis notes that a social imaginary gives people and society an understanding of their place in the world—"an original investment by society of the world and itself with meaning." And, he says, the

324 | JACK LULE

social imaginary specifies "a particular importance and particular place in the universe constituted by a given society" (p. 128). It is an important line. I think the changes wrought by globalization and new media are causing numerous societies, from the United States to China to Egypt to Afghanistan to France, to consider their particular importance and place in the universe.

As a political scientist, Benedict Anderson (1991) has interests different from psychoanalysts and social theorists. Anderson's primary focus is on the origin of nations and nationalism. His question is key: He wonders how a group of people, though spread across a vast expanse of land, come to conceive of themselves as a "nation." He points out that "the nation" is a relatively modern idea, developed in the late 18th century to replace monarchies and religious empires (pp. 11–12). Yet within a fairly short amount of time, people began to see themselves vividly as part of a nation. People's loyalty and dedication to the nation became so strong that they would kill and die for it. How does such a belief take hold?

Anderson's answer, like the psychoanalysts', leads him to the imagination. He says that nations are the result of "imagined communities," a concept now used regularly throughout the humanities and social sciences. People will never meet face to face with all or even most of the other members of their nation, Anderson says, but they can *imagine* themselves as one; "in the minds of each lives the image of their communion" (p. 6).

This imaginary, Anderson (1991) theorizes, comes about largely through the media, or, more specifically for Anderson's historical analysis, "print-capitalism" (p. 52). In the dawn of the printing press, publishers of books, newspapers, and magazines, looking for the largest audiences, printed their materials in a common vernacular and made them accessible across the land. Readers who might be divided by local dialects were brought together around a common print language—and common topics. People became aware of other people, places, and events in their own nation. They were aware that others were reading and responding to the same things. They began to understand themselves as a nation and see differences between their nation and others. Anderson concludes that print capitalism "created the possibility of a new form of imagined community," which set the stage for the modern nation (p. 46).

The Canadian philosopher Charles Taylor (2004) found Anderson's concept enormously useful for his scholarship on people's understandings of society and social relations. Though interested in the construction of society, not especially the nation, Taylor draws upon Anderson and proposes, with language similar to Castoriadis's, that *modern social imaginaries* are the ways in which people conceive their societies. "I speak of *imaginary* because I'm talking about the way ordinary people 'imagine' their social surroundings, and this is often not expressed in theoretical terms; it is carried in images, stories, and legends" (p. 23).

Taylor's (2004) conception differs somewhat from that of Castoriadis, whose focus is on the dominant imaginary of the group. Taylor's focus is on the beliefs and practices of average people in daily life. He says, "Our social imaginary at any given time is complex. It incorporates a sense of the normal expectations that we have of one another, the kind of common understanding which enables us to carry out the collective practices that make up our social life. This incorporates some sense of how we all fit together in carrying out the common practice" (p. 24).

That potent phrase—"how we all fit together"—gets richly complicated in the context of globalization and news media. In our time, who, precisely, is "we"?

The World as Imagined Community

The imaginary, thus far, has been used by these theorists to understand how individuals and societies imagine themselves and the world. In Castoriadis's words, the imaginary captures the "particular importance and particular place in the universe constituted by a given society" (1987, p. 128). Globalization, however, seems to call for new understandings and new imaginings. Indeed, sociologist Roland Robertson (1992) defines globalization in part as "the intensification of consciousness of the world as a whole" (p. 8). Anthony Giddens (1990), too, speaks of "the intensification of worldwide social relations" (p. 64).

People increasingly work, act, study, communicate, move, and get information from around the globe. It is the world, rather than the village or state, that becomes their frame of reference. In Taylor's terms, "the sense of how we all fit together" is increasingly global. "We" may actually now mean the people of the world. Yet is this new? Actually, no. The feeling of working, acting, and belonging to the world did not arise in our era of globalization. In other eras, globalization awakened similar impulses. Privileged people called "cosmopolitans"—literally from the Greek, *kosmopolit⁻es*, citizen of the cosmos—were those who had traveled and perhaps studied abroad, had knowledge of other people and lands, read news of others places, and felt themselves part of the larger world.

Two differences, however, mark our era of globalization. The first difference, alluded to by Robertson and Giddens, is the intensification or intensity of the understanding and consciousness of the world. We can see vividly and instantly into every corner of the world. News media are central to this intensification. The power and scope of mass media now bring the world to our living rooms and offices. The tools of interactive communication, such as cell phones and the computer, allow regular communication and communion with others around the globe. In our era, we feel more intensely the closeness of the world. The second difference is the expansion and acceleration of global social, economic, and political relations. Acts of globalization have been going on for centuries. However, because of the spread and growth of communication technology, as well as lower costs for travel and technology and rising incomes in many areas of the world, more people than ever are participating in global activities.

Being cosmopolitan is thus no longer a rare attribute but a marked feature of modern life. The immigrant, study-abroad student, account executive, pilot, poet, tourist, cable news viewer, Twitter follower, and many others feel themselves *of the world*. Can we therefore speak of an emerging global imaginary?

Appadurai (1996), a cultural anthropologist, argues that new advances and possibilities in media and migration indeed have caused a "rupture" in social relations that allows for new ways of imagining ourselves and the world. He writes that "electronic mediation and mass migration mark the world of the present not as technically new forces but as ones that seem to impel (and sometimes compel) the work of the imagination" (p. 4).

Appadurai (1996) realizes that media and migration are not new, that not everyone has access to new media, and that not everyone migrates. Yet, he says, the explosive expansion and commingling of media and migration are new. Few people are untouched by advances in media, and few people do not have a friend, relative, or coworker who has come back and forth from distant lands. The work of the imagination now takes place in this global context and becomes "a space of contestation in which individuals and groups seek to annex the global into their own practices of the modern" (p. 22). The imagination is vital and alive, Appadurai says, "a staging ground for action" (p. 7). And he emphasizes that this view of the imagination must be different from Anderson's. It is "explicitly transnational—even postnational" (p. 22).

For Manfred Steger (2008), the stirring of the "postnational imagination" is *The Rise of the Global Imaginary*, the felicitous title of his book. Like Appadurai, Steger recognizes how images, people, and material now circulate more freely across national boundaries, creating a "new sense of 'the global'" (p. 10). He says "globalization was never merely a matter of increasing flows of capital and goods across national boundaries. Rather, it constitutes a multidimensional set of processes in which images, sound bites, metaphors, myths, symbols and spatial arrangements of globality were just as important as economic and technological dynamics" (p. 11).

Steger (2008) emphasizes the importance of the awareness and apprehension of this new globality. The result is an "intensifying 'subjective' recognition of a shrinking world" (pp. 10–11). Steger sees the resulting imaginary as "no longer exclusively articulations of the national imaginary." Indeed, as the national increasingly gives way to the global, the result is a "dawning global imaginary" (p. 12). To return to Anderson's terms, the imagined community is now the globe.

GLOBAL IMAGINARY TO GLOBAL VILLAGE

A global imaginary sounds like a 21st-century idea, but media scholar Marshall McLuhan prefigured the concept as early as the 1960s with his notion of the "global village." McLuhan was a determinedly controversial personality. His work on media spanned four decades, from the 1950s to his death in 1980, but he rose to prominence in the 1960s and 1970s, during the height of television's popularity and the dawning of computers. He became an international celebrity. He appeared on magazine covers and television talk shows. He portrayed himself in the Woody Allen film *Annie Hall*. *Wired* magazine lists him on its masthead as "patron saint."

In academic circles of the time, however, McLuhan was often a subject of derision and degradation. Perhaps because of his celebrity, his outlandish style, and his broad, sweeping declarations, McLuhan earned the scorn of many scholars. Yet his works continued to be referenced and his ideas debated. And as media continued to develop in ways anticipated by his writings, McLuhan edged back into the academy (Stille, 2000).

Numerous theorists on globalization now cite the value of McLuhan's work. Manuel Castells's title, *The Internet Galaxy,* pays tribute to McLuhan's *The Gutenberg Galaxy*. Elsewhere, Castells has defended McLuhan. He says, "McLuhan was a genius. The fact that he was not an empirical researcher, but a theorist, has allowed people to think that they can dismiss his insights" (Rantanen, 2005a, p. 142). Anthony Giddens too has recognized McLuhan's role. Giddens's explorations of how globalization and media transformed space and time derive in part from his study of McLuhan and the Toronto school tradition (Rantanen, 2005b, p. 66). And McLuhan's work continues to find traction in studies of media and globalization (Dixon, 2009; Fishko, 2014; Levinson, 1999; Marchessault, 2005; Powe, 2014; Theal, 2001).

Why do people still find value in McLuhan? In a series of works, *The Mechanical Bride* (1951), *The Gutenberg Galaxy* (1962), *Understanding Media* (1964), and others, McLuhan develops a complex and controversial approach to media. Influenced by his colleague at the University of Toronto, Harold Innis, McLuhan's primary focus is on the transformative effects that electronic media are having on humankind. McLuhan argues that the medium itself is far more important than any content it carries (1964, pp. 23–39; Grosswiler, 2010). Indeed, he says, the media physically affect the human central nervous system. They influence the way the brain works and how it processes information. They create new patterns of thought and behavior. For example, he argues that people and societies of the printing press era were shaped by that medium. And people and societies are being shaped in new ways by electronic media. In one of his well-known, provocative dictums, he says, "The medium is the message" (1964, p. 23; Fishko, 2014).

In a related theme, McLuhan also argues that electronic media are "abolishing" space and time (1964, p. 3). What does he mean? He says humans around the world can see one another and speak with one another as if they are in the same space at the same time—space and time no longer separate people. From that basis, he develops perhaps his most important concept. With the world "made smaller" by electronic media and free from the restrictions of space and time, he says, "the human family now exists under conditions of a 'global village'" (1962, p. 31). It is a striking metaphor. "The new electronic interdependence recreates the world in the image of a global village" (1962, p. 31; 1964, pp. 34, 93).

McLuhan's son Eric believes the term derived from James Joyce's *Finnegans Wake* or Wyndham Lewis's *America and Cosmic Man*, which has the line, "The earth has become one big village, with telephones laid on from one end to the other, and air transport, both speedy and safe" (E. McLuhan, 2010). Regardless of its origins, the phrase now regularly appears in common and academic use. "Global Village" is the name of an entertainment and shopping venue in Dubailand, a Habitat for Humanity project, a summer program for young entrepreneurs, a worldwide phone service, and countless other entities. A recent Google search finds 5.68 million results. To recall McLuhan's original argument in such a context is daunting. Yet serious reflection on the global village may offer ways of apprehending the present and future shape of a rising global imaginary being shaped by news media and globalization.

Regaining Babel

McLuhan places the global village within the Judeo-Christian metaphor of Babel. In the Biblical story of Babel, vain humans are unified and powerful and try to erect a monument to themselves. But the Lord sees their plans and confounds their language so that they can no longer understand one another. Humanity becomes divided and scattered across the globe. The site of ruin, where humanity was once united in common language, is to be known as Babel.

For McLuhan, media allowed humans to recover the unity they lost at Babel. With humans sharing news stories, television images, photographs, films, advertising, video, and more, and with computers able to provide instant translation, language no longer needs to divide humans. McLuhan (1964) was exceedingly optimistic:

> Language as the technology of human extension, whose powers of division and separation we know so well, may have been the "Tower of Babel" by which men sought to scale the highest heavens. Today computers hold out the promise of a means of instant translation of any code or language into any other code or language. The computer, in short, promises by technology a Pentecostal condition of universal understanding and unity. (p. 80)

The utopian vision—"a Pentecostal condition of universal understanding and unity"—is striking. McLuhan even imagines the possibility of a kind of collective unconscious, shared by all humans. That is, we would know what each other is thinking and feeling and would exist together in peace. He says (1964):

> The next logical step would seem to be, not to translate, but to by-pass languages in favor of a general cosmic consciousness, which might be very like the collective unconscious dreamt of by Bergson. The condition of "weightlessness," that biologists say promises a physical immortality, may be paralleled by the conditions of speechlessness that could confer a perpetuity of collective harmony and peace. (p. 80)

The Technological Sublime

McLuhan eventually backed away from this glorious, almost ecstatic vision of the future. Writings that appeared after his death underscore later concerns about the effect of global media on humankind (McLuhan & Fiore, 1997). However, *Understanding Media* remains McLuhan's most influential work, and its impact continues to be felt. McLuhan had bequeathed to the world a provocative metaphor. The overall global imaginary anticipated by McLuhan is one in which people, through new media, recognize and reclaim their common humanity in a world that evolves into paradisal collective harmony and peace. His imaginary resonates with lofty visions, idealistic hopes in humanity, and fervent confidence in the power of media technology.

It seems overblown, perhaps, but McLuhan had simply placed himself in a long line of writers and public figures who celebrate and anticipate the role of technology, particularly communication technology, in human life. For example, with language that intriguingly anticipates a global village, Samuel Morse told the U.S. Congress that his telegraph could "diffuse, with the speed of thought, a knowledge of all that is occurring throughout the land; making, in fact, one neighborhood of the whole country" (Czitrom, 1982, p. 12). And it is good to recall that the completion of the first transatlantic telegraph cable in 1858 was greeted by celebrations, bonfires, fireworks, and pageants on both sides of the Atlantic. New York City hosted a mammoth parade, called the largest ever to that point. Just for the telegraph (Czitrom, 1982, p. 12).

Each new technological advance—the telegraph, telephone, film, radio, television, satellite, computer, Internet, cell phone—seems to inspire these redemptive dreams of community and peace. The many books that chronicled the rise of globalization near the turn of the century credited and celebrated media technology, especially digital media, and can be understood in this tradition. Thomas Friedman (1999), in *The Lexus and the Olive Tree*, glowingly defines globalization as "the inexorable integration of markets, nation-states and technologies to a degree never witnessed before—in a way that is enabling individuals, corporations, and nation-states to reach around the world farther, faster, deeper and cheaper than ever before" (p. 9). Friedman (2005) also offers a hearty embrace of technology in *The World Is Flat*: "*I am a technological determinist! Guilty as charged*" (p. 536). Another writer of the same period, Keniche Ohmae (1999), similarly heralds opportunities in a "borderless world" in which business is "carried out through a network of offices and entrepreneurial individuals, connected to each other by crisscrossing lines of communication rather than lines of authority" (p. 99). As Bill Gates, founder of Microsoft, said in an interview, "Never before in history has innovation offered promise of so much to so many in so short a time" ("The Last Page," 2010).

Decades ago, Leo Marx, a historian of technology, identified such representations as "the rhetoric of the technological sublime"—treatises that look to technology to bring about a renewed sense of community, equality, humane labor, peace across borders, and other aspirations (Marx, 2000, p. 193). Media scholars James Carey and John J. Quirk (2009) updated the phrase in the 1970s, with the ascension of television and the Internet, as "the rhetoric of the electrical sublime" (p. 94).

From its first appearance in *The Gutenberg Galaxy*, even as the words entered common parlance, the "global village" has often been summarily dispatched as more rhetoric of the technological and the electrical sublime. The cozy concept of the village and the transcendental characterization of its contours have been criticized and satirized in the academic and popular press, and indeed the debate over the concept continues to this day (Dixon, 2009, pp. 1–26; Douglas, 2006; Marchessault, 2005, pp. 202–221; Porter, 2015).

LEWIS MUMFORD

However, as we have seen, the global village is still a powerful metaphor. Dismissing the metaphor does not make it go away. Much more interesting and important, especially for a study of news media and globalization, is the analysis and censure leveled by Lewis Mumford, another historian of science and technology. Mumford was writing in the same era as McLuhan. Rather than simply deriding and dismissing the metaphor of the global village or its utopian dimensions, Mumford took the metaphor seriously. He laid out what he saw as dark and sinister implications of the global village. Mumford's vision thus can be understood as an alternate global imaginary, an imaginary that may offer insights into the shape of news media and globalization in our time—a time that surely seems quite distant from cosmic, collective harmony and peace.

The Pentagon of Power

Mumford was a writer of enormous breadth, producing work on urban issues, architecture, literature, technology, and science. Born in 1895, Mumford lived and chronicled the technological advances of the 20th century. Like others, he first marveled at the tremendous advances in media technology of the time—film, radio, telephone, and television. In his early writings on media technology and society, Mumford (1951, 1967) evokes the technological sublime in language that actually might have guided McLuhan toward the global village. With the development of "the telephone and radio and ultimately television," Mumford writes, "all the inhabitants of the planet could theoretically be linked together for instantaneous communications as closely as the inhabitants of a village" (1951, p. 236).

McLuhan was deeply and admittedly affected by Mumford's early work and cites him throughout his books. James Carey (1997) has provided an insightful analysis that demonstrates the influence of Mumford on many of McLuhan's most important ideas, from media as extensions of man to the abolishment of time and space to the effect of media on human senses to the global village. McLuhan greatly appreciated the power of Mumford's insights.

However, the appreciation was not returned. Mumford had watched with ever-deepening dismay as media technology was used not for the betterment of humankind but the betterment of corporations and the military. Rather than for peace and prosperity, technology was being used for the pursuit of profit and power. Mumford's original fervor for media technology helped fuel a palpable rage over the betrayal. He excoriated what he termed "the pentagon of power"—political absolutism, property, productivity, profit, and publicity (Mumford, 1970). You can almost hear him sputtering the words. And as McLuhan seemed to legitimize and even celebrate the exploitation of media technology by those at the nexus of the pentagon, Mumford turned his considerable talents and scorn on him.

Mumford was enraged, in particular, that McLuhan's elevation of electronic media could lead to the repudiation of language and the written word. He depicts a resulting grotesque world of disorder, ignorance and entropy, "expressed with psychedelic extravagance by Professor Marshall McLuhan and his followers" (1970, p. 293). The criticism gets more intense. Mumford says, "McLuhan's trancelike vaticinations" offer a world of instantaneous planetary communication in which "mankind as a whole will return to the

pre-primitive level, sharing mindless sensations and pre-linguistic communion." Mumford goes on to paint McLuhan's celebration of electronic media
as a "burning of the books," such as "the public bonfires lighted by the Nazis"
(p. 293). He writes:

> But it remained for McLuhan to picture as technology's ultimate gift a more absolute
> mode of control: one that will achieve total illiteracy, with no permanent record except
> that officially committed to the computer, and open only to those permitted access to
> this facility. This repudiation of an independent written and printed record means noth-
> ing less than the erasure of man's diffused, multi-brained collective memory. (p. 294)

Mumford sees special danger in McLuhan's conception of the global village.
For Mumford, a global village would mean "total cultural dissolution" (p. 295).
He acknowledges that electronic communication has "added a new dimension to human capability and practical cooperation." But, he says, "immediate
intercourse on a worldwide basis does not necessarily mean a less trivial or
parochial personality." In fact, Mumford says, "The lifting of restrictions upon
close human intercourse" has been dangerous and increased the areas of friction and mobilized warlike mass reactions (p. 295).

He looks back over the history of media technology and transportation
and notes that the introduction of each technology was accompanied by hopes
of worldwide solidarity and political unity. "In the course of two centuries,"
he says, "these hopes have been discredited. As the technical gains have been
consolidated, moral disruptions, antagonisms, and collective massacres have
become more flagrant, not in local conflicts alone but on a global scale" (p.
296). His blunt conclusion: "Audio-visual tribalism (McLuhan's 'global village') is a humbug," an "electronic illusion" that would lead to wars, massacres, excommunication of cultures, authoritarian control, subjugation of large
populations by the military and corporate elite, and worldwide division—"the
electronic Tower of Babel" (pp. 297–298). Mumford thus completes his exco-
riation by turning back upon McLuhan the beloved metaphor of Babel.

CONCLUSION: A GLOBAL VILLAGE OF BABEL

For Mumford, the stakes were high and the danger absolute in academic theorizing over media and a global imaginary. What can today's readers interested
in intercultural ethics conclude? First, the individual and social imaginaries
described by Lacan, Castoriadis, Anderson, and Taylor surely are being aug-
mented with increased awareness of globality. As Appadurai and Steger suggest, the economic, cultural, and political processes of globalization in our
time have combined with continued advances in media technology to produce
a rising global imaginary.

The deep divide between Mumford and McLuhan can then be understood in this context. Each writer offers a starkly different vision of the results of the global imaginary. Whose vision best aids our understanding of the globe today? Close to 50 years after their acrimonious debate, we can declare: They both were right.

McLuhan was right. Our era of globalization has indeed seen the realization of the global village. A dawning global imaginary has been made possible in which people can and do imagine themselves as sharing life on the planet in the same way that people long ago understood themselves as sharing life in the village. Travel from one end to the other is expensive but not difficult. News and communication are instantaneous. People share stories, songs, videos, images, myths, and more. They are dependent upon one another for resources, goods, and trading, and they compete in those areas as well. The "global village" has entered common parlance because it captures for many people their conception of the world today—the globe as imagined community. Globalization and media have partnered over time and, in our time, have created the conditions by which the globe can be imagined as a village.

However, Mumford too was right. This global village is no utopia or paradise, as McLuhan first prophesied. Nor does the global village suggest a "flat world" or a "borderless world" with access and opportunity for all. Mumford's ferocious critique has proved too true. It does not ultimately deny our now-emerging global village. It shreds McLuhan's transcendental depiction of life in that village. Rather than the restoration of unity before Babel that McLuhan foresaw, the dawning global imaginary offers a village dominated by corporate and military elites, a village characterized not by understanding, unity, or community but a village torn by contest, control, suffering, struggle, and separation—a return to Babel itself.

As Mumford warned, more contact does not mean more peace, more communication does not mean more community, and more trade does not mean more cooperation. Power and profit, themes that haunt Mumford's work but play little part in McLuhan's, have confounded humankind again. Unlike Innis, his mentor, McLuhan paid little heed to economics, power, politics, and the likely collision of global and local cultures. He did not at first apprehend how these forces would polarize life in the global village, dividing it into a Babel of contesting languages, opposing ideologies and beliefs, and savage struggles for resources and power.

Arjun Appadurai (1996) has also sought to capture the dystopian potential of the global village. He writes:

> We are now aware that with media, each time we are tempted to speak of the global village, we must be reminded that media create communities with "no sense of place." The world we live in now seems rhizomic, even schizophrenic, calling for theories of

rootlessness, alienation, and psychological distance between individuals and groups on the one hand, and fantasies (or nightmares) of electronic propinquity on the other. (p. 29)

Perhaps with some irony, the new media, which have contributed to the polarized, divided village, bring us incessant reminders of the chaos around us. With tens of thousands of the globe's children dying each day from starvation and disease, with one billion people living in desperate poverty, with contemplation and reflection throttled by incessant and omnipresent media, with holy lands cleaved by hatred, with families torn asunder, with giant slums growing each day outside the world's biggest cities, with violence and terror haunting terminals and stations, with journalists beheaded in the name of religion, a global village of "universal understanding and unity" seems a pathetic and preposterous absurdity.

McLuhan himself, seemingly from the grave, came to endorse a stark, darker vision of the global village. *The Global Village: Transformations in World Life and Media in the 21st Century* was published almost 10 years after McLuhan's death, co-written by McLuhan and Bruce Powers (1989). The authors appear eager to disavow the transcendental enthusiasm of McLuhan's more celebrated work. They describe a world of "massive unemployment in the industrial nations, a destruction of all privacy, and a planetary disequilibrium keyed to continent-wide propaganda skirmishes conducted through the new-found utility of interactive satellites" (p. 102). They also see a future of cable channels divided by culture and language, banks retooled for money handling to different cultures, neighborhood schools each with a diverse language, and ethnicities congregated in self-integrated barrios. In their home United States, they say, cities will harbor "a gestaltic political conglomeration of whites, blacks, Asians, and Hispanics fighting with each other for what is left of the economic pie in a nation of a declining birthrate of native-born Americans and an aging white population" (p. 85). Worldwide, they see "centers everywhere and margins nowhere in a new tribalism" (p. 95). And finally, one possible result of "global media networking," they suggest in a cryptic warning, is that it "brings back Tower of Babel" (p. 120). Cosmic, collective harmony, in this look back, has been throttled before birth.

Aided then by the insights of both Mumford and McLuhan, the contours of an emerging world come into view. We are being drawn closer and closer together, but that closeness is yielding friction and division. The historical, ongoing but erratic economic, cultural, and political processes of globalization, combined with electronic and digital news media, pulled and twisted by humankind's hubris, vanity, and greed, are yielding a cheerless, bleak perspective of an emerging world, a global village of Babel. In communication studies, intercultural perspectives have particular relevance and urgency.

NOTES

1. Jack Lule (2011) is author of *Globalization and Media: Global Village of Babel*, from which this chapter is adapted.
2. Barbara Strauss (2006) reviews the same theorists in her study of the imaginary. Though Strauss' study focused on anthropological applications, her insights into theorizing of the imaginary are of great interest.

BIBLIOGRAPHY

Anderson, B. (1991). *Imagined communities: Reflections on the origin and spread of nationalism.* New York: Verso. (Originally published 1983)

Appadurai, A. (1996). *Modernity at large: Cultural dimensions of globalization.* Minneapolis: University of Minnesota Press.

Carey, J. W. (1997). The roots of modern media analysis: Lewis Mumford and Marshall McLuhan." In E. S. Munson & C. A. Warren (Eds.), *James Carey: A critical reader* (pp. 34–59). Minneapolis: University of Minnesota Press.

Carey, J. W., & Quirk, J. J. (2009). The mythos of the electronic revolution. In J. W. Carey, *Communication as culture: Essays on media and society* (pp. 87–108). New York: Routledge.

Castoriadis, C. (1987). *The imaginary institution of society.* Trans. Kathleen Blarney. Cambridge, UK: Polity. (Originally published 1975)

Czitrom, D. J. (1982). *Media and the American mind: From Morse to McLuhan.* Chapel Hill: University of North Carolina Press.

Dixon, K. (2009). *The global village revisited: Art, politics, and television talk shows.* Lanham, MD: Rowman & Littlefield.

Douglas, S. (2006). The turn within: The irony of technology in a globalized world. *American Quarterly, 58*(3), 619–638.

Durante, T. (2015). The visual archive project of the global imaginary. Retrieved from http://www.the-visual-archive-project-of-the-global-imaginary.com/visual-global-imaginary/

Fishko, S. (2014). The medium is the message at 50. *On the Media.* Retrieved from http://www.onthemedia.org/story/medium-message-50/

Friedman, T. (1999). *The Lexus and the olive tree.* New York: Farrar, Straus & Giroux.

Friedman, T. (2005). *The world is flat.* New York: Farrar, Straus & Giroux.

Giddens, A. (1990). *The consequences of modernity.* Cambridge, UK: Polity.

Grosswiler, P. (Ed.). (2010). *Transforming McLuhan: Cultural, critical and postmodern perspectives.* New York: Peter Lang.

Kadry, A. (2014). Gender and Tahrir Square: Contesting the state and imagining a new nation. *Journal for Cultural Research, 18*(4). Retrieved from http://www.tandfonline.com/doi/abs/10.1080/14797585.2014.982922#.VQx8WGTF_P5

Lacan, J. (1968). *The language of the self: The function of language in psychoanalysis.* Trans. A. Wilden. Baltimore, MD: Johns Hopkins University Press. (Original publication 1956)

Lacan, J. (1977). The function and field of speech and language in psychoanalysis. In *Ecrits: A selection* (pp. 30–113). Trans. A. Sheridan. New York: Norton. (Originally published 1953)

Levinson, P. (1999). *Digital McLuhan: A guide to the information millennium.* New York: Routledge.

Lule, J. (2011). *Globalization and media: Global village of Babel*. New York: Rowman & Littlefield.

Marchessault, J. (2005). *Marshall McLuhan: Cosmic media*. Thousand Oaks, CA: Sage.

Marx, L. (2000). *The machine in the garden: Technology and the pastoral idea in America*. New York: Oxford University Press. (Originally published 1964)

McLuhan, E. (2010). The source of the term, global village. *McLuhan Studies, 2*. Retrieved from http://www.chass.utoronto.ca/mcluhan-studies/mstudies.htm.

McLuhan, M. (1951). *The mechanical bride: Folklore of industrial man*. New York: Vanguard.

McLuhan, M. (1962). *The Gutenberg galaxy: The making of typographic man*. London: Routledge.

McLuhan, M. (1964). *Understanding media: The extensions of man*. New York: McGraw-Hill.

McLuhan, M., & Fiore, Q. (1997). *War and peace in the global village: An inventory of some of the current spastic situations that could be eliminated by more feedforward*. New York: Hardwired.

McLuhan, M., & Powers, B. (1989). *The global village: Transformations in world life and media in the 21st century*. New York: Oxford University Press.

Mumford, L. (1951). *Conduct of life*. New York: Harcourt Brace Jovanovich.

Mumford, L. (1967). *The myth of the machine*, vol. 1, *Technics and human development*. New York: Harcourt Brace Jovanovich.

Mumford, L. (1970). *The myth of the machine*, vol. 2, *The pentagon of power*. New York: Harcourt Brace Jovanovich.

Ohmae, K. (1999). *The borderless world: Power and strategy in the interlinked economy*. New York: HarperCollins.

Porter, P. (2015). *The global village myth: Distance, war and the limits of power*. Washington, DC: Georgetown University Press.

Powe, B. W. (2014). *Marshall McLuhan and Northrop Frye: Apocalypse and alchemy*. Toronto: University of Toronto Press.

Rantanen, T. (2005a). The message is the medium: An interview with Manuel Castells. *Global Media and Communication, 1*(2), 135–147.

Rantanen, T. (2005b). Giddens and the "G"-word: An interview with Anthony Giddens. *Global Media and Communication, 1*(1), 63–77.

Robertson, R. (1992). *Globalization: Social theory and global culture*. Thousand Oaks, CA: Sage.

Steger, M. (2008). *The rise of the global imaginary: Political ideologies from the French revolution to the global war on terror*. New York: Oxford University Press.

Stille, A. (2000, October 14). Marshall McLuhan is back from the dustbin of history. *New York Times*, pp. A17, A19.

Strauss, B. (2006). The imaginary. *Anthropological Theory, 6*(3), 322–344.

Taylor, C. (2004). *Modern social imaginaries*. Durham, NC: Duke University Press.

The Last Page. (2010, Spring). *21st century manufacturing technology*. Retrieved from http://www.capacity-magazine.com/wmspage.cfm?parm1=438

Theall, D. F. (2001). *The virtual McLuhan*. Montreal: McGill-Queen's University Press.

CHAPTER EIGHTEEN

The Ethics OF Human Dignity IN A Multicultural World

CLIFFORD CHRISTIANS

For communication ethics to be effective in today's global era, it must be international and multicultural in scope, rather than centered on Western individualism. The sacredness of the human species is the starting point of this new ethics, and grounded in this universal norm is the ethical principle of human dignity. With this ethical principle understood in terms of human existence, rather than the legal order, our thinking shifts from human rights to our intrinsic worthiness. Morality in intercultural conflict is not reduced to the procedural justice of fairness but is committed to nonviolence and seeks restoration. When human dignity is grounded in the worth of humanity as a whole, we have a framework for avoiding the divisiveness of appeals to individual interests, community practices, and national prerogatives. The ethics of human dignity is presented as a cross-cultural standard for the news media today, but it is not abstract and idealistic. Because it works close to the ground of everyday experience, this chapter applies it to intercultural struggles in international journalism: Africa (Darfur humanitarian crisis), the U.S. (Native Americans at Wounded Knee), and Europe (Denmark's Islamic cartoon controversy).

THE QUESTION OF UNIVERSALS

The question of universals in ethics is a complicated one (Ward & Wasserman, 2010). But universals are the foundation for an ethics of intercultural communication.

Having diverse communities judged by universal norms follows the intellectual strategy of Jürgen Habermas (1984, 1990, cf. 1993). For an ethics of discourse to operate effectively in the public sphere, he presumed an ideal speech situation as its context. Competing normative claims can only be adjudicated in the public sphere under ideal speech conditions such as reciprocity and openness. Presuming an inherent desire in speech acts for mutual understanding, Habermas argues for an ideal discourse of full participation, mutuality, and reciprocity as a goal for citizens and a critical standard for public communication (cf. Ruta, 2014). In *Moral Consciousness and Communicative Action* (1990), Habermas argues that the principle of universalization acts as a rule of argumentation and is implicitly presupposed by human discourse (pp. 86–94). In moral consciousness, universals are the bridging principle that makes intercultural agreement possible (pp. 57–68).

Kwasi Wiredu (1996) writes out of an African philosophical perspective. The human species lives by language. It is through the intrinsic self-reflexivity of natural language that we arbitrate our values and establish our differences and similarities. The shared lingual character of our existence makes intercultural communication possible. Through the commonness of our biological-cultural identity as *homines sapientes*, we can believe that there are universals, notwithstanding that we live in local communities. In his words, "human beings cannot live by particulars or universals alone, but by some combination of both. Without universals intercultural communication must be impossible, while our natural formations are in the vernacular" (pp. 1, 9).

All languages are similar in their phonemic complexity, and all languages serve not merely functional roles but cultural formation. All humans learn languages at the same age. All languages enable abstraction, inference, deduction, and induction. All languages can be learned and translated by native speakers of other languages; in fact, some human beings in every language are bilingual. In Wiredu's terms, as lingual beings, we are sympathetically impartial to other cultures. Human beings have a basic natural sympathy for their kind, so that while they celebrate their own language and way of life, in principle they are predisposed to respect the cultures of their fellow human beings. Languages everywhere are communal and give all peoples an identity. Through the commonness we share as lingual beings, we can believe that there are universals at the same time as we live in particular cultures.

The idea of *ren / jen* in Confucius enriches intercultural media ethics also. Confucius uses *ren* (humanity) as the term for virtue in general. Humaneness (*ren*) is the key virtue in the *Analects*. It has a variety of translations, such as perfect virtue, goodness, and human-heartedness. However, it does not mean individual attainment—such as generosity or compassion—but refers to the manifestations of being human. It derives from a person's essential humanity.

Before Confucius, the idea of humanness did not have ethical importance, and its centrality is certainly one of the great innovations of the *Analects*.[1]

In grounding his theory in virtue, Confucius turned on its head the traditional idea of a superior person born into an aristocratic family. Human excellence is seen as depending on our native humanness (*ren*) rather than on social position. The idea that human excellence is a function of character rather than birth, upbringing, dynasty, or achievement was revolutionary then and remains so today (cf. Bell, 2008).

Byun and Lee (2002) argue that Confucian humaneness challenges the narrow Western notion of human rights set largely in legal terms. For them, Confucianism provides a much more expansive and compassionate morality than does individual rights: equilibrium, harmony and *ren* are based on a holistic understanding of human nature. Whereas the Occident values the rights-based morality of political philosophy (liberalism), the Confucian tradition is framed by mutual regard and respect toward the social order, that is, toward community-oriented responsibilities (cf. de Bary, 1998). As Confucius puts it in the *Analects*, "It is humaneness which is the attraction of a neighborhood. If from choice one does not dwell in humaneness, where does one obtain wisdom?" (IV.1). While individual rights represent one tradition, "dwelling in humaneness" belongs to the human species as a whole.

Through universal norms, we raise questions about cultural values that are exclusionary and oppressive. Cultures need norms beyond their own values to be self-critical. "Only an 'outside' lets us know that we are limited and defined by those limitations; only an 'outside' shapes us" and enables us to evaluate and move forward constructively (Fleischacker, 1992, p. 223). In synchronicity with the intellectual traditions from around the world that affirm universal, cross-cultural norms, this chapter develops an ethics of multiculturalism rooted in our common humanity.

THEORIZING THE ETHICS OF INTERCULTURAL COMMUNICATION

The great challenge in media ethics at present is globalizing it (Ward, 2015). Media ethics historically has been monocultural, largely Western, and gendered male. We ought to develop a multicultural, comparative model instead. To do so, we need to reconstruct the character of theorizing.

Theories are not *ex nihilo*. They are not conceptually immaculate, arising out of nothing. Theories are not abstract theorems, without context. We identify inconsistencies and conundrums in existing conventions and theorize how to start over. Einstein did not formulate $E = mc^2$ in purity but in opposition to Newtonian physics. Noam Chomsky's transformational linguistics is contrary to psychology's behaviorism. The relationalism of feminist theory contradicts John Locke's dichotomy between individual and society. Theories ought to be understood as an inside perspective on reality and not as an examination of external events. Thomas Kuhn (1969) calls this "revolutionary science"—the constructing of paradigms—rather than the "normal science" of verifying that propositions are externally and internally valid.

Individual autonomy has been the axis of most ethical theory to date. Universal human solidarity, its radical opposite, ought to be the centerpiece of media ethics instead. Universal imperatives have been discredited. Abstract ethical principles conceived in the Western mind but presumed true for all cultures are now rejected. Formal abstractions are no longer seen as neutral but imperialistic—exposed as the morality of a dominant educated class. A new kind of universal is needed. For a new ethical theory appropriate to a multicultural world, the problem of individual autonomy must be turned on its head, and its opposite become the starting point—universal human solidarity.

The narrative turn in the communications discipline is salutary. Through stories, we constitute ways of living in common. They are symbolic frameworks that organize human experience. People tell stories about who they are and what they care about. The stories of Nelson Mandela's 26 years in jail, the Selma march for civil rights in the United States, Deng Xiaoping's black cat/white cat and crossing-the-river stories, and the demolition of the Berlin wall are fodder for social change. In narrative ethics, moral values are situated in the cultural context rather than anchored by philosophical abstractions. Contextual values replace ethical absolutes. The domain of ethics shifts from principles to story, from formal logic to community formation.

Narrative ethics stakes out its territory in radically different terms than the ethics of rationalism. It points us in the right direction, but in the end it is co-opted by the status quo. After providing a thick reading of how societies work in a natural setting, narrative ethics is mute on which valuing to value. Whatever is identified experimentally cannot in itself yield normative guidelines. If phenomena situated in immediate space and present time are presumed to contain everything of importance, the search outside the momentary and particular is meaningless.

The narrative paradigm yields arbitrary definitions of goodness, as if to say, "This is good because I say it is good" or "This is good because most people in a social group identify it as good." For a century, philosophers have recognized the fallacy of deriving "ought" statements from "is" statements. To assert prescriptive claims from an experiential base entails a contradiction (Christians, 1995, pp. 126–127). Rather than superficial attention to courtesies, quirks in language, and unusual habits, a deep understanding of culture is necessary in transnational communication. Cultures are complex and multilayered; they express our worldviews and make life meaningful. But the demands of cultural diversity cannot become moral relativism without making a category mistake (cf. Paul, Miller, & Paul, 1994).

No culture takes a laissez-faire approach to morality. Some values are culturally distinctive, but that does not mean all cultural values are relative. Polygamy is practiced in some societies, with various types of monogamy in most. However, in no culture do men have free play with women. Some societies practice euthanasia or capital punishment, but no culture has a hunting season for people—"your hunting license permits you to shoot three in October" (Christians, 2011). For communication ethics to be meaningful over the long term, we have to recover the idea of moral universals itself. But our mandate is not communication ethics of any sort under any conditions. As the global information society takes shape, the only legitimate option is an ethics that is culturally inclusive.

The sacredness of life is a credible attempt to shift the field unequivocally from individual autonomy to universal humanity. The sacredness of life is not a metaphysical given but a core belief about human existence (*ren*). It unveils the inner character of complex cultures. As Aristotle established for all thinking beings, infinite regression is impossible. One cannot proceed intellectually without taking something as given. All human knowledge needs an unmoved mover.

With universal theory, there is a frame of reference for interpreting and measuring communities. Standards are essential for forming the common good. Communities turn in on themselves. Not all communities are legitimate. Conflicts between people groups and among nation states need principles outside them for their resolution. Without protonorms of universal scope, ethical theory and professional practice are trapped in the distributive fallacy, one ideological bloc presuming to speak for the whole. The question is whether our communities, in their values and practices, affirm the sacredness of life.

Sacredness of Life

In a study of ethical principles in 13 countries across four continents, the sacredness of human life was consistently identified as a universal value (Christians & Traber, 1997; cf. Christians, 2008). The rationale for human action was affirmed to be reverence for life on earth. Veneration of human life represents a universalism from the ground up. Various societies articulate this protonorm in different terms and illustrate it locally in multiple ways, but every culture can bring to the table this fundamental norm for ordering political relationships and social institutions such as the media.

The German philosopher Hans Jonas turns to nature for grounding a moral responsibility that is global in scope and self-evident regardless of cultures and competing ideologies.[2] Natural reality has a moral claim on us for its own sake and in its own right. In his perspective, purpose is embedded in the animate world, and its purposiveness is evident in "bringing forth life; nature evinces at least one determinate goal—life itself" (Jonas, 1984, p. 74). Thus, Jonas concludes, "showing the immanence of purpose in nature, ... with the gaining of this premise, the decisive battle for ethics has already been won" (p. 78). There is at least one generality of universal scope underlying systematic ethics. The philosophical rationale for human action is reverence for life on earth, for the physical realm that makes human civilization possible. The sacredness of life, evident in nature itself, is the basis for a responsibility that is global in scope and self-evident regardless of cultures and competing ideologies.

The veneration of human life is a protonorm—*proto* in Greek meaning underneath. Sacredness of life is to ethics what the proto-SinoTibetan is to language. Proto-SinoTibetan is the lingual predecessor underlying Chinese in all its variations and dialects, plus the Sinitic and Tibeto-Burman languages, as we know them in history.

Reverence for life on earth establishes a level playing floor for cross-cultural collaboration on the ethical foundations of responsible communication. Our human livelihood, in fact, is rooted in the principle that "We have inescapable claims on one another which cannot be renounced except at the costs of our humanity. ... Universal solidarity is the basic principle of ethics and the normative core of all human communication" (Peukert, 1981, pp. 10–11). The primal sacredness of life is a protonorm of common oneness. This universal protonorm anchors community values and professional ethics.

As Confucius made clear in the *Analects*, virtue arises from our being. The notion of protonorms is a way of rooting our universals in ontology rather than in the rationalist propositions of the Western tradition. Out of this primordial generality, basic ethical principles emerge such as human dignity.

Human Dignity

Diversity is one of the central issues in journalism ethics at present. Indigenous languages and ethnicity have come into their own. Ethnicity has replaced class struggle as the most powerful force of the 21st century. One's culture is more salient at present than one's nationality. Muslim immigrants are the fastest-growing segment of the population in France, and they are not interested in full assimilation into French language and politics. A total of 30,000 Navajo Indians live in Los Angeles, isolated from their native nation and culture. The nomadic Fulani, searching for good pasture throughout sub-Saharan West Africa, are held together by clan fidelity, but their political future is bleak. In the United States, 1.5 million people from across the globe become new citizens every year, but debates over immigration policy are acrimonious and irresolute. In contrast to the melting pot of the previous century, immigrants to the United States today insist on maintaining their own cultures, religions, and languages.

On a global scale, according to anthropologists, nearly 20,000 culture groups are locked away from the social mainstream. For the most part, these hidden peoples exist without recognition or adequate representation. Urdu-speaking Muslims are aliens in the state of Punjab in India. There are 14 groups of Taiwanese aborigines living in Taiwan, some of whom have migrated to the Fujian province on the mainland; their legal status is controversial. Since winning independence in 1989, the Belorussians have had little success in creating a sovereign state; for 70 years, their history and language had not been taught. Their identity crisis reaches even to the parliament in Minsk. Only the remnants of Mayan culture survive in the Yucatan peninsula of Mexico, obscured under the government's official commitment to the Spanish language and to nationalism. Anthony Cortese (1990) documents how deeply moral commitments are embedded in social relations—his cross-cultural evidence including among others an Israeli kibbutz, Kenyan village leaders, Tibetan monks, and folk societies in Papua New Guinea and India. Ethnic identity is now considered essential to cultural vitality and, indeed, survival. As a result, social institutions such as the mass media are challenged to develop cultural pluralism in their thinking, organizational structure, and reporting practices (cf. LeCompte & Schensul, 2015).

The ethical principle of dignity is of primary importance to media ethics across the globe. Different cultural traditions affirm human dignity in a variety of ways, but together they insist that all human beings have sacred status without exception. In Confucianism, we are to live in harmony with others because the human species is unique, requiring from within itself regard for its members as a whole. In African communalistic societies, *likute* is loyalty to the community's reputation, to tribal honor. In Latin American societies, insistence on cultural identity is an affirmation of the unique worth of human beings. Native American Indian discourse is steeped in reverence for life and interconnectedness among all living forms, so that we live in solidarity with others as equal partners in the web of life. In Islam, every person has the right to honor and a good reputation. In Judeo-Christian ethics, all human beings without exception deserve respect because all are made in the image of God.

From the cultural diversity perspective, one understands the ongoing vitality of the Universal Declaration of Human Rights issued by the United Nations General Assembly in 1948. As the preamble states: "Recognition of the inherent dignity and of the equal and inalienable rights of all members of the human family is the foundation of freedom, justice and peace in the world." The ethics of cultural diversity declares that everyone has sacred status with no exceptions for religion, class, gender, age, or ethnicity. The common sacredness of all human beings regardless of merit or achievement is not only considered a fact but a shared commitment.

In the ethics of human dignity, justice ought to be grounded in the inherent dignity of the human species. On account of possessing certain properties, all humans have worth. And that worth is sufficient for having rights we are owed. There does not have to be something else that confers these rights (Wolterstorff, 2008, p. 36). On account of a person's worth, someone comes into my presence bearing claims against me. Receiving one's due arises from one's intrinsic worth. It is not a privilege for which one has gratitude. The universal generalization that torture of children is unjust arises from humanity's intrinsic value, not because right order has been established in criminal law. Intrinsic worth is ontologically prior to legal mechanisms of conferral.

With the sacredness of life as the overarching protonorm, the ethical principle of human dignity is emphasized in working on ethnic diversity, racist language in news, and sexism in advertising. Gender equality in hiring and eliminating racism in organizational culture are no longer dismissed as political correctness but seen as moral imperatives. Human dignity takes seriously the decisive contexts of gender, race, class, and religion. While globalization lays a grid over the globe and pulls it toward uniformity around consumption and media technology, local voices are becoming more strident than ever. International media ethics continues to emphasize the normative principle of human dignity. When this principle becomes a priority in the news media, multiculturalism and ethnic pluralism will be enhanced.

With cultural identity coming into its own from Miami, Florida, to East Asia, is ethnic conflict inevitable? The Hutu and Tutsi massacres in Rwanda, killing in the streets of a Chechen village, and brutal warfare in Bosnia have not been stories about tribal disputes only but also about ethnic cleansing. Without a commitment to the common human good, we will not avoid tribalism. The issue for ethical journalism is not communal values per se but universal ones—not the common good understood as the community's good but *communis* in its richest universal meaning. A community's polychromatic voices are increasingly seen worldwide as essential for a healthy globe, and the media's ability to represent those voices well is an important arena for professional development and enriching codes of ethics (Glasser, Awad, & Kim, 2009; Ross & Lester, 2011).

Obviously news cannot be ethical unless the challenge of cultural diversity is met, and this requires a fundamental shift from homogeneity to recognition. The basic issue is whether political systems discriminate against their citizens in an unethical manner when major institutions fail to account for the identity of their members. In what sense should the specific central and cultural features of Asian Americans, Buddhists, the 55 minority groups in

China, Jews, the physically disabled, or children publicly matter? Should not public institutions ensure that all citizens share an equal right to the nation's wealth and due process without regard to race, gender, education, or religion?

The Canadian philosopher Charles Taylor, from the province of French-speaking Quebec, considers the issue of recognizing multicultural groups politically as among the most urgent and vexing on the social agenda, in our case on the media's agenda. Beneath the rhetoric is a fundamental philosophical dispute about the ethics of recognition. As Taylor (Taylor et al., 1994) puts it, "Nonrecognition or miscrecognition can inflict harm, imprisoning someone in a false, distorted and reduced mode of being. Due recognition is not just a courtesy we owe people. It is a vital human need" (p. 26). Guaranteeing that people have their own voice, define their own identity, and are respected as equals on their own terms is a fundamental challenge for society and for the news media. This foundational issue regarding the character of cultural identity needs resolution for cultural pluralism to meet the ultimate standard of the sacredness of life.

MEDIA CASES WITH HUMAN DIGNITY THE ISSUE

Language makes community possible; it is the public agent through which our identity is realized. The lingual dimension forms humans and their relationships into meaningful units, and its vitality or oppression inevitably conditions our well-being. In that sense, the media as our primary form of public communication are a crucial arena through which ethnic pluralism is represented and understood. I introduce three illustrations from the media to illustrate how the ethics of human dignity promotes ethnic pluralism.

Humanitarian Crisis in Darfur

The international news media often deal with intercultural conflict outside a nation's borders but of direct domestic concern. And in these transnational settings, typically the interests of several nations converge. Comparative research is necessary to analyze whether the representations of the news media are meeting the ethical standard of human dignity. Darfur is an illustration of comparative intercultural controversy, where the news media based in China, the United States, and Great Britain overlap. It serves as a testing ground for human dignity as the fundamental principle in intercultural news.

China has been the world's leading importer of Sudanese oil and a major trading partner with Sudan and South Sudan, and therefore with a national interest in having the *People's Daily* and *China Daily* cover it. The United Nations has called Darfur one of the greatest humanitarian crises of the 21st century, and with the United Nations headquarters located in New York, the coverage of its actions and deliberations on Darfur are of special importance to the *New York Times.* The BBC, with its home in the former colonizing country, pays special attention to Darfur's history and Sudanese politics.

Darfur for several hundred years was an independent Islamic sultanate with a population of Arabs and black African tribes—both of them Muslim. Darfur was annexed to Sudan by the British in 1916. Since its independence in 1956, both the Darfur region and Sudan have been embroiled in intercultural conflict. In 1962, a decade-long civil war broke out between the Arabs residing in the North and the Africans living in the South. After 11 years of peace, another civil war erupted, this time raging on for two decades. One of the largest and longest civil wars in history, more than two million have died and millions have been displaced, often to neighboring Chad and the Central African Republic.

Bloody conflict appeared to be calming down when, in February of 2003, a rebellion occurred in Darfur, an area plagued not only by drought and desertification but by continued tensions between the farmers and nomads who inhabit the area. The rebels began attacking government targets, claiming that the government in Khartoum was discriminating against them because of their black African identity. The Sudanese government retaliated by employing local Arab militias to quash the uprising—nicknamed the *Janjaweed* (translated as "the evil horsemen"). After the government conducted air strikes on targeted villages, the *Janjaweed* descended on the area, murdering and raping anyone left alive. To ensure that no one returned, the militias burned any remaining structures and poisoned the water supply. By backing the militias, the Sudanese government has been engaging in ethnic cleansing while at the same time denying responsibility for the human rights violations. Khartoum claims the violence is due to tribal conflicts (cf. Onishi, 2015).

In research that is now a classic in its comprehensiveness and depth, *The Geopolitics of Representation in Foreign News* compares the news coverage of Darfur from seven countries between 2003 and 2005 (Mody, 2010). Darfur was chosen as an icon of armed conflict since the end of the Cold War and the scene of the first genocide of the 21st century. From the footprint of this chapter on human dignity, the news media that are included for comparison are two newspapers, the Chinese-language *People's Daily* and the *New York Times,* and two online media operations, the English-language *China Daily Online* and the *BBC.co.uk.*

Geopolitics of Representation of Foreign News reinforces important findings in comparative journalism studies. News organizations are limited in presenting international news because of their preoccupation with events that have direct domestic linkage. News outlets will hesitate to cover stories that offend their sources of revenue or that show these sources in a negative light.

With China's high national interest in keeping good relations with Sudan and South Sudan for reasons of commerce, the *People's Daily* and *China Daily Online* restricted themselves to hard news stories. (As evidence of its national interest, China protected Sudan from sanctions for the Darfur massacre in the UN Security Council.) Mody (2010) concludes that national interests are still a significant predictor of news coverage in all countries but notable in both the *New York Times* and *BBC.co.uk*, despite the claim "that they are the watchdogs against state abuse of power" (p. 322).

The four news media showed different emphases because of their location, ownership structures, and intended audience. The charge of genocide made by UN Resident and Humanitarian Coordinator Mukesh Kapila and then by the United States was discussed most frequently in the *New York Times*. The *BBC.com.uk* most often identified race and ethnicity as the causes of the civil war, a sensitivity perhaps because of its location in the predominantly white Caucasian North. The *People's Daily* quoted only two news sources, the Khartoum government and the African Union, for its Chinese-speaking domestic audience, whereas the *China Daily Online* with its international English-speaking audience frequently quoted United Nations sources. Among the causes of the conflict, the *People's Daily* generally targeted the Darfuri rebels, with the other three news media referring regularly to the Khartoum government.

Despite such differences in nuance and detail, Mody (2010) concludes that the predominant emphasis for these news organizations was the day-to-day brutality. The conflict was bloody and dramatic in character, drawing the news to the sensational—gang rape, bombings, murder, burned-out villages, children slaughtered in daylight. As typical of international journalism as a whole, Mody calls the news organizations here "the one-eyed Cyclops" who address one major crisis at a time as a series of visible events.

In Mody's (2010) research, all of the news media are weak on the humanitarian dimension of the crisis. The *New York Times* emphasizes the dramatically political and includes the economic. *China Daily Online* and the *People's Daily* are focused on the political and economic also. *BBC.com.uk* scores well on Mody's comprehensiveness index but is preoccupied with the complicated politics and includes the economic as relevant. Such standard definitions of news are not adequate. Fairness and accuracy are important, but not sufficient. Accuracy is required on the details, but the complications are enormous when dealing with the causes, definitions, and consequences of human abuse.

The ethics of human dignity insists on thick description, on seeing beneath the surface to the heart of the matter. The deeper reading of human dignity discloses the attitudes, culture, and language of the abused without simplistic judgments. As Michael McDevitt (2010) puts it, in contrast to the watchdog role, journalism mobilizes the public conscience by identification with the victims. Violence from the oppressor and counter-violence in return from the oppressed will continue unless the dehumanization that drives it can be overcome. Human dignity is a different guiding principle in which ethnicities and religions are respected rather than polarized. In S. Keen's terms, "We first kill people with our minds, before we kill them with weapons" (quoted in Sadig & Guta, 2011, p. 616). The ethics of human dignity teaches us that a change in language and attitudes is required for changes to occur in policy and institutions.

American Indians at Wounded Knee

The classic case of Wounded Knee in the United States is a second illustration of how the ethics of human dignity works in intercultural communication involving various media.[4]

South Dakota's Sioux Indian Reservation at Pine Ridge was a site of despair and frustration in 1973. Most of the adults on the reservation were unemployed, rates of suicide and alcoholism were high, health care was substandard, and poverty was relentless. But the newly elected tribal leader, Dick Wilson, seemed more interested in helping his family and friends than in improving conditions on the reservation for those he was elected to serve. Tensions had been growing steadily for three weeks, ever since a group of Native Americans clashed with the police in nearby Custer, South Dakota. They protested the light, second-degree manslaughter charge against a white man accused of stabbing and killing Raymond Yellow Thunder.

On the night of February 27, 1973, American Indian Movement (AIM) activists occupied the site of Wounded Knee, inside the Pine Ridge Reservation. AIM leaders Dennis Banks and Russell Means seized the local trading post, museum, church, and other buildings—along with several hostages from the few white families living nearby. By the following morning, the Federal Bureau of Investigation (FBI), the Bureau of Indian Affairs (BIA), and federal marshals surrounded Wounded Knee. A siege had begun, with the government hoping to seal off supplies and force a peaceful surrender.

Media coverage exploded. Journalism crews from across America and around the world arrived to cover the developing events. For the first time in history, broadcast news carried the story every weekday night for 10 weeks.

The problems at Wounded Knee were momentous and dramatic. To make these problems known, the 200 Native Americans set up their bunkers and prepared to hold their ground by violence if necessary. They gathered considerable public support, trading on sympathy for the slaughter of Chief Big Foot at this location in 1890 by the U.S. Seventh Cavalry. This was the last open hostility between American Indians and the U.S. government until now—83 years later. According to Russell Means,

> Wounded Knee would always remain the haunting symbol of the white man's murderous treachery and of our nation's stoic grief. At Wounded Knee, on ground consecrated with the blood of our ancestors, we would make our stand. At Wounded Knee, as nowhere else, the spirits of Big Foot and his martyred people would protect us. (Means & Wolf, 1995, p. 253)

Small-arms fire erupted regularly between the two groups, and after four weeks, it turned injurious. On March 11, an FBI agent was shot and paralyzed from the waist down and a Native American injured as gunfire erupted at a roadblock outside town. A marshal was seriously wounded on March 2, and two Indians were killed in gunfire as the siege wore on into April. Finally, after the 10th week, on May 6, with supplies and morale nearly gone, the Native Americans negotiated an armistice and ended the war.

An incredible 75% of the U.S. population followed the story on television, but Indian attorney Ramon Roubideaux was unimpressed: "Only the sensational stuff got on the air. The facts never really emerged that this was an uprising against Washington's Bureau of Indian Affairs and its puppet government here at Pine Ridge" (Hickey, 1973, p. 34). A young Oglala Sioux bitterly criticized the press for news reports that framed the standoff as a "Wild West gunfight between the marshals and Indians" (Hickey, 1973, p. 34). Some reporters did break through the fog with substantive accounts. NBC's Fred Briggs used charts and photos to describe the trail of broken treaties that reduced the vast Indian territory to a few small tracts of land called "reservations." CBS's Richard Threlkeld understood that AIM really sought a revolution in Indian attitudes. ABC's Ron Miller laid vivid hold of life on the Pine Ridge Reservation itself by getting inside Indian politics and culture and describing what was happening through the natives' eyes. But, on balance, journalists followed the technological imperatives of television, showing the battle action. Journalists on the scene did not fully comprehend the subtleties or historical nuances of tribal government. Reporters complained that their more precise accounts often were reduced and distorted by heavy editing. The siege ended from weariness, not because the story was fully aired or understood. The press could have unveiled a political complaint to be discussed sensibly and thoroughly; instead it was caught up in the daily drama of quoting accessible sources and finding attractive visuals.

It has been argued that Wounded Knee is a tipping point in American Indian history. After nearly two centuries as U.S. citizens, this cultural group began establishing its voice. The protestors and their supporters at Wounded Knee confirmed that "we are Indians; we should be who we are and we need to communicate it." Although the leaders' decisions and actions during the 10-week occupation were often controversial, Wounded Knee is typically said to have sparked a revival of Native American languages, culture, religion, and education.

But the AIM leader at Wounded Knee, Russell Means, considers the issues of intercultural communication here more complicated. He participated in protest marches many times before Wounded Knee. He and Native Americans occupied Mount Rushmore, the sacred grounds of the Lakota. AIM protested Plymouth Rock and organized the "Longest Walk," a march on Washington to challenge government sterilization programs of Native American women. The occupations, marches, and protest assemblies at historic sites caught people's attention, but often they veered into violence before the voice of the Native Americans was heard completely.

Russell Means's own pathway in intercultural communication illustrates how the ethics of human dignity can be fulfilled for minority cultures. He abandoned the protest strategy and began using other forms of communication he thought would be more effective. He turned to film, for example, initiating an acting career as the title character Chingachgook in *The Last of the Mohicans* ("Russell Means, the Movie," 2014). He became the voice of Chief Powhatan in Disney's *Pocahontas*. He starred in the HBO documentary *Paha Sapa: The Struggle for the Black Hills* and in *Black Cloud*, a film about a Navajo Olympic athlete. He began to act in several television broadcasts, including such documentaries as "Incident at Oglala" and "Images of Indians." He narrated the video *Wounded Heart: Pine Ridge and the Sioux*. He opened a production business for creating CD-ROMs, short films and documentaries, magazines, books, television shows, and animated children's series. He narrated the music album on Soar Records, *Electric Warrior*.[5]

He returned to Pine Ridge to live and helped build a health clinic on Indian lands at Porcupine, South Dakota. A grant from the Corporation for Public Broadcasting funded a new AM radio station for Pine Ridge. He emphasized schools on the reservations, with special attention to teaching Lakota youth their native language and culture. All his projects have slowed since he died of throat cancer on October 12, 2012. But they leave behind for minority cultures a legacy of ideas for implementing the ethics of human dignity in intercultural communication.

Muhammad Cartoon Controversy

The third application of the ethics of human dignity is to the well-known Muhammad cartoon controversy.

On September 30, 2005, the *Jyllands-Posten*, Denmark's largest newspaper, published a series of 12 cartoons depicting the Prophet Muhammad. Fleming-Rose, *Jyllands-Posten*'s culture editor, commissioned the cartoons in response to the incidents of self-censorship and intimidation within Islam he observed in Denmark and across Europe. He wanted moderate Muslims now living in a democratic country to speak out in favor of healthy criticism. He insisted that the paper had a tradition of satire with the royal family and public figures, and that the cartoonists were treating Islam in the same way they treat Christianity, Hinduism, Buddhism, and other religions (Debatin, 2007).

Although there have been irreverent portrayals of the Prophet Muhammad by Europeans since the Middle Ages, the right-of-center *Jyllands-Posten* was known for its anti-immigration stance, and publication of the cartoons appeared to many Muslims as racial hatred toward a disrespected community. The act of even creating an image of Muhammad is blasphemous according to the Sunni Islam tradition, so not surprisingly, many Muslims were outraged for that reason alone. To a neutral observer, some of the cartoons were mild and innocuous. A few were aimed at the editor's call for cartoons, not at Muhammad directly. One showed Muhammad as a Bedouin flanked by two women in burqas. Another showed him standing at the gates of heaven telling newly arrived suicide bombers that heaven has run out of virgins. Muhammad is defined by a crescent and star—not "Muhammad, peace be upon him," but a scheming conqueror of Christian Europe (and the universe). And in the most offensive cartoon, Muhammad is wearing a bomb-shaped turban, complete with burning fuse—a reference to the Aladdin story. Those who took offense at the cartoons viewed their publication as yet another instance of Western intolerance of and prejudice against Islamic culture ("Muhammad Cartoon Gallery," 2006).

In mid-November, some Danish fundamentalist imams set off on a journey through the Middle East. They took with them the 12 cartoons, 10 others from a November publication of the Danish *Weekend Avisen*, and three more of unknown origin (one showing Muhammad with a pig's nose). The imams' visit to the Middle East and their inclusion of additional incendiary cartoons were the major cause of the worldwide turmoil that ensued (Exum, 2007). In late January, the imam of the Grand Mosque of Mecca issued an ultimatum: "He who vilifies the Prophet should be killed." Thousands of angry demonstrators marched through the streets of Cairo, Karachi, Istanbul, Tehran, and several cities in Afghanistan. Danes were ordered to flee Lebanon after mobs burned the Danish consulates in Damascus and Beirut. The Danish cartoonists were threatened with beheading. On January 30, 2006, gunmen raided the European Union's office in Gaza, demanding an apology for allowing the paper to publish the cartoons. The Danish newspaper apologized, but Danish Prime Minister Anders Rogh Rasmussen defended freedom of speech as essential to democracy. In a show of support for freedom of the press, papers in Spain, Germany, Italy, and France reprinted the cartoons the following day.

The truth is not on the surface. The meaning is said to be a dispute over freedom of speech and freedom of religion, with both sides correct and the controversy unending. The media make cartoon publication and the violent aftermath the news frame, but the truth is not in the cartoons.

The truth on the deep level of human dignity is modernity. The *Jyllands-Posten* acts out of modernity without shame, and Muslim culture struggles over its encounter with it. Neither is giving the principle of human dignity priority. Neutrality and reason are modernity's values, not those of human dignity. Modernity, the post-medieval world, is industrial and scientific rather than agrarian. Modernity means secularism, experimentation, and procedures rather than norms from outside. Modernity is a majority culture that disrespects cultures outside it.

Modernist culture was the issue for Fleming Rose and the other newspapers that published the cartoons, that is, individual rights, and a utilitarian ethics that serves the majority rather than the few. And fanaticism is unacceptable in a modernist society. The religious belief of Islam is pre-modern, antiquated.

And there is a struggle over modernism for Islamic culture. Islam is being pushed to the world stage, engulfed by global technology, put into context with the ruling power of the industrial nations of the planet—modernist culture. The threat is not a brazen newspaper in Denmark but a majority culture seeking to destroy Islam's very rationale.

Regarding the ethics of human dignity, the *Jyllands-Posten* and the news organizations across Europe and North America, and for the violent of Muhammad's followers, the challenge is identical (Kunelius, 2009). The ethics of human dignity is the radical opposite of modernism's ideology. It reminds the *Jyllands-Posten* of the intrinsic worthiness of the human species instead of individual rights. To Islam, this ethics reminds them that all human beings are created in the image of Allah and therefore sacred. Instead of the shrill ideology of secular modernism, in opposition to the fundamentalist ideology of the pre-modern imams, ethical intercultural communication highlights the golden truth—all human beings have sacred status. The ethics of human dignity appeals to our universal common humanity rather than to Eurocentric ideology on the one hand and Islamic ideology on the other.

Instead of Fleming's modernist utilitarianism, and instead of Islam's divine commands, the ethics of human dignity considers the publishing of the cartoons unethical and the violent response also (cf. Debatin, 2007).

CONCLUSION

Intercultural communication ethics at this juncture has to respond to both the rapid globalization of communications and the reassertion of local identities. It is caught in the contradictory trends of cultural homogenization and cultural resistance. As we theorize the ethics of intercultural communications, it is the integration of globalization and ethnicity that is today's extraordinary challenge. Through the sacredness of life, we can make our way constructively at the intersection of the global and multicultural.

The socially responsible media are brought to judgment before the ultimate test: Do they sustain life, enhance it long term, contribute to human well-being as a whole? In other words, does intercultural discourse connect the issues to universal norms? Do reporters and editors graft the deeper questions underneath the stories of cultural struggle onto our human oneness? If so, our moral imagination is invigorated, and the ethical media worldwide enable readers and viewers and new media users to resonate with other human beings who also struggle in their consciences with human values of a similar sort. Media professionals have enormous opportunities for putting the universal protonorm to work—that is, the sacredness of life—when they live by the ethics of human dignity. In the process, they enlarge for cultures, races, and ethnic groups their understanding of what it means to be human.

NOTES

1. In his work on human rights and Asian values, China scholar William de Bary (1980) resists the "individualistic West" and "communitarian Asia" dualism. While endorsing the standard conclusion that Japan, Singapore, Taiwan, South Korea, and the People's Republic have been deeply influenced by Confucianism, he elaborates on the nuances and applications through the major dynasties in China and accounts for different kinds of allegiance to Confucianism in different periods (p. 13). He looks for evidences of Confucian humanity under various conditions. For China, two cases are of special interest to him as evidence of Confucian virtue congealed in *ren*: (1) Community schools in villages, outside the bureaucratic system, were rooted in both the moral uplift of the *Great Learning* and Confucian values (ch. 4, pp. 41–57). (2) The ritual of compacts (*xiangyue*) survived into the 20th century, where members of communities entered into a contract of voluntarianism, mutual aid in distress, rotating leadership, engagement in rites and customs to limit the intervention of the state in local affairs (ch. 5, pp. 58–59). These examples are "authentically Confucian" in that they illustrate "the wide range of efforts by Confucians to strengthen community life and build consensual fiduciary institutions" (p. 13) by acting out of common oneness (*ren*).

2. This summary of Hans Jonas is based on a fuller review of his "purposiveness of life" in Christians (1997, pp. 6–8).

3. Haydar Sadig has developed the most comprehensive understanding of the history and ethics of the Darfur controversy, including strategies for peace in Sudan and South Sudan (e.g., Sadig & Guta, 2011).

4. For a full account of Wounded Knee and Russell Means, see Christians, Fackler, and Ferré (2012, ch. 12). For Wounded Knee as a case study for ethics, see "Case 17: Ten Weeks at Wounded Knee," Christians et al. (2011). For background, see also the University of Illinois publication *The Politics of Hallowed Ground: Wounded Knee and the Struggle for Indian Sovereignty* (Gonzalez & Cook-Lynn, 1998).

5. For a complete filmography of Russell Means's acting and other media work, see http.www. russellmeans.com.

BIBLIOGRAPHY

Azzam, M. (2006, April). Cartoons, confrontation and a cry for respect. *The World Today, Research Library, 62*(4), 7–8.

Bell, D. (2008). *China's new Confucianism: Politics and everyday life in a changing society.* Princeton, NJ: Princeton University Press.

Byun, D.-H., & Lee, K. (2002). Confucian values, ethics and legacies in history. In S. Bracci & C. Christians (Eds.), *Moral engagement in public life: Theorists for contemporary ethics* (pp. 73–96). Berlin: Peter Lang.

Christians, C. (1995). The naturalistic fallacy in contemporary interactionist-interpretive research. *Studies in Symbolic Interactionism, 19*, 125–130.

Christians, C. (1997). The ethics of being in a communications context. In C. Christians & M. Traber (Eds.), *Communication ethics and universal values* (pp. 3–23). Thousand Oaks, CA: Sage.

Christians, C. (2008). The ethics of universal being. In S. J. A. Ward & H. Wasserman (Eds.), *Media ethics beyond borders: A global perspective* (pp. 6–23). Johannesburg: Heinemann. Reprinted by New York: Routledge (2010).

Christians, C. (2011). Cultural diversity and moral relativism in communication ethics. In A. G. Nikolaev (Ed.), *Ethical issues in international communication* (pp. 23–34). New York: Palgrave Macmillan.

Christians, C., Fackler, M. & Ferré, J. (2012). *Ethics for public communication: Defining moments in media history.* New York: Oxford University Press.

Christians, C., Fackler, M., Richardson, K. B., Kreshel, P., & Woods, R. (2011). *Media ethics: Cases and moral reasoning* (9th ed.). New York: Pearson.

Cortese, A. J. (1990). *Ethnic ethics: The restructuring of moral theory.* Albany: State University of New York Press.

de Bary, W. T. (1998). *Asian values and human rights: A Confucian communitarian perspective.* Cambridge, UK: Cambridge University Press.

Debatin, B. (2007). *De Karikaturenstreit und die Pressefreiheit: Wert- und Normenkonflikte in der globalen Medienkultur. [The Cartoon Debate and Freedom of the Press: Value and Norm Conflict in Global Media Culture.]* Stuttgart: LIT Verlag.

Exum, A. (2007). Arabic-language media and the Danish cartoon crisis. *Media Development, 2*, 30–33.

Fleischacker, S. (1992). *Integrity and moral relativism.* Leiden, Netherlands: E. J. Brill.

Glasser, T. L., Awad, I., & Kim, J. W. (2009). The claims of multiculturalism and journalism's promise of diversity. *Journal of Communication, 59*(1), 57–78.

Gonzalez, M., & Cook-Lynn, E. (1998). *The politics of hallowed ground: Wounded Knee and the struggle for Indian sovereignty.* Urbana: University of Illinois Press.

Habermas, J. (1984). *The theory of communicative action. Vol. I: Reason and the rationalization of society.* Trans. T. McCarthy. Boston, MA: Beacon Press.

Habermas, J. (1990). *Moral consciousness and communicative action.* Trans. C. Lenhardt & S. W. Nicholsen. Cambridge, MA: MIT Press.

Habermas, J. (1993). *Justification and application: Remarks on discourse ethics.* Trans. C. Cronin. Cambridge, MA: MIT Press.

Hickey, N. (1973, December 8). Only the sensational stuff got on the air. *TV Guide*, December 8, p. 34. For details of and community on this case, see the other three articles in Hickey's series: Was the truth buried at Wounded Knee? (December 1, pp. 7–12); Cameras over here! (December 15, pp. 43–49); Our media blitz is here to stay (December 22, pp. 21–23).

Jonas, H. (1984). *The imperative of responsibility [Macht oder Ohnmacht der Subjektivität? Das Lieb-Seele Problem im Vorfeld des Prinzips Verantwortung]*. Chicago: University of Chicago Press.

Kuhn, T. S. (1996). *The structure of scientific revolutions* (3rd ed.) Chicago: University of Chicago Press.

Kunelius, R. (2009). Lessons of being drawn in: On global free speech, communication theory and the Mohammed cartoons. In A. Kierulf & H. Rønning (Eds.), *Freedom of speech abridged? Cultural, legal and philosophical challenges* (pp. 139–151). Gøteborg, Sweden: University of Gothenburg Nordicom.

LeCompte, M. D., & Shensul, J. J. (2015). *Ethics in ethnography: A mixed methods approach* (2nd ed.). Lanham, MD: Alta Mira Press.

McDevitt, M. (2010). Journalistic influence in moral mobilization. In B. Mody (Ed.), *The geopolitics of representation in foreign news: Explaining Darfur* (pp. 45–63). Lanham, MD: Rowman & Littlefield.

Means, R., & Wolf, M. J. (1995). *Where white men fear to tread: The autobiography of Russell Means*. New York: St. Martin's.

Mody, B. (2010). *The geopolitics of representation in foreign news: Explaining Darfur*. Lanham, MD: Rowman & Littlefield.

Muhammad Cartoon Gallery. (2006, May 30). *Online Human Events*. Retrieved from http://www.humaneventsonline.com/sarticle.php?id=12146

Onishi, N. (2015, June 15). Sudanese leader's bid to avoid arrest is tested in South Africa. *New York Times*, pp. A1, A7.

Paul, E. F., Miller, F. D., & Paul, J. (Eds.). (1994). *Cultural pluralism and moral knowledge*. Cambridge, UK: Cambridge University Press.

Peukert, H. (1981). Universal solidarity as the goal of communication. *Media Development*, *28*(4), 10–12.

Ross, S. D., & Lester, P. M. (2011). *Images that injure: Pictorial stereotypes in the media* (3rd ed.). New York: Praeger.

"Russell Means, the Movie." (2014, January 23). *Indian Country Today Media Network.com*.

Ruta, C. (2014, June 18). Habermas: A philosopher for the public. *DW Akademie*.

Sadig, H. B., & Guta, H. A. (2011). Peace communication in Sudan: Toward infusing a new Islamic perspective. In R. S. Fortner & P. M. Fackler (Eds.), *The handbook of global communication and media ethics* (pp. 617–622). Malden, MA: Wiley Blackwell.

Taylor, C., Appiah, K. A., Habermas, J., Rockefeller, S. C., Walzer, M., & Wolf, S. (1994). *Multiculturalism: Examining the politics of recognition*. Princeton, NJ: Princeton University Press.

Ward, S. J. A. (2015). *Radical media ethics: A global approach*. Malden, MA: Wiley Blackwell.

Ward, S. J. A., & Wasserman, H. (Eds.). (2010). *Media ethics beyond borders: A global perspective*. New York: Routledge.

Wiredu, K. (1996). *Cultural universals and particulars: An African perspective*. Bloomington: Indiana University Press.

Wolterstorff, N. (2008). *Justice: Rights and wrongs*. Princeton, NJ: Princeton University Press.

CHAPTER NINETEEN

How Is Intercultural Communication Possible?

BO SHAN

How we communicate with the other, that is, how communication bridges the chasms of gender, nationality, race, ethnicity, language, and culture, has been a core issue puzzling the intercultural communication of human beings. It contains four fundamental questions: Am I able to communicate? How can the relationship of "me, us, and them" be made free and balanced? How are both cultural diversity and unity possible? And how should we understand the media's dual cultural role as bridge and gap? Based on these four issues, we can rely on multidimensional cross-cultural communicative thinking to explore the possible solutions for intercultural communication.

1. AM I ABLE TO COMMUNICATE?

Communication, like "logos," has become a term covering the reality of today's world. It retains the meaning of "common" from the Latin word *communis*, but it actually represents a typical concept from the 20th century. Much different from the previous turning points of the centuries, people took trains and boats, made phone calls, listened to phonographs, watched movies, and walked into the 20th century with the rhythm of the industrialized, urbanized, and commercialized age. However, the paradox is that we also fell into the chasm of communication at the same time as we walked into the legendary world created by communication technologies. Therefore, we had to resort to war and violence many times more than previous ages to resolve the conflicts between different cultures. The unbearable estrangement and isolation among people in modern civilizations, an expansion of the communicative chasm with the rapid progress of communication technology—and the communication problems between different nationalities, groups, religions, classes, male and female, old and young—all accumulated gradually so that people had to depend on communication. Thinkers and scholars of different disciplines—Marxists, Freudian psychologists, existentialists, feminists, anti-imperialists, sociologists, linguistic philosophers—all tried to study the tragedies, comedies, and absurdities of communication failures (Peters, 1999, p. 263).

Communication study, even at its early stage, presented a dramatic picture, as many modern writers including T. S. Eliot, Hemingway, and Kafka joined in discussing communication failures. Then communication study gradually concerned the production, processing, and effects of signs, the sharing of meanings, and the political economy of communication. Positivist scholars constructed scientific laws of communication, information researchers focused on the human capability to receive and absorb information, and humanists designed a communication utopia while at the same time criticizing industrialized communication. The meaning of communication has thus become more and more pluralistic, containing various parts of signs, languages, narrations, interactivities, relations, feedbacks, transmissions, contacts, and exchanges. It not only defines the transmission of information in natural spaces but also the communication-and-exchange relations of human beings, the shared cultural worlds of people, social interactive rituals, and the subsistence from and re-creation of culture.

However, communication has become complicated and confusing in three intercultural contexts: First, in the context of "different cultures," how can we equally know the other yet reflect ourselves? Second, across cultures or in the "cross-cultural domains," how can we start dialogue and collaborations that engage cultural diversity and interaction? Third, in the "trans-cultural" or "beyond cultural" context,[1] how can we create vital public cultural spaces beyond divisive cultural debris? Maybe everything is possible as long as we are ready to explore. In terms of communicating with the other, we would more likely agree with John Durham Peters (1999), who regards communication as an adventure without guarantees (p. 253). We aspire to communication, hope to talk to others with open hearts and also be understood by others. Sadly, such delightful communication is rare compared with awkward talks or even the desperate failure of communicating with others. Typically, we step into an isolated world full of misunderstanding, prejudice, discrimination, arrogance, and fraud.

Therefore, we have to admit that communication's role as bridge is actually an illusion, while communication's expansion of gaps is more often a cruel reality. Like the Little Match Girl of Andersen's fairytales, we also try to warm ourselves with prayers and hope but fail to expel real coldness and ignorance. We then, on one hand, start fantasies of communicating with angels, saints, ancestors, and heaven, and finally transform into an illusive self by relying on "telepathy"—"the transmission of ideas from one brain to the other without the help of any already known channels of meaning." We rely on "telepthesia," which allows people who are culturally distant to perceive shared meanings. On the other hand, we try to look for a realistic way of "pseudo-communication" by enduring differences, escaping from freedom, or giving up our own personalities. During the communicative experiences with people from diverse cultural backgrounds, our tragic destiny is even worse in that the competitive relations of cultural power constructed by the epistemological dichotomy of "us" and "them" evolve into dominant relations of cultural power. Or our communicative experiences fall into the absurd stage depicted by Raymond Williams that we neither speak to others nor communicate with others, with the result that our conversations are perhaps more like talking to ourselves in front of others (Williams, 1989, p. 12). The theme song of the 2008 Beijing Olympics "You and me, heart by heart" expressed the theme of intercultural communication and has the good aspiration of removing the dilemma of the subject-and-object dichotomy. But this good aspiration turned out to be illusory when certain political issues intervened.

These realities give us a reason to question whether I am able to communicate. The doubt itself reflects a rational mind that at least indicates that we will try to look for new ways to communicate. However, Peters correctly denied this possibility by saying that we should ask not whether we are able to communicate, but whether we can care about each other and treat each other fairly and leniently (Peters, 1999, p. 273). His intention is to change the perspective of the question from self-centered subjective communication to intersubjective communication. The issue then becomes the question of whether I have the moral ability for intersubjective communication. Our doubt reveals the human mind by seeking moral values, discovering the moral need of caring about each other, and improving our morality of mutual care to rescue human communication. But how our moral rationality applies to the communication process is still a problem to be resolved. One thing worth noting is that human communication is not merely a moral issue but also a cultural, social, linguistic, political, media, and psychological issue. To simplify a complicated issue into a moral issue would possibly fall into the shallow pattern of preaching and resort to a utopian imagination.

Whether I am able to communicate is indeed a problem of practical reason or a problem of moral reason in communication. It was actually proposed much earlier by Kant when he was thinking about the difference of the other. A cosmopolitan citizen should think about and act toward the other from the following three aspects: first, think independently; second, think from the other's perspective; and third, do not violate one's real thoughts (Sandkül-her, 2003). Influenced by Kant, Henri Bergson (2008) introduced the idea "politeness of spirit" or "experience the other's life, forget oneself" (p. 23). The subjective moral value of "respecting others" has transferred to "thinking from others," which means I should not treat others from the good will of my own culture (such as freedom, quality, and love in Western cultures and benevolence, righteousness, manners, wisdom, and credit in Chinese culture) but understand what kind of good will others need. However, how would this become possible in intercultural communication?

Based on human nature, the fundamental reason that I am able to com-municate and interact with others is because I am free. I have the ability of free choice, respect the others' right of free choice, and therefore reach the unlimited possibility of intercultural subsistence and self-development. On this premise, all motivations for moral behavior in intercultural communica-tion lie in one's freedom to surmount the constraints of the actual self. These constraints include desires for possessing materials and controlling others and restrictions from one's personality, habits, cultural prejudice, and customs. To surmount these constraints requires that we truly understand the other's cul-ture and diverse cultures so we can jump out of our own cultural prejudice. Surmounting these controls means further that to maintain our self-respect, we confirm the possibility of self-cultural creation and unlimited develop-ment. In the freedom perspective, we respect others as we look for the self-developing general benevolence to think from the others' point of view; we cast off the prejudice of self-centered thinking and the confusion of no think-ing as though it prevents pride and bias. The moral behavior of respecting others is expressed by searching for all possible cultural perspectives and the creating of new cultures.

In Jürgen Habermas's communicative rationality, I have the awareness of moral rationality. My rationality is not only a purposive rationality (or instru-mental rationality) but also a communicative rationality. The former presumes that we influence others intentionally to achieve certain goals while the latter presumes that we all have a common communicative rationality and willingly seek truth through interactive communication. If this communication process can avoid oppressive social powers, and all people involved in this process can have the same chance to act through words of their free-will choices and mutually question the authenticity and rationality of their words, then effec-tive communication can be achieved (Habermas, 1994, p. 218). Here I, as the subject of communication rationality, am not the self-centered subject of instrumental rationality but the subject of mutual communication, the subject of mutual respect and openness in the debate of ideas. Therefore, this is the essence of and an ideal realm of human communication. This form of human communication constructs a communicative value based on intersubjectivity and becomes a powerful critique of the distorted communication caused by the intervention of oppressive social powers and pseudo-communication caused by the suppression of the communicative ability of the underprivileged.

Under the circumstances of communicative rationality, I should adapt to a concrete understanding toward other cultures. As expressed in anthropological terms, this adaptation means "to have contextualized understanding toward the local knowledge of other cultures" (Geertz, 1973). Ethnographic interviewees look for "encountering cultures and sub-cultures of different views." For example, they have to be aware of differences between the already-known cultures and now-experienced new cultures and have to be open toward the totally different cultures. This is the basis of intercultural communication, but how would it be possible? Theoretically, "to have contextualized understanding toward the local knowledge of other cultures" is only a one-dimensional understanding and therefore does not necessarily lead to two-dimensional interactive understanding.

We then need to discover the possibility of communication from the idea of "reciprocal understanding" in anthropology (Le Pichon, 1995). This means that only understanding from dialogue and collaboration can go beyond the constraints regarding the understanding of other cultures as knowledge and interests, and therefore there is the possibility of constructing intercultural communication relationships.

We could also look for the possibility of intercultural communication in the sociologist's concept of "reciprocal interdependence," which means that group collaborations are achieved through mutual adaptation and interactivity through the continuing pursuit of new information and ideas so as to gradually open visions for accomplishing tasks (Thompson, 1967). Collaborations are accomplished because we integrate resources of knowledge related to present goals and together work on strategies and plans (Graham, 1995). At the same time, people in communications have a kind of pro-social emotion that includes shame, guilt, sympathy, the sensitivity of social punishment, and the expectation of punishment to betrayers. This pro-social emotion would urge individuals relying on constructive communication to achieve collaborations.

Why would people have this pro-social emotion? Economists provide another way of understanding it. If people do not have this pro-social emotion, we will all become anti-social no matter how much we try to strengthen social contact through legal and formal mechanisms, and human society would no longer exist. Pro-social emotion comes from the trust built through frequent communications, and this emotion shapes the individual's altruistic tendency to reduce free-rider behavior. Groups can then reduce the cost and maintain a higher advantage in external competitions. Therefore pro-social emotion can be expressed, diffused, and inherited (Bowles & Gintis, 2004, pp. 17–28). However, pro-social emotion can bring damage to individuals too and result in their paying a higher cost. Therefore, to maintain the inherent advantage of pro-social emotion, groups must have certain individuals who require equality of collaboration and punish those who are not cooperative despite the high price they have to pay for this. These individuals have a strong reciprocity.

2. HOW CAN THE RELATIONSHIP OF "ME, US, AND THEM" BE MADE FREE AND HARMONIOUS?

In our daily communication "I" act upon my identity in a group and define people by in-group and out-group, or us and them. For example, we are American, they are Chinese; we are white and they are black; we are men and they are women; we are heterosexual and they are homosexual; we are Christians and they are Buddhists (Lie, 2015), and so forth. These classifications play a positive role in defining a person's social position. But they also bring negative consequences, such as intergroup discrimination, racism, nationalism, political conflict, and violence, all of which are significant social problems hindering our development.

Although the most difficult thing in our lives is to "know ourselves," "I" always tries to express "who I am" (such as I am Chinese) in interpersonal communication. I try to define my existence with certain group characters (such as Chinese characteristics) and differentiate myself from others who do not share the same group features (such as non-Chinese characteristics). What I do not know is that the unique "me" has been replaced by a collective "me" and a conceptual "me," and that real "me" has been shielded by "us"; that is, an individual has been shielded by a group. From a sociological perspective, a society is constructed by the communication of individuals. Therefore, I have to give up part of my personality to be consistent with the group's public values when I am in a group, which means I not only examine others from the group's perspective but also define myself from it, too. At the same time, communication takes place among individuals of different social identities. I am unable to understand myself if the reference is myself. Instead, I have to find out the possible potential "me" through communication with others.

But to maintain my freedom, "I" cast off social norms and live across different groups. Thus "I" keep a distance with the original group and start to reflect the original "I." Influenced by "group subconsciousness," this would mean an essential psychological change, and I would involuntarily lose my self-consciousness to become a being of low intelligence. My personality is suppressed by groups to a various extent, and I would allow the group spirit to replace my own even without any outside force. Therefore, my personality reveals more of those inherited primitive instincts and those simplified conformity mindsets. I accept willingly paranoid and prejudiced control and never agree that truth, especially "social truth," can only be "grown through discussions." I always tend to transfer complicated issues into simple concepts on the style of slogans and endow my ideals and prejudice with imperious qualities when I realize my opinions are in the dominant position. If not, I will have an inner anxiety and cannot help giving up my stances. I realize, though I am aware of the inner group problem, that those who are skeptical and tend to explain problems through reasoning and discussion have no status in groups (Le Bon, 2008).

I am, without a doubt, a socialized being. Communications between me and innumerable other individuals compose society. Communication occurs among individuals of different social distance, but I always look for easier conversation targets. Thus communication mostly occurs among similar individuals, and their effective communications produce more homogeneous thoughts, attitudes, and behaviors in individuals. This type of communication gradually becomes steady and shapes certain cultural and social structures. Without much trace, "I" becomes "us" then and establishes a stable relationship with groups. When groups employ homogeneous communication to be more influential and to enforce a more stable social structure, "I" then has to disappear into groups to enjoy a steady mind and the pleasure of social trust and cooperation.

The East and the West have clear cultural differences in how "I" fits into groups. In the West, "I" am an independent being relative to others. There is an unavoidable distance between us so that individuals compete and cooperate through social contracts. Western individuals form various types of reciprocal groups to compete for economic, social, and cultural capital, or escape from freedom and frustration to build communities whose homogeneity and stability lie in social contracts. While in the East, I am an insignificant and humble being represented by relationships with others, and I do not have absolute value. Individual value lies in relationships (including family ties, ethnic, national and religious relations, and so forth), while group homogeneity and stability rely on beliefs and relationships.

However, whether in the East or in the West, there is an internal intensive relation between individuals and groups. Individuals grow self-perception and self-image through communication; they present and exchange their identities by communication so that their identities can be manifested in groups and networks. Thus the relational identity of me with others is represented through interactive deliberation, which is beyond individuals to form group identity and is therefore identified as inner group membership (Hecht, 1993, pp. 76–82).

On the one hand, individuals have a sense of belonging and a determined expression of "who I am," while on the other hand, due to the stereotyped and labeled process of fitting into groups, individuals also fall into suppressive status and lose their ability to reflect and create, and also their awareness and capability of intercultural communication. "I" am not a being who could have free communication with other beings. More than that, "I," possessed by group spirit, develop an illusion that "our" cultural values, spirits, beliefs, customs, and moral principles would be solely most supreme. Then I grow an "authoritarian personality" full of prejudice and national superiority, which tragically leads to antagonism and the exclusion of other groups. Therefore, how to maintain a harmonious relationship between individuals and groups and how to make free communication among people possible have become the fundamental propositions of identity in communication research.

Identity on the whole has individual, societal, and group attributes, which means the communication of personal identity is actually a trinitarian activity combining personal identity, group identity, and cross-group identity. As "I" have free will, I can express my identity freely and at the same time belong to a certain group, share meanings and values with others, and also live across different groups, realize personal values, make unique creations, and adapt into social cultures through my cross-group identities. For instance, I can choose to live with an American cultural group or an Arabic cultural group while at the same time retaining characteristics of a Chinese cultural group. I can join in a group of cultural diasporas or return to local cultures. However, the more freedom I pursue, the heavier pressure I have to bear. "I," regarded as a "stranger," have to face double disavowal and feel repeated loneliness because of the expansion of "social distance." So how "I" develop intercultural sensitivity—a capability to deal with cultural differences flexibly in the intercultural context—how to conquer anxiety and uncertainty to eliminate prejudice from different groups, and how to process equal face-to-face negotiation become key problems of whether "I" can have communication freedom.

However, the problem is not over yet, as the biases hidden deeply in our consciousness such as Orientalism, neo-racism, fundamentalism, and flowing consumerism often pop out in front of "me." This urges people to change power dominating relations among different races and dispel various power dominances through institutional force. But struggle is merely a means of intergroup communication; harmony is the purpose. In this sense, struggle is not considered wisdom, because both sides, confined by self-interest or inner group interest, demarcate and entrench their cultural domains without surpassing themselves. On the contrary, harmony is the wisdom that not only distinguishes who I am and who they are but also thinks beyond diverse groups on how to resume the freedom of living across groups and what our collaborations can achieve. Everyone could become a fundamental-ist in conflicts when we continuously reaffirm those solid boundaries of "us" and "them," friends and foes, God's elect and the cursed, the superior and the inferior. In striving for group interest, we gradually adapt into blurred cultural boundaries caused by flowing consumerism and fall into the power system of capital. We then forget the values of culture but shield with cultural nihilism the relations of power dominance in cultural groups.

Wisdom is to deal with the problem of how the relationship of "me, us, and them" becomes free and harmonious. The possible solutions for bring-ing wisdom back might be summarized as follows: First, advocate cultural pluralism or "differences" while also supporting the individual's freedom to approve or disapprove certain cultures, the freedom to approve multi-cultures, freedom to approve certain parts of particular cultures and disapprove other parts, and, most importantly, imposing none of one's own choices on oth-ers (Qin, 2004). Second, build the equal status of communicative groups within specific contexts, maintaining intergroup communication, observing and adjusting the effectiveness of intergroup communication. Third, reduce the potential tensions of intergroup communication and the negative con-sequences of intergroup cooperation due to diversities and differences, and a better understanding of and harnessing of diversities. Fourth, dispel the power relations of dominant groups by the systematic power of laws, poli-cies, and management, monitor the biochemical crisis caused by assimilation, isolation, and marginalization, and protect diversity and the interactivity of ethnic groups.

3. HOW ARE BOTH CULTURAL DIVERSITY AND UNITY POSSIBLE?

The awkwardness of human beings' aspirations and the failure of communica-tion are reflected by the word "Babel," which originates from the 11th chapter of the Bible. In the Babel story, after the flood, people surviving from Noah's ark tried to build the tower of Babel to meet God, who was so angry about this that he disarranged human languages and accents. Thousands of languages then appeared in the world, each of which has various dialects and accents, making it impossible to reconcile thinking. Thus discrepancies emerged among cultures, and problems of disagreements and suspicions came one after another, so that communication became an everlasting difficulty for human beings. The word "Babel" means "chaos" in Hebrew, which is the real portrayal of human communication. The movie *Babel* digs out the allegorical meaning of this biblical story and displays the chaos of modern communication: Two kids shot an American tourist unintentionally when playing, and the accident became political in the Arabic country of Morocco, where the bewildering communication finally dragged the world into terrorist attacks.

Though suffering from "chaos," humans should thank God for diverse cultures and lives. It is God's worry of humans replacing him that actually stopped the human race's foolish ambition and the potential cultural exhaustion caused by homogeneity of languages, thought, and behavior. After hard exploration, humans have gradually achieved a consensus about cultural diversity. Sociologists in the industrialized and colonized 19th century started to realize humanity's interdependence, and anthropologists hesitated between cultural relativism (equality of different cultures) and cultural universalism in understanding cultural diversity.

In the post-colonial era of the 1970s, ethnic minorities, especially national minorities and immigrant ethnic groups, were required frequently to recognize their cultural identities and tolerate cultural differences (Kymlicka, 1995; Mattelart, 2014), which made "cultural diversity" an international issue. Ever since the end of the 20th century, UNESCO has introduced cultural diversity into its organizational principles and regarded it as the major theoretical support for maintaining a balanced "cultural geographical system." At the Thirty-First United Nations Congress in 2001 in Paris, representatives from different countries passed the "Universal Declaration on Cultural Diversity" in which the first article pointed out that "cultural diversity" is "the common heritage of humanity" and is as necessary for humankind as biodiversity is for nature (Mattelart, 2005, pp. 11–14).

Comparing cultural diversity with biodiversity reveals the positive significance of an "ecology" mindset. Ecology ponders how organisms maintain a complicated social contract for quantity and distribution and emphasizes how the interactivity of different elements produces a balanced and healthy environment (Postman, 2000, p. 2). But the comparison is also clumsy because it reminds us of a "chain of being" and the survival of the fittest. This then would introduce the relations of power dominance into cultural diversity, so that so-called diversity would tend to preserve cultural differences in competitions and would tend to bring in the power of cultural dominance as the order of diverse cultures. Therefore, we mistakenly regard the American cultural melting pot as diversity when it actually aims for assimilation. We take racial segregation, which is based on absoluteness of racial and cultural differences, for diversity. And we consider the structure of mainstream and peripheral culture as diversity. In fact, the comprehensive understanding of cultural diversity is to preserve the right of cultural difference and equal competition while at the same time to protect the right of interactive cultural communication and free creation.

Following the logic of the ecological mindset, a UNESCO report depicted the relation of diversity and unity as "one of the characteristics of development, the balance of diversity and unity, is significantly important to the future of human beings" (Lazlo, 1993, p. 1). These words reflect the political rationality of culture and seek perfect format and structure. However, the problem of the unity of cultural diversity does not lie in the perfection of format and structure but faces a more serious problem: Who dominates the unity of cultural diversity? Or, what sort of powers are relevant? To whom is unity meaningful? Why does the policy of pluralism—which actually allows a privileged few to control our economy, society, and culture while most of the marginalized are still marginalized—become a hypocritical political strategy? When facing these questions, we sense that diverse culture is in danger of certain ideologies such as universalism and neo-racism.

One of the hidden but also evident possibilities of the unity of cultural diversity is that diversified cultures are united by a power-dominant system of ideologies. This analysis is meaningful in rethinking social structures and regaining human subjectivity. But on the other hand, it also denies the possibility of intercultural communication. If people are just prisoners of their thoughts and follow ideologies to communicate, understand, and speak, then the puppet subjects of ideologies do not need intercultural communication but only to be conquered by and obey certain ideologies. In this sense, intercultural communication becomes totally unrealizable due to ideological hegemony, and therefore it turns out to be a false proposition. We are trying hard to look for universal values as the foundation for intercultural communication but finally find that universal values are shrouded by ideologies. In the end, our consciousness either is decided or conquered so that cultures become homogeneous, or it is differentiated or conflicted so that cultural differences become the front lines of public conflicts.

What we can do is realize that diverse cultures united by a power-dominant system of ideologies is just one noteworthy possibility. It is neither life's entire part nor cultures' destiny. One proposition closer to cultural life itself should be: diversified cultures are united by an "articulated entirety." According to Stuart Hall, "articulation" means that under certain conditions, we "can" articulate two different elements into an integrated format while the retaining rings are not forever necessarily bound, decided, absolute, and essential. The discourse of "integration" is actually the articulation of different and dissimilar elements that do not have absolute attributions and therefore are re-articulated in different ways (Tang, 1998). In this sense, unity is not the result but a process of articulation, a process of "seeking for unity from differentiations." That is to say, despite the existence of differences and splits, the fact that diversity has become an essential character of culture does not mean the end of meaning but the production of meaning by articulations (Slack, 1996). Therefore, our cultural identities are not preexisting endowments but articulations of cultural competition. Articulation can make ideologies become shared meanings, but ideologies cannot predetermine the results of articulation since people can remove the "retaining rings" at any time. So articulation also implies hope because it is not unchanging, and it can be removed and reconstructed.

From the perspective of articulation, we can understand the possible unity of cultural diversity as follows:

> First, the possibility of the unity of cultural diversity lies in the process of cultural adaptation. One challenge people often face is to establish a long-term connection between their spiritual worlds (needs, ideas, and so forth) and the outside world (environment, others, and so forth). We deal with the challenge under specific contexts where individuals shape their surrounding environments (every one affects surrounding things) and are shaped by surrounding environments (every one changes with surrounding things). The encounters between immigrants and members of the host country become a plural cultural context where immigrants' cultural adaptation strategies will be articulated through contradictions and conflicts with the requests of host country members toward the immigrants' adaptation. People of different cultural backgrounds try to win their alliances through building up cultural identities, which is the way of assembling split cultures and also for hegemonic struggles. "Co-culture" and "third culture" therefore become a possible pattern of cultural adaptation.

Second, the possibility of the unity of cultural diversity also lies in the fact that languages, as cultural codes, have the natural tendency of seeking generality among discrepancies. That is to say, though linguistic forms are different, translation makes possible the communication of people who speak different languages in various fields. This proves that human intellectual perception has generality, or intercultural communication would be a "mission impossible." The character and confines of ethnic and group discourses and the human capability of overcoming obstacles of language and thought through criticizing and reflecting their own thinking to build up intellectual generalities would be a possible way of achieving unity for cultural diversity.

Third, the possibility of unity for cultural diversity also lies in our intercultural capability that is represented by how individuals can create interactive cultural consensus based on specific contexts, personalities, goals, and expectations, and by empathy, that is, the ability to think, feel, experience, and express their emotions from the stances of others.

4. HOW SHOULD WE UNDERSTAND THE MEDIA'S DUAL CULTURAL ROLE AS BRIDGE AND GAP?

In mediated societies, interpersonal relations surge. On the one hand, the distance of time and space between us shortens or even disappears, and communications between us and others are much more frequent. We have more freedom no matter with whom we choose to communicate or the nature of our communications. In this sense, communication extends boundlessly to become a "bridge." On the other hand, the semiotic reality created by the media and the information, knowledge, and symbolic saturations caused by the communication explosion have separated people from objective realities and from real histories and cultures. As a consequence, we are fond of a certain type of communication rather than a different one. We prefer a certain kind of perception and ignore the integrated one. We wander around the visual constructions of culture promoted by the media and walk away from the real contacts of cultures. We get used to "face-to-face" communication constructed by the media and lose real face-to-face interactive communications among people. From these perspectives, communication has an omnipresent "gap."

We feel more acutely that the media-created environment has changed the world from the original survival and development mode of humans. The media have also changed our cognitive schema toward the world and have shaken to some extent the development foundation of traditional society. Particularly through the research of media ecology we found that different media affect our perceptions, emotions, cognitions, and values all the time, forcing us to play different roles and construct our perceptions and behaviors. The "time-and-space bias" of Harold Innis, the "sensory preferences" represented by Marshall McLuhan's statement of "the medium is the message," or "technopoly" proposed by Neil Postman all refer to one proposition: The media are in control. We then have a new understanding: Media control and the mediated control hardly make humans free of the "caveman" designation. Even in that primitive age, human beings tried to pursue brightness and knowledge to become a rational person, and to harness one's emotions and desires. However, it can never be expected that technology, along the nature of rational control, sets, affects and dominates our social lives and transforms humans into the "cavemen" of mediated societies. The dual cultural role of media as both bridge and gap is actually two sides of the coin of media control: As a boundless bridge, it controls the channel, both means and ways, while as an omnipresent gap, it expands perceptual and cultural deviations.

Generally speaking, to separate rationality from human naturalness and enable rationality as an independent spirit was the achievement of the Greeks. As a result, science and the pursuit of science and technology became the greatest capacity of human beings. Humans took a big step forward but bore a loss, too, because the original integration of human beings was segmented. Independent rationality became regarded as a sacred part of humanness that breaks away from our animality and is beyond human corporeality, substance, and limitation. On the contrary, characterized by abstraction, indirectness, and universality, humans' rationality presents a binary opposition with irrationality and therefore gains validity as a control of irrationality.

In the *Phaedrus*, Plato designed the well-known myth about the soul to reveal the control of rationality: Rationality, as the driver of a two-wheeled horse-drawn chariot, grasps the reins of a white horse and a black horse. Representing human bravery and sentiment, the white horse is tamed to the order of rationality, while the black horse, representing desire and lust, follows the orders of whips. The most significant thing rationality has to control is human sentiment and lust through a technological imagination of reins and whips to shape a sacred and eternal human being. Embedding controls and coercive ideas in reins and whips symbolizes an extensive and intensive control of emotions and lusts, which in this way shows a control bias. Now from language, sign characters, print media, electronic media to the Internet, mediated technology, as the boundless reins and invisible whips, controls our emotional and cultural world.

Kant said humans' rationality, like a lithe pigeon, always longs for giving up our emotional world and flying freely (Kant, 2007). Actually the media are like a lithe pigeon flying with its free feathers in the human communication world. When the media pigeon feels the resistance of distance, it envisions communicating without distance; when it feels the resistance of differentiation, it tries to communicate within the vacuum of hearts. It is beyond people's emotional and cultural world and leads us into a symbolic world, a "pseudo-environment" and an abstract life. However, it never realizes that when all the resistances are gone, when abandoning the human sensory and cultural world, real communication will be dispelled as well, replaced by a biased communication and a suppositional community. Thus, in the mediated environment technology creates, intercultural communication becomes an essential pursuit.

The lithe pigeon of the media does not care about our reflection and critique but always tricks us into taking risks in communicating and leads us to indulge ourselves in faddish feelings, meaning sharing, and virtual interactions. In the end, it aggravates people's sensory and cultural preferences and dissolves intercultural communication in the following three ways: First, by producing popular and stylish meaning, demolishing cultural differences and making co-shared illusions through commercialized and market-oriented operational systems. Second, by exaggerating cultural differences, reducing abundant cultural connotations, ignoring cultural changes, intersections and penetrations, protruding essentialist and absolutist abstractions, and abandoning the human being's sensational and cultural worlds from the perspective of stereotyping, standardizing, and labeling representations. Third, by enveloping the human emotional and cultural world through the production of cultural interests and preferences, such as personalized media styles, "fans" of certain media contents, and stylish forms of communication. As a result, every culture is changed to media culture and every media culture to the directed culture of internal interests and preferences. Therefore, persons who seem to communicate with the world are actually living in the world of their own cultural interest and preference with the consequence that intercultural communication becomes a luxury illusion.

The above three ways can be summarized as mandatory and non-mandatory strategies of media control. For the mandatory strategy, media control defines concepts, knowledge, difference, and media space that people obtain from their social lives and produces cultural interests and preferences. For the non-mandatory strategy, it constructs homogeneous, abstract, and commercialized relationships of cultural dominance through tempting, deceptive, and fascinating media landscapes.

We can learn through these three ways that the dual role of media as bridge and gap actually contains the governance concept of technological rationality, which is an anti-human governance. To make intercultural communication possible, this anti-human governance of media technology has to be eliminated and its rational bias resisted. It means primarily to return to the concept of "the complete human" and dispel the one-dimensional idea of imagining humans as rational or irrational. One has to know that the person, controlled either by rationality or by desire and emotion, is a partial person. Though moderate rationalism is helpful for any society and any age, we have to understand profoundly the internal and possible limitations of rationality. We need to see that conventions and taboos will appear when a society is controlled and managed by rationality. We would then involuntarily have less and less thinking, or even stop thinking at all. The real need for social dynamics is the "overall, free development of people," that is, a complete person who is absolutely not a "lonely self" but a lively individual establishing various relations with the world and actively interacting with society. This is not a "passive self" led by the media landscape and technical reason, but subjects of communication who are fully developing their natural potential and social relations.

SOLUTIONS FOR AN INTERCULTURAL COMMUNICATION MINDSET

Intercultural communication changes people's way of thinking. We can imagine "hell is other people"—and estrangements between people are common and universal due to the failure of communication—but this will confine our freedom of communication. If we want to restore our communicative freedom, we have to recognize that the failure of communication indicates its limitations under certain circumstances but also predicates the possible direction of communication. We will also have to know that our complaints about communication represent our infinite aspiration of eliminating estrangements between people. This kind of aspiration is widespread and universal in diversified groups, and constitutes a free sky for communication.

Following this train of thought, intercultural communication constructs another way of thinking. First, the subject-object mindset of "me and him" has to change into the intersubjectivity mindset of "me and you" with the logic that any communication should have intersubjectivity to become the content of communication subjects. The meaning of communication is not produced by subjects themselves but by subjects and intersubjects, since in interpersonal communication, we see ourselves in terms of others and see others in terms of ourselves.

In the second place, intercultural communication converts intersubjectivity into inter-culturality to build up a cultural reciprocal structure. It improves every individual's capacity to surpass oneself, interact with other cultures, and construct a complete self-consciousness.

Third, intercultural communication makes cultural interactivity the basis of "starting from the other" by believing that the human direct-life reality is to communicate with others. Therefore, a subjective perspective cannot solve the problem of encountering others, and it is only a unitary angle of viewing issues. While an objective and universal perspective means observing things from no angle at all, only "starting from the other" can suspend one's preference and then be able to see, hear, and understand the other to construct a multidimensional perspective of culture.

Fourth, intercultural communication constructs intercultural political problems from free cultural pluralism by protecting cultural diversity and the cultural right of choice and by opposing cultural segregation and isolation under the guise of cultural diversity. It tries to convert the passive communication freedom of avoiding other's interference, enjoying independent and equal space in the positive communicative freedom of seeking the balance of right and obligation through cooperation.

Fifth, intercultural communication is regarded as a practical reason to pursue ethical fusion between cultures, respecting the differentiations and histories of cultural ethics but also trying to construct the diversified interactive relationships of cultural ethics. And that leads to a sixth way of thinking in intercultural communication. It provides a contextual understanding toward other cultures and possible intersections between cultures. In so doing, it reveals potential clashes of cultures and builds up an interactive mechanism through cultural articulation.

Intercultural communication enriches the rationality and wisdom of communication, of exchange, transmission, and understanding in the open space of communication. It tells people who suffer from communication frustration that between us, there is no other way but to communicate, and that all possibilities emerge in practice.

NOTE

1. There are three different English concepts of the word "cross-culture": cross-cultural, inter-cultural, and trans-cultural. Therefore, the word actually consists of three kinds of cross-cultural study. Specifically, these three compound words are formed by the same root "cultural" with three different prefixes: "inter-," "cross-," and "trans-." Here, "inter-" typically includes "in the middle of," "between," or "in" and "inter-cultural" generally represents "differences between different cultures." "Cross-" mainly consists of "crossing," "through," or "crossover"; "cross-cultural" generally means "the common field of different cultures or cross-cultural territory," "involving a variety of cultures or cultural geographies." "Trans-" means to be more than the current state, and its dimensions can be imagined or transcendent; it mainly consists of "crossing," "through," "beyond," "be better than," "transformation." "Trans-cultural" usually means "suitable for a variety of cultures" and "beyond culture."

BIBLIOGRAPHY

Bergson, H. (2008). *La politesse*. Paris: Rivages Poche.

Bowles, S., & Gintis, H. (Eds.). (2004). The evolution of strong reciprocity: Cooperation in heterogeneous populations. *Theoretical Population Biology, 65*(1), 17–28.

Geertz, C. (1973). *The interpretation of cultures*. New York: Basic Books.

Graham, M. P. (Ed.). (1995). *Mary Parker Follett: Prophet of management*. Cambridge, MA: Harvard Business School.

Habermas, J. (1994). *The theory of communicative action*. vol. 1. Trans. T. McCarthy. Boston, MA: Beacon.

Hecht, M. L. (1993). A research odyssey: Toward the development of a communication theory of identity. *Communication Monographs, 60*, 76–82.

Kant, I. (2007). *Critique of pure reason*. Whitefish, MT: Kessinger.

Kymlicka, W. (1995). *Multicultural citizenship: A liberal theory of minority rights*. Oxford, UK: Oxford University Press.

Laszlo, E. (1993). *The multicultural planet—The report of a UNESCO International Expert Group*. Paris: Oneworld.

Le Bon, G. (2008). *The crowd: A study of the popular mind*. Teddington, UK: Echo Library.

Le Pichon, A. (1995, September 12–17). *The sound of the rain: Poetic reason and reciprocal understanding*. A Centennial Conference at International House: the University of Chicago.

Lie, S. (2015). "Messengers of the good news": Discourse of Chinese Indonesian evangelical Christian identity. *China Media Research, 11*(1), 87–98.

Mattelart, A. (2005). The cultural diversity: Between history and geopolitics. In B. Shan & Y. Shi (Eds.), *Intercultural communication* (pp. 11–14). Wuhan University Press.

Mattelart, T. (2014). "Diversity" policies, integration and internal security: The case of France. *Global Media & Communication, 10*(3), 275–287.

Peters, J. D. (1999). *Speaking into the air: A history of the idea of communication*. Chicago: University of Chicago Press.

Postman, N. (2000). *The humanism of media ecology*. Keynote speech at the first annual convention of the Media Ecology Association.

Qin, Hui (2004). Right of difference or right of cultural choice? Comment on *Le Racisme* by Pierre-André Taguief. *Nanfang Weekly*, no. 1384.

Sandkülher, H. J. (2003, November 20). Monde Arabe & Monde Occidental: Un dialogue philosophique par une approche transculturelle. *Journée de la Philosophie à L'UNESCO*, Paris : UNESCO.

Slack, J. D. (1996). The theory and method of articulation in cultural studies. In D. Morley & K.-H. Chen (Eds.), *Stuart Hall: Critical dialogues in cultural studies* (pp. 112–127). London: Routledge.

Tang, W. (1998). *Cultural study: Interviewing Hall*. Taipei: Yuan-Liou Publishing.

Thompson, J. D. (1967). *Organizations in action*. New York: McGraw-Hill.

Williams, R. (1989). Drama in a dramatized society." In A. O'Connor (Ed.), *Raymond Williams on television: Selected writings*. London: Routledge.

Contributors

Valerie Alia is Professor Emerita and a playwright living in Toronto, Canada. She was Distinguished Professor of Canadian Culture at Western Washington University, Running Stream Professor of Ethics and Identity at Leeds Metropolitan University, and a research associate of the Scott Polar Research Institute at Cambridge University. Her books include *The New Media Nation: Indigenous Peoples and Global Communication* and *Media Ethics and Social Change.*

David E. Boeyink is an Associate Professor (retired), Indiana University School of Journalism. Boeyink's research focuses on how journalists make decisions on controversial cases in the newsroom. He co-authored *Making Hard Choices in Journalism Ethics* (2010) with Sandra Borden.

Sandra L. Borden, Professor, School of Communication, co-directs Western Michigan University's Center for the Study of Ethics in Society. Her 2007 book, *Journalism as Practice: MacIntyre, Virtue Ethics and the Press*, won the Clifford G. Christians Ethics Research Award and the National Communication Association's top book award in applied ethics.

Clifford Christians (Ph.D., Litt.D., D.H.L.) is Research Professor of Communications, Professor of Journalism, and Professor of Media Studies Emeritus at the University of Illinois, Urbana-Champaign, where he was Director of the Institute of Communications Research and Head of the Ph.D. in Communications for 16 years. His recent publications as co-author include *Ethics for Public Communication, Normative Theories of the Media,* and *Communication Theories in a Multicultural World.*

Romayne Smith Fullerton, Ph.D., is an Associate Professor at the University of Western Ontario, Canada. She is an interdisciplinary scholar whose research interests and publications broadly encompass gender, minority issues, and journalism ethics. Along with Maggie Jones Patterson, she is writing a book about international crime coverage.

Hugues Hotier (Ph.D. in Linguistics, Ph.D. in Information and Communication Science) is Professor Emeritus at the University of Bordeaux, France. He is an adjunct professor at the International University of Dakar, Senegal. He researches mainly on intercultural communication and communication within business enterprises. His latest publication is *France Chine Interculturalité et communication* (October 2013).

Xinya Liu is a Ph.D. candidate, School of Journalism and Communication, Wuhan University. She was a visiting Ph.D. student at the University of Gothenburg, Sweden. Her research interests are comparative journalism and intercultural communication.

Xue Liu, Ph.D., is Assistant Professor, School of Journalism and Communication, and Researcher in the Center for Intercultural Research, Wuhan University. He was a Visiting Scholar and Freeman Fellow at the University of Illinois, Urbana-Champaign. His research interests are intercultural communication, comparative journalism, and international communication.

Xuewei Liu is Lecturer, School of International Education, and a Postdoctoral Fellow, College of Chinese Language and Literature, Wuhan University. Her Ph.D. and M.A. are from the School of Journalism and Communication, Wuhan University. Her research interests are intercultural communication, subcultural studies, new media and politics, and teaching Chinese as a second language.

Jack Lule, Professor and Chair of Journalism & Communication and Director of Global Studies at Lehigh University, is the author of *Globalization and Media: Global Village of Babel* (Rowman & Littlefield) and *Daily News, Eternal Stories: The Mythological Role of Journalism* (Guilford Press). He is also author of more than 50 scholarly articles and book chapters and the recipient of numerous teaching awards.

Donald Matheson is an Associate Professor in Media and Communication at the University of Canterbury, Aotearoa, New Zealand. He is the author of *Media Discourses* and the co-author of *Digital War Reporting.* He is co-editor of *Ethical Space: The International Journal of Communication Ethics* and writes on journalism practice, with particular emphasis on digital developments, ethics, and discourse practices.

Margaret Jones Patterson, Professor of Journalism at Duquesne University, does research in media ethics, gender, crime, and intercultural issues. She has co-authored three books, as well as articles, book chapters, and papers. She and Romayne Smith Fullerton are working on a book about crime coverage.

Patrick Lee Plaisance is a former U.S. journalist and a professor at Colorado State University. He is editor of the *Journal of Media Ethics* and is author of *Media Ethics: Key Principles for Responsible Practice* (Sage) and *Virtue in Media: The Moral Psychology of Excellence in News and Public Relations* (Routledge).

Chris Roberts (Ph.D., South Carolina, 2007), a longtime journalist, is now Associate Professor of Journalism at the University of Alabama. He is co-author (with Jay Black) of *Doing Ethics in Media: Theories and Practical Applications* (Routledge, 2011), and has published in *The Journal of Mass Media Ethics, Ethical Space: The International Journal of Communication Ethics,* and other journals.

Hemant Shah is Professor in the School of Journalism and Mass Communication at the University of Wisconsin–Madison. Shah's research is on the role of mass media in various types of social change, including construction of social identities, creation of racial anxiety, and the formation of social movements. He is the author of *Newspaper Coverage of Interethnic Conflict: Competing Visions of America* (Sage, 2004) and *Production of Modernization* (Temple University Press, 2011).

Bo Shan, Ph.D., is Professor and Vice Dean, School of Journalism and Communication, Head, Media Development Research Center, and Head, Center for Intercultural Research, Wuhan University. His research interests are in intercultural communication, comparative journalism, cultural conflict, and communication ethics. His representative publications include *The Problems and Possibilities in Intercultural Communication, The Spiritual Space of Junyi Tang's Philosophy, On Comparison Between Chinese and Western Journalism, Chinese Journalism and Communication in the Twentieth Century: On Applied Journalism,* etc.

Jiamei Tang is Associate Professor, School of Journalism and Communication, Guangdong University of Foreign Studies, PRC. She has an M.A. from University of Leeds and an M.A. from University of Manchester,

UK, and has a Ph.D. from Wuhan University. She was a Visiting Scholar at the University of Central Lancashire. Her research interests are international journalism, media ethics, and media translation.

Jingcao Xiao is Lecturer, School of Journalism and Communication, Wuhan University. His Ph.D. is from the School of Philosophy, Wuhan University. His research interests are moral philosophy and applied ethics.

Jing Xin is Postdoctoral Fellow, School of Journalism and Communication, Wuhan University, PRC. Ph.D., BA (Hons.), Department of Media and Communication, University of Canterbury, New Zealand. She is the author of *The Chinese Approach to Web Journalism*. Her research interests include journalism studies in new media, cross-cultural studies, and comparative journalism studies.

Dan Yang, Ph.D., is Lecturer, School of Humanities and Social Sciences, Huazhong Agricultural University, PRC. Her research interests are intercultural communications, comparative journalism, and interpersonal communication.

Index

Intersections in Communications and Culture

Global Approaches and Transdisciplinary Perspectives

General Editors: Cameron McCarthy & Angharad N. Valdivia

An Institute of Communications Research, University of Illinois Commemorative Series

This series aims to publish a range of new critical scholarship that seeks to engage and transcend the disciplinary isolationism and genre confinement that now characterizes so much of contemporary research in communication studies and related fields. The editors are particularly interested in manuscripts that address the broad intersections, movement, and hybrid trajectories that currently define the encounters between human groups in modern institutions and societies and the way these dynamic intersections are coded and represented in contemporary popular cultural forms and in the organization of knowledge. Works that emphasize methodological nuance, texture and dialogue across traditions and disciplines (communications, feminist studies, area and ethnic studies, arts, humanities, sciences, education, philosophy, etc.) and that engage the dynamics of variation, diversity and discontinuity in the local and international settings are strongly encouraged.

LIST OF TOPICS

- Multidisciplinary Media Studies
- Cultural Studies
- Gender, Race, & Class
- Postcolonialism
- Globalization
- Diaspora Studies
- Border Studies
- Popular Culture
- Art & Representation
- Body Politics
- Governing Practices

- Histories of the Present
- Health (Policy) Studies
- Space and Identity
- (Im)migration
- Global Ethnographies
- Public Intellectuals
- World Music
- Virtual Identity Studies
- Queer Theory
- Critical Multiculturalism

Manuscripts should be sent to:

Cameron McCarthy OR Angharad N. Valdivia
Institute of Communications Research
University of Illinois at Urbana-Champaign
222B Armory Bldg., 555 E. Armory Avenue
Champaign, IL 61820

To order other books in this series, please contact our Customer Service Department:

(800) 770-LANG (within the U.S.)
(212) 647-7706 (outside the U.S.)
(212) 647-7707 FAX

Or browse online by series:
www.peterlang.com